D1577189

4 974052 000

Chitrál Charlie

By the same author

The Colonel's Table

On Laffan's Plain

Reveille & Retribution

Spit & Polish

Friend & Foe

K-Boat Catastrophe – The Battle of the Isle of May

Chitrál Charlie

The Life and Times
of a Victorian Soldier

**The Slow Rise and Swift Fall of Major General
Sir Charles Townshend KCB DSO**

N.S. Nash

Pen & Sword
MILITARY

WILTSHIRE LIBRARIES

This edition published by
Pen & Sword Military
an imprint of
Pen & Sword Books Ltd
47 Church Street
Barnsley
South Yorkshire
S70 2AS

Copyright © N. S. Nash 2010

ISBN 978 1 84884 276 2

The right of N. S. Nash to be identified as Author of this Work has been asserted by him in accordance with the Copyright, Designs and Patents Act 1988.

A CIP catalogue record for this book is available from the British Library

All rights reserved. No part of this book may be reproduced or transmitted in any form or by any means, electronic or mechanical including photocopying, recording or by any information storage and retrieval system, without permission from the Publisher in writing.

Typeset in Ehrhardt

Printed and bound in England by CPI Antony Rowe

Pen & Sword Books Ltd incorporates the imprints of Pen & Sword Aviation, Pen & Sword Maritime, Pen & Sword Military, Wharncliffe Local History, Pen & Sword Select, Pen & Sword Military Classics and Leo Cooper.

For a complete list of Pen & Sword titles please contact
PEN & SWORD BOOKS LIMITED
47 Church Street, Barnsley, South Yorkshire, S70 2AS, England
E-mail: enquiries@pen-and-sword.co.uk
Website: www.pen-and-sword.co.uk

Contents

Maps and Figures vii
Preface viii
Acknowledgements ix

1   1861 and 1919. The Beginning and Almost the End . . 1
2   1861–1885. Egypt and the Sudan 5
3   1886–1893. India and the Hunza-Nagar Expedition . . 28
4   1893–1895. The Chitrál Campaign 54
5   3 March–20 April 1895. Besieged in Chitrál 71
6   1895–1898. Celebrity and Return to the Sudan 93
7   1899–1900. India and South Africa 118
8   1900-1903. Service in the United Kingdom and the
     Canadian Expedition 132
9   1903–1908. India 141
10   1909–1911. South Africa 150
11   1911–1914. Major General's Command, the Territorial
     Army and India 154
12   1915–1916. The Campaign in Mesopotamia 164
13   October–November 1915. The Advance to
     Ctesiphon and the Retreat to Kut 195
14   November 1915–April 1916. Besieged 220
15   April 1916–October 1918. Prisoner of War 271
16   1918–1924. Soldier to Civilian 282
17   1924–2010. Epilogue 308

Appendix I – 'Mesopotamia' by Rudyard Kipling 316
Bibliography 317
Index 318

The newly promoted Major General C.V.F. Townshend CB DSO
Photographed in India in 1911, aged fifty. *(Barker)*

Maps and Figures

Fig 1.   Map of Egypt and the Sudan *c*.1885   10

Fig 2.   Sketch map of the theatre of operations for the

relief of Karthoum   18

Fig 3.   The juxtaposition of the forts at Nilt, Maiun and Thol   39

Fig 4.   Family tree of Shak Afzul II   57

Fig 5.   Sketch map of Chitrál fort   74

Fig 6.   The routes taken by the relief columns of Low and Kelly   85

Fig 7.   Map of Mesopotamia and the River Tigris   165

Fig 8.   Sketch map of the Battle of Kurna   171

Fig 9.   Sketch map of the Battle of Kut-al-Amara   191

Fig 10.   Sketch map of the Advance to Ctesiphon   203

Fig 11.   The Battle of Ctesiphon. (CVFT)   206

Fig 12.   Sketch map of Kut   231

Fig 13.   Townshend's last message   266

Preface

Originally I set out to write a book about ineptitude in high places and, in my investigation, I explored the debacle of the campaign in Mesopotamia and the eventual surrender of Kut in 1916. This latter event interested me in the complex personality of the British commander at Kut, Major General Charles Townshend.

The more I looked into the life of this man the more I was intrigued by him. He was clearly brilliant and brave and, on the face of it, he had all the attributes of a hero. Indeed at one point in his young life he had achieved hero status and public adulation.

Then he threw it away. I hope that this book explains how although, perhaps, not why.

I decided to write a biography of Townshend. I am not the first and there have been two others. The first of these, by a family member, was written in 1928, and the most recent over forty years ago. The great man himself wrote two books and the second of these was entitled *My Campaign in Mesopotamia*. These sources are among many others that have provided me with the background for this book and I have drawn where possible, and predominantly, upon contemporary sources.

It is hoped that the plethora of photographs, maps and illustrations will serve to bring to life the events of so long ago, to feed the reader's appetite and cause him or her to marvel at the courage, tenacity and endurance of the Victorian soldiers and their successors who built and defended an empire. These men deserved the very best of officers and, in the main, that is what they got. However, there were exceptions, as this book reveals.

Townshend has long passed out of living memory but, back in 1967, Russell Braddon wrote an excellent book called *The Siege*. This is, specifically, about the siege of Kut and, in his research for his book (which I thoroughly commend), Braddon interviewed over sixty soldiers who had known Townshend and served under him. It is consequently a very valuable resource. Those sixty soldiers have all now gone to join their commander and are no longer available to reiterate their testimony. I take note of the evidence but do not concur, entirely, with Braddon's bleak view of Townshend.

If you, the reader, stay with me to the bitter end then it is for you to make a judgment on this brave, bright and ambitious officer.

Tank Nash
North Berwick

Acknowledgements

The production of this book would not have been possible without the unstinting support of Lieutenant Colonel W.W.T. Gowans who read my typescript and offered invaluable advice. Also Mr Bobby Gainher my skilled, painstaking editor at Pen & Sword who corrected and enhanced my text.

I am indebted to Colonel Ali Amir, the Army and Air Force attaché at the Pakistan High Commission in London who secured for me the photograph of modern Chitrál, and to my meticulous researcher, Mr Jeff Birch, who trawled through the National Archives on my behalf.

The photographs and illustrations are reproduced from books listed in the bibliography, most of which are over a hundred years old, and I am grateful to Mr David Wheeler for his help in matters photographic. The sources of illustrations are acknowledged where possible, however, copyright holders of unattributed photographs should contact the publisher.

Wherever possible I have included the words of those present at the events described – including much from the personal diary of Charles Townshend. This source is identified as a footnote or in the body of the text.

Two previous biographies of Townshend provided an outline framework for this book, especially in the chronology of his life. All the interpretation, judgments and opinions expressed are mine alone unless otherwise specified.

Chapter 1

1861 and 1919

The Beginning and Almost the End

Late summer 1919 found Britain deep in the throes of depression. Almost a year on from 'the eleventh hour of the eleventh day of the eleventh month' there was precious little to celebrate. Millions of families were bereaved; hundreds of thousands of men were crippled and destitute. The country was bankrupt and across the Channel anarchy was running rife in Europe – there was no guarantee that insurrection would not spread to Great Britain.

However, in central London, a well-dressed man, modestly affluent, with a neatly trimmed moustache, in his late fifties, gave a satisfied sigh. He put down a pen and set to one side the typescript of a large document of his authorship. He had been meticulous in writing the book and just as precise in making all the necessary corrections to this, a publisher's proof. The finished opus, his work of 200,000 words, was now ready for the printer, the press and a public that, he judged, was eager to hear his side of a complicated story.

The following day he made his way to 62 St Martin's Lane and to the premises of the publishers, Thornton Butterworth Ltd. Here he was greeted with the deference that he considered to be his due and after grave formalities and the shaking of hands, he gave the corrected draft to one of the firm's principals. With it went his hopes for the restitution of his damaged reputation.

He was gratified to be assured that the book's success was not in doubt because although his pension was adequate, it was not sufficient to support the lifestyle which he had hitherto enjoyed. Any extra income that might be generated by sales of the book would be most welcome.

The book was to be entitled *My Campaign in Mesopotamia* and it first saw light of day three months later, in February 1920. The author was Major General Sir Charles Townshend KCB DSO, and the book was designed to quell the rising tide of criticism of him that had followed his exploits in Mesopotamia.

The book did not have the desired effect – quite the opposite, in fact. It

1

was viewed as a mere apologia. Townshend had thirsted for glory all his life and, in addition, had worked assiduously to obtain an elevated station in his country's establishment and the approbation of his peers. He had manipulated, politicked, lied and laboured mightily to achieve all three but, ultimately, he failed to achieve any of them.

It was all really rather sad.

This book is a cautionary tale and it shows how a soldier with an extrovert personality, considerable talent and ample courage was eventually brought down by his driving ambition and hubris.

The British Army has, over the last 350 years or so, produced general officers of every hue. There have been a minority who, by any yardstick, might be termed 'brilliant' and, if they also had enviable human qualities then they were much admired. In that bracket Field Marshal Bill Slim springs to mind. Montgomery was arguably a more skilled strategist yet he was also a rather disagreeable man. He makes the brilliant category – just. But then, Slims are few and far between.

Generals are made by the circumstances of the day, few of which they can influence. It is blindingly obvious that the successful general must have survived the politicking of a peacetime army even to get to the 'start line'. In wartime his ability to excel is dependent upon the political aims of his government, the support of his military superiors, the quality of his soldiers, the capacity of his logistic tail and, by no means least, the quality of his opposition. He has to seek success and commensurate glory by playing, to best advantage, the hand he is dealt in terms of the theatre of operations and a multitude of other factors he cannot control – not least of these the weather – as Napoleon and von Paulus would testify.

The officer who has vision, can control vast forces with skill, tenacity, efficiency and enjoy a fair share of luck, whilst spending the lives of his soldiers very frugally, deservedly becomes a legend. Such men are few and far between. Arguably, Wellington fails the last of these tests and so too, by a very wide margin, do Field Marshals Haig and French. Marshal Foch, brilliant though he might have been, wasted the flower of French youth.

Defeat in the field is to consign a general to the scrap heap of military history. Being removed from command is also professional death. Percival, who cravenly capitulated in Singapore, not only surrendered his sword but his reputation as well. Hamilton, the painfully inept commander at Gallipoli, deservedly ruined his reputation, but his heroic incompetence cost thousands of lives along the way. Nixon, whose crass ineptitude triggered the debacle at Kut, the greatest defeat suffered by the British

Army since Kabul in 1842, has been rightfully damned. Buller, who plays a part in this narrative, was grossly overpromoted and failed miserably in South Africa. There would be very few defeated or sacked generals in the 'Generals' Hall of Fame' – if such a ghastly thing existed. The officer who is besieged is, by definition, on the defensive and his future is in the balance. Some lose their lives and of these Gordon at Khartoum is an example. However, some officers emerge as heroes and Colonel Baden-Powell, who survived at Mafeking and went on to reap international fame, is an unusual case.

A country has every right to expect competence from its generals and the vast majority of British generals have been 'good enough', with many of those 'very good indeed', bordering on 'excellent.' The downside is that there have been more than enough disastrous British generals. Between them, they have filled military cemeteries all over the world.

There is one overriding principle that is imbued in all British officers and willingly embraced by all. That is, that the care of their soldiers is always and unequivocally the single highest priority. The officer's personal comfort and convenience comes a very distant last. It is this principle that is at the root of a soldier's reciprocal regard for his officer.

No officer takes the Queen's shilling on the basis that he will serve out his engagement as a second lieutenant – even if the system allowed it, which it does not. It is entirely appropriate for an officer to aspire to further promotion and there is not a regular lieutenant now or ever, who did not aspire to the crowns of a major. Every lieutenant colonel, in his heart of hearts, can see himself as a brigadier or better. Nevertheless it has always been an unspoken custom of the Service that an officer conceals his ambition, for to do otherwise is to invite ridicule from his peers and the suspicion of his seniors.

In April 1991, the author once remarked to General Sir Patrick Howard-Dobson, a very distinguished former Quarter Master General and a man deeply respected by all who came within his sphere, 'You really couldn't have done any better, could you?' The great man smiled wryly and said softly in reply, 'Well, to be honest I'd have liked to be Chief of the General Staff [CGS].' So it would seem that ambition is not quelled by advancement even when it is achieved at the highest level and by the most civilized of men.

The system that promotes officers in the Armed Forces has developed and become increasingly sophisticated over the last 140 years. It dates back to 1871 when the system of purchase of commissions, in place since 1660, was abolished.

Since 1871 there has been any number of poor decisions that led to inept officers being elevated to positions well beyond their capacity. No doubt ICI, Microsoft, British Airways, Shell, BP and certainly every British bank have made similar mistakes. Generally, however, the mistakes of multinational corporations do not cost men their lives. This book examines the career of an officer who had most of the attributes that would see him safely to the very top of the military tree.

Charles Townshend had a long family history with a record of service to the Crown. He was quick witted, outgoing, gallant and professionally adept. The young man had every reason to be modestly ambitious.

Ambitious he was. But, sadly, there was no discernible modesty about it.

Chapter 2

1861–1885

Egypt and the Sudan

'A man of character in peace is a man of courage in war.'

Lord Moran in *The Anatomy of Courage*

A biography is traditionally started at the subject's birth and this author sees no reason to make an exception here. 'Chitrál Charlie' was christened Charles Vere Ferrers Townshend (CVFT) and he was born at Great Union Street, Southwark in London on 21 February 1861. He was the eldest son of Charles Thornton Townshend (1840–1889) and his first wife, Louisa Townshend (née Graham), an Australian. Charles Thornton Townshend (CTT) was painfully young and, although only twenty-one, he had been married for two years. In the view of the family he had married below his station.

He was a railway clerk in impecunious circumstances, who suffered intolerably from gout. He headed a lower middle-class family without obvious pretensions, despite the background of his wider family. Whilst Charles and his younger brother Augustus were growing up the family lived in an unprepossessing property at 144 Orchard Road, Brentford. Young Charles spent much of his childhood just across the river from The National Archive which, located at Kew, is now the repository of that small boy's entire hopes, fears and ambitions. It also holds the complete record of his ultimate fall from grace.

He might have been influenced by his family history which, it was claimed, could be traced back to a Sir Roger Townshend, Bt., of Raynham. This worthy was a 'Justice of the Common Pleas' and a successful fifteenth-century lawyer. The 3rd baronet was a prominent Royalist during the Civil War and another forebear, the 1st Marquess, fought at Fontenoy and Dettingen. He was with Wolfe at Quebec, rose to field marshal and was the role model for young Charles.

The wider Townshend family which had, at one time, been as affluent as it was influential, was in decline and when the 5th Marquess succeeded to

5

the title, the family seat, Raynham Hall in Norfolk, was under threat. Charles Thornton Townshend (CTT) was the great-grandson of the 1st Marquess Townshend and the heir presumptive to the title. This was at least until the birth of John James Dudley Stuart Townshend (1866–1921) who, in time, would become the 6th Marquess. Nevertheless, young Charles (CVFT) still had the possibility, perhaps even the likelihood, of one day being Lord Townshend and the 7th Marquess. This was an aspiration that was to be an important factor for much of his life. As the 6th Marquess grew to manhood he certainly showed no intention of taking a wife, a most satisfactory non-event as far as CVFT was concerned.

Charles Townshend was fortunate in that his grandfather, the Revd Lord George Osborne Townshend, brother of the 4th Marquess, appreciated the fact that when his (CVFT's) father died, all that would separate young Charles from the title was his bachelor cousin. Grandfather Townshend, aware of his responsibilities to the boy, produced the funds to educate a potential marquess in an appropriate manner. He sent Charles to Cranleigh School in Surrey when he was twelve but for only a year, as he left Cranleigh a year later to take up a cadetship in the Royal Navy.

Soon after his admittance into the Royal Navy his mother Louisa died, a crushing blow to any young man. The regime at HMS *Britannia*, the Royal Naval College, or for that matter at RMC Sandhurst, was part academic, part sporting, part the development of military skills. The academic element required cadets to study military history. That syllabus fired in Townshend an interest in the subject that was to last him the rest of his life. It could be said that his anxiety to contribute to that history was his Achilles heel.

Any aspirations to be a naval officer young Charles might have entertained came to naught because in 1881 he opted to be commissioned into the Royal Marine Light Infantry – he would become a 'sea soldier'.

Well, for a while anyway.[1]

Most of the cadets attending *Britannia* and Sandhurst came from comfortable middle and upper-class families, and the officer cadre of the Armed Forces that they joined in the late nineteenth century was homogeneous. Townshend made up for his very modest means by trading gently upon his aristocratic aspirations and, with his outgoing, easy personality he fitted into the mould. His commission would have described him as 'Trusty and well beloved', and a military luminary of the day signed the document on behalf of the Queen. That commission was probably framed and decorated a wall in his parents' modest home.

C.V.F. Townshend had found his niche and he would have been

described as 'army barmy' – if that epithet can be ascribed to a Royal Marine. He was the epitome of the young officer. He was an extrovert with a relaxed, almost casual manner, a veneer of social polish, ample charm and a quick wit to boot. But, even at the age of twenty, he was ruthlessly ambitious. An 'ambitious second lieutenant' was a beast neither known nor recognized in the Royal Marines or the Army in 1881. It is similarly a beast, thankfully, still rare in the twenty-first century. The very phrase is an absurd contradiction in terms.

The golden age of Victorian empire building was at its zenith – there were opportunities aplenty for a young officer to demonstrate his worth. Charles had a brief spell in Egypt late in 1882 and then a further few weeks in the spring of 1883. Although this was routine garrison duty it was a useful period for a young officer to find his feet and gain confidence in the authority he now exercised over men, many of whom were much his senior in age.

From his earliest youth Charles was a social networker and, by his early twenties, he had started to cultivate a circle of theatrical friends. Charles had an attractive personality, was a gifted raconteur, played the banjo and is reported to have been most entertaining company. For the moment, though, Charles Townshend was not stimulated by garrison duty in that environment, either in the UK or in a hot, unsanitary desert country, neither of which provided an obvious opportunity that would bring him to notice. He applied to transfer from the Royal Navy to the Indian Staff Corps, an organization somewhat removed from the activities of the Royal Marines.

The Indian Staff Corps was a branch of the British Indian Army during colonial rule, having been formed in 1861 to unify the Bombay, Madras and Bengal constituents of the Indian Army at that time. Over time it became a sort of military clearing house.

The principal purpose of the Corps, despite its misleading name, was to provide officers for locally recruited native regiments and for appointments on headquarters at every level. It had the additional role of acting as a conduit for those suitably qualified officers of the Indian Army who sought political or civil administrative positions.

Townshend and those of his generation would have viewed service in the ISC as making them, in effect, members of the regular cadre of the Indian Army. In Townshend's case it was certainly a more attractive billet than the Royal Marines.

When an officer is commissioned into his corps or regiment he joins a family and this usually engenders a feeling of affection for the cap badge and those others who wear it. This affection – perhaps 'comradeship' is a better word – is reciprocated in a very understated and 'frightfully British sort of way'. Accordingly, to transfer, although perfectly acceptable, is nevertheless not a matter to be undertaken lightly. It is not unlike a 'military divorce' – in that an important and potentially life-long association is severed, albeit in a civilized manner, but with scant regret from either party.

Charles Townshend was to develop 'transferring' into something approaching an art form. He saw it as a means of securing advancement and was rather like the motorway driver who chops and changes lanes to the irritation of all his fellow motorists. 'Transfers in' were not always made particularly welcome: first, because their motives were suspect; second, because they took their place in the regimental roll according to their seniority. This caused those who were junior to be displaced and moved lower in the order of precedence – with the attendant angst. Their peer group saw them, quite correctly, as competitors in the promotion race and a source of more, if unspoken, angst. All in all this did not make the incomer a fancied runner in the popularity stakes. Accordingly, only the very thick skinned would choose to put themselves through this particular mill. Townshend was to go through this process time and again and, in doing so, became an officer without regimental roots, and the comfort and support that the regimental family provides. The inveterate 'transfer in' becomes something of a pariah and is seen, by some, as a professional predator – this would have been a fair judgment of Charles Townshend.

To his chagrin the transfer sought so avidly did not take effect. An habitual and devoted correspondent all his life, letters had to suffice for these theatrical friends who had to be left behind when, in 1884, a 'Special Service Battalion' was raised for service in the Middle East – Egypt. It was now that he started to keep a diary, a document he maintained until two days before his demise. It was this diary that his cousin, Erroll Sherson, lent upon heavily in writing his biography of Charles and which is quoted in this book.

The Battalion, some 500 strong, included a detachment of 200 men, Townshend and one other officer, from Plymouth. The composite battalion embarked on the P&O troopship *Poonah*. There then followed an interminable but not uncomfortable voyage during which he was able to make his social mark with his wide repertoire of songs and risqué ditties, accompanying himself on the banjo – he was clearly an accomplished entertainer and, given that all entertainment on a trooper had to be generated by the passengers, he basked in his popularity whilst elsewhere life was rather more earnest.

*   *   *

On 4 February 1884, Valentine Baker, in command of an Egyptian force of 3,500, marched from Suakin to relieve the beleaguered garrisons of Tokar and Sinkat but on his way he encountered a group of Sudanese under the command of Osman Digna at El Teb (not shown on the map on Page 10).

Colonel Baker was an interesting character. He had been dismissed from the British Army in 1875 after an alleged assault on a young woman in a railway carriage. It brought his career to an end and he served a year in prison. He then served as a contract officer with the Turkish Army (as a lieutenant general) and later commanded the Egyptian Police, a quasi-military organization. It was in this capacity that he marched from Suakin.

At El Teb the Sudanese numbered around a 1,000, but the Egyptian soldiers were ill-disciplined. They panicked, scattered and were butchered piecemeal. Only 700 men survived. It was a disaster and it got worse because Baker's surviving troops were mutinous and he was unable to complete his mission to relieve the two garrisons. The Sinkat garrison resolved to fight its way through to Suakin, but it was overwhelmed by the Mahdist strength and ferocity and massacred. The Tokar garrison, sensibly, adopted Plan 'B' and surrendered – another disaster.

These defeats of the imperial power had to be reversed and, on 21 February 1884, Lieutenant General Sir Gerald Graham VC GCB GCMG (1831–1899), an officer of the Royal Engineers, led a force of 4,500 men with artillery and machine guns back to El Teb. There was a bloody encounter but Graham's men were up to the job and they defeated the Mahdists, killing 2,000 while suffering only thirty killed and 142 wounded themselves.

A little over three weeks later, on 13 March, Graham brought Osman Digna to battle again at a place called Tamai (or Tamanieh) and inflicted a further heavy defeat. Osman Digna lost 4,000 men killed, the British 120. Osman Digna escaped, but the pious hope that his influence and that of the Mahdi would now decline was not to be. The Sudanese were made of stern stuff and they were utterly devoted to their cause, as Townshend was soon to discover at close quarters.

Poonah's first stop was in Malta and it was here Townshend heard that the expected violence in Sudan had finally erupted, and had led to the massacre of the British-controlled Egyptian garrison at Sinkat. The immediate consequence was that the British Government resolved to mount an expedition to deal with Achmet Shemsedden, who had pronounced himself to be 'The Mahdi' and an Islamic prophet. He sought the violent overthrow of the Government and the establishment of an Islamic Utopia. Elsewhere,

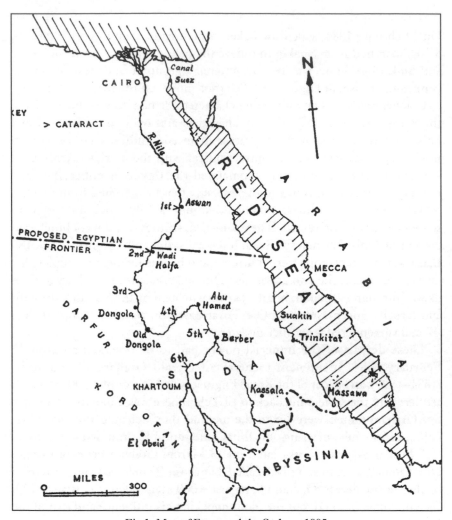

Fig 1. Map of Egypt and the Sudan c.1885.

a young man eagerly anticipated the action for which he had joined.

The obstacles to his plans were that the Sudan was ruled from Cairo which, in turn, was firmly under the aegis of Britain. There was widespread dissatisfaction in the Sudan about the manner in which the country was governed and with hindsight it is clear that the local people had a genuine grievance. The Mahdi, not unreasonably, set out to improve matters. However, the elimination of all non-believers was a first objective. This was a non-negotiable aim and now, 125 years on, the largely

Christian West is still facing a similarly intractable and irreconcilable foe. The Mahdi's rhetoric had translated into violence and it had it to be confronted. In the meantime multitudes of poor and uneducated Sudanese tribesmen flocked to his banner because not to do so triggered life-threatening consequences.

The P & O troopship was but a happy memory when the marines continued their journey and were transported from Malta to Alexandria in a vessel called the *Gilsland*. Charles Townshend confided in his diary that the conditions aboard this 'pig boat' made 'our life loathsome'.[2]

Townshend's battalion disembarked gratefully in Alexandria and marched off to its permanent barracks in Ramleh, close enough to the flesh-pots of the city to offer diversions for active and lusty young men. The barracks were 'splendid but in a filthy state'.[3] A busy social life ensued with a constant round of cocktail and dinner parties to alleviate the chore of garrison duties. The sun shone, there was ample to eat and drink and, much more important, there was a pleasing plethora of attractive girls or available married women. Without a doubt Townshend was a ladies' man, and who can blame a 23-year-old bachelor for that? He commented that, 'The French women were unquestionably handsome and devilishly well dressed . . . The French detested us since they are jealous of the English in Egypt.' He added that, 'The Greeks do not dislike us.' Certainly not, and one Greek girl in particular very much took Townshend's fancy.

Townshend enjoyed the social round and in his diary made constant comments on the girls who came within his social sphere, and even on those who were not. He commented, 'Saw Hassim Pasha's twelve wives out for a walk, with a black slave to keep guard. One pretty little girl among them looked round at us looking very nice and raised her veil.' This was all very well but the drinking and dancing were doing nothing to progress his career and as weeks wore on there was no indication that the Battalion was going to be employed in the Sudan.

CVFT once more moved into 'transfer out' mode, particularly 'as there seems to be no chance of going to the front and getting a medal'.[4] He continued to pursue the Indian Staff Corps as option number one, having carefully researched the Corps and the opportunities that it could provide. To achieve his aim he lobbied all and sundry both within his chain of command and outside it if he thought it might be productive. However, the administrative wheels moved very slowly and in the meantime he had to continue to serve alongside brother officers who, in effect, he was 'rejecting'. Perhaps that word is too strong but his attitude to the Royal Marines would not have added anything to his popularity.

By early March his relationship with the Greek girl had deepened and he admitted to being 'awfully mashed', which in the parlance of that era meant that he was in love or close to that happy state. This could so easily have been a turning point for the better in his life and he recognized that there were decisions to take. He lived on his pay, aided by a small allowance from his uncle; marriage was a major financial commitment. The good news was that the girl's father was not only very well heeled, but that he looked on Townshend's suit with favour.

Townshend was a calculating man, not a person readily ruled by his heart, and he doubtless did an 'appreciation of the situation', a system whereby army officers weighed up, in a logical manner, the pros and cons of any course of action. This was usually in a tactical situation but it was just as applicable here. One of the factors to be considered and weighed was that Townshend had it 'on the vine' that the girl's father would *not* (author's italics) be providing a handsome dowry if she married a non-Greek. This had an adverse effect upon the lady's attraction and rapidly diminished his ardour. Coldly and without any apparent remorse, Townshend terminated the romance and broke a heart along the way. History does not tell us what happened to the Greek girl but perhaps she had a lucky escape.

In early April, Townshend was able to make a permanent break with his former amour when the Battalion was warned for service in the Sudan to rescue General Gordon who was holed up in Khartoum. On 3 May 1884, the Battalion was embarked on the *Orantes* and shipped to Suakin, a small, horribly squalid port, but a key British garrison town on the Red Sea, about 40 miles south of Port Sudan. This was to be the base from which the pacification of the country was to be attempted. The voyage was all too short and when the destination hove into sight, Suakin looked attractive. Closer inspection showed it to be rather different and it was with mounting horror that the Royal Marines viewed their new home.

Suakin was grim.

It was bone numbingly poor, the dirt and squalor turned the strongest stomach and gave succour to uncounted clouds of flies that promptly transferred their unwanted affections to the marines as they came ashore.

It was early May 1884 and on the 7th of that month, soon after disembarking, Townshend confided in his diary that, 'The local population seem to be friendly enough, mostly jet black and the women especially are very fine, very handsome with very fine teeth, they are always laughing and merry.'

The port lay under the guns of a warship but the marines were not best pleased to be assigned to the trench system that encircled El Geyf, a village that lay on the landward end of the causeway. Townshend was having none of this and he manipulated himself into an ad hoc unit of mounted infantry. This spared him having to share the crashing boredom of his fellow officers who were confined to manning the trenches. The mounted unit gave Charles some freedom of action.

Meanwhile, the health of the British troops started to suffer under the unremitting 120°F temperature, the maddening, ever-present swarms of flies and the insanitary conditions in which they existed. To these discomforts had to be added the presence of a wily, determined and courageous foe.

It was on 18 July that Townshend achieved one of his ambitions – he saw action for the first time and he revelled in it. He was commanding a mounted patrol along a desert road and, taking the chance to water the horses and his men, he called a halt at a well. Whilst the patrol was dismounted, mounted Arabs were spotted about a mile away and Townshend, calling his men to order, determined to investigate the unknown party. He set off in pursuit but the two groups were evenly mounted and Townshend could not make headway. He had to resort to long-range shooting from the saddle – a nugatory exercise if there ever was one. 'It was like something from the Wild West.'[5]

After about an hour, with horses at the end of their tether and the gap between the two parties lengthening by the minute, Townshend sent three men on ahead. They saw one of the Arabs drop behind the main body and a trooper rode around him to cut off his retreat. The Arab rode at his adversary and at close range shot him from the saddle. This was the signal for the body of Arabs to turn back in order to spear the wounded man to death – and they still had time to make off on their original course. Townshend followed and discovered he had been led into an 'ambuscade'. He extricated his patrol from that situation without loss and set out to return to the doubtful delights of Suakin. About eight miles from home and with his horses 'done up', Townshend was confronted by about 200 men, camel mounted, barring his route.

They were demonstrably hostile – very hostile.

Townshend ordered his men to dismount and he put down what he described as 'biting fire'. This caused the opposition to dismount and take cover. Their camels, wise beasts that they were, lay down too. Whilst he had the initiative and the Arabs were unprepared, Townshend remounted his men and they made a dash around the enemy flank to their rear, from where fire was re-opened on a disconcerted, uncoordinated foe. Townshend took full advantage of the situation and sprinted for Suakin, hotly pursued.

There was an inconclusive running fight for three miles. Nevertheless, the body of the Egyptian trooper was recovered, a safe haven was reached at last and, in Townshend's words, 'A regular crowd of everyone who possessed a gee [horse] was at the wells to greet us. Woodhouse, the Governor, Colonel Ozzard, *tout le monde* . . . and about 1500 friendlies.'

Townshend was very pleased with himself but his patrol had achieved no military aim and had cost a life. The only minor benefit of Townshend's patrol was that it brought him to the attention of the establishment. For an ambitious man this was highly satisfactory. He recorded several days later that, 'My official report has been sent on to Cairo to (the) Commander–in–Chief and my name has been brought before Sir John Hay. Reports of native scouts say we killed 12 of their men.'

A few days later, on 23 July, four of Osman Digna's spies, who had infiltrated Suakin masquerading as pilgrims, were brought from the cells in the cavalry camp. The Egyptian soldiers were paraded in a hollow square and one of the spies was publicly hanged. His demise was witnessed by the other three. Townshend said soberly, 'This is the first man I have seen hung (sic) and he died without a kick and hung there until sundown.' It was not to be the last.

Soon after, Charles Townshend returned to his constant quest for the military Holy Grail and noted on 16 August, 'Have applied for a commission in the Cavalry. I don't think for a moment that I will get it but Woodhouse [his commanding officer] is going to back me up.' Moving quickly and, quite incorrectly, outside the chain of command Townshend also appealed to his grandmother, and made no bones about it – he wanted her to pull some well-connected strings and clear his way for a new number one aim – his desired transfer to the cavalry. For the moment the Indian Staff Corps was set aside.

Manifestly, Grandmother failed in her mission because the young man, who alleged that he wanted to be with horses, was sent with unconscious official humour and two other Royal Marine officers to the Egyptian Camel Corps on 24 October 1884. The good news was that his unit was assigned to General Wolseley's mission to rescue Gordon from the besieged city of Khartoum. Townshend and his unit had been alerted for this very same mission back in May and five months of heroic inactivity had followed. Any sense of urgency was missing and that deficiency was a feature of the expedition from start to finish – little wonder that Gordon was in extremis.

Travel in this part of the world was an exhausting business and the Nile as a thoroughfare was a mixed blessing with its series of cataracts. It was also the only reliable water source. Townshend and his party had to navigate up the Nile, under sail, which was all very agreeable – when the wind blew. When it did not the boats were towed by the passengers. Townshend remarked what hard work this was and from 14 November until the 19th he spent long hours taking his turn on the end of a tow rope.

On arrival at his destination he found that the facilities were nil and it was every bit as hot and miserable as Suakin. In the next two weeks he integrated with his new unit, honed his camel-riding skills and cheerfully made the best of what life had to offer. The relief column set out on its odyssey on 2 December 1884 heading for Dongola 200 miles up the Nile. The march was unopposed but very demanding on man and beast alike. Water was at a premium, strict water discipline was applied and the penalty for taking an unauthorized mouthful was draconian. There was one potentially serious incident and Charles Townshend commented on 15 December, 'Marched with the RA at 7am. The road from here to Dongola is through a vast plain of hard sand. My banjo had a narrow shave today. The camel on which it was carried fell down dead from heat, without any warning. However, through providence, the banjo escaped!'

The rescue of Gordon was now a pressing matter but the expeditionary force to rescue him faced huge administrative and logistic problems. The upper Nile provided the access but not the least of the problems was the acquisition of sufficient boats and boatmen to carry the main body. The sketch map (Fig 2) on page 18 shows that, about 60 miles south of Dongola, at Debbeh, the Nile creates a pocket of land by swinging away to the east and making a large loop before resuming its former direction.

It took ten long days to reach Dongola and after a brief rest the force pressed on to Korti. Brigadier Sir Herbert Stewart KCB (1843–1885) was in command of the 'Desert Column'. Townshend and his unit were part of Stewart's force which also embodied four light field pieces and a small group of navy blue jackets whose task, among others, was to man a Gardner machine gun. Named as Stewart's successor if he fell in action was an unlikely character called Colonel Fred Burnaby. Burnaby was a dilettante, adventurer, traveller and author. By dint of his seniority alone he was the Colonel of the Blues. He was an inexperienced soldier and his rank made him dangerous.

The master plan was for General Sir Garnet Wolseley, who commanded the main British force known as the 'River Column', to move on the river directly from Korti to Khartoum while, in the meantime, Stewart was to cut across country aiming to reach Khartoum by the most direct route. This short cut would take him past the wells at Abu Klea (or Abu Tulayh). These were about 20 miles north of Metemneh on the river and no more than a resting place with a water source, used by caravans crossing the Bayuda Desert of Sudan. Its only claim to fame in January 1885 was that it happened to be on the route of Stewart's force of about 1,500 men marching to relieve Gordon.

That all sounds straightforward, but it was not.

First, the Desert Column had to cross the 200-yard-wide River Nile where there was neither a ford nor a bridge. The banks were steep, high and unscaleable by camels. The beasts had to be lowered onto dhows, sailed or rowed across the river and then hoisted ashore – it was a process that was very slow and labour intensive. The camels did not enjoy it either and their active opposition did not help. The Desert Column formed up on 30 December having had a far from happy Christmas.

That morning the column paraded before and marched past their Commander-in-Chief with bands playing, colours flying and bayonets fixed. Briefly, very briefly, a soldier's life did not seem to be too bad. However, the march to Khartoum was arduous and was made largely at night through long grass that tugged at the men and their equipment. It was a complication that exhausted men did not need and whenever the column halted men fell asleep on the spot. This was hazardous as anyone left behind could expect no quarter from the Arabs tagging along well to the rear. The soldiers had expected to replenish their water bottles at various wells along their route, but at El Howeiyat the well was all but dry and they had to press on another 20 miles to Gakdul, where fortunately there was water in abundance. Morale was instantly raised and the column paused for an inexplicable twelve days. Quite why Stewart should have idled his time away is not clear but, by doing so, he lost impetus and the initiative.

Eventually, as the much-refreshed Desert Column resumed its advance and approached the wells at Abu Klea, Stewart realized that the Mahdists were in occupation of the wells in considerable numbers. He could not wait to be attacked as he had already come 43 waterless miles and had to seize this, the next watering place without delay. In any case the Dervishes ahead of him blocked his route to Metemneh and so battle was inevitable.

The Dervishes did not make a frontal attack and contented themselves with sporadic sniping. Stewart decided to bivouac for the night, painfully aware that the need for water was most urgent and to get it he was going to have to fight for it. Nevertheless, men who are rested fight a deal better than those who have just marched 20 miles across a desert in 120°F.

Townshend and his company passed an uneasy night in the zariba, a defensive work constructed of small trees, bushes, rocks and sand. They shared their accommodation with their camels and endured the long-range sniping which was worryingly effective, particularly so among the animals. It also prevented sleep.

Who knew what the morrow might bring?

Dawn found Stewart's force secure in its zariba, thirsty and threatened on all sides. He employed artillery to disperse the larger groups of Dervishes but that was only a temporary measure. It was a curious period – the zariba was threatened but not attacked. However, Stewart did not have time on his side, there was a pressing need to take the wells and water was his prime aim. If the Dervish army would not attack him then he would attack it and to do that, he had to advance.

The force moved out of the zariba, formed square and with the reserve water, ammunition and medical supplies carried by camels and horses it moved with ponderous deliberation toward the enemy concentration. It should be appreciated that the 'square' was not merely a defensive device. It provided all-round defence but it was completely mobile and, providing it was well commanded, it was a formidable offensive formation.

There were rather less than 1,500 bayonets now facing a foe estimated at 15,000 strong. Not all of the opposition were carrying mere swords and spears   they had 1,000 or more rifles, some of which were the much-admired Remington. Townshend took his place at the centre of his company and no doubt his stomach churned as he saw the mass of the enemy upon whom he and his comrades were advancing.

Stewart was a seasoned and skilled campaigner and, exuding calm, he deployed to the front of his square two companies of mounted infantry and two companies of guardsmen, with three guns of the Royal Artillery. The left face composed a company of the Heavy Camel Regiment and two companies of mounted infantry. On the right were two further companies of the Household Brigade and the Royal Marines, and the balance of the Royal Sussex. The square was completed with four companies of the Heavy Camel Regiment and the Naval 'Brigade'. The small naval party with their Gardner machine gun was kept in reserve.

The square braced itself for the inevitable onslaught.

An infantry square was not an immobile entity and this one moved forward in a forlorn attempt to outflank the enemy. Incoming fire started to take its toll and in the opening few moments of the engagement a marine near Townshend fell, choking on his own blood before death mercifully claimed him. The movement of the square was uneven and in the process a gap opened at the rear left corner of the formation. To cover the gap and to eliminate the danger that the gap now presented, the Gardner gun, a potent weapon, was run out to the left flank of the square to provide covering fire.

Meanwhile the sergeant majors, in their varied regional accents, controlled their men, dressed their ranks, imbued them with a sense of calm and purpose, and timed the discharge of their devastating volley fire. The discipline that comes from training and the instant reaction to a command that is the product of that discipline was seen at its very best at Abu Klea on 17 January 1885.

The square closed behind the Gardner party leaving it exposed and in the open. Stewart responded by deploying two companies of his Heavy Camel Regiment out of the square to support the Gardner gun. After only

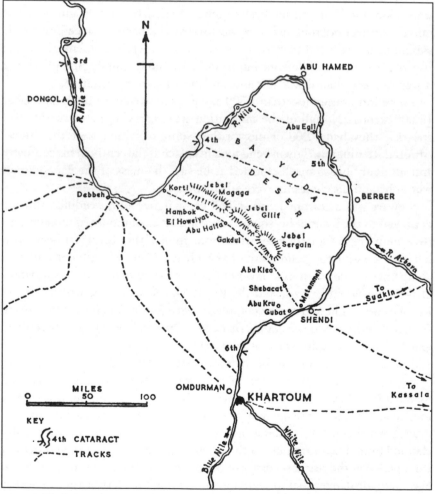

Fig 2. Sketch map of the theatre of operations for the relief of Khartoum.

about 70 rounds had been fired – a miniscule delivery from a machine gun, the gun jammed. The crew tried frantically to clear the stoppage but the Dervishes were on top of them and the sailors were fighting for their very lives. It was unfortunate that Colonel Burnaby had been placed in command of the square's rear face, which included the Blues.

'Burnaby, for the first time commanding troops in battle gave a wildly ill-judged order. He told the dragoons to break square and wheel outwards so that their rifles would bear on the enemy approaching. But the Dervishes on the higher ground at once perceived the opening in the rear of the British square and rushed towards it.'[6]

A large group of Dervishes were able to force their way through the perimeter of the square where they then found the interior to be full of frightened and irritated camels. The Dervishes were obstructed by the live-stock and unable to force a passage. The fight became a contest between the bayonet and the sword and spear, all of which were wielded with desperate urgency and on equal terms. Superior firepower counted for nothing here. Men fell and were trampled underfoot, the sand was stained with blood and the screams of the wounded, and animals made the scene something akin to hell. Burnaby would have had a lot to answer for had he lived, but he fell outside the square and alongside a number of others who lost their lives as a result of his folly. He took a lance through the neck, suffered a dozen other wounds and died in the arms of a young trooper from the Bays. 'Oh Sir,' cried the trooper to Lord Binning who had come to help, 'here is the bravest man in England.'[7] Meanwhile the impetus of the Dervish assault pushed the naval party back into the face of the square where they were re-absorbed.

Townshend was in the very thick of this desperate hand-to-hand fighting and he said, afterwards:

> The square became a mob, huddled back to back retreating from the Arabs, who were now among us cutting and slashing with their long straight swords and stabbing the men with their long spears like so many sheep. The crush was so great that at one time I could not get my arms to my sides, and remained with sword and pistol up in the air doing my utmost to keep my feet.

The British square was broken. This was a very rare event and, in desperate circumstances, desperate measures were called for. Accordingly, the troops in the rear ranks, with commendable discipline, turned about and opened fire into the mêlée of Dervishes and camels behind them. The fire was absolutely destructive and the intruders were killed to the last man. The carnage was awful, with dead and dying men inextricably mixed with wounded, shrieking camels. A critical situation was saved but it had been a close thing.

Townshend acknowledged the extraordinary bravery of the Dervishes and commented that, as the skillfully controlled fire of the square finally caused c.. .. .y mass to melt away:

> About five of their Sheikhs came charging at our square on horse back. It was a wonderful sight those five Arabs coming on at a mad gallop waving their swords over their heads and apparently bullet proof as one whole side of the square was firing at them. They were shot down one by one. The last man galloped around the flank about 40 yards from the bayonets. It was incredible. All the men blazed away at him. When only a few yards from us horse and man came over a tremendous crash and neither stirred again.

The surviving Dervishes, faced with a complete and stable square, were obliged to withdraw, hastened on their way by the Gardner gun, now back in action, and in fine voice. The Royal Artillery added to the body count and the battle, very hard fought in the first ten minutes, had become a rout.

The Royal Navy contingent, forty strong and from HMS *Alexandra*, had been in the thick of the action. From this party, two officers and six ratings were killed and seven were wounded in the first serious battle of the campaign – a high percentage of casualties from such a small a contingent. Lord Charles Beresford was one of the minor casualties. He was one of several RN officers who were to achieve national fame in the early twentieth century. He was 'scratched' on the left hand by a spear as he managed to duck under the Gardner gun.

The battle had been very brief and those who were present insisted that the whole affair lasted a scant fifteen minutes from start to finish. Casualties for the British were nine officers and 65 other ranks killed, and over 100 wounded. The Mahdists lost 1,100 dead. Using the enemy dead as the yardstick it probably means that 2,000 to 3,000 or more were wounded. This is testimony to the intensity of the struggle during that hectic quarter-of-an-hour of fighting. Among the Dervish dead was Musa wad Helu, one of the Mahdist chiefs. Charles Townshend had fought in and survived one of the bloodiest encounters of the age. The enemy wounded littered the landscape. No prisoners were taken as a wounded Arab proved still to be a devoted and dangerous enemy – it seemed that the Arabs preferred to meet their maker rather than accept the ministrations of the medics.

*   *   *

In the early twenty-first century the Western world and all non-Islamic countries are under the same threat of extreme violence that the Mahdi preached in the 1880s. The differences are that, in the Sudan, soldiers fought soldiers and certainly the British respected their opponents for their unvarnished self-sacrifice. Today, the latter-day Mahdists do not depend on swords and spears – their weapon is the bomb and their targets are anyone and everyone, sometimes brother Muslims, who are in the wrong place at the wrong time.

Rudyard Kipling, that great admirer of the British soldier, recognized the manner in which the Dervishes had broken into the square. In his own inimitable style and in words that would doubtless give deep offence to those who are governed by today's politically correct standards, he famously wrote:

> So 'ere's to you Fuzzy-Wuzzy, at your 'ome in the Soudan;
> You're a pore benighted 'eathen but a first-class fighting man;
> An 'ere's to you Fuzzy-Wuzzy. With your 'ayrick 'ead of 'air
> You big, black, bounding begger – for you broke the British square.

Townshend and his fellow officers would subscribe fully to these lines of verse because their adversary had been totally committed and inexpressibly brave in the face of overwhelming firepower. But bravery was not enough and the immediate British objective had been taken. Stewart moved on swiftly to the wells at Abu Klea. The water was not cool and crystal clear but no one complained, and the soldiers and surviving animals drank deeply of the brackish, lukewarm water.

Ever the professional analyst Townshend commented adversely upon the effectiveness of the issue sword bayonet which, by their 'blunt headed' design, were of little use for a stabbing action. He believed that the sword bayonet was 'useful for cutting grass but that was about all'. He also noted, accurately, that during the battle a number of rifles had jammed because they were choked with dust. He said that it was a matter of routine for marines to bind a cloth around the breach of their rifles and expressed surprise that it was not a fundamental precaution taken by all desert troops. He always kept a silk handkerchief wrapped around his revolver even inside its leather holster.

The battle having been won, Stewart spent that night and the following day at Abu Klea resting his men. Thus it was that he set out on the evening of 18 January 1885 to complete his march to the Nile.

The route was much more rugged than that experienced on earlier marches. The column was obliged to march across a limitless sandy plain covered in black rocks that had absorbed the heat during the day and now exuded it during the night. The going was very difficult, the surface broken and a hazard to feet and hooves. It was all the more trying as Stewart had ordered his column to march at night so that many of the hazards were not identified until an ankle was turned, a leg broken or a camel load shed. The column lost all cohesion as control disappeared in the anonymous black wasteland. Men who stopped and fell asleep, slept eternally as the Dervishes following on behind cut to ribbons any soldier that they came across. It was a long and unpleasant night.

Came the dawn of 19 January and the Nile, glistening and very blue under a cloudless sky, lay before them. Smoke was issuing from the funnels of two river steamers which were presumed to be Gordon's. The column closed up, Townshend called the roll of his company and Stewart prepared for the final approach to Metemneh. His visit to the town was clearly to be contested as swarms of Arabs were seen converging on the column's line of advance. Their estimated number was 20,000. Townshend described what happened next in his diary entry for the day:

> We were ordered to halt and form a zariba as fast as we could, and saw with rage that we should have to repeat our tactics of the previous day and fight not only to win, but for water and our lives. A breast work of biscuit boxes and camel saddles was made, but before this was completed and our camels double knee lashed inside the square the bullets of their riflemen began to sing about us as they crept closer and closer. There was a small rise in the ground about 200 yards in front of our square and, hearing Burleigh, the correspondent, point this out and suggest that it should be occupied, I at once asked permission to go and make a breast work. About a half a dozen of us officers and Burleigh ran as hard as we could with camel saddles and boxes to the knoll piling them one on the other. It was warm work, for their riflemen only 400 yards distant devoted all their energies to us. Not a man would have reached the Nile had not the enemy foolishly charged us. Their riflemen were all around us in the bush and the sand hills were blackened with sightseers from Metemneh: They would have become very active if we had been defeated! Those crowds of people who had come to look on reminded me of field days at Portsmouth.
>
>   It was about sunset when the rush took place, and on they came as they did at Abu Klea. We opened fire, the men beginning without

orders. The charge of the Arabs seemed to melt away under it and not a man got nearer than thirty yards of the square.

With the Gardner gun operating smoothly in the hands of the RN contingent, the gunners served their field guns and sprayed the advancing Dervish mass with white-hot shrapnel to terrible effect. Townshend continued:

> The cheering was tremendous as the enemy, including the spectators from the villages began to fly in all directions. The wounded Arabs lying about were all bayoneted, for it was found that they would slash at our men as they lay wounded on the ground, and one of our marines had his brains blown out by a wounded Arab who was apparently dead.

But the battle was not yet won. Among the casualties in this first encounter was the commander, Brigadier Sir Herbert Stewart, who was shot in the stomach, a wound that led to his death several days later. Burnaby, his named successor, was dead which was probably as well, as with him in command, disaster would have beckoned. In the meantime, Colonel Sir Charles Wilson, a sapper officer, assumed command. This was on the express wish of Lord Charles Beresford who, although outranking Wilson, was a naval officer and discommoded by the wound he had suffered at Abu Klea.

Wilson inherited a problem. The route to the river was still blocked and he was going to have to fight his way through to the river steamers, both so tantalizingly close. He had two options: the first was to advance by leapfrogging from zariba to zariba. This would be much slower and would involve labour on a massive scale. The other option was to adopt Stewart's tactics at Abu Klea and advance to the river in a square. Wilson opted for the 'square option'.

He left fifty men in the current zariba base and with his square formed and stable, the body set off at a measured pace for the village of Abu Kru. There was only a handful of camels still alive and these were burdened with water and ammunition, but more importantly, they carried the wounded, of which twenty-five were stretcher cases.

The square had moved forward only a few paces when the Mahdi's men rose in a mass and swept down on the small but well-disciplined British force. The fire from the square was as accurate, controlled and as effective as it had been forty-eight hours earlier. The firing of volleys converted hundreds of brave and determined Arabs into small bundles of lifeless rags with only the wind to stir them. They were not deterred, however, and death apparently held no fear as many gave their lives in a series of fruitless charges. These constant charges inevitably slowed Wilson's pace of advance and the first awful and bloody mile took an hour. Behind the square there was a swathe of dead with several similarly dead camels among them. The battle followed its repetitive course and, on both sides, the butcher's bill grew ever larger.

There was yet one more charge, more volley fire and then . . . silence. The Mahdists had run their course and they were broken. The square moved quickly and in late afternoon it reached the River Nile with only token resistance. The men went down to drink by companies, probably a drink most of them would remember for the rest of their lives. The following day the village of Gubat, about two miles from Metemneh, was occupied and there was a welcome chance to regroup. The wounded were left at Gubat with a strong guard and the remainder marched the six miles or so back to their start point. There were dead to be buried and equipment to be recovered. A team of strapping guardsmen carried Sir Herbert Stewart who was suffering the particular agony that comes from a gut wound.

On 21 January, Wilson took the village of Abu Kru and this nondescript little place lent its name to the battle of two days before. The battle of Abu Klea is well known but its rather bloodier successor less so. Charles Townshend fought through both and in the process commanded a company with skill and determination. He had cause to take pride in the part he had played.

Before Colonel Wilson could take any decisions he had to try and ascertain the exact state of affairs at Khartoum. The steamers which had arrived from Khartoum were just ordinary Nile paddle steamboats, which had been converted by Gordon into very formidable gunboats. They were clad with heavy wooden beams and crude iron plates, both proof against small-arms fire. A large fortification had been constructed on the forecastle and another similar defence work adorned the quarterdeck.. The evidence of the action the two boats had already been engaged in was the plethora of bullet holes that riddled the funnels and the splinter marks that scarred the wooden cladding.

The crew reported that Gordon was holding on and this gave Wilson every hope of reaching the besieged general. It was on this basis that Colonel Wilson and twenty men set off for Khartoum in one steamer, while Beresford mounted his Gardner in the other and followed on. Given that the city was invested by a large enemy army, Wilson was something of an optimist if he really thought that two boats and less than 100 men could resolve the dire situation. As it happens, not only was it an absurd venture but it was a forlorn hope because Gordon was already dead and his garrison had been put to the sword. But Wilson was blissfully unaware of the gravity of the situation in Khartoum when he set off.

The death of Gordon was not the end of the campaign as Wilson's steamer was wrecked by gunfire about 40 miles from Gubat where the main channel of the river ran only 100 yards below an enemy position. Wilson and his crew abandoned the boat, still under fire, and took refuge on an island in the river. Beresford set out to rescue them in his steamer, the *Sofia*, a vessel that even undamaged could only manage 4 knots, flat out, against the current. As he approached the island and the same enemy breastworks he too came under fire and, by unhappy chance, the enemy dropped a shell straight into the boiler room. *Sofia* stopped abruptly and Beresford was obliged to anchor in full sight of the enemy.

The enemy fire was countered and suppressed by the Gardner gun which fired 6,000 rounds and glowed as it heated under the pressure. Whilst this rain of fire was directed at the enemy breastwork, a man called Henry Benbow laboured mightily to repair the boiler. Benbow was without doubt the 'man of the match' and, incredibly against all the odds, he succeeded in getting the boilers working. When darkness fell *Sofia* raised steam and got under way; however, the Arabs were alerted by the sound of the engine and the display of sparks issuing from the funnel. Once more fire was brought down on the little boat – it was hardly a ship but it battled upriver on what seemed to be a hopeless mission.

Beresford, like a character from a boys' comic, made his way to the island, took aboard Wilson and his men and then retraced his course downriver and back past the main enemy position. Beresford suspected treachery and so when they got close to the point of extreme danger he told the pilot that, if he got the boat through he would give him £200, but added the warning that, if the boat grounded, he would, 'Blow your brains out'. So saying, the naval officer drew his revolver, cocked it and placed it against the pilot's head. This proved to be sufficient incentive for the pilot to focus on matters in hand and the party, in their shot-holed boat, got through. Amazingly, given all the lead that had been flying around, only two men were killed and an officer wounded.

Townshend was unaware of the Wilson saga because several days before, on 23 January, he accompanied a convoy which started for Gakdul and reached Abu Klea at midday next day. Townshend commented:

> The garrison had made a fort with a zariba in which was the hospital. Surgeon McGill of the Guards was doing well, and so was Lyall of the

R.A., whom we thought to find dead. St. Vincent and Guthrie had died of their wounds. . . . We resumed our march for Gakdul, crossing the battlefield of 17 January. The bodies were decomposing and the stench was very bad. We lived on half rations during this march and reached Gakdul on 26 January.

The same day that Townshend arrived in Gakdul, Wilson's water-borne sally was seen to be far too late – Khartoum had fallen on 26 January 1885 after a siege of 317 days and Gordon was dead at the Mahdi's hand. The object of the expeditionary force had been to relieve Khartoum and save Gordon; it had failed in its aim. Despite massive effort and sacrifice it had all been in vain and, one wonders, would it have been different if Stewart had not lingered for those twelve days in early January, and if his preparations had not been so dilatory?

In mid–February, Colonel Redvers Buller made a belated appearance in the theatre. This rising military star was related to Townshend by dint of his marriage to Audrey, the daughter of the 4th Marquess, and Audrey was a first cousin. He did not fully realize what he was taking on when he married into the family – he was to find that he had acquired a demanding military cousin who, over the years to come, would exploit their connection and Buller's fame entirely to his advantage.

The expedition was abandoned and withdrew across the Bayuda desert, but not before Townshend had had his first taste of a full-scale battle – two, in fact, in which he had acquitted himself well. Indeed, well enough to be 'mentioned in despatches'. There is no evidence of this 'Mention' on his service record, but that might just be a clerical error. It is to his credit that despite any criticism ever made of him, his personal courage was never questioned. He was every inch the professional soldier and he never shirked his duty in confronting his country's enemies.

Townshend observed, shrewdly, the wave of national emotion that was generated around Gordon as he held out in Khartoum, and the mere fact of his being besieged that had made him a national hero. Gordon's death served to accentuate the reverence in which he was held. Townshend was to be involved in two further sieges and in both, the hero status of the besieged was to be underscored. Unfortunately all sieges are, by their very nature, defensive and although they might be lifted they can very rarely be hailed as 'victory'. A possible exception might be 'The Lines of Torres Vedras' which were a series of defence works built by Wellington, around the town of Torres Vedras, in 1809 to resist Massena's advance in 1810.

Massena's army starved in its siege lines and eventually was obliged to withdraw. It was the exception that proved the rule.

In May 1885, Charles Townshend was taken seriously ill with enteric fever and sent down the Nile with a 'sick convoy', his condition worsened and by the time he reached Wadi Halfa he had also contracted dysentery. He left Egypt and the Sudan in the summer and arrived home in England in August. This was all a rather anticlimactic end to an arduous and exciting campaign.

Notes
1. Townshend's personal file, PRO/WO/76/258, the content of which he read and signed as correct in 1906 shows him as a graduate of the RMC, Sandhurst. The *Oxford Dictionary of National Biography* incorrectly avers that he went to Dartmouth RNC, but Dartmouth has no record of CVFT. The RNC was housed in wooden hulks on the River Dart, one of which was HMS *Britannia,* until 1905. It seems to be a most unlikely place in which to train infantry officers. Erroll Sherson and A.J. Barker also recorded that CVFT was a graduate of Dartmouth. On checking Navy Lists, for the years 1873-5, no record of him could be found. It is possible that he entered the Navy, was sent to *Britannia* and subsequently moved on to Sandhurst for further training. Naval and Marine cadets were listed together in the Navy Lists, but their place of training was not recorded.
2. CVFT.
3. CVFT.
4. The civilian reader should be aware that there are only two means of rewarding servicemen and women for their service. The first of these is 'promotion', but that is severely limited by the constraints of the organizational structure. The second is a 'medal' which, although of no intrinsic value, does serve to advertise a soldier's experience, service and sometimes gallantry. The value of medals as an incentive should not be underestimated. In commercial life it is all so simple – a good performance attracts a cash bonus.
5. A.J. Barker.
6. Hastings, *Warriors*.
7. Ibid.

Chapter 3

1886 – 1893

India and the Hunza-Nagar expedition

'The soldier is a peculiar being that can alone be brought to the height of efficiency by inducing him to believe that he belongs to a regiment infinitely superior to the others round him.'

Field Marshal Lord Wolseley

On 15 January 1886, Townshend achieved one of his aims and was gazetted to the Indian Staff Corps (ISC), being attached to the Central Indian Horse (CIH). After five years his time as a marine was over. He seemed to have achieved two objects and the CIH promised to be 'just up his alley'. He was joyfully shipped out to pastures new – in the event they were as hot, dusty and insanitary as those he had left behind in the Sudan. Nevertheless, the North-West Frontier of India was an exciting place to be and much to be preferred over Colchester, York or Aldershot.

First, there was the expensive meeting with the regimental tailor, and finally there came the generous welcome at Regimental Headquarters and the pleasure of meeting new faces in new settings, and a vastly different way of life. Three years of regimental duty followed, with only intermittent episodes of excitement in a great deal of endless routine.

An army overseas is very different to an army at home. It is more close knit, more interdependent, more cohesive and often more social. For the time being it was peaceful, although it transpired that India was perhaps not all it was cracked up to be. Certainly, the grass was not noticeably any greener, although the short bouts of active patrolling that were part of the routine of the North-West Frontier were welcomed.

In the late nineteenth century, the British Army in India devoted much of its energy to an extraordinary schedule of unit moves which involved great cost and enormous human effort. Looking back, and with hindsight, one does wonder what was achieved by these exhausting peregrinations. The road from Lucknow to Peshawar is a thousand miles of almost geometrically straight road. It was along this 'Grand Trunk Road' that regiments and battalions marched north-west or south-east from canton-ment to cantonment under a hot sun, 12 miles a day – sometimes 15 – all of this through clouds of choking dust that made the exercise an unattractive way to spend a summer day.

At the day's end a bivouac area was reached where first and foremost the horses had to be fed, watered, groomed and made comfortable. This was before there could be any thought of pitching camp or getting food; the needs of the men were low down the order of priorities and that of the officers even lower. After a brew, it was back to care for the horses and atten-tion to 'stables' and the saddlery. It was only at this late stage in the day that the officers were able to attend to themselves. By 1886, Townshend should have been totally imbued with the culture that put horses first, soldiers second and officers a very poor third.

In all this, the role of the subaltern was to see that the march routine was observed and this, absolutely, was not Townshend's idea of fun. He thirsted for command, in action, fighting the enemies of the Crown. In his some-what immature judgment the day–to-day administration of the Raj was undemanding and very boring. It probably was, but then a soldier has to play the cards he has been dealt.

He settled down for long enough to attend riding classes; this time it was horses and not camels. Whatever it was, it was a far cry from the Royal Marines. Ever the professional, he applied himself to learning Hindustani, a second linguistic string to his bow as he was already fluent in French. In due course he would pass the army intermediate examination in Arabic.

It was too good to last and after three years the novelty of the Indian Army was beginning to wear thin. He started to recall the advantages of service in Egypt and began writing to ask Buller if he could use his influence to secure for him an appointment with the Khedive's army.

The likelihood is that, back in Whitehall at the War Office, there was now a burgeoning file. The cover would have been emblazoned with Townshend's name and inside the buff-coloured cover, on the fly-leaf, there would have been a summary of the contents. Buller's intercessions on Townshend's behalf, and Charles Townshend's litany of complaints about his lot and his repeated requests for either a change of employment, cap badge, theatre or station were dutifully preserved. In addition, as the file was circulated routinely for comment to the various branches that had some interest in Townshend, staff officers had added comments on each of the various folios. Not all of these were to his credit. Townshend was now well advanced in building a reputation – but it was not quite what he had in mind.

In June 1889 he took some leave, rode the 74 miles to the nearest rail head and made his way to the hill station and resort of Simla. There was every chance he would find lots of pretty girls, but the holiday was suddenly blighted when news came of the death of his father, Charles Thornton Townshend.

For anyone the death of a parent comes as a shock and the cause of deep distress. In this case Townshend had not seen his father for six years and Erroll Sherson, who edited the diaries, either, discretely or unintentionally, left out any expressions of regret or indication of emotion made by his cousin. Perhaps CVFT simply did not put to paper any expression of remorse. Either way, Townshend's emotions on the death of his parent are not recorded. We can but speculate that their relationship was distant and six years apart will not have helped. It did not pass unnoticed by Charles that the death of his father had moved him up the Townshend pecking order and he was now heir presumptive to the title. His younger cousin was still steadfastly, wonderfully and most satisfactorily unmarried.

Perhaps it was the death of his father, but something disturbed him sufficiently that he suspended writing his diary for a month. When he eventually resumed his daily record, a lady, only identified as 'EH', became the subject of constant entries. They rode out together and he spent much of his time in her company He wrote of any number of engagements at the home of 'Mrs H' – doubtless the mother of the young lady. On 28 July 1889, he notes, 'engaged to EH'. By any yardstick this was a whirlwind romance – he had known the girl little more than a month.

After his leave and tender farewells to his intended bride there was a brief spell back at his duty station before he left once more, this time for England. By all accounts he was, as ever, the life and soul of the party on the troopship in which his banjo was put to good use. On arrival in England he wasted no time in going to Cheltenham to visit the brothers and sisters of EH, as well as attending to his professional duty, not the least of which was reporting in to the India Office. Whilst in London he was able to deal with the issues raised by the death of his father. But much more fun, he was able take up again the rather racy and bohemian life that is a feature of the theatre world.

EH was out of sight and sufficiently out of mind for Charles Townshend to pursue an attractive actress known only as 'My Very Dear L'. Neither EH nor L is ever fully identified in his diary. He corresponded with EH until mid-1891 and so their relationship was of about two years' duration. It must have been a curious engagement because there was no talk of marriage and no evidence that they ever met again. EH then left the scene quite unheralded and there is not even a brief diary entry to mark her departure. Charles Townshend was not the first to have his head turned by a holiday romance, but clearly there was much more to it than that.

Townshend's return to UK was for serious business and from October 1889 until December 1890 his service record[1] notes that he attended a musketry course at Hythe. Whilst at home he took leave, having been abroad for six years. During these six years he had seen active service in command of a company, had broadened his experience and grown to the full bloom of manhood. Braddon describes Townshend as 'a tall, ugly man with an ovate skull.'[2] In fact Townshend was 5 foot 10 inches in height and, as his photographs testify, he was certainly no uglier than any other man on the Clapham omnibus – not that Townshend was inclined to take such a conveyance.

Townshend, by now permanently ensconced in India, decided that, after all, he really rather preferred Egypt. During his next nine years whilst on the establishment of the Indian Army he devoted considerable energy in manoeuvring to get out of India – but without success. He bored his brother officers to death as he complained incessantly about his lot – one that of course they shared but in rather more stoic manner. However, on 28 May 1890, he notes that, 'Colonel Buller writes me asking if I will take the Egyptian Army if offered for two years; have said I will.' Life was looking up and he still had several more months to enjoy all that the London scene had to offer. Sundry, but anonymous ladies helped him to pass the time agreeably.

The job in Egypt was delayed and Christmas 1890 was spent in Agra with the CIH. Townshend had to be patient and in the meantime he made full use of the opportunities for hunting big game and his diary records the part he played in reducing the population of tigers and panthers. Hunting the big cats was not without risk and that was the attraction of the 'sport.' Although Townshend was an expert shot he obviously relished the danger and one diary entry says:

> Just returning from the river beat I shot a tiger. As you can imagine, I am very pleased. I was sitting on the ground on a path under a steep cliff and suddenly I heard a step behind me, I turned round and there was the tiger looking at me about twelve yards away. Without getting up I screwed myself round and fired killing him dead with an explosive bullet through his heart. I expect if I had only wounded him slightly he would have killed me.

This entry has a curious tone and it reads as if it was written to a third person.

On 25 June 1891, his commanding officer received a telegram from the Acting Governor General, Central India, which said, 'Colonel Durand applies urgently for the services of Lieutenant Townshend at Gilgit, and the Viceroy wishes him to go at once. Please send Townshend at once and report time of departure.'

There is no explanation why this Colonel Durand should seek the services of an obscure subaltern and the direct involvement of no lesser person than the Viceroy in this matter is nothing less than extraordinary.

Townshend and 'Curly' Stewart, a Gurkha officer, had to make their way to Gilgit from Peshawar. This journey took three weeks and on their route, which had no road or even a track, they climbed over the Tragbal Pass (11,000ft) and the Dorikun Pass (13,500ft). This was the same route taken by the supply trains that provisioned the garrison at Gilgit and its sub-stations. Townshend and Stewart made the journey safely and Charles Townshend took up his new appointment with great enthusiasm.

In 1888, the Gilgit Agency had been established on the North-West Frontier of India, an event, political in nature, that had been a matter of no interest to a young officer like Townshend. Neither was it of the slightest interest that a Colonel A.G. Durand had been installed as 'The Agent' with a surgeon to work on his staff – a Surgeon–Major George Robertson. Unknown to him, both men were to play a part in Townshend's future.

Durand was an expert on the social, domestic and diplomatic scene in this inhospitable part of the world and he remarked, 'Diplomacy in the Hindu-Kush is an interesting game to watch; the men intrigue from their cradle; it is an amusement as well as the business of life. For an Englishman the only safe course is the honest one; he must think pretty carefully before he speaks, and then speak plainly.'[3]

This was the backcloth against which that telegram arrived. One can conclude that either the CIH wished to be rid of Charles, or his reputation as a fighting soldier had gone before him. He discovered from Durand that he had been selected to command the 1st (or Raga Pertab) Battalion of the Imperial Kashmir Contingent. This was an element of the 20,000 strong 'Imperial Service Troops' created by Lord Dufferin to harness the warrior characteristics of the disparate tribes of the frontier region.

'Battalion' is something of a misnomer and a rather grandiose title for what was, in effect, a locally enlisted defence force of 583 all ranks. These men were largely untrained, of doubtful quality and were not natural soldiers. Nevertheless, this was an important career move for a young man, still only a lieutenant, but thirty years of age and serving in close proximity to the Agent himself. It was an opportunity too good to miss.

Command of a locally enlisted battalion called for a special sort of leadership because his men, although they accepted the authority of a British officer, still required that officer to demonstrate his worthiness of their respect.

Townshend was in a very demanding post. For success he had to display guile, courage, diplomacy and fine judgment. He had the task of converting tough, unsophisticated hillmen into a semblance of soldiers. They would all have been conversant with firearms but not the modern weapons with which they were now issued, mostly Snider rifles.

Townshend had to instil the discipline in his men, not only to obey fire orders, but also teach them how fire was used tactically. Rudimentary First Aid, low-level tactics and bayonet fighting were on the curriculum. Field hygiene was also high on Townshend's priority list, if not on that of his soldiers; Colonel Durand had commented on the distasteful smell of the hill people of the Hindu Kush who viewed bathing and personal cleanliness as quite unnecessary and no more than a quaint British aberration. It is a hard fact that, over the last 400 years, as many British soldiers and sailors have died from disease as from enemy action. It was well understood that keeping bodily clean and maintaining a pure water source were both fundamental to operational effectiveness. Logistics are never a very attractive topic but the maintenance of an army in the field in 1891, as now, required food, transport, water, clothing, bedding and accommodation. The men had to be paid and all their needs catered for. The mules too had to be cared for. Townshend did not work single-handed and he had, in his support, Kasmiri officers, but he was the Commanding Officer, the 'Boss.' He alone was responsible.

His diary entry for 14 August 1891 gives an indication of what he was up against:

> Sent for the Adjutant[4] and asked him what was doing in the regiment? It had as yet done no battalion drill, no musketry, no outpost duties nor advance or rear guards – in fact no duties of 'detached order' of any kind. Bayonet exercise had never been done, but they do the manual and firing exercise. Saw a few recruits at evening drill, a dirty looking lot. Took the Adjutant down to the range and explained to him many things and how I wanted them done to get the regiment in proper trim for active service in November.

This period of his career should have embedded, even more deeply, in his mind the absolute priority to be given to the well-being of his soldiers. All in all Townshend was being tested and although he was a high-grade officer it is difficult to imagine a young officer being so exposed today.

A very welcome opportunity to distinguish himself arose soon after taking command. This was when his battalion was selected, by Durand, to join the Hunza-Nagar expedition, an operation that was to be the overture to one of the most important episodes in Townshend's career. Some background on the political situation would be appropriate.

Hunza and Nagar were two small states situated on the North-West Frontier of Kashmir and they were administered by the British from their base at Gilgit. They were in a state of constant conflict with each other and had been for generations, even though the two states were inhabited by people of the same ethnicity and religious persuasion. Neither state was of any particular significance until about 1889 when 'The Great Game' was being played out between Great Britain and Russia in the forbidding and rugged country of Kashmir. It was then, as part of 'The Great Game', that Hunza and Nagar took their place on the playing field of international politics.

This stretch of frontier was known as the region of the eastern Hindu-Kush; from east to west it was 500 miles long and from north to south about 150 miles broad – 75,000 square miles of bleak and, in places, impassable terrain.

In 1891 all of these states of the area were either directly under the rule of, or tributary to, Kashmir and Kashmir acknowledged the suzerainty of the Queen. The single feature that gave this section of the frontier such importance was that it was in close proximity to the Russian outposts.

It was a difficult area to access. Gilgit, which is roughly at its centre, lies 400 miles north of the line of the railway at Rawal Pindi (now Rawalpindi) in the Punjab. The only road to India over which the British had permanent control, ran over two passes of 14,000ft and 11,300ft; these were often blocked by deep snow and impassable for weeks on end. A 'road' did run up the Indus valley whereby strong men might reach Srinagar after a hike of 400 miles. However this road, in effect little more than a goat track, ran through the territory of hostile tribes, all of whom had a particular and very specific aversion to Europeans.

Thomas Cook did not recommend this route.

Everything had to be carried by porters along this ill-defined goat track. Conscription as a porter was tantamount to a death sentence and the fatality rate among the unfortunate coolies, who were all pressed men, was very high because no arrangements were made to care for them.

On every supply train men froze as they crossed the high passes, they drowned fording the rushing mountain torrents and they succumbed to plague, smallpox, cholera and dysentery which they contracted in the verminous camps that offered them scant shelter along the way. It was by this ill-favoured route that Townshend and Stewart had joined their duty station.

From a soldier's point of view the area administered from Gilgit was vulnerable. It was far from an ideal place in which to garrison troops as it was beset with communication and logistic difficulties. The policy of HM Government is rarely altered to accommodate military considerations and so Gilgit was maintained as a hub of Empire, and Townshend and many others had to live with the problems. This was particularly so as Russian activity was increasing and its influence expanding, to the detriment of Britain's prestige. It was strategically important for Britain to hold fast to its sphere of influence. It was this evaluation that had led to the original establishment of the Gilgit Agency and the eventual occupation of Chitrál.

Chitrál is a place that figures large in this narrative as it was there that Townshend was to establish his reputation. This obscure village, which is now a flourishing town with a permanent garrison and an airport, was to be of great significance in the shaping of Charles Townshend, of which we will hear much more later.

Chalt was the closest British outpost to the villages of Hunza and Nagar, which are on opposite banks of the Kanjut River. They almost face each other and each was the capital of a 'robber state'.[5] Between them they could raise about 5,000 men although they were entirely independent of each other and usually mutually antagonistic other than when they combined against a common foe – usually the Indian Empire.

The Kings or Thums of these two states were the ungrateful recipients of a small subsidy from the Government of India and another from the Maharajah of Kashmir. Despite this they had, in the past, attempted to seize Gilgit and had once actually succeeded in capturing the fort at Chalt – they were eventually driven out, taking the fort's guns with them.

It was a curious arrangement for two rival nations to exist facing each other over a narrow ravine with precipitous sides only scaleable at a few points on either side – each of these accesses being very closely guarded. The ravine extended for 30 miles along the Kanjut river valley, and along its length the forts of Hunza faced those of Nagar, with hostility between the two always a possibility.

At the gateway to this interesting piece of country two strongpoints guarded access to the valley and these were the fortified villages of Nilt and

Maiun (or Mayun). Notwithstanding the fact that the two states were usually at loggerheads with each other, they always combined to resist any incursion by a third party. It all seems to defy common sense but a great deal of life on the Frontier did not correspond to life in more civilized parts of the world.

E.F. Knight, in his forthright manner, described the Thums (Kings) of these two states as 'ignorant and blood-thirsty scoundrels, faithless to their treaty obligations and incapable of respecting anything but force. They were absolute monarchs and murdered and sold at will their subjects into captivity at their own sweet will.' He went on to say that 'patricide and fratricide were hereditary failings of both royal lines.'

These were certainly not the sort of chaps with whom one would choose to do business but, it was people like this that Townshend had to deal with.

In May 1891, Rajah Uzr Khan, the Thum of Nagar, murdered his two brothers because he was jealous of their relatively civilized relationship with Colonel Durand. To add to his infamy he then recommenced his attacks on travellers, and kidnapped and sold into slavery some people living very close to Chalt. Soon thereafter he combined with the Thum of Hunza and they marched on Chalt.

Colonel Durand thwarted this particular act of aggression by rapidly reinforcing the garrison with 200 men and the threat evaporated. It was a characteristic of warfare on the Frontier, in that opponents of the British often 'talked a good game' but capitulated in the face of a determined opposition.

Durand could not tolerate this sort of conduct but nevertheless offered almost conciliatory terms. He advised the two Thums that in order to ensure the safety of British garrisons a new fort was to be erected at Chalt and a military road, practicable for mules, would be built from Gilgit to Hunza and Nagar, and beyond, should this be judged expedient, to defend the high passes of the Hindu Kush. The route was down the Kanjut valley. Durand, a very practical soldier/diplomat, did not entertain any hopes that the road scheme would be accepted without opposition and he had no illusions – an expedition would have to be mounted.

Not least of the unstated objects of the expedition would be to re-assert Britain's dominance of the region, which could not tolerate the defiant attitude being displayed by the Hunza and Nagar chiefs towards the British in general and Durand in particular. An informant who was a source of high-quality intelligence revealed that Hunza and Nagar were proposing to attack several British outposts in a coordinated operation. It became ever clearer that there had to be a demonstration of the Empire's will. The Hunza-Nagar

Expedition of 1891 was the result, mounted under the command of Colonel Algernon Durand, the well-established Political Agent and the personification of the British presence.

On 29 October 1891, Durand inspected Townshend's battalion and expressed great satisfaction with what he saw. He told Townshend that he was to command his unit in the forthcoming campaign and allotted him British subalterns, Widdicombe and Williams. The Battalion advanced to Chalt on 7 November and in his diary Townshend wrote admiringly of the beauty of the valley which was full of fruit trees. He said, 'I have never seen such a pretty place.' On 15 November, a messenger arrived bearing a letter from the Rajah of Hunza. The letter said that he understood that the British were going to make war and he'd be obliged if they would indicate when they were coming. It was an interesting insight into the attitude of a foe that seemed to see the forthcoming contest as a sort of military sporting event. He might just as easily have enquired who would provide the oranges at half time.

On 17 November, Townshend was recalled to Gilgit and Durand told him that after the campaign he was going to install him as Military Governor of Hunza. This was riches beyond even the imagination or aspirations of Charles Townshend. 'I did not know how to thank him,' he recorded, obviously delighted. First, the command of a battalion and now, *ipso facto*, King of Hunza – what next? None of this could happen until Durand had imposed his will and there were stern times ahead.

On 29 November, Townshend was given the task of turning the enemy flank with the 5th Gurkhas and 200 men of his own battalion. 'Quite a nice little command,' he thought and for him the expedition could not start soon enough. He did not have long to wait and on 1 December 1891, the Hunza-Nagar Field Force marched from Chalt on the first leg.

Durand had raised a force of 2,000 men but he had to reinforce the garrisons at Gilgit, Boonji and Astor. Similarly he had to secure several other strategic points on his line of advance and by the time he left Chalt his force was down to about 1,000 men, with a considerable train of porters and muleteers in support.

These minor Victorian wars, of which Hunza-Nagar is typical, are now reduced to merely a few lines in unopened history books, but they were vicious, uncompromising affairs. There was little compassion or chivalry on the North-West Frontier, and British soldiers and their locally enlisted comrades died unheralded and alone.

Durand was an enterprising and skilled soldier and this he demonstrated by wasting no time in grasping the nettle. He chose the Nagar side of the River Kanjut as the line of his advance on the twin strongholds of Nilt and Mayun. The drawback to this decision was that the safety of his force would be dependent upon his holding a bridge in his rear; this had to be guarded and the provision of the guard force further depleted his numbers. The going was much easier on the Nagar side of the river and he anticipated reaching his first objective, the fort of Nilt, in only one day's march.

The task facing Durand was difficult. Nilt had been strongly fortified, and if the force was to have access to water it was essential to storm the enemy position on the day that his force arrived. This was because the only track to the fort ran several hundred feet above the river for some miles and there was no way down to the water within a reasonable distance of the fort.

Durand was as dependent upon the River Kanjut as Stewart had been on the River Nile, for without water Durand knew that he could not maintain his force in front of Nilt. With the first streak of dawn on 2 December the little force, now a little short of 1,000 men, two mountain guns and a Gatling machine gun, fell in and, Townshend included, set about its work. It was a painfully small force but the shrewd commander commented that, 'A larger force could not have been fed in the country; a smaller could not have undertaken the job.'

He was absolutely right in his judgment.

The opposition was estimated at some 4–5,000 men who, although indifferently armed, were nevertheless very skilful and dangerous enemies – particularly when established behind stone walls. It is a measure of Durand's confidence that he was prepared to take on an entrenched enemy that outnumbered him by a margin of about 5:1. An assaulting force would normally seek a 3:1 superiority. Durand was either an intrepid and skilled soldier, or a fool – the next few days would be the judge of that.

The initial advance was unopposed, but the path had been cut away in places and some spirited road building by the sappers was necessary. Consequently the march was slightly delayed, so that it was about midday before Durand and his men crossed the last rising ground and saw Nilt with Maiun, or Mayun, high on the cliffs ahead of them. The fort stood at the junction of the river with a vast ravine that descended from the snows of Rakaposhi.[6] The cliffs forming the ravine, as well as those arising from the river bank, were some 300 feet in height.

The ground posed Durand with some daunting problems. Flags fluttered from the walls of Nilt and a burst of cheering and a roll of drums made it clear that the Field Force was expected. Men could be seen hurrying into the fort and entering the sangars (stone breastworks) on the high hills

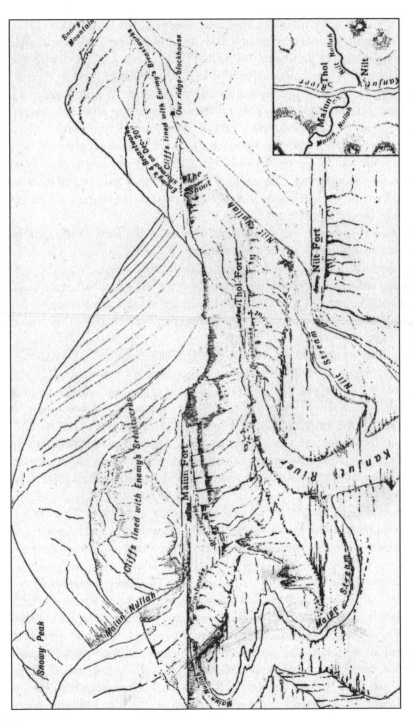

Fig 3. A contemporaneous field sketch showing the juxtaposition of the forts at Nilt, Maiun and Thol. A map would not provide the same feel for the ground. (Knight)

behind the town. Nilt was to be the first objective, overlooked as it is by a ridge. Durand sent a party to secure the ridge and to establish a blockhouse there from which to dominate the fort. This was accomplished with the expenditure of a great deal of effort but with no casualties.

Notwithstanding the occupation of the ridge above it, Nilt remained a significant defensive position. The inhabitants of the fort lived in a warren of substantial, stone-built houses, two or three storeys high with narrow twisting lanes, alleys really, in between. The whole was surrounded by a massive stone wall 12 feet thick and about 20 feet high, with towers at intervals around the perimeter. The roofs of the buildings were covered in stone slabs and virtually impregnable to shellfire. Durand was facing a tough nut that might be difficult to crack.

The fort at Nilt followed the pattern of most of the forts in the Hindu-Kush which were generally square, with towers at the corners. The solid walls, often 10 to 15 feet thick for some feet from the base, were built of stones and mud strengthened by timbers, but the towers, which were high, were usually relatively flimsy, and the loosening of the timber frame could bring them down. The sketch on Page 39 gives an impression of the ground and the difficulty that Durand faced.

A curiosity of Durand's force was that it was accompanied by six civilians one of whom, a Mr Spedding, was an engineer by profession. He was appointed Chief Engineer with the local rank of captain and he made a splendid contribution to the expedition by supervising the improvement of the tracks that the force had to use. The others, as far as can be ascertained, were 'just along for the ride'. Nevertheless, Durand made use of these miscellaneous civilians by making them temporary officers and assigning them military duties. They all accepted their new responsibilities gladly and with great enthusiasm.

Edward Knight was one of these worthies. He was 'a very experienced war correspondent'[7] by profession and clearly something of a character. He was engaged in a trek across northern Kashmir with a friend called Beech – two archetypal Englishmen who had brought their golf clubs on their trek. Knight records the difficulties experienced in playing a variation of the Royal and Ancient game on the foothills of the Hindu Kush where the 'fairways' were less than sympathetic and often very seriously steep. The lie of the ball on a rock-strewn hillside was not always agreeable and one must assume that 'preferred lies' were allowed. Despite this no doubt he and Beech faced any number of 'unplayable lies'. They must have carried a large stock of golf balls because the 'lost ball' rate would have been high but, as the 'course' was unmeasured, the good news was that they did not have to submit a card to the Secretary of their home club! There was no formal golf course that conformed to the accepted norm for perhaps 1,000 miles or more in any direction. When called for service to the Crown by Durand, Beech laid down his golf clubs and was promptly appointed Provost Marshal.

Knight, who had an abiding interest in matters military, became an infantry officer and was placed under the command of Charles Townshend; he took to soldiering like a duck to water and proved to be an asset. He took charge of the troops placed under him and from all accounts he not only thoroughly enjoyed the exercise but he acquitted himself well. Knight was able to observe Townshend from close quarters in the weeks that followed and wrote a vivid description of the battles for Nilt and Thol in his book *Where three empires meet.*[8] It is a readable account and Knight's journalistic background is quite evident. The measure of the quality of Knight's book is that Durand commended it as an accurate record and did not, himself, write a detailed account of the two engagements.

Durand's intention was to test the corner of a tower with his light mountain guns, in the hopes of causing the tower to collapse, providing a vulnerable point susceptible to an attack. He also decided that if this first initiative failed then Lieutenant Aylmer RE, with a handful of sappers, covered by the Gurkhas, were to make a dash for the gate and blow it in with guncotton. The moment the fort was taken the Body Guard Regiment, which was held in reserve, was to be pushed past it into the ravine behind to take the defences on the far side.

It was decided to move the guns as close as possible and when fire was opened the enemy replied with ill-directed small-arms fire that caused only a few casualties for they were firing at well-concealed targets. Unfortunately one of the few casualties was Durand who was shot through the thigh. The bullet was of the home-made variety – a garnet encased in lead, but no less lethal for all that. Notwithstanding the provenance of the bullet, the initial prognosis was that it was a mortal wound. However, Durand survived and the bullet was removed that evening.

The fire on the tower proved to be ineffective and it was discovered, after the event, that the tower was not a hollow structure but had been built of solid stone to the very top. Despite this setback and his painful wound Durand decided to commit his infantry. Orders were given, and a covering party of Gurkhas dashed forward and lined the last of the terrace walls that faced the fort. They opened effective fire on the loopholes of the fort, under cover of which Lieutenant Aylmer and his party of sappers crossed the open ground and threw themselves into the ditch.

The gate of the fort was in the centre of the main wall but it was hidden from view by a six-foot curtain wall, built on the edge of the surrounding ditch. The enemy had loopholed this wall but, curiously, had omitted to defend it. The ditch was full of abattis, a barricade of felled trees, with branches pointed towards the enemy. In later conflicts the trees were often reinforced with barbed wire. Obviously the object was to hamper an enemy's advance and well-constructed abattis are often impassable.

In this case the abattis stretched the length of the ditch and beyond, forming a major barrier and restricting access to the curtain wall of the fort. Nevertheless a path was eventually found, through the barrier, which led to a small door set into the curtain wall. This door gave access to the passage between the curtain and main walls. The door was under heavy fire from the sangars across the ravine, but it was quickly prised open, incredibly with the loss of only one man. Aylmer and his small party found themselves in a position of relative calm for the enemy had failed to direct flanking fire to cover the passageway, and Aylmer had time to prepare a demolition charge to destroy the main gate.

Aylmer laid his guncotton, lit the fuse and stepped back under the wall; but the fuse did not burn and after an agonizing wait it was clear that the demolition charge had failed. Aylmer appreciated that he had to return, cut the fuse and relight it. To do so would take cold courage but, without hesitation, the young sapper officer rose to the challenge. He returned to the demolition charge and coolly and methodically reset the fuse. It was a critical time because, by now, the defenders had realized what Aylmer was about and were firing through loopholes in the main gate itself. Aylmer was wounded twice. Nevertheless, he completed his task, lit the fuse and withdrew, sprinkling blood in his tracks. There was an anxious pause as the fuse burned down and then a sudden, violent explosion as the heavy gate disappeared in a cloud of flame and dust.

The little party, including the wounded Aylmer, dashed through the miasma of smoke and dust and was, at once, engaged in a furious hand-to-hand fight in the tunnel that led through the main wall behind the gate. It was then that Lieutenant Boisragon, who was commanding the Gurkhas, found that he had only half a dozen men with him; the rest were still struggling through the abattis and had missed the only possible path. His bugler was engaged with his rifle and bayonet in the thick of the conflict fighting for his life and he had not thought of sounding the 'advance', which would have indicated that the fort was taken.

The attackers, although very small in number, had ample courage and they held their own, grimly repelling determined and repeated attacks, and taking casualties as the time ticked by. Eventually Boisragon gathered his men, regrouped and returned with Gurkha reinforcements. The hillmen from Nepal had their kukris unsheathed and this boded ill for the defenders. The small force poured into the narrow alleys of the fort and the defenders wilted under the refreshed assault. Whilst this desperate fight was going on inside the fort, 'A fire was kept up from the loopholes of our supports, the detachment of the Ragu Pertab Regiment now came up led by Lieutenant Townshend and the fort was soon swarming with our men.'[9]

The ensuing fight was brief, during which the Wazir of Nagar was killed and the fort finally fell. Lieutenant Badcock was severely wounded and Aylmer was desperately wounded, having now been hit in three places. The struggle had lasted twenty minutes. It had seemed like hours. British losses were six killed and 27 wounded. The enemy lost 80 killed.

The principal leaders of the enemy and a high proportion of the garrison escaped, threading their way through the maze of alleys in the fort and making their exit up a steep 'nullah', or ravine, behind the fort. As they climbed they became targets for Townshend's men who, in turn, were recipients of return fire from sangars even further up the mountain; the fort at Nilt was occupied, and stocks of grain, weapons and much more of the hand-made ammunition were found. The water supply was assured and, as the long-range sniping lapsed, Townshend busied himself with the host of tasks that follow any engagement. Clearly, there was more action yet to come as the forts of Thol and Maiun, each high on their precipitous cliffs, still posed very formidable obstacles.

The sketch map at Fig 3 (Knight) illustrates the problem, but not shown is the severity of the Nilt nullah which separated the Field Force in Nilt and the defenders of Thol. To the upper right of the sketch are the strategically important sangars overlooking Thol.

The next obstacle was Fort Thol and no one relished the thought of a frontal assault. The fort was dominated by four major breastworks high above the town at the top of precipitous cliffs. The enemy had clear line of sight and if the fort was to be taken these well-defended sangars had to be eliminated. The principal defence of the sangars was the awesome cliffs and the enemy had diverted a stream so that it sprayed on one of the possible approaches and encased it in a sheet of unscaleable ice.

The next phase of the expedition had an unsavoury feel to it. Townshend looking at the ground with a soldier's eye had no illusions as to what confronted him and his comrades and he was far from happy. His command had shrunk to a shadow of its former self and his diary for the next few days gives a flavour of the situation on 8 December as he recorded:

8th Dec. This is the most awful day I think I ever spent in my life! We moved off from camp at 4.30 a.m. Got into the nullah below Nilt Fort and waited for daybreak—our guns then got to work on the fort to pound down the sangars on the precipitous cliffs in front (of Thol fort). No effect after an hour,[10] and then we got orders to stay where we were as an attack would be made, and there we stayed all day, not being able to get out without losing a lot of men from the fire of the sangars.

9th Dec. A messenger came in from the enemy at Mayun this morning. The purport of this letter was that Safdar Ali Khan did not want war and only wanted to watch what went on between England, Russia and China. Also that we ought not to think a lot of ourselves because we had taken Nilt.

11th Dec. Built a sangar last night without getting a shot fired at us . . . After getting near the point along the river, I halted the party and went on with Manners-Smith and got around the point over the rocks and down a gully onto the sand in front of the enemy sangars. Having seen it was practicable for the men, I left Manners-Smith to watch and went back to fetch the men. Built sandbag redoubt called 'Townshend's sangar'. The men worked as silently as they could in the shadow of the rocks filling the sandbags and stacking them. The enemy never heard us and we got away at about 1 o'clock, leaving a Jemadar and 8 sepoys to occupy it.

He notes that on 13 December he was able to 'send a sketch or two to *The Illustrated London News*'. This is the first reference to such activity, and although an avid correspondent, hitherto his penmanship had been purely social.

There were three courses open to the British. The first was to push up the river bed and thus turn the enemy's position on the Nagar bank and by so doing make an approach to Thol, or to find a way up the cliffs in front and destroy his line of defensive sangars by direct attack. This was an unpalatable option as it had been discovered that the principal route up the cliff had been destroyed and four officers and forty men were killed in an abortive feint. There was yet another extreme alternative and that was to blow up the captured fort at Nilt, retire to Chalt and await the arrival, perhaps six months later or perhaps never, of help from India. Durand considered this option but swiftly rejected it, as he well knew that if he adopted this action it would inflame the frontier with grave consequences for the overall British position in 'The Great Game'.

Reconnaissance patrols probed at night but without success and no route could be found up the precipitous cliffs upon which Thol stood. The feasibility of moving troops up the river bed and of turning the enemy's position was next considered. This was fraught with danger as the British troops would have had to pass, for 600 yards, under a line of cliffs that provided excellent observation and firing points for the enemy securely emplaced there and above them in Maiun. The cliffs into the river were some hundreds of feet high. Only at rare intervals did a path lead up a ravine to the plateau above, and down these well-known passes the enemy had again poured water, which froze and converted the paths into sheets of ice – a novel, practical and very effective form of defence. To storm up such paths was impossible and the enemy, ever on the alert, redoubled the difficulty by sending down fireballs at night into the river bed, which illuminated it and deterred any build-up of troops. The second alternative, after careful consideration, had to be abandoned.

A way had to be found up the cliffs opposite Nilt to deliver a direct assault. Every night reconnaissance patrols were pushed up the great ravine leading to the glaciers of Rakapushi, and the opposing cliff was fully explored. One particularly intrepid reconnaissance was made by Lieutenant J.McD. Baird, 24th Bengal Infantry, but despite his determination to put himself in danger by making his way to positions directly under the occupied sangars, his exploration failed.

The impasse lasted for eighteen days during which no route to the top of the cliffs could be found, not least because the enemy's posts ran right up to the glaciers, and the cliffs became more forbidding the further the attackers searched. Finally, a little Dogra sepoy called Nagdu succeeded in climbing 1,200ft up the cliff, and in so doing he found a practicable path. His initiative and daring allowed preparations to be made for the final assault on 20 December 1891.

The absence of the wounded Durand, who had by now been evacuated to Gilgit, had required Dr Robertson to take on political responsibilities, whilst Captain L.J.E. Bradshaw, 35th Bengal Infantry, was given military command. It is curious that the most senior officer below that of the Colonel was a captain.

In the event, the attack on Thol was led by Captain Colin Mackenzie of the Seaforth Highlanders. This was because Bradshaw was absent in Gilgit dealing with a supply problem – an extraordinary priority for a commander in the field to take when in the face of the enemy and with an attack pending.

Mackenzie took the chance offered to him and he resolved to mount his attack at once. Before daybreak on 20 December, a covering party took up a position facing across the ravine to four well-constructed enemy sangars. A hundred and thirty-five men, all selected marksmen, under Charles Townshend (with Knight at his side), and Lieutenants Malony and Baird, had the job of ensuring that the sangars were not reinforced once the assault went in.

Mackenzie gave the order to open fire and the four sangars were each subjected to carefully controlled, accurate fire. The range was about 450 yards; to hit a target at that range with the unsophisticated open sights then in service called for a high degree of marksmanship. Townshend described it thus:

> 30 picked shots from each formation paraded on the ridge and fired on the enemy sangars with such accuracy that there was no response. Manners-Smith and Taylor with 100 men then scaled the cliff having been concealed all night in a ravine. Under this cover and led by the resourceful Nagdu, Lieutenant Manners-Smith in command of a small body of Kashmiri troops made an assault up the cliffs, 1200 feet high.

They assaulted the sangars one by one and with great élan took them all, losing only two men wounded. As the enemy vacated their redoubts and fled up the mountain so they exposed themselves to the fire of the marksmen on the ridge. Meanwhile, Manners-Smith and his party accounted for twenty of the enemy in one sangar alone.

It transpired that the attacking column had not been detected by the enemy until more than half of the ascent was completed and this proved to be crucial to success. With the element of surprise on its side the assault party escaped the danger of an avalanche of stones hurled down from the sangars covering the path.

Once taken, the enemy's line was fatally pierced. The opposition abandoned their positions, all organization evaporated and the survivors fled. Townshend observed in his diary:

> My regiment was the advance guards to take the Ziarat, this was a shrine that had been fortified as a strong point. 113 of the enemy surrendered to us when we got to the lower sangar. I thought that only about 15 men would be in it: my surprise was great on jumping down from the roof to find 100 men. They laid down arms when I told them; my men didn't come for 15 minutes, as the ascent was so difficult. I then went on in skirmishing order occupying the Ziarat and carried

one sangar with the bayonet . . . kept advancing on Thol fort by rushes
. . . we rushed in to find no one in it!

The campaign was over. Within two days Nagar was reoccupied, the
Hunza Chief and Uzr Khan, his henchman, escaped northwards across the
frontier. As Colonel Durand said, 'The result of the little war may best be
summed up in the words of a well-known Russian statesman, who said when
he heard of our occupation of Hunza: "*Ils nous ont fermé la porte au nez*"
(They have slammed the door in our faces).'

It had been a successful, economical operation and success was in large
part due to the gallantry of a number of officers and men. Accordingly,
decorations were distributed in reward. Aylmer, Boisragon and Manners-
Smith received the Victoria Cross,[11] and a number of Orders of Merit, the
equivalent to the Victoria Cross in the native army, were distributed among
the rank and file.

Peace was declared, order was restored and Townshend was installed as
the Military Governor of Hunza. He had played a key role in the capture of
the hill forts at Nilt and Thol, and thereafter resistance evaporated; Maiun
and Hunza surrendered. Colonel Durand was impressed with Townshend's
command ability and observed that he conducted himself in a sufficiently
commendable manner as to merit a second 'Mention'.[12] Townshend knew
Fenton Aylmer,[13] Guy Boisragon[14] and John Manners-Smith[15] well. He
would not have been human if he did not envy them their glory and wonder
how close he had been to similar distinction. By chance, Aylmer's career
was to be closely tied to that of CVFT some twenty-five years later.

Townshend was on a 'high'. He was lord of all he surveyed at Hunza –
although, frankly, it did not amount to much. Then, at the turn of the year,
he was promoted to captain. Ah now! A captain, two mentions, an independent command, a military governor no less and the icing on the cake was
that his cousin, the current Lord Townshend, was still not married – what
more could a man ask for?

Christmas 1891 was spent at 'Hunza Castle' as Townshend chose to call
his new domain, and in somewhat grandiose manner he 'issued a proclamation that Hunza now belongs to the British Government and that as long
as the inhabitants obey the British officer at Hunza all will go well for them'.
Who is to say the effect all this power would have had on a young man if he
had been left to rule his kingdom for long? The local population had com-
pliantly accepted British rule and consequently there was no military part
to be played. Surgeon-Major Robertson, now the Political Officer for the

area, had the reins, so Townshend's reign was short lived and he was recalled to reassume command of his Raga Pertab Regiment.

By 1892 CVFT's personality and personal characteristics were well developed. He would have been demonstrating the character traits that would merely come more pronounced as he got older and more senior – seniority would make him all the more difficult to deal with. It was said of Townshend, certainly after his death and possibly well before, that 'His military career was marred by his arrogance, egotism, ambition and intense dislike for routine soldiering, which did not endear him to his fellow officers.'[16] Arrogance is not, in itself, a fatal flaw. Most successful men display it to some degree or other. It springs from self-belief and the confidence generated by achievements already accomplished. Townshend got the balance wrong and the price he paid was eventually to lose the approbation of his peers. That makes for a lonely and unhappy man.

His sojourn in Hunza was very brief and uneventful, but it did give him the chance to catch up with his correspondence and to give further attention to the strategic aims and tactical successes of his hero, Napoleon Bonaparte. In a letter to a lady friend, obviously an actress, he indicated that he was still trying to transfer out of the Indian Army and back into the Egyptian Army. He also voiced his discontent to be so distanced from young women, a predictable moan that might have been echoed by any man in his forced state of celibacy.

In February 1892, Townshend was sent off to Skardu, a small town in Kashmir about 160 miles south east of Gilgit and the same distance from Srinagar – what was more, there were no available women there either. It was a sexual and social desert.

There was little chance of any military action either and he found himself enmeshed in the unremarkable garrison duties that he loathed. Erroll Sherson picked out a small incident that took place on 9 March when his soldier cousin showed some perfectly normal human compassion to two wretched prisoners who were incarcerated for the offence of being 'found sleeping when on sentry'. That was a serious offence, but Townshend discovered that they were imprisoned in appalling conditions and corrected the matter – and so he should. Any officer would have done the same and should have been damned if he had not.

June was a tedious month marked only by the banning of a man who 'had the insolence to send me a letter saying that he would proceed against me in Civil Court for refusing a petition. The man concerned had previously been convicted of stirring up insurrection against his commanding officer.'

It is presumed that the commanding officer concerned was CVFT because Townshend continued, 'Sent for Baskat Ali, kicked him out of the office and the orderlies ducked him in the pond. Have ordered that he has 24 hours to clear out of Skardu and if not he will be imprisoned.'

The same month he wrote to the Marquess to thank him for his financial support over the previous eleven years and said that now he had captain's pay he could get by. It was very irritating for Townshend, the prolific letter writer, not to receive reciprocal mail. He had none of the distractions of his London friends and they clearly did not respond very frequently. The man was lonely and mail was important. The following month when the postmaster said he had no mail 'I beat the postmaster.'[17] That was the same day that his battalion was ordered to leave Skardu and so a reason to celebrate. The postmaster doubtless joined in the celebrations, bruises permitting.

An MP called Henry Du Prè Labouchère (1831–1912), who was a blatant self-publicist, made damaging remarks in the House ridiculing the process by which officers were 'mentioned' in despatches. He alleged that, in many cases, the officers concerned had merely been doing their duty. He was a rich man and a failed diplomat, having been dismissed from the diplomatic service. He was a Liberal but failed to make his mark, politically, not least because Queen Victoria in 1892 forbade the recently returned Gladstone to offer him an office in government. Labouchère launched his attack on the system and made specific mention of Townshend, who had had a 'mention' for having brought the Raga Pertab Battalion to a creditable state of discipline and efficiency in peacetime. Townshend was outraged at this slur and wrote furiously in his diary: 'Well, I commanded the regiment in the campaign, was made Military Governor of Hunza and commanded the party in pursuit of Safdar Ali. If I had not the right to be mentioned in despatches, I don't know who had!'

In the twenty-first century a 'mention' for any action in peacetime would attract similar odium because, by definition, despatches are only written by a commander on active service, and it follows that the individual has to be on active service to qualify. But this was not the case in the 1890s. Today there are more sophisticated means of rewarding hard work. Durand, who wrote the despatch, would have done better to link Townshend only to the successful way he had commanded, in action, during the Hunza-Nagar campaign, where a mention was almost certainly very well earned. Two days later the honours and awards for that campaign were published: Durand got a CB and there were the three VCs already mentioned.

*   *   *

There was no time to brood because on 2 August 1892, Townshend, at the head of his battalion, marched down from Skardu to Srinagar. This was one of those unit moves that the Indian Army inflicted on itself at regular intervals. Townshend's personal effects required the services of 30 coolies; there was also a coolie for each of his sepoys, 46 for the officers, 64 for the NCOs, 160 to carry tentage, spare rifles and sundries, 74 to carry the rations, 13 for the hospital and 369 for the 'Irregular Corps', which is one way of describing the camp followers – just under 1,000 in total. Before he left he had had to deal with a request from the Rajah of Skardu who wanted a testimonial to say that he had behaved well. Townshend was not going to go that far and contented himself by averring that the Rajah 'was a keen sportsman and played polo'. Once established in the new duty station Townshend turned once more to his ever present priority – his career.

Although he had been so delighted to be given command of the Battalion in June 1891, only 15 months later he was prepared to give up this prestigious appointment if there was another, brighter opportunity on the horizon. He was due to take six months leave in 1893 and, given his attraction to the bright lights, pretty women and the social whirl that would be his for the taking, he was surely looking forward in anticipation of good times to come. His leave would fall neatly when his tour in command had expired. However, he opted to relinquish command early. Curiously, there is no mention in his diary of his handover of the Battalion and no reference to any sort of leaving party. It is rare indeed for soldiers to allow their commanding officer to just pack up and leave because his departure marks the end of an era and, as such, is an important event. It is invariably marked in some way. The degree is a measurement of the affection in which he is held and even martinets who are respected and not loved are given a send-off – if perhaps a little muted. Either Townshend was the exception to the rule and he did just pack up and leave, or whatever arrangements were made on his behalf left him sufficiently unmoved as to leave them unrecorded. Of this brief phase in his life there is nothing.

Nothing!

For most officers, leaving a unit that one had trained, and moreover one had served with in action, would have emotional overtones. Affection and concern for his men would manifest itself. That would be normal. In this respect Townshend was, apparently, not normal. He decided to forgo his leave, possibly on the advice of his grandmother who continued to 'wheel and deal' on his behalf, although these 'out-of-the-chain-of-command' negotiations would have won him few admirers among those who were aware of them. He very much wanted to get back to Gilgit under the eye of Durand. He telegraphed to Buller that he had decided to return to Poonah and on 26 October 1892 he took over command of 4 Squadron CIH.

His old chum, the very gallant Manners-Smith, now appointed as Political Officer in Khotal, wrote to say that, in his view, Durand would be happy to have him back at Gilgit. Townshend needed no second bidding and quickly got off a letter to Durand asking him to bid for him. Manners-Smith's judgment, although encouraging, was poor and Durand wrote back to a say, 'Thank you but no thank you. I have my full complement of officers.'

It is difficult to accept that an officer, just appointed to command a squadron, should apparently bypass his commanding officer and seek employment with another senior officer, who compounded the situation by replying to him privately.

Townshend was diverted from his machinations during March 1893 with the need to study for his promotion examinations, probably the very important 'Captain to Major'. Just two days before the examination day, and very unexpectedly, Durand wrote to say that he had applied for Townshend to be attached to him in Gilgit.

On 14 April, Curly Stewart, working in Simla and now an intelligence officer, told Townshend that very soon he would get his orders from the Foreign and not the Military department. Sure enough, two days later the Commandant CIH confirmed that CVFT was to move to Gilgit. One suspects that the Commandant, certainly a colonel, was irritated with both Durand and Townshend and only too happy to forgo the unenthusiastic services of the latter.

The journey to Gilgit from Poona took fourteen long and strenuous days. He started out on 4 May 1893 and must have wondered whether his sacred career was worth the daily struggle through thick snow, freezing conditions, cutting wind and minimal shelter at night. To these difficulties could be added the management of recalcitrant coolies. He wrote: 'I determined to push on . . . the coolies did not seem to see it and chucked their loads down on the road, but on my punching the ringleader they all rushed and took up their loads.' It would seem from this and other diary entries that Townshend was prepared to resort to fisticuffs as and when he deemed it necessary. He should not be damned for that because these were unsophisticated times and he was dealing with unsophisticated people. This style of 'management' was still commonplace when the author joined the British Army nearly seventy years later.

Notes
1. PRO/WO/ 76/258.
2. Braddon, *The Siege*.
3. Durand, *The making of a frontier*.
4. The Adjutant is the Commanding Officer's personal assistant. It is a pres... ; appointment and in this case it would seem to have been filled by a Kashmiri officer.
5. Knight, *Where three empires meet*.
6. Rakaposhi is in the Karakoram mountain range situated in the Nagar Valley about 60 miles north of Gilgit. It is the 27th highest in the world. Rakaposhi was first climbed in 1958 by Mike Banks and Tom Patey.
7. CVFT.
8. Edward Fredrick Knight (1852–1925) was born in Hammersmith and was the foreign and war correspondent for *The Times*. He was an intrepid man and made it his business to be in the thick of the action. This led to him losing an arm during the war in South Africa. He wrote several books of which one was *Where three empires meet*, published in 1892.
9. E.F. Knight.
10. These guns were only easily transported light mountain guns and they fired a 7lb shell. It is little wonder that they had no effect upon stone-built defences.
11. The Victoria Cross (vc, instituted 1854) was one of only three medals available for gallantry in 1891. The others were the Distinguished Service Order (dso, instituted 1888) and Distinguished Conduct Medal (dcm, instituted 1855). This latter medal was usually awarded to other ranks. The VC was awarded relatively more generously before 1900 than since, say, 1918.
12. *London Gazette*, 21 June 1892.
13. Later, Lieutenant General Sir Fenton Aylmer vc kcb (1862–1935).
14. Later, Brigadier G.H. Boisragon vc (1864–1931). His citation stated: 'For his conspicuous bravery in the assault and capture of the Nilt Fort, on 2nd December 1891. This Officer led the assault with dash and determination, and forced his way through difficult obstacles to the inner gate, when he returned for reinforcements, moving intrepidly to and fro under a heavy cross-fire until he had collected sufficient men to relieve the hard pressed storming party and drive the enemy from the fort.'

15. Later, Lieutenant Colonel John Manners-Smith VC CIE CVO (1864 –1920).
16. *Oxford Dictionary of National Biography*. Oxford University Press, 2004–2008.
17. CVFT, 31 July 1892.

Chapter 4

1893–1895

The Chitrál Campaign

In April 1893, Townshend's appointment to the command of Fort Gupis was promulgated. Gupis is located almost 7,000ft up in the Hindu Kush in an isolated and very mountainous area of what is now Pakistan. It is midway between Gilgit, then the seat of British regional power, and Chitrál. Gupis was on the way to nowhere and life was unvarnished. The new incumbent described his station on arrival on 25 May as 'Situated about one mile beyond Gupis at the entrance to the Yasin valley. Position of the fort is extremely bad, commanded on all sides within easy musketry and even matchlock range and not very close to water.' This last phrase is key because, without water, there is no military position that can be viable for very long. Throughout CVFT's lengthy career, military success, even survival, depended upon access to water. The rivers Kanjut, Kunar, Nile and Tigris all played an important part in his life. He described Gupis to a girlfriend as 'This . . . most awful place. You never saw such a desert. Just see if you can find it on a map.' Two days later his friend, Curly Stewart, visited and Townshend wasted no time in telling him, 'what a rat trap the fort was and how a determined enemy could make it very hot for us'.

He enumerated his responsibilities in his diary and they were, among others: accounting for expenditure of cash and materiel; liaising with the Political Officers at Gilgit and Chitrál; obtaining intelligence on the movement of the mountain tribes; drilling the garrison and keeping the men fit; the repair and maintenance of the fort and the roads around it; building new roads; providing escorts for treasure passing through his domain; hearing and adjudicating in local disputes. This is a comprehensive list and a heavy burden of responsibility for young shoulders.

The tribal system that operated throughout the frontier region was a rich brew of inter-tribal jealousy, corruption and intrigue. There was a sparse overlay of British administration supported by an even thinner military presence. Throughout the region outbreaks of violence, although often not aimed at the British, had to be quelled by people like Townshend, in minor wars like Hunza-Nagar.

The Hon George Curzon[1] visited Gupis and made an interesting assessment of his host. He had this to say about Captain C.V.F. Townshend:

> The British officer in command rode out to greet me and offered me the modest hospitality of the fort. In his company I visited the lines inside the fort, the keep containing the officers' quarters, school stores and magazine . . . Even more vividly, however, than the inspection of the garrison do I remember the night spent with my somewhat unusual host. He combined with an absorbing interest in military science and an equal familiarity with the writings of Hamley and Clausewitz and the strategy of Hannibal, Marlborough and the Emperor Napoleon, an interest in the gayer side of existence in which Paris was to him the hub and symbol. On the walls of his mud dwelling were pinned somewhat daring coloured illustrations from Parisian journals of the lighter type: and he regaled us through a long evening with French songs to the accompaniment of a banjo.

That is a remarkably accurate summation of Townshend by a very shrewd man. It highlighted his most agreeable characteristics and there is no doubt that Curzon was impressed. On the other hand, Townshend could recognize a valuable contact when he saw one and in the years ahead would use Curzon, just as he used Buller.

In late 1894, Townshend was hard at work preparing for the Staff College examination and in the process wrote to a titled relative explaining that, 'If it were worked properly', a recommendation from the Duke of Cambridge and another from Sir Redvers Buller would help. The recipient of the letter would have been left in no doubt as to the part he had to play in *working it properly* (author's italics).

The small initials *psc* against an officer's name in the Army List was seen as a prerequisite for advancement to the upper echelons of the Army. The first hurdle, and the highest, was to pass the entrance examination. Thereafter the officer would spend an intensive year studying the profession of arms. 'Passed Staff College' was the desired result and an officer with those three important initials permanently affixed to his name could face the future with confidence. As was his wont, Townshend did not waste time dealing with the lower orders – he went first class! The Duke was the Head of the Army, and Buller was on his way up the military ladder. The sheer brass neck that Townshend demonstrated here in which, as a very junior officer, he sought to involve senior officers in his career machinations borders on the breathtaking.

Early December 1893 brought a Captain Campbell to Gupis. This officer was the 'Inspecting officer of Imperial Service Troops' and his function was to establish the battle worthiness of units such as Townshend's. The inspection went well and Townshend exalted in his diary:

> I showed him the firing, bayonet and manual, physical drill, attack and a hill parade, taking the men up the cliff and along the platform south of the fort and then home. Not a man fell out. The men were absolutely perfect at everything; I would pit them confidently against any British Indian regiment. Campbell was delighted and the British Agent, who looked on, said to me 'It reflects the highest credit on you to have brought the men to such a pitch of efficiency.' He has written all about it to Colonel Durand. I am delighted, I must say. It repays me for all the trouble and doing regular drill sergeant's work at morning and evening parades for the last five months. The British Agent was especially pleased with the way we scaled the mountain side and said afterwards, 'those are the men for us.'

On New Year's Day 1895, and miles away, there was a squalid murder that was to have far-reaching consequences for Charles Townshend, for it was to propel him into the nation's consciousness.

It is necessary to digress briefly to provide some background to what was a very complex situation in order to place Townshend in his correct context.

At the time of the murder CVFT was no more than one of many junior British officers administering the outer extremities of the Indian Empire. In a few short weeks he moved to the centre of a military/politico stage that quickly attracted international attention and figured in headlines world-wide.

The ruling family in Chitrál were habitual murderers and examination of the family tree (Fig 4), produced by Dr Robertson in 1899, tells much of the story at a glance.[2] Colonel Algernon Durand assessed the patriarch and Mehtar (King) Amán-ul-Mulk as 'an exceptional man who for 40 years had been the chief personality on the frontier; he had ruled a united Chitrál for forty years.'

That said, the Mehtar was steeped in treachery; his hands were crimson with the blood of his nearest relations; he had murdered two out of three of his brothers; the third was in exile in Kabul. He was continuously plotting to get his refugee relations to return to his country, with small success, for they well knew theirs would be a very short shrift.

In this remote area, well beyond the aegis of any formal code of law and order, it was always a case of kill or be killed amongst the sons of a ruling chief, especially after their father's death. Polygamy and the pernicious habit of parcelling out a kingdom among the sons into governorships during a ruler's lifetime invariably led to war; when one brother fell into the hands of another there was only ever one result.

Amán-ul-Mulk was by modern standards a monster and of similar ilk to Idi Amin, Robert Mugabe and Saddam Hussein. Notwithstanding all of that, Durand commented further on Amán in the following terms: 'Any man more thoroughly competent to conduct affairs I have never met. The Mehtar's views on the condition of frontier affairs were interesting, and his knowledge of men and matters varied far and wide.'

Amán-ul-Mulk was probably poisoned by one of his sons and no tears were shed for him, despite Durand's charitable words. The man was an ogre. He was one of many and he begat others. Winston Churchill remarked that 'Amán's sons were all equally ferocious, ambitious and unscrupulous.' How right he was.

With Amán dead, his brother, Sher Afzul now claimed to be Mehtar and the local people, who saw little unusual in this latest bout of violence, were

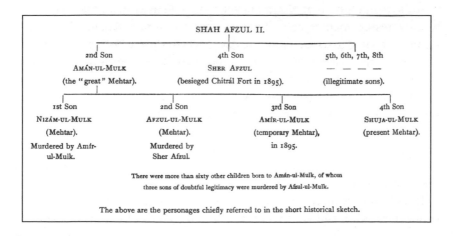

Fig 4. Family tree of Shah Afzul II. Taken from Robertson, *Chitrál. The story of a minor siege.*

perfectly prepared to accept him. However, Sher Afzul's hold on the throne did not last long and he was challenged by the eldest son of Amán, Nizám-ul-Mulk, the natural heir who, having been usurped by Sher Afzul, was currently living in Kashmir. Despite Nizám's unpopularity at all levels, and his reputation as a coward, he not only summoned up enough courage to challenge Sher Afzul but managed to gather sufficient support to mount a spirited attack that succeeded in driving Sher Afzul back into exile.

It was not to be for very long.

Nizám-ul-Mulk filled the power vacuum and took his rightful place as Mehtar. He was not very good at the job. He was a handsome and extrovert personality but a heavy drinker and as such was frequently drunk, a characteristic that was anathema to his Muslim subjects who eschewed alcohol. Nizám was apparently very attractive to women, but their availability was of no interest to him – indeed he was repelled by women because he was an aggressive homosexual.

His subjects were not overly enthused by his lifestyle or his corruption but, nevertheless, Nizám-ul-Mulk survived for just over three years until 1 January 1895.

Very early in his reign, Dr George Robertson,[3] now employed as a Political Officer, formed a mission and visited Chitrál to congratulate Nizám on his succession, and to promise him the same subsidy paid to his late father. When Robertson arrived in Chitrál it was clear that not only was Nizám cordially hated by his subjects, but they also utterly mistrusted the British who were supporting him.

Robertson found that Nizám, never a brave man even on a good day, was in a distressed mental state. This was because Umra Khan,[4] the ruler of Jandol (who had married one of the daughters of the old Amán-ul-Mulk and was a brother-in-law of Nizám's), was not only anxious to annex Chitrál but seemed about to take steps to achieve his aim. Umra Khan was no light-weight. He was variously described as 'The most expert and enterprising soldier on the North-West Frontier' and in a Gilgit Agency report, dated 28 April 1890, he had been called 'the most important man between Chitrál and Peshawar'.

The local populace was cautious, knowing that Sher Afzul was lurking in the wings and that Umra Khan too was in a position to invade Chitrál.

It took all of Robertson's considerable political negotiating skills to rally support for Nizám and, over a period of four months, he went well towards stabilizing Nizám's position. Eventually, the situation was sufficiently secure for Robertson to return to Kashmir, leaving behind two British officers and a small detachment of regular Sikh Indian Army troops.

*   *   *

Whilst all these nefarious, convoluted and homicidal events were taking place, life in Gupis had been peaceful. Indeed it had been for two uneventful years and Townshend had been free to concentrate on the training of his troops and to study the campaigns of the Great Captains. His diary recorded little but routine and a letter from 'home' was the high spot of the week. This was all soon to change and as the news of events in Chitrál filtered out, the British administration reacted as quickly as the difficult terrain, poor communications and icy weather conditions would permit.

Nizám had kept a precarious hold on his throne until 1 January 1895, but then he fell victim to his not very bright 19-year-old brother Amir-ul-Mulk. The murder took place whilst the brothers were out hawking. 'Nizám's turban had worked loose and fell off, and he stooped to pick it up. As he bent forward Amir-ul-Mulk tried to shoot him. His gun misfired, but at a signal from his master, one of Amir's retainers shot the Mehtar in the back.'[5] Amir announced to the incredulous Chitrális present that he was now Mehtar and, as they saluted him, his brother expired nearby in the dust.

Robertson got news of the assassination but nothing of the safety of the small garrison in Chitrál. The commander in Chitrál was Lieutenant Gurdon, an extraordinary young man in every way. He and his men were in extreme danger in the volatile circumstances that prevailed because there was a vociferous faction calling for the elimination of Gurdon and his soldiers. Skilfully, he kept a lid on the boiling emotions around him; no violence took place and the young officer refused to give Amir any formal recognition or support until he had received orders from Gilgit. He showed a quality of judgment and maturity beyond his years and eventually got a message to Robertson saying that any pre-emptive move by Townshend from Gupis would not be necessary. However, his message to Townshend had the effect of bringing reinforcements of fifty Sikh riflemen to Chitrál.

Amir, having murdered his brother, was now overwhelmed, not only by what he had done, but by the apparent success that now was his. He worried how the Raj would react and he recognized that, domestically, he was now a prime target for assassination. Amir turned to Umra Khan, explained what had happened and asked for support from his brother–in–law. Umra Khan was a political beast and he could see that Chitrál was a prize ready to be taken. It was effectively leaderless and, ostensibly to support the inadequate Amir, he formed an army of his 3,000 Pathans, and marched on Chitrál. It was a major expedition to be undertaken in winter and in the face of heavy and persistent snow. His route lay across forbidding territory and a 10,000-foot pass.

The Chitrális had mixed feelings about this incursion by Umra Khan because the Pathans had been their natural enemies for countless generations and it was for debate as to who was the most formidable foe, Umra Khan and his followers or the British.

Events moved quickly, the leaderless Chitrális could offer no worthwhile defence and their fort at Kila Drosh soon fell, providing Umra Khan with a firm base for future expansion when the time was right. Large numbers of Chitrális thought that they could see the writing on the wall and, pragmatically putting self-interest first, threw in their lot with Umra Khan and swelled his force.

News of the killing of Nizám had by now reached the exiled Sher Afzul. He escaped from the benign house arrest in which he was held by the Emir of Afghanistan and linked up with Umra Khan at Kila Drosh. They formed a formidable alliance.

Sher Afzul was already a big player in the world of assassination and frontier intrigue, and initially he became the main protagonist. His unconcealed antagonism toward the British boded ill and Dr Robertson, the political master of that part of the North-West Frontier, based in Gilgit, determined to return to Chitrál and occupy it in force.

The operations leading to the occupation of Chitrál, although relatively small in scale, were widespread and led to many acts of bravery and endurance that have no place in this biography of Townshend, as he was not involved. Suffice it to say that Dr Robertson received the news of the assassination of Nizám on 6 January 1895. On 15 January, accompanied by Captain Campbell, he started to march from Gilgit to Chitrál with a mixed force of Kashmiris and Sikhs. He and Campbell joined up with Townshend on 21 January en route. Captain C.P. Campbell CIH, a member of Townshend's current regiment, was senior to Townshend and, as was and is the custom of the Service, he took precedence and military command. This was the same Campbell who had inspected Townshend's battalion a couple of years earlier.

At Rahman, the Resident was told that Umra Kahn of Jandol, with 3–4,000 men, had taken the fort at Kila Drosh. The situation was clearly worsening but Robertson, Campbell and Townshend had no option but to press on and, after nine days' march, the fort at Mastuj hove into welcome view. The Resident and his party had a day's rest at Mastuj and moved on to Chitrál on 27 January, a four-day march away. This group now consisted of Robertson, Captain Campbell, Captain Townshend, Lieutenant Harley and Surgeon-Captain Whitchurch. There were 183 rank and file who would reinforce the garrison at Chitrál, which was currently commanded by

Lieutenant Gurdon with his fifty-eight Sikhs and 199 Kashmiris. On the face of it this would provide a garrison of six officers and 440 locally enlisted officers and soldiers.

All across the North-West Frontier bodies of men were on the move to counter the threat; plans were being made to mount a large-scale expedition. It was like a large military chess board with soldiers being shuffled like chess men across some of the most inhospitable terrain on the planet.

So very many years later, it is worth pausing to consider how tiny was the number of soldiers charged with the control of such a vast, rugged area in a hostile environment. Enormous command responsibility was given to very junior officers and little wonder that it bred self-reliant, confident and in some cases arrogant men.

The physical effort made by Robertson's party should not pass unnoticed. 'A four-day march away' is a brief and glib phrase, but it conceals enormous effort and organization. The men had to advance with an appropriate appreciation of the tactical situation at any given point on the route. Campbell deployed the vulnerable column to best advantage and spread his few officers in such a way as to ensure that any attack would draw a considered and effective response. The column had to halt at night, seek shelter, men had to be fed and sentries posted. This was not a stroll in the park but it was an advance through difficult terrain that was more than likely hostile. Campbell conducted the march in exemplary style and Gurdon was delighted to welcome the party on 31 January.

Gurdon opened with the bad news. First he told Robertson that the road behind them to Mastuj was now closed. Then he confirmed that Umra Khan had defeated the loyal Chitrális at Kila Drosh and that there were a number of the wounded survivors of that action in his hospital. Whitchurch immediately had his hands full.

Very significantly, Amir-ul-Mulk, the self-proclaimed Mehtar, did not greet Robertson by lining the road, and this departure from the norm sent a clear message. Instead he sent his very young brother, Shuja-ul-Mulk,[6] to say that he was 'too preoccupied with military duties' to greet the Resident. Townshend described the small boy who bore the message as 'a dignified little lad'. Amir had stationed himself at the far end of the Chitrál valley, about 15 miles beyond the fort, in a strategically commanding position overlooking the defile into the valley. This posture was contradictory because Amir had already sought the active support of Umra and his dispositions were now illogically designed to resist any further advance by Umra from that direction.

Umra Khan had been warned by the British government in 1891, 1893 and again in 1895 not to interfere in the affairs of Chitrál, which was a protected state under the suzerainty of Kashmir. Nevertheless, Umra Khan, taking full advantage of the unrest caused by the rash of murders, had invaded the Chitrál valley with Jhandoli troops, led by his general, Abdul Majid Khan, and attacked the Chitráli people.

The British Government issued a proclamation to all the people in Chitrál and in the adjoining states of Swat and Bajuar, in which it said: 'The Government is determined to use force to compel him [Umra] to retire if he disregards the last warning . . . As soon as that object has been attained the force will be withdrawn.'

The Chitráli people were, however, ambivalent. Some saw Umra Khan as a saviour worthy of devoted support, whereas others considered him to be a pillaging, ruthless invader. Their attitude could be likened to that of the Iraqis post the US/UK invasion of 2003. Things started to look ominous when, on 25 February, the majority of Chitrális started to change their allegiance in favour of Sher Afzul, and this thoroughly unpleasant character and his adherents soon took up position in the vicinity of the fort.

Sher Afzul had arrived at Chitrál at the head of an unknown number of troops, and a confrontation seemed to be increasingly likely and imminent. This was especially so when, on 27 February, Sher Afzul demanded in the most peremptory manner that Robertson and the garrison leave the area of the fort and return to Gilgit.

This was a demand that could not possibly be accepted and had to be confronted. Dr Robertson was unquestionably the senior person and this political decision was his alone but, ostensibly, military matters were the responsibility of Captain Campbell. As Campbell was the military commander there should have been a clear separation in his role and that of Robertson.

Unfortunately there was no such demarcation line.

The local atmosphere was such that outlying picquets were recalled and three days later, the British officers cautiously consolidated their position; on 1 March, they camped in and close around the fort at Chitrál.

Things now looked even bleaker.

The following day, Amir-ul-Mulk was placed in confinement by Robertson, which was prudent because his loyalty was highly suspect. Robertson then recognized his even younger brother, Shuja-ul-Mulk, the erstwhile messenger, as temporary Mehtar, but with the proviso that this was only until such time as the Government could rule on the status of Shuja-ul-Mulk.

Robertson managed the accession of Shuja with some dignified theatre, leading him to the throne and then inviting all the leading Chitrális to kiss the hand of their new, painfully young, Mehtar. Townshend noted 'the grace and dignity of the little fellow on suddenly being made King and the way he received the homage of the nobles'. The scene impressed Townshend and he owned that 'I could not help feeling sorry for Amir', the now deposed and incarcerated former incumbent of the throne. Robertson then announced that the personal safety of Shuja was the responsibility of Captain Townshend.

It had not been a good day for Amir, but his henchman, the assassin of Nizám, had a rather worse one – his day was spoiled when he was summarily executed. History does not record his name.

Robertson sent a letter to Sher Afzul to say that he must either come to Chitrál and pay homage to his nephew or leave the country. It was unlikely that Sher Afzul would find either alternative attractive and Robertson, by his uncompromising stance, certainly hardened Sher Afzul's resolve. Armed conflict was bound to be the product.

The British Agent, a medical doctor by profession, clearly harboured military ambitions and in the past had been involved in several engagements. However, when employed in his medical capacity he had non-combatant status and was not in command. But, by now, he was employed in a political role and used his acknowledged seniority to take military decisions for which he was untrained. This must have been difficult for Campbell but he did not have the moral courage to gainsay Robertson and, regrettably, acquiesced to Robertson's amateur wishes.

Robertson decided that it was necessary for the position of Sher Afzul and his force to be identified and the number of his troops calculated. To this end he determined to reconnoitre the situation in force. At 1545 hrs on 3 March, Campbell was 'invited', although in practice he was instructed, to lead 200 men and four officers (Captains Townshend and Baird, Lieutenant Gurdon and Surgeon-Captain Whitchurch) on this large-scale reconnaissance. Lieutenant Gurdon went in his capacity of 'Political Officer', although how he would exercise his political acumen in a firefight was unclear then, and is still unclear today. The force of 200 plus was, in Robertson's words, 'more than half the garrison'. The presence of Whitchurch was curious. It was then and is now unusual for a medical officer to accompany a patrol of this type because medical officers are too valuable for them to be put at unnecessary risk.

Robertson, who was ill at this time with dysentery, allowed the force to leave the security of the fort, and then as he described it, he 'rose from my sick bed and putting a cloak over my night clothes rode out after the party' – although quite why he never explained, and if he was seeking admiration he would find none here.

Chitrál is situated in the tree-covered valley of the broad and swift flowing River Kunar. The valley is about two miles wide, overlooked by towering mountains, and it was home to a population who lived in a series of small hamlets that were sprinkled over the fertile valley floor. As the Commanding Officer, Campbell should not have been involved in this operation and should have delegated the responsibility to one of his sub-ordinates. He could, and probably should, have put Townshend in overall command.

Campbell had Robertson breathing down his neck and the function of command was split. As it was, Campbell directed Baird to take the high ground to the west which Campbell saw as critical to his very simplistic plan. Campbell, meanwhile, took the bulk of his force and occupied a semi-circular ridge of high ground with extensive line of sight to the south. He then made a serious error when, having determined that a warehouse about 600 yards south of the fort was a key point, he ordered Townshend and 100 men to descend from the commanding heights and advance towards it. A little later, Campbell had second thoughts and sent a clarifying message to Townshend but it did not reach him. Townshend was now 'advancing to contact' and, in effect, inviting fire.

Robertson, the architect of this excursion remarked later,[7] 'Townshend, who, following out his original instructions, eventually came upon the enemy at somewhat of a disadvantage.'

This was probably the understatement of the decade.

Gurdon laid down his political hat, put back on his service cap and was immediately sent off with a letter to Baird from Dr Robertson. It was strange employment for an officer but, that apart, it would seem that Campbell was now a commander in name only. The authority was Robertson's, so was the responsibility, and it was he who made the immediate tactical decisions. The letter to Baird, in Robertson's words, 'embodied my wishes that a single shot be fired over the heads of the men at the farther side of the ravine, when, if they proved to be enemies and not simple villagers, they were to be steadily volleyed and driven back'.

The note has been lost but Robertson justified himself by adding, 'There is no doubt that it (the letter) conveyed exactly what was intended. Unluckily the written word of the English language is not always incapable of misconception and the mood of the reader at times influences his grasp of its meaning.'

The double negatives here are typical of Robertson and little wonder that he was misunderstood. Baird, a capable and hitherto competent officer was facing a large body of men across a ravine at the bottom of which ran a swiftly flowing stream. He read his instructions, duly fired the single shot and promptly received a volley in return. Then, recalling Campbell's earlier words that the men across the ravine were 'to be turned out' of their positions, he decided that he was expected to descend into the stream at the bottom of the ravine, cross it and attack up the opposite slope. Gurdon was not a little alarmed at this interpretation of the order, suggested that Baird had misread the letter and urged caution. Baird overruled Gurdon and also dismissed his suggestion that he bring up reinforcements. Given the order to move forward, the majority of Baird's men saw the folly of the order, declined and took cover. Foolishly, the two officers with only thirteen men scrambled up the opposing steep slope. The enemy reversed the tactic, crossed the ravine further down and occupied the very ground that Baird had just left. Baird was now in a trap of his own making. His force was split by the ravine, he had a large party of hostiles between him and the fort and both elements were at serious risk.

The small party of fifteen came under fire and within moments ten were casualties. All save a Gurkha officer called Badri Nar Singh, Gurdon and three sepoys were unwounded. Baird had been hit and seriously wounded; his fox terrier who had accompanied him was shot dead. Gurdon sent off one of the surviving sepoys to find Surgeon Captain Whitchurch and in the meantime organized the fire of his tiny party against a vastly superior enemy which was in a most advantageous position.

Whitchurch, with commendable courage, made his way forward, eventually reached Baird and organized his removal. Meanwhile, and with similar bravery, Gurdon rounded up the remainder of the recalcitrant and unwilling company, 'on the bank of the torrent'.[8]

He awaited the next development and it did not take long to materialize. Sher Afzul's men made a concerted rush at the reunited and depleted company and in doing so split the company again. Half, under Badri Nar Singh, were forced back down the road that had given Whitchurch access to Baird, the other half, under Gurdon, were obliged to move higher up the hillside. With enemy above and below, they were not only surrounded but burdened by their wounded who could not be left on the field.

Robertson and Campbell, about a mile away, were unaware of these events; Townshend too was in blissful ignorance as he moved across the convex Chitráli plain and, as expected, drew enemy fire. Campbell decided to go forward to direct Townshend's attack – interference that was almost certainly not well received by Charles Townshend. CVFT did not specifically comment in his diary but merely said that Campbell, having given the order, returned to bring up reinforcements who were pinned down 150 yards to the rear.

Townshend had by now occupied his first objective, a cluster of buildings and walls. Ahead was a further grouping of houses, which was probably large enough to be more accurately described as a 'village', and was alleged to be where Sher Afzul and his large force were based. Townshend urged his men to advance but the advance was contested and Townshend's company came under brisk rifle fire when about 200 yards from their objective. Two hundred yards is a range at which a target can be readily identified and also hit with ease by even a moderate marksman, as the British Army was to discover on this particular evening and again in South Africa and Flanders in the years ahead.

The company 'took cover behind a low stone-revetted bank',[9] but the Chitrális were better than moderate marksmen and Townshend's casualties began to mount. Townshend heard the firing from the high ground over to his right and fully expected Baird and his company to attack the village from that flank. However, Baird was in no condition to do anything except keep a tenacious hold on life.

As Townshend realized that the enemy were seeking to outflank him in the gathering dusk, Campbell shouted to him to rush the village. To reinforce his instruction Campbell moved closer to Townshend with 'about half a dozen men'[10] and in doing so he had to climb over a ruined wall. At the top of the wall he stopped and started to focus his field glasses, a position in which he was the ideal, stationary target. He was duly shot – in the knee. It was an agonizing wound.

That single, indifferently aimed round was to change Townshend's life for ever.

CVFT immediately reassumed command, ordered the fixing of bayonets and started to lead the charge over the 200-yard gap to the village. It was a long 200 yards and two Kashmiri officers immediately fell dead at his side; the defensive fire was rapid and effective, so much so that the company of 100 men was badly depleted and the charge quickly lost its impetus as men took cover among the rocks that littered the ground. The assault had failed and Townshend and his men were pinned down.

The coming darkness provided welcome increasing cover and Townshend, pragmatically, very prudently and skilfully withdrew his men back to the north and the direction of the fort. He and his survivors were still under fire from, what transpired to have been, a force several times larger than his. It was perhaps as well that Charles Townshend and his Kashmiris had not reached their objective because if they had they would have been butchered to the last man.

The withdrawal was not easily accomplished and Townshend was subjected to harassing fire all the way – further casualties were taken and not all the wounded could be recovered. One overweight wounded soldier offered to pay his comrades to bring him in but they failed, and he was easy prey to the knives of the pursuers. There was a host of tragic and gallant episodes enacted during what was, by now, an out-and-out retreat.

Meanwhile the remnants of Baird's company were in serious trouble, about 1½ miles from the fort, as was Surgeon-Captain Whitchurch, who was trying to bring in the wounded Baird. The enemy, who vastly outnumbered the British force, infiltrated their line and, as night fell, the party of Gurkhas and Kashmiri rifles was completely isolated. There was a desperate need to get Captain Baird to a place of safety and the wounded officer was placed on a litter. The soldiers stuck to the task but three were killed and a fourth was badly wounded in the process. The doctor abandoned the litter, took the wounded Baird on his back and struck out for the fort.

The enemy had made the direct route to their haven impassable and so a much longer route was selected, of some three miles, over broken ground to be traversed in the dark. The darkness was a problem but it also served to cloak the movement of the returning party along a route exposed to constant and heavy rifle fire, from an enemy who still had the advantage of the high ground.

Time after time, in order to force a way over walls held by a more than usually obstinate group of the enemy, Whitchurch had to lay down his burden and charge an enemy position with his men, after which he would once more lift up Baird and continue on the journey.

The walls of the fort were eventually reached but, when safety was at hand, Baird was shot for a third time. Only seven survivors of Baird's optimistic little party that had sallied forth several hours earlier answered to their names at roll call that evening. Baird was mortally wounded but, before he died, he reported the incredible devotion of Whitchurch to his patient and asked that such gallantry should be recognized. Baird died the next day. Much later, the Resident wrote in his report: 'It is difficult to write temperately about Whitchurch.'[11]

That was in the future, but meanwhile Dr Robertson continued to control matters around him and commented that, 'I was desperately weak and suffering, and was alternately doubled up with pain.' It is difficult to sympathize with Robertson as he had no need to have exposed himself. His incapacity and self-indulgence placed a burden on those about him.

Slowly, most of the wounded, including Campbell, were recovered and what remained of the original 200 struggled back to the fort. The battle had been brief. It had failed to achieve anything and had cost far too many lives. The entire event was ill considered by Robertson, and Campbell's planning seems, at best, to have been optimistic and simplistic. The operation was never likely to provide an accurate estimate of enemy strength – whether or not the opposition amounted to 1,000 or 5,000 made little practical difference. Townshend commented later that, 'The enemy were computed at 1000 to 1200 of whom 500 had Martinis and many had Sniders.'

It was a bad decision to leave the protection of the fort for such an unnecessary purpose. However, its one significant effect was that the bullet that disabled Campbell had now placed Townshend in command at Chitrál and started him on the ladder to the fame and fortune that is the right of a public hero. His nickname 'Chitrál Charlie' can be traced back to this unsatisfactory and inconclusive action – perhaps to the moment Campbell stood on that wall and presented such an easy target.

Townshend was to comment later that the rate of fire inflicted upon him and his men on that fateful evening was greater than anything he had experienced at Abu-Klea and Gubat on the Nile, or the Hunza-Nagar campaign. The officers present and who survived commented upon the skilful fieldcraft of the enemy, all of whom made most excellent use of ground and only rarely presented a target.

Whitchurch, Gurdon and Townshend emerged from the debacle with honour. The same cannot be said for Robertson, although he cheerfully reported that, notwithstanding his lack of any medical practice for several years he treated Campbell's wound. 'I was assured long afterwards,' he said, 'by the most famous surgeon in London, that my prompt, if vigorous action probably saved Campbell's leg and enabled him, less than two years afterwards, to make one of the champion polo team of the Indian Cavalry.'

It is to be expected that any author of a book, describing events in which he had a central part, will put a gloss on his contribution. Robertson's book is certainly no exception. He restricts his more eloquent praise to officers who were not in competition for any of the glory that was to be distributed later. He speaks highly of Baird (dead) . . . 'Kindness, gentle manners . . . no braver or more dashing officer in the army . . . chivalrous, fighting disposition'; Gurdon (very junior) is 'cool, as his clear head sees danger'. Campbell (wounded and having relinquished command) 'was the ideal of a man brimming over with fight'. Whitchurch, a doctor, and undeniably the bravest of the brave, Robertson lauds most generously. On Townshend he is curiously completely silent and it is reasonable to assume that the fort at Chitrál was rather too small for the egos of two arrogant men.

In 1895, Robertson was forty-three and Townshend was thirty-four. The age gap between them is about the same as one might find between a lieutenant colonel and a captain/major. Robertson was much travelled, adept in the ways of the local people and very confident in his ability to make military judgments. He certainly viewed Townshend as the subordinate he undoubtedly was, but gave the younger man little credit for his background and experience. Townshend deferred to Robertson and did not challenge his authority until Robertson strayed once into purely military matters. Charles Townshend possibly saw Robertson, in modern parlance, as 'a bog-standard civilian' who interfered in matters not of his concern. The following days and nights promised to be lively if not turbulent. Robertson wrote his book long after the event but Townshend, shrewdly, kept a contemporaneous record.

Notes
1. George Nathaniel Curzon, 1st Marquess Curzon of Keddlestone KG GCSI GCIE PC (1859–1925) was a British Conservative statesman who served as Viceroy of India and Foreign Secretary. He was to be involved with CVFT, on and off, over the next twenty-five years.
2. From Robertson, *Chitrál. The story of a minor siege.*
3. George Scott Robertson (1852–1916) qualified in medicine at Westminster Medical School and, in 1878, joined the Indian Medical Service. He served through the Afghan War (1879–80) and in 1888 became the Agency Surgeon in Gilgit. In 1893, he was appointed Political Agent (sometimes referred to as 'British Agent') for Chitrál. His military rank in 1895 was Surgeon-Major. Robertson, despite his calling, was employed in a political, quasi-diplomatic role and took precedence over all other military officers. For the sake of continuity he is referred to as 'Dr Robertson' throughout.
4. Umra Khan (1860–1903), described by Colonel Durand as 'The Napoleon of Bajour', became the ruler of Jandol when he murdered his brother the incumbent. He conducted himself in the same ruthless and corrupt manner as the rest of his extended family.
5. Thomson, *The Chitrál Campaign.*
6. British soldiers called Shuja-ul-Mulk 'Sugar and milk'. In 1919 Mehtar was granted the title of 'His Highness' and was created KCIE. In 1936, Sir Shuja-ul-Mulk died after forty-one years of rule. He was

succeeded by his eldest son, Sir Nasir-ul-Mulk, born in 1898 (Shuja, his father, was then aged between seventeen and nineteen). Nasir served for a year with a British regiment in India and was granted the rank of Honorary Major in the British Indian Army in late 1939. Sir Nasir-ul-Mulk died in 1943. Chitrál became an integral part of Pakistan on 1 January 1971. (Mohammad Afzal Khan)

7. Robertson, op. cit., p. 195.
8. Ibid.
9. Ibid.
10. CVFT.
11. Harry Frederick Whitchurch, Indian (Bengal) Medical Service, attached to the 24th Bengal Native Infantry. He was born in September 1866 and joined the Army in 1888 having recently qualified at St Bartholomew's. Surgeon–Major Whitchurch died in 1907.

Chapter 5
3 March–20 April 1895
Besieged in Chitrál

'Don't bellyache at out what you have not got, but get on and make
certain that you do your utmost with what you have got.'
Field Marshal Lord Harding of Petherton, on 'Leadership'

The dead had been left on the field and, when the roll was called, it became
clear that 30 per cent of the men engaged in the action were casualties. That
is sixty in total and of these half were killed, a very high percentage. It later
transpired that enemy losses were one killed and fourteen wounded.

The arithmetic says it all.

It was evident that the garrison was surrounded by a foe that outnumbered it by something of the order of 5:1 so there was no sensible way
that the fight could be taken to the enemy. The only realistic options were
either to sit it out and wait for relief, or seek a negotiated settlement.

An extract from Robertson's diary sums up the reasons for the defeat, or
at least as he saw it:

> The true reason of our defeat was – that we found the enemy too strong
> and too well-armed for us. There were other reasons also. Our men
> behaved well on the whole. A large number behaved splendidly; an
> almost equal number behaved indifferently: the one party counterbal-
> anced the other. But it was quite clear that the Raghunath (the name of
> the Kashmir regiment) Sepoys had not the faintest idea of musketry.
> Their shooting was terribly wild – atrociously bad. They fumbled with
> their rifles, let them off at all manner of unexpected times, dropped their
> ammunition about, and behaved, many of them, as if they had never
> before fired a shot. There is reason to suppose that some of our men, at
> any rate, were hit by the wild, un-aimed shooting of our own men.

This latter statement does not reflect well on Townshend who Robertson
knew had been responsible for training. Robertson added, as an

71

afterthought, that the men were, 'hampered by their heavy greatcoats and that it was a warm afternoon'. That statement begs the obvious question, 'Why were greatcoats worn?' And 'who so ordered?' Townshend, in his diary, comments similarly and one can speculate that when the men paraded in greatcoats no one had the wit or wisdom to tell them to take them off. On the face of it, it was a minor decision but then who was to take the decision – Campbell or Robertson?

Inevitably, after the defeat of the previous day, from 4 March 1895 the fort at Chitrál was besieged and Captain Charles Townshend was in military command. Campbell, although wounded, was available to give advice to Robertson and duly did so, which did not make things any easier for Townshend. Writing of Charles Townshend, H.C. Thompson said:

> Captain Townshend assumed command. Fortunately it was not his first experience of war; he was in the square at Abu Klea, and served in the Hunza-Nagar campaign and what was of infinitely more importance at the present juncture, although a cavalry officer, he had made a special theoretical study of fortification, but had also acquired a certain practical knowledge of it for he was employed only last year in building the fort at Gupis. This knowledge now stood the Chitrál garrison in good stead.

These were early days but nevertheless perhaps a good example of 'horses for courses'. The situation was undesirable and difficult but it was by no means hopeless. The fort was a defensible position. It was about 80 yards square with walls 25 feet high. It had four towers each a further 25 feet higher than the walls. The fort was situated about 40 yards from the aforementioned Chitrál or Kunar River which flowed along its north face. A fifth tower, known as the 'Water Tower', outside that north face of the fort was strategically placed to protect the route down to the river and the vital water source. Some time before the fort was invested Captain Campbell had converted a rough, rocky and steep path down the cliffs to the riverside into a tunnel from the isolated Water Tower. The distance from the end of the tunnel to the water's edge depended upon the state of the river which fluctuated with the seasons. A great marble rock was incorporated into the scheme. With a perimeter of over 320 yards the defenders were, of necessity, thinly spread and their field of fire was restricted by various single-storey, agricultural buildings scattered around the area just beyond the walls of the fort, which they had been unable to demolish before the outbreak of hostilities The enemy established himself in these outhouses and loopholed them. Thus they were close to the walls of the fort, sheltered from view and direct fire.

The walls of the fort were 8 feet thick and constructed of stone within a timber framework – not unlike those in Hunza and Nagar. The stone in both walls and towers was laid in the manner of a dry stone wall and so, clearly, the timber frame was a weakness in the structure – especially in the towers. Abdul Majid Khan knew this and in the weeks that followed he made repeated attempts to fire the towers. On the north–eastern corner of the fort and facing the river were some stables, part of which the defenders promptly demolished, and part of which they reinforced and loopholed as an integral part of the garrison's defences. This measure also enhanced the secure access to the river. The western aspect of the fort was marked by yet more stables and these, for the most part, were demolished leaving only a small strongpoint to cover the western wall.

To the south was a wall surrounding a garden; to the east was a second garden, 140 yards long, also surrounded by a wall. Between these two gardens and only about 40 yards south-east was a substantial building described as 'a summer house'.[1] Abdul Majid Khan occupied this building and, later in the siege, it would become the scene of a bloody engagement when it became the base from which a sap was built towards the Gun Tower.

The fort had been built in the lowest part of the river valley, albeit at an elevation of 3,700ft, and all about it the land rose and provided those occupying the high ground with a clear view of the fort and its inhabitants. Dominating the entire scene was the permanently snow-covered Tirich Mir, the highest mountain in the Hindu Kush, 25,289ft, at whose foot Chitrál crouched. On the western side of the fort was a grove of large trees, the branches of which overhung the walls of the fort. These trees should have been felled but there were not the axes and saws to do the job. These overhanging branches provided an easy route into the fort by a moderately agile enemy but, throughout the siege, the route was never exploited.

There were five British officers: Townshend, Surgeon-Captain Whitchurch, Lieutenants Harley and Gurdon, and Captain Colin Campbell who was incapacitated but in good voice. The Resident, Dr Robertson, was not a combatant officer but it was accepted by all that he was 'in charge' although not 'in command'.

Townshend probably carried in his knapsack a copy of *The Army List*, that most invaluable of documents and the ambitious officer's bible. 'Seniority' is not entirely the name of the game but Campbell had commanded by dint of his seniority. However, now he was completely in-capacitated, he was obliged, no matter how reluctantly, to pass

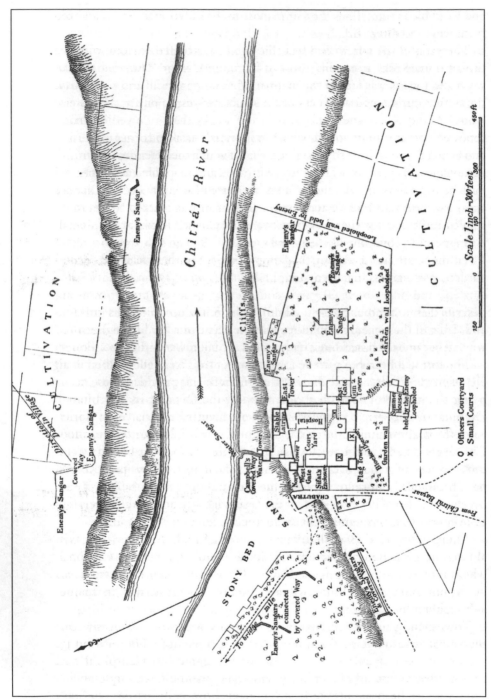

Fig 5. Sketch map of Chitrál fort. (Robertson)

responsibility and authority formally to Townshend. The other captain, the doctor, did not count as he was technically a 'non-combatant'. That said, the extraordinary bravery of Dr Whitchurch was now well known and this man was a very combatant non-combatant. In effect there were now only three combatant officers, all of whom were very junior.

The joker in the pack was Dr Robertson, who insisted on a military role when it suited him and he gave the impression that he was the fount of all initiatives and decisions. In his account of the siege and the events leading up to it Robertson claims responsibility for everything. He relied heavily upon a hereditary rajah called Sifat Badádur who he saw in the role of 'musáhib'. This is an aide-de-camp and normally an appointment on the staff of a major general or above. Perhaps Robertson had delusions of grandeur. This young man had apparently saved Robertson's life in the Indus valley in 1892 and had been with him ever since. Sifat's relationship with Robertson distanced the Resident from the officers and may have been, in part, the reason he suggests that the officers present did no more than respond to his commands. Certainly, he credits none with any initiative. His book, wonderfully detailed though it is, is nevertheless a vainglorious epistle. The historian is obliged to read between the lines in an effort to distribute the credit more equably.

Townshend probably found his relationship with Robertson difficult to manage, but he could see no profit in confrontation and accordingly he avoided conflict. He revelled in a situation tailor made for an officer seeking to win fame and glory, and he rose to the challenge despite Robertson's constant interference. The next few weeks established him as a man to watch. As a student of military history, Townshend would have known that, although a siege is arduous for the besieged, it is the relief force that usually suffers the greater number of casualties, and a relief force was now being raised to lift the siege of Chitrál. Townshend calculated that he had sufficient food for ten weeks on half rations, but highest in his priorities was safeguarding access to the river.

Townshend's opponents were skilled soldiers. Some of the enemy were equipped with the high-quality, long-range Martini-Henry and the remainder with the much less effective Snider rifles. They were experienced in the art of besieging which was almost a routine exercise in this part of the world; well armed and with ample logistical support, they were formidable foes who would contest vigorously any attempt to rescue the occupants of Chitrál fort.

Townshend had under his command a grand total of 543 people, of whom 370 were combatants.[2] The non-combatants included about ninety whose loyalty was sufficiently doubtful that Townshend considered it prudent to guard them. Of his soldiers, the ninety men of 14th Sikhs commanded by Lieutenant Harley formed the backbone of his force and the part they played in the defence of Chitrál drew plaudits from all the survivors. The senior Sikh was Gurmukh Singh who was an example, not only to his soldiers, but also to the 301 surviving men of the 4th Kashmir Rifles who made up the bulk of the defenders. These 4th Kashmirs had been trained by Townshend and they were composed of Dogras and Gurkhas, but they had been severely mauled on 3 March when hostilities had first broken out and the quality of their future performance was unknown.

CVFT considered his priorities and they were first and foremost to establish a system to counter any attempt by Abdul Majid Khan to set fire to the timber in the towers – especially that of the Water Tower and those on the south-east face. He selected fire picquets, organized their duty roster, and placed water and beaters close to the most vulnerable spots. Next he had to deal with the potential enemy within. The loyalty of the ninety Chitrális was an issue. They had to be fed and watered but they also had to be watched. The guarding of these people bit into Townshend's slender resources and, with hindsight, one wonders why he did not expel the entire group. The Resident who, incidentally, reported that there were only fifty-two people to guard would have been the decision maker on this issue and he may have judged that to expel the Chitrális might, just might, provoke a massacre. They stayed on as a constant stone in Townshend's military shoe.

Siege conditions generate all the elements for disease – 543 human beings and an unknown number of horses and mules produce, on a day-to-day basis, an unattractive and considerable quantity of faeces. A man serving in a well-nourished British unit produces 2.4 lb of faeces and urine per day. In a company position this amounts to a total of one ton per week.[3] The greater percentage of this will be urine. Chitrál fort was home to many more than just one company; the denizens were not European and not 'well nourished'. However, despite the subsequent restricted of rations there was still a considerable pile of ordure to be disposed of daily. The latrines used by Chitrális in a normal peacetime setting, never very sanitary, had been demolished as part of the priority of making the fort assault proof. A new site for the latrines had to be found because otherwise an unutterably awful stench would be the price to be paid.

Robertson rather pompously claims that it was he who gave instructions on the placing of the latrines. He decided that this was to be outside the walls of the fort in the old and now fortified stables on the river side. Townshend, rather weakly acknowledged the primacy of Robertson, and did as he was bidden. If he had misgivings, there is no record of them and he put in place arrangements for his men to dig the new latrines as best they could in the rocky surface of the stable floor. Perhaps he counted himself fortunate to have with him two doctors, both able to contribute to the garrison's best efforts in this regard.

The fort was within 40 yards of the river which was the sole water source. The stables located outside the main walls of the fort were even closer to the river. It was an asinine decision to place the communal latrines in the stables and so close to the water. As the siege extended, the stable area became hopelessly and horribly fouled with liquid sewage lying on the rocky surface, and eventually running down the steep slope into the river. This was cholera, dysentery and death just waiting to happen.

The decision was all the more ill judged because the northern face of the fort, including the Water Tower and Campbell's covered way, were absolutely critical to the defence of the garrison. The increased fortification of the stables and the additional soldiers stationed there are evidence of this criticality. Moreover, the massive quantity of ordure produced over a protracted period was sufficient, eventually, to make this key stable area untenable for any length of time. Men on duty in this place had to be relieved at regular intervals to allow them to breathe clean air. The awfulness of the daily defecation that had to be exercised in this evil latrine must have been an active constituent in any constipation experienced by the garrison, but all sources are silent on that particular subject.

So much for the military, or for that matter the medical, skills of Dr Robertson.

The matter of feeding his command was addressed when a Sikh under Harley's command let it be known that he could fabricate hand mills for the grinding of grain. That sounds a fairly simple measure but the mechanics must have been rather more difficult. The detail of how these mills were made has not survived but unfortunately the only stones available were the wrong sort. The ground grain became mixed with 'gritty particles' which did nothing for the teeth and good health of the besieged.

To make best use of the fighting men, Townshend (or Robertson) organized his Punyal levies, and sixteen were incorporated together with his forty servants and camp followers into work parties whose task was to relieve the fighting element of any domestic or routine chores. The infantry was thus able to focus on manning the perimeter and to this end a formalized disposition of the men was issued.

The enemy had clear line of sight into the fort from the surrounding hills and from the outset of the siege were able to bring fire on any movement within the ramparts. This sniping was effective as it was deleterious to morale and casualties rose. Townshend determined to screen his people from sight and to this end started the construction of overhead cover and traverses. According to a contemporary account, he also set about the construction of several parados. These were banks built up behind a trench or fortification to give protection from the rear.

All manner of material was employed to screen and protect the defenders. Beams from demolished buildings, mule saddles, empty ammunition boxes, sandbags, old blankets and carpets were utilized to provide either cover from fire or, at the least, cover from view. The enemy kept up a persistent fusillade before Townshend could erect his screens and, during the night, constructed a series of sangars on the other side of the River Kunar. This provided the enemy with secure firing points that were quite safe from a frontal assault across the river – not that Townshend would have contemplated such a folly.

Nightfall brought with it extreme danger as the enemy could approach the fort under its cover. Townshend (or Robertson), alert to this threat, caused the manufacture of fireballs made of resinous wood and soaked in kerosene oil. The quantity of wood required would have been prodigious and its provision must have presented a logistic problem. Nevertheless, these fireballs were duly placed at intervals around the walls and were to be thrown over the wall to provide illumination in the event of a night attack, a defensive device that Townshend had experienced in the Hunza-Nagar campaign. What Townshend would not have given for half a dozen Very pistols?[4] They were coming into use but had not reached isolated outposts like Gupis from whence Townshend had come.

Of Townshend's measures, the one most immediately to have a beneficial effect was the screening of the interior of the fort from sight. The enemy could still rake the area but could no longer pick out a specific target, and their occasional random unaimed fire was markedly less lethal. The defenders knew that they were in for the long haul and the conservation of ammunition was apparent to all. There were about 350 rounds per man armed with the Martini-Henry and about 280 for those with the Snider. Given that half rations was to be the norm, the garrison had sufficient food for two months. However, a decision was taken later, on 1 May, to go to quarter rations and that gave the garrison the means to hold out until June.

The fireballs were to be complemented by what was described as 'a kind of machicoulis' – a projecting gallery on top of a castle wall that has openings in the floor through which boiling liquids and projectiles could be directed at an attacker. On the machicoulis, piles of faggots were kept alight to provide permanent illumination.

The balance of Townshend's fighting increment consisted of a mobile reserve of thirty-five, available for instant deployment wherever a threat was perceived. This left a residue of about 170 bayonets uncommitted but to be used for sallies and counter-attacks. The merits of leaving a defended position to attack an enemy holding surrounding high ground are few and far between and, prudently, Townshend decided that this was a tactic to be adopted only in extremis.

The siege started in earnest on 4 March, on which day Baird was first buried. He was later to be reinterred (a photograph of this follows) and a second letter arrived from Sher Afzul saying that he would guarantee the safety of the garrison if it evacuated Chitrál and returned to Gilgit. He added that his recognition as Mehtar was a prerequisite. Robertson gave this message short shrift. It was to be the first of many written and verbal messages from the besiegers.

Robertson and Townshend separately commented on the very low morale of the Kashmiris immediately following the defeat of 3 March. They had taken a severe drubbing and their value in the next fight was an unknown. Townshend observed that:

> There is no doubt that they are very much shaken by their losses on the 3rd. They were tried very highly, they had never been on service before and they got the highest possible test when they had to assault (with only about 50 men) a strong village filled with enemy riflemen, and across the open! I do not know what troops could have done it.

On 6 March, and as an aid to improve morale, fourteen men including the gallant Badri Nar Singh were formally paraded and the garrison was told that they were to be recommended for the Order of Merit for their courage in remaining with Dr Whitchurch. This decoration, divided into three classes, carried with it a life pension, which in the longer term was more significant than the medal. Additional feats of bravery could bring promotion in the order and more money. The selection of the fourteen was somewhat random, but it had the desired effect.

Later that day, and under a white flag, Umra Khan sent an envoy to speak to Dr Robertson. A protracted debate followed in which the envoy sought to explain that Umra Khan's presence on the hills around the fort, together with 1,000 men, was in order to provide support for the garrison and to intervene if any collision should occur between Sher Afzul's troops and the garrison. Robertson in this situation was doing what he did best and Townshend could only look on as the labyrinthine negotiations were conducted with graciousness on both sides. Robertson sent the envoy away 'with a flea in his ear' having rejected the offer to abandon the fort and return to Gilgit with the garrison, under the protection of Umra Khan. This was the third message to Robertson to be followed by many more, all of which combined to protract the siege in the garrison's favour as forces were being marshalled to relieve it.

The first week of the siege was remarkably peaceful. Sher Afzul, Umra Khan and Abdul Majid Khan knew perfectly well that time was on their side and had every reason to expect to starve the garrison into submission. Robertson, who thought that the rest of the world had no idea of the circumstances at Chitrál, called for volunteers to carry a message and four brave men stepped forward. They were despatched on successive days charged with making their way to a friendly force. On 7 March, the last of these men slipped out of the fort, his mission being to establish whether or not his predecessors had got through the cordon. The Messenger was to report back and to gain entrance to the fort by way of the marble rock. Townshend ensured that the sentries would be warned to look out for him. He was a bad choice because he went straight to Sher Afzul and briefed him on the conditions in the fort. Sher Afzul exploited the situation and a miscreant who had been condemned was offered his life if he took the messenger's place.

It was an offer difficult to refuse and accordingly, on 8 March, the unwilling substitute approached the Marble Rock and made his way up the tunnel to the Water Tower. He laid a fire but he was too hurried and the fire did not take hold. It was quickly extinguished and the spy made his escape. The degree of sympathy he received at the hands of Sher Afzul after his failed mission is not recorded.

Lieutenant Harley volunteered on 10 March to take six of his Sikhs, swim the river and take the enemy's water sangar. Townshend, correctly, declined the offer, noting: 'I would not let him go. We have so few men – only ninety of 14th Sikhs, the men we rely on, and only three British officers.' This little episode speaks volumes for the courage of Harley, courage he was to demonstrate again in the future.

The constant exchange of correspondence between the two sides with the occasional exchange of envoys generated apparently endless negotiations which were conducted with a show of enormous courtesy on both sides, even though there was precious little honesty on offer. Sher Afzul's aim was to be recognized as Mehtar of Chitrál, and Robertson's was to prevent any such thing. Umra Khan conducted quite separate negotiations, always assuring Robertson that all this hostility really was nothing to do with him. These meetings and exchanges of correspondence played into the hands of Robertson who was in no hurry – in fact the longer the talks went on the more likely it was that relief would arrive. Townshend could contribute little to the debate and he probably was not consulted anyway; on the other hand Sifat was constantly consulted. The former just got on with the day-to-day tasks of maintaining a fort under siege without any immediate prospect of relief.

On 11 March a man bearing yet another letter from Sher Afzul asserted, but was not believed, that two British detachments had been overwhelmed: the first at Reshun, three days' march from Chitrál on the left bank of the Mastuj River, and the other a little beyond the village. The envoy claimed that, at Reshun, one officer and forty sepoys were killed, with sixty cases of 'treasure' and twenty boxes of cartridges being taken. He said that ten men, the survivors, were still defending themselves in a fortified house. The news got worse because the letter bearer went on to allege that, in the second clash, sixty-two men were killed and barely a dozen had survived by entrenching themselves in a cave by the river's edge. Two officers had been taken prisoner. To add authenticity to his story he named the officers as Lieutenants Edwardes and Fowler.
   As icing on the military cake, the man told Robertson that his first three messengers had all been captured and as a result none of his messages had got through; they languished in one of Sher Afzul's highly uncomfortable jails. The mention of 'treasure' was sufficiently fanciful for Robertson to be inclined to reject the story out of hand, but there was sufficient credibility in much of the rest to convince him that there had, indeed, been a disaster. Sadly, the facts turned out to be much as Afzul's messenger had claimed. The story of their most gallant action at Reshun is well worth telling but it has no place here as it has no direct relevance to Charles Townshend, who probably knew both officers if only by name. Sher Afzul now intended to use the two officers as pawns in his negotiations with Robertson.

Abdul Majid Khan, the besieging general, had correctly identified the importance to the defenders of the protected route to the river and knew that if he could cut this the survival of the garrison would be in doubt. Thus, on 14 March, Townshend's men were obliged to repel a particularly determined assault on the waterway. Majid Kahn was the commander on the ground, but Umra Khan was the strategist and guiding light. He was a most skilled besieger, was not content to allow the defenders to while away their time eating up precious food and playing cards, and made constant probes of the defences. He did not permit his men to fire their weapons unless they had a target, but the opportunity target was always engaged and that served to keep the nerves of all those confined in the fort on edge. Communication with the outside world had ceased and Robertson and Townshend had no idea what, if anything was being done to rescue them. Townshend and his two officers split the hours in the day between them, but rarely did any of them enjoy an uninterrupted sleep, and this lack of sleep, poor diet and constant tension started to have an effect.

On 15 March Sher Afzul proposed a truce and the following day forwarded a letter from Edwardes to Robertson. Edwardes confirmed all of Robertson's worst fears, causing Townshend to comment: 'The B.A. [Robertson] talking to me this evening said that he did not mind his plans having failed, the only thing he regretted was the death of poor Baird.'

Apparently Robertson felt that he must do everything and anything to save the lives of Edwardes and Fowler and, incidentally, any of their surviving soldiers. His aim was to extract the garrison from Chitrál 'as honourably' as he was able. The lives of the two officers were one issue, but a considerable quantity of ammunition and engineering stores had fallen into the hands of the Chitrális which, no doubt, would be turned against the fort in due course. The truce of three days was extended to five days and was marked by white flags being hoisted on one of the fort's towers, and by Sher Afzul on Lieutenant Gurdon's house. During that period low-grade intelligence, little more than a rumour, said that Sher Afzul was in effect a prisoner of Umra Khan.

On 19 March two very conciliatory letters arrived at the fort; one from Umra Khan, the other from Sher Afzul. They said that the two British officers would be delivered to the fort 'tomorrow' and that the Chitrális had been beaten by the British relief force that was now advancing. Robertson sent an envoy called Munshi Amir Ali to visit the two officers, a visit readily agreed by Umra Khan. On his return it was reported that the two men were being well taken care of but that only twelve of their men from a complement of sixty had survived.

The five-day truce was welcomed by the denizens of Chitrál; it was like a holiday. They could stroll along the ramparts and show themselves without fear of attracting a bullet from any of the multiplicity of sangars that by now ringed the fort.

*   *   *

It was two weeks into the siege and the middle of March when the news of the investment of Chitrál reached the Government of India, which realized that there was a potentially explosive situation and that Chitrál was the 'blue touch paper'. If Chitrál fell it would bode ill for any number of other similarly vulnerable British outposts.

The relief of the besieged garrison was put in hand. Major General Sir Robert Cunliffe Low, who was in command of Lucknow District, was given orders to march from Nowshera on the Kabul River in north-east Peshawar to lift the siege at Chitrál. The news of the siege had reached the newspapers – public opinion was swiftly voiced and it was very positive in tone. The action of Umra Kahn and Sher Afzul was seen as an affront to the entire British Empire, and the Indian Raj in particular. Decisive action was required, nay demanded.

By 19 March, Low had mobilized a division of 15,000 men, supported by 28,000 requisitioned pack animals and an uncounted multitude of camp followers to carry, cut forage, cook and serve in a host of capacities. Low was a very seasoned soldier and had spent his entire military career in India. He knew a bit about sieges having experienced those of Delhi and Lucknow during the Mutiny. In Europe the news of Britain's difficulties in Chitrál was greeted with satisfaction by all Anglophobes, and there were many of these – not least in France.

In Russia events were observed with 'interest' and, given that Low's advance to Chitrál might be by way of the Dorah Pass, a pass that was the likely access for a Russian invasion, there was speculation in *The Times* that the object of the expedition was less to defeat a few thousand ill-disciplined tribesmen or rescue a few hundred soldiers, but more to deter the multitude of Russians waiting to attack British India.

On 22 March, whilst Low was well advanced with his plans, over 200 miles away as an eagle might fly a Lieut Colonel J.G. Kelly, commanding the 32nd Pioneers at Bunji, about 40 miles east of Gilgit, was also advancing to the rescue.

On 21 March, Townshend noted in his diary:

The BA has told me about the capture of Fowler and Edwardes. It was a truce. On the day after the truce was declared the Chitrális invited the two officers to a game of polo. When they appeared they were at once knocked down and bound. That to me is not a surprising matter. As for the sepoys, it is said that the enemy killed 35 of them and the rest are slaves . . . How will these officers explain the fact that they left their sepoys and quitted the post where they had been barricaded and besieged in a little house for six days to see a game of polo at the invitation of the enemy?

In Chitrál the truce had run its course, hostilities recommenced and men on both sides continued to die – more outside the walls than within. Most of them had very little idea of what the whole affair was all about. The truce had benefited Sher Afzul nothing, but it had provided the besieged with more breathing space and, every day, help was getting closer. The enemy, now refreshed, returned to the fray and were as persistent as ever. Abdul Majid Khan was proactive, mounting a feint on the north-west tower and putting in a determined attack on the Water Tower. This latter attack was so successful that the enemy succeeded in lighting a fire alongside the Water Tower. The fire was extinguished by the defenders but it had been a dangerous situation. During the truce and afterwards, when fire was being exchanged all the while, Sher Afzul was trying to persuade Robertson to retire to Mastuj.

It was an impasse and neither would give an inch to the other. Robertson emerges from these labyrinthine negotiations with great credit because it would have been all too easy to succumb to the honeyed words of his adversaries, but then he was a deal worldlier than Fowler and Edwards.

The weather turned for the worse, rain fell in sheets and it had a deleterious effect upon the fragile walls of the fort, which crumbled under the flow of water. The interior of the fort became a quagmire and raw sewage flowed freely in the latrine area. It was necessary for working parties to labour in the torrential rain shoring up vulnerable sections of the walls. Everything was wet and morale took a corresponding dip. Townshend said very bleakly, on 24 March, 'There is nothing for the horses to eat, so we eat the horses.'

A Union flag was fabricated on 29 March from oddments of material and this was hoisted on the south-east tower in a show of defiance. It was no more than a symbol, but then that is all a flag ever is. However, symbols can be potent in the right context and this was just such a case. To the defenders it seemed that after the hoisting of the flag their luck changed for the better.

On 31 March, new enemy sangars appeared and there were signs of an increase in sapping to such extent that a week later they had approached to no more than 30 yards of the fort's main gate. The enemy fabricated giant bundles of brushwood fascines and this work was serviced in a covered sangar that extended 200 yards to the rear. Robertson decided that it was time to demonstrate his military acumen and said to Townshend that he

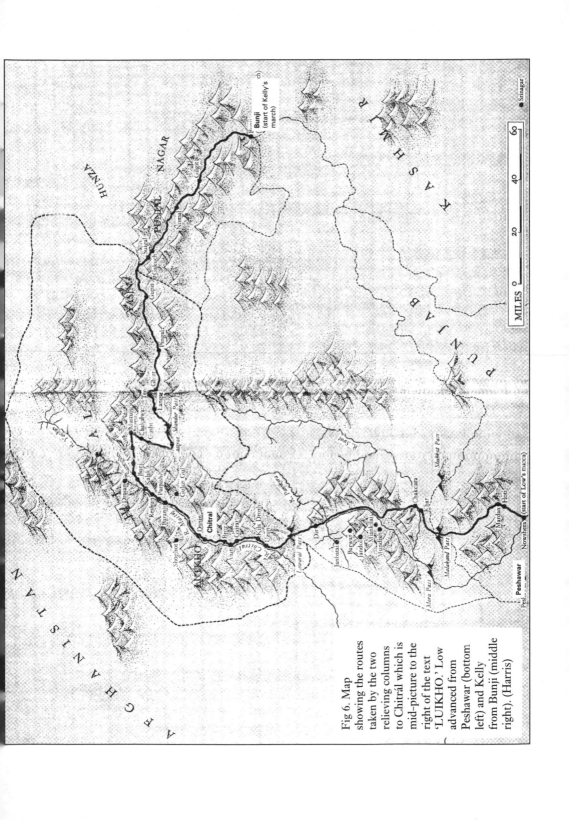

Fig 6. Map showing the routes taken by the two relieving columns to Chitral which is mid-picture to the right of the text 'LUIKHO.' Low advanced from Peshawar (bottom left) and Kelly from Bunji (middle right). (Harris)

thought that, 'we might rush the two sangars in front of the fort and then go up the ridge.'⁵ Townshend would have none of it but, anxious not to 'come to a misunderstanding', he remained silent until Robertson persisted by saying that he was concerned about what others might think of them. Townshend had had enough of this and 'I told him straight that we had done our duty and would continue to do it; that I did my duty, and what I thought to be sound, and did not care what anybody said or thought.'

The absurd suggestion that Townshend should mount a sally from the safety of the fort and up a defended ridge was quietly shelved. He probably saved fifty lives in the process. It is interesting to note that throughout this siege, Townshend, although more than capable of taking decisions often referred them to Robertson for confirmation. It was a characteristic that would be seen again in late 1915.

By 3 April, ghee had run out which was serious as ghee was to Indian soldiers what meat was to a European. In explanation, ghee is made by simmering unsalted butter in a large pot until all the water has boiled off and the protein has settled to the bottom. Unlike butter, the ghee that is thus formed can be stored for extended periods without refrigeration. It is an important constituent in many Asian cuisines.

There was only a little rum left but Townshend ordered that a dram was to be given to the Sikhs every fourth day, and a quarter of an ounce of tea to every Kashmiri every other day. Townshend noted in his diary on that same date:

> What will happen in the way of sickness when it gets hot I do not know or care to reflect upon much: the stenches in this awful fort are simply appalling already. How the men in the stable picquet do not get ill coming off duty I can't imagine. I feel sick every time I go to the stables to inspect the picquet.

On 7 April, at 0500 hrs, there were a series of well co-ordinated, vigorous attacks. In the first, yet another attempt was made to take the waterway, however the Sikhs stationed in that critical area met the assault and repulsed it with considerable loss to the enemy. At the same time, and on the southern side, there was an approach in force together with an attempt to fire the south-east tower. The summer house had been the base for this fire-raising team and they had come prepared with ample kindling for the task. The tower took fire and it was five hours before it was extinguished. The defenders suffered eight men wounded, one of whom was the British Agent, Dr Robertson, who was shot in the arm. It may be stating the obvious but, once again, he had no place in the firing line because his death would have precipitated a major crisis.

The vulnerability of the towers had already been recognized and so additional steps were taken to thwart any further incursions. Wooden pipes were constructed to allow a flow of water onto any fire and, in addition, heaps of sand and earth placed to smother a fire at its source. Stones were stockpiled to drop on the enemy. Given that the defenders were well armed it is curious that they would, from choice, throw a stone when a round from a Martini-Henry would be provide a more pleasing and permanent result.

It was as well that the defences of the towers had been beefed up because on 8 April the enemy renewed its efforts to fire the south-east tower, again taking casualties, but without success.

On 10 April another victim was felled by the skill of the Chitráli snipers and 'Ghazi' Townshend's dog was hit for the second time, on this occasion in his body. His former wound was through in the loose skin that covered his stomach. History does not tell us the fate of the little dog and, if he succumbed to his wounds, his master did not record it.

Much more serious was Townshend's uncompromising position over a Kashmiri sentry found sleeping at his post on 13 April. He made it clear that the man would be tried by court martial and, if found guilty, sentenced to death. This was a very serious offence for the self-evident reason that the offender put all of his comrades at risk. Men were executed during the First World War for the same offence. There is no record of the outcome of this case and the probability is that the charge was dropped in the euphoria that was to follow.

The siege was by now well advanced but losses inside the fort had been surprisingly light: four men had been killed and seventeen wounded within the walls. The body count among the besiegers was very many times greater. The conditions in the fort were now deeply unpleasant. The unutterably dreadful stench has been much mentioned but in addition the men themselves smelt, food was meagre and the health of the garrison started to suffer. At any one time there were sixty-six to seventy men in the hospital and Dr Whitchurch was not equipped to deal with ill-health on this scale.

17 April was marked by the sound of drumming during the night and it seemed to emanate from the summer house, a mere 40 yards from the wall. It was surmised that the drumming was designed to mask some other activity, probably the sound of picks and shovels. It did not take long for the distinctive sound of digging to be distinguished and the conclusion drawn by the defenders was that their adversaries were attempting to under-mine the tower and, what was more, were making excellent progress. The

mine was within 10 feet of the walls and there was certainly no time to sink a counter mine.

Townshend was obliged to take action against the mine immediately and decided to make a sally. Forty Sikhs and sixty of the Kashmiri were swiftly detailed off under the command of Lieutenant Harley, who was charged with rushing the summer house to blow up the mine. The excursion was to be conducted in silence and no weapons were to be fired. Townshend briefed each member of the party personally and explained that the objective had to be taken at the point of the bayonet.

This was the single most critical point in the siege. The penalty that would be paid if Harley and his men failed was the probable fall of the fort and, consequently, the death of the inhabitants – the mission was as important as that. Young Harley, courageous as he was, realized just how much depended upon his leadership, tenacity and skill.

At 1600 hrs the small garden gate – about 80 yards from the summer house – was quietly opened and Harley slipped out at the head of his men whom he now led in a mad dash for their objective. They were seen at once and came under accurate fire, not only from the summer house but also from any of the sangars that could bring a weapon to bear. Several men dropped only yards from the gate but the main body swept on and cleared the summer house, whose occupants withdrew, but only to an alternative position behind a garden wall from which they continued to fire upon Harley's party. The mouth of the mine was inside the summer house and, according to all contemporary accounts, on hearing the tumult above, thirty-five of the enemy inside the tunnel made their way to the surface only to be bayoneted one by one as they emerged squinting in the late afternoon, spring sunshine.

How these thirty-five men managed to fit into a tunnel at most 15 to 20 yards long and quite what they were able to achieve in such a confined space is not explained. The figure of thirty-five is open to question but it is quoted confidently by several sources.

In the meantime, Townshend brought down a brisk controlled fire on all the sangars that were engaging his party and at the same time responded to an enemy thrust toward the stables.

Harley placed powder bags in the mine and when these detonated, the effect was all that he had hoped for. The explosion collapsed the tunnel and reduced it to a sunken trench about 30 yards long from the summer house to that point just ten yards from the walls. Harley rallied his men, re-organized, slew any enemy to hand and withdrew his party, under control, to the garden gate. It was just after 1700 hrs and it had been a hectic but productive hour, although Harley had lost eight men killed and thirteen wounded.

There is no doubt that Townshend had made a correct decision and Harley had carried out his mission in the most exemplary manner. Enemy losses were very considerable. Townshend and Harley estimated that they had killed or seriously wounded sixty or more whilst eliminating a serious threat. The morale of the garrison had been boosted and it had been made clear to the opposition that it still had a long way to go in its quest to take Chitrál fort and its inhabitants.

Lieutenant Harley was, quite rightly, the hero of the hour because his sally had probably saved the lives of the entire garrison. It is interesting to compare his performance with those of the winners of the VC during the Hunza-Nagar expedition.

Ostensibly to prevent another attempt at mining, Townshend ordered the digging of a subterranean tunnel around the tower to act as a first line of defence. The merits of this measure are not clear. Neither is it clear how the tunnel was to be manned but, as it happened, it was never put to the test.

The night of 18 April was, like many, others crystal clear and very cold. Shouts were heard outside the wall and Gurdon, the officer on duty, made his way to the parapet to see the individual doing the shouting. It was a man who claimed that he had important news. He asked to enter the fort and, with some reluctance, a gate was opened. The man explained that Sher Afzul and the Jhandoli had withdrawn because a British force was only two days' march away. The garrison could scarcely believe the story but not for a moment did Townshend allow the degree of vigilance to drop. The following morning it was confirmed that the sangars were abandoned and the enemy had indeed fled.

The garrison moved beyond the confines of the fort, weapons were unloaded and a degree of normality restored. A priority was the digging of new latrines. Campbell and others who were sick or wounded could be moved from the stygian depths of the fort into daylight. Parties were organized to forage for food and morale was sky high when, twenty-four hours later, on 20 April 1895, Colonel Kelly arrived in the valley with his relief force from Gilgit. Soon after, Captain Baird was reburied.

Lieutenant Colonel J.G. Kelly had assumed military command throughout the Gilgit agency on 22 March and, having made arrangements for the security of Gilgit, he left on a march of 220 miles to Chitrál. His assets eventually totalled 590 soldiers supplemented by porters and muleteers; he had in addition two mountain guns. During the arduous march Kelly had been hindered by the loss of many of his porters who lost interest in the expedition and deserted.

Kelly made first for Mastuj, about 50 miles north-east of Chitrál, but blizzard conditions forced him back. He tried again but conditions at the Shandar Pass had worsened considerably and Kelly's force failed in its first attempt to cross. Deep snow was beyond the capacity of the mules and they and any ponies were abandoned. The guns were manhandled through snow 4 feet deep by men who did not have the benefit of efficient bad-weather clothing. The consequence was that forty-three men suffered frostbite and a further sixty-three snow blindness.

The enemy had determined that Shandar was impassable and so it came as a disagreeable surprise to the 400–500 at Chakalwat to be confronted by Kelly on 9 April with part of his force and the two vital guns. Kelly's disciplined soldiers routed the more numerous enemy and later that day lifted the siege of Mastuj, which had by now been invested for eighteen days. Four days later, on 13 April, a much more significant action was fought at Nisa Gol when 1,500 of the enemy, entrenched in a strong position, were decisively beaten by Kelly's well-coordinated force – now 622 strong. The two mountain guns were again employed to great effect and the decision to manhandle them, despite the cost, was more than vindicated.

Kelly's force reached the River Kunar on 17 April but found that the bridge had been destroyed. His troops had to ford the icy and swift-flowing river which was breast deep. The weather was very cold and there were no means to dry clothes. Fording a river in this part of the world was not an exercise to be undertaken lightly, but needs must when the devil drives.

The relief of Chitrál was by now almost assured. Umra Khan and Sher Afzul commanded many times the modest force commanded by Kelly, and it is extraordinary that they did not stay and give battle. The bloody events of 3 March were proof enough that they would have given a very good account of themselves. However, they melted away and Kelly received a rapturous welcome when he made his weary way to the gate of Chitrál fort on 20 April. His march from Gilgit had taken twenty-nine days and from start to finish it had been a splendid feat of arms.

The relief of Chitrál was an epic in itself and the subject of several books. General Low's contested advance from Peshawar alone was a remarkable military campaign, and Kelly's not one whit less praiseworthy but, as Townshend was no more than a beneficiary of the bravery of these two groups of gallant soldiers, the extended story of Low and Kelly has no place here.

Kelly's arrival drew to a close the 46-day siege. There was no doubt that the men of the hour were Robertson and Townshend. Both were feted as heroes. For Townshend it was a high point in his life and the whole business of siege warfare became a matter that thereafter he studied at length. He had seen the failure at Khartoum, but had now experienced the other side of the coin. He probably concluded that sieges were not necessarily all bad.

In mid-July the India Office announced that Surgeon-Major George Scott Robertson CSI, of the Indian Medical Services and British Agent in Gilgit, was to be Knight Commander of the Most Exalted Order of the Star of India (KCSI). At the same time the War Office in London announced that the military players in this minor epic would also reap their reward. Lieutenant Colonel James Graves Kelly was made Brevet[6] Colonel and appointed ADC to HM The Queen, and he and Townshend were appointed Companions of the Most Honourable Order of the Bath (CB). For a lieutenant colonel in command a CB was probably, in its day, about right but for a junior captain a CB was unprecedented – a DSO would have been much more appropriate. In addition Townshend was 'mentioned'[7] for the third time and made Brevet Major, as was Campbell. Gurdon and Harley were decorated with the DSO. Whitchurch, of course, received the Victoria Cross.

Notes
1.   Robertson.
2.   The numbers in the garrison and their status varies depending on the source used. For example, Mohammed Afzul Khan in his book, *Chitrál & Kafirstan, a personal study*, asserts that 'There were 419 fighting men.' Robertson says there were a total of 550 with a fighting strength of 340. The precise arithmetic cannot be determined as every contemporary source differs very widely.
3.   Corrigan, *Mud Blood and Poppycock*.
4.   Edward Wilson Very (1847–1910), an American, patented, in 1877, the flare gun that to this day bears his name. It fires a white flare for illumination and coloured flares for signalling.
5.   CVFT.
6.   There were two avenues for promotion in the British infantry and cavalry and these were the 'Regimental List' and the 'Army List.' Brevet rank applied only to the Army List. It was an award, ostensibly for meritorious service, but patronage and good fortune were also factors.

The number of brevet ranks in the Army was loosely controlled by the Commander–in-Chief but there was no prescribed allocation for any particular rank. Those promoted 'brevet' wore the badges of rank and accoutrements of their brevet rank, and were granted army seniority in this rank. The downside was that they retained the pay and responsibilities of their lower regimental rank. The significant benefit enjoyed by brevets was that they were accumulating seniority in the brevet rank, whilst their peers, without brevet, depended on regimental seniority only. It was a clumsy system that generated frustration and irritation, and its merits are difficult to discern. Quite rightly it was eventually discontinued.

The Foot Guards were, inevitably, different. A brevet system operated but officers of the Household Division carried army rank one level above regimental rank at ensign and lieutenant level, and two levels above at captain. This was an enormous career advantage and, in part, explains why so many officers of the Foot Guards were eventually promoted to general rank.

7.   *London Gazette*, 16 July 1895

Chapter 6

1895–1898

Celebrity and Return to the Sudan

Townshend returned to England as a celebrity. He was feted everywhere he went and basked in public and official approval. It was heady wine for a young man and Townshend's already well-developed ego was boosted by unabashed public adulation. He took a boyish delight in his fame and who can blame him for trying to recreate the situation later in life.

His cousins, the St Aubyns, were in London when he arrived and their circle made a fuss of Charles Townshend. He dined at 29 Bruton St with Sir Redvers and Lady Buller, and soon after was sent for by Prince George, Duke of Cambridge,[1] who with Lord Lansdowne, questioned him closely about events in Chitrál. They then enquired of this young officer his views about the future of the fort and the manner in which it should be held. Townshend was mightily flattered and was more than happy to express his opinion. He said that 'One battalion of infantry – a British Indian regiment and one mountain battery were sufficient to hold Chitrál . . . The old Duke was very nice to me, shook hands and made me sit down beside him. He appeared to be very old but quite clear in his intellect and vigorous. He complimented me very much.'

At the time the retention of Chitrál or otherwise was a political hot potato and Townshend had to steer a careful course. His diary recounts meetings with any number of distinguished soldiers and politicians, and he found that opinions were divided. His mentor Sir Redvers Buller was against the retention of Chitrál and it would have been imprudent for Charles Townshend to be seen to be in the opposition camp. Townshend confided in his diary: 'As far as my opinion is worth anything, I think that it was a mistake to go to Chitrál in the first place, but for that the political authorities were answerable. But, having gone there and fought we could not retreat and it was right to retain Chitrál.'

The measure of young Charles Townshend's extraordinary social success was that he felt entirely at ease in hosting a supper at The Savoy for George Curzon, the Under-Secretary of State for Foreign Affairs, General

Kitchener,[2] Younghusband,[3] Bean St Aubyn (a cousin), Captain Campbell, Sir Saville Crossly[4] and Arthur Roberts.[5] This was quite a batting order and an expensive evening for a man on captain's pay. The host commented on what 'a very merry supper party it was!'

This supper party has to be put into its social and military context. Captains do not usually socialize, other than on the most superficial level, with generals. Generals, if invited to dine with a captain, would usually find that they had other engagements to attend to. In this case two generals, a member of the Government, a distinguished traveller and an actor who was a household name, all came to his table. The social standing of Charles Townshend by far exceeded his rank and station in life. It is a measure of the impact that his service at Chitrál had had at every level.

It did not end here, for his next port of call was Marlborough House and a meeting with the Prince of Wales, who discussed Chitrál with the young hero and then turned to the affairs of the Townshend clan, not least to the still gloriously, happily and unmarried Marquess. During a very sociable and agreeable meeting the Prince said that if Townshend wanted to transfer into the Guards he, the Prince, would see what he could do! This was an offer difficult to refuse but after consulting Buller, who judged such a move to be 'suicidal', he was advised to stick with the Indian Army.

The icing on the cake was when he was invited to lunch at Osborne with the Queen, no less. After the meal, a private investiture followed at which the Sovereign placed the ribbon of the CB around his neck and invited him to kiss her hand. The following week he dined at Osborne at a table littered with luminaries, spent ten minutes alone with his Queen, and later that evening had a lengthy conversation with the Marquess of Lorne who was knowledgeable about the famous 1st Marquess Townshend, victor of Quebec who took over command from Wolfe when he fell on the Heights of Abraham

The social whirl continued apace and there were invitations from Guards officers who had served with him in previous campaigns, the Camel Corps and the Royal Marines. He stayed in several country houses, widened his circle of friends and did not miss any opportunity to attend and be seen at the theatre. He went to see Arthur Roberts no less than eighteen times in the current hit *Gentleman Joe* – he must have known the script off by heart.

Family affairs came to the fore in late November 1895 when he stayed at Balls Park, a property belonging to Lord Townshend which was rented out. Townshend was chagrined that the family had fallen on such hard times that the current Marquess could not afford to live either in Balls Park in Hertfordshire or Raynham Hall in Norfolk. The plan was that both properties were to be sold with the land around them. Townshend mused that perhaps, in the future, he might be able to restore the family prestige and fortune.

A Chitrál exhibition was to be staged at Olympia in December and, on 6 December, accompanied by Curly Stewart, Charles Townshend went to look it over. The scenery painter enquired if he was Major Townshend, saying he recognized him from a painting in a book by Younghusband. Townshend conceded that it was 'all very flattering'.[6]

Christmas came and went, but the best sort of belated present was a telegram from General Sir Herbert Kitchener which read: 'Can offer command battalion if you come to Egypt February 23rd. You to arrange Indian Government. Am sending application home. Kitchener.'

Things must have been very different in 1896 and for a commander-in-chief to deal, on a personal basis, with a mere major is noteworthy. More noteworthy still was that Kitchener made an 'offer' of an appointment to an officer who was neither under his command, nor for that matter even in his Army.

Today officers and soldiers go where they are sent and the scenario described above would be highly unlikely. There is no place for a prima donna like Townshend in the twenty-first century. To put this matter into balance, if Townshend had not been a first-rate leader with a track record to prove it, Kitchener would most certainly not have made the approach. Nevertheless, this was just the opportunity Charles Townshend wanted to advance his career, well realizing that it was active service that was the key to success and glory. However, to achieve his aim he had first to pull any number of well-connected strings. He was never inhibited in this regard and moved into top gear, subjecting the India Office in both London and Delhi with telegrams requesting his release – with predictable success.

He returned to Cairo, as bidden, on 11 February 1896 and was given command of the 12th Sudanese Battalion. His fame preceded him and he was lionized when he joined the station. It was very agreeable, but this degree of public attention is best given to a man with his feet firmly on the ground and who is without delusions of grandeur. Charles Townshend was probably not best equipped to cope.

On 21 February 1896, his thirty-fifth birthday, he reported to Kitchener. At this meeting the Sirdar congratulated Townshend 'on gaining the command of about the best regiment in the Egyptian Army'. Townshend met Major Hector Macdonald and they dined together. Macdonald was the elder by four years and an interesting character. He had risen from the ranks of the Seaforth Highlanders, which in itself was testament to his ability, and was to be Townshend's commander as Major, acting Brigadier.

Three days later Charles Townshend lunched with Evelyn Baring, 1st Earl Cromer (1841–1917). Cromer was, in effect, the ruler of Egypt. A most distinguished civil administrator, he ranked alongside Lord Curzon in status in Victorian Britain. By giving of his time to Townshend he paid the young officer an enormous compliment. It got even better when CVFT was presented to the Khedive. The day finished with a dance at a major hotel and, he noted with satisfaction, that 'it was all very well done. Lots of pretty women.'

Townshend had to date thoroughly deserved his swift advance. He was an assiduous student of the profession of arms and was already a skilful exponent of that profession. Any preferment he had been given had been on the recommendation of others, and his three 'Mentions' were drafted by officers by far his senior. It is true that he constantly manipulated the system to his perceived advantage, but his admirers would counter that charge by saying that any officer who seeks to confront his country's foes is not to be damned for wanting to do his duty. Unfortunately, for all Townshend's admirable ability, his lively personality and his undoubted bravery, he was not a very attractive person. His ambition was all consuming and almost certainly completely unnecessary. In fact, he was good enough to achieve high rank in any circumstances and, had he curbed his rampant ambition, he might just have made some military friends along the way.

Overtly ambitious officers, generation on generation, have one characteristic in common and that is their belief that one of the paths to success is through the patronage of their seniors. To this end the cultivation of people of influence becomes a priority. In the unattractive parlance of the twenty-first century it is called 'brown nosing' – one cannot think why. Townshend was adept and energetic in this activity. He established a wide circle of correspondents and used them to his advantage throughout his career. Buller, Kitchener, Durand, Robertson and Aylmer were all very useful contacts who might yet be exploited in the years ahead.

Townshend's arrival in Egypt was particularly well timed because only a few weeks later his battalion was included in Kitchener's expedition to reconquer the Sudan. The start of the expedition was precipitated by the massive defeat of the Italians at Adowa on 1 March 1896 by the Mahdists who, capitalizing on their success, became overtly aggressive. The British Government, anxious to relieve the pressure on the Italians and to restore European prestige, urged Kitchener to make a start.

Townshend was highly unamused when his battalion was issued new rifles on 14 April and he waxed eloquent in his diary on the matter, complaining that:

The new rifles we have taken over are so full of sand that in many cases it is impossible to ease the springs, the blocks are set so high up . . . It shows a lack of practical knowledge . . . now I have at once ordered that the whole Battalion be set on cleaning rifles. The armourer to whom I have lent thirty men to help, is to clean 100 rifles a day – all companies to parade two hours a day under their company officers, cleaning rifles.

All in all this sounds like a great deal of cleaning for unsophisticated weapons, perhaps 'overkill' might best describe his response.

The Nile was at a very low level, the hot season was fast approaching and it was quite the wrong time of the year to embark on operations in this merciless environment (see Fig 1 on Page 10). Advancing on Dongola in northern Sudan was nevertheless the order of the day. South of Wadi Halfa, the Nile has created an awesome gorge about one hundred miles long with remarkable rock formations. The Nile is only navigable when it is in flood and, when it is not, islands and isolated rocks rear out of the water, making movement by water largely impractical.

The expedition set off on foot and made its arduous, uncomfortable and painstaking way up through Dongola province to Akasha where it was intended to establish a base for future operations. Akasha had the attraction that it was on a narrow-gauge, single-track railway line, albeit recently torn up by the Mahdists. Kitchener determined to repair the railway and applied enormous resources to the rebuilding and defence of the line. Blockhouses were built at intervals and units, Townshend's included, were passed up this route over the following months, and dug in between Sarras and Akasha.

There was an indecisive skirmish on 1 May and the enemy retreated towards the small settlement of Ferkeh, a small fortified village on the banks of the Nile. It was here that Townshend fought in the first major engagement of the campaign at the Battle of Ferkch (or Firket) five weeks later, on 7 June 1896.

Kitchener's Anglo-Egyptian force of about 9,000 men (included in its inventory were three batteries of field guns and one of Maxim machine guns) was confronted by 3,000 Mahdist soldiers at Ferkeh. The enemy was under the command of the two tribal chiefs, or Emirs, Hammuda and Osman Azrak.

Kitchener wasted no time and determined to attack Ferkeh on two fronts. Accordingly, he deployed his infantry to approach along the bank of the Nile from the north whilst his camel-mounted cavalry and horse artillery attacked from the south-east. The force then made a night march on 6/7 June and were in position to make an assault at dawn on 7 June. The Mahdists were unprepared for the ferocity of the opening barrage of artillery – the first shell killed eight men – and the speed and ruthless application of force by Kitchener's infantry and cavalry.

Surprise was total and the Mahdist response was weak, uncoordinated and ineffective. Hammuda was killed and although Osman Azrak fled and lived to fight another day, many of his men stayed at their posts and died there – at the point of a bayonet. Townshend had been ordered to move his unit to cut off the enemy retreat and noted: 'when we topped the rise I deployed on the move, moving into line, and could see the Dervishes in white groups coming out of a nullah in the rocks in front, but evidently wavering. I poured hot fire into them, and they fled left and right.'

The entire operation had lasted under three hours and by 0720 hrs, to quote Townshend, 'the show was over.' The British/Egyptian force suffered twenty killed and about eighty wounded, but the Mahdists losses were variously estimated at between 900 and 1,200. The Sirdar visited Townshend and his battalion that morning, obviously well pleased with the morning's work and Townshend's part in it. CVFT's name duly appeared in the *London Gazette* of 11 November 1896 when he was 'mentioned' for the fourth time. On this occasion it was for his conduct at the actions at Ferkeh and later at El Hapi.

Townshend's battalion formed part of Hector Macdonald's brigade and it would seem that these two men, despite their earlier meeting, did not 'hit it off'. But Macdonald was the senior and was in command. Townshend complained in his diary on 22 July:

> Macdonald wrote officially to me yesterday to stop my Battalion holding 'Zikers' at night. These zikers are religious ceremonial laments for the wives dead at Halfa. About 30 women of this Battalion have up to date died at Halfa. I wrote back to Macdonald to the effect that I understood that the custom in Sudanese regiments was to allow the men to hold a ziker up to ten at night, and naturally I did not care to interfere with the religious customs of natives. However, in accordance with his wishes I had ordered that there should be no zikers or any noise whatever after lights out at 9pm. I think that Macdonald is very mistaken to interfere in any way in matters of this kind. Natives

talk of these things and resent interference. In two cases where I sent two men for summary court martial (both of them richly deserving it) Macdonald had refused and ordered me to punish them regimentally.

The relationship between these two men was further marred when a month later the Nile had risen high enough to be navigable and Kitchener was able to order a further advance to the south. Inexplicably Macdonald then issued his brigade with a series of orders for a march to the north from whence they had come. This was unnecessary and absurd. The subsequent march back to Wadi Halfa was a nightmare.[7]

There were insufficient camels and those allocated were loaded with everything, except water. Any respect Townshend had had for Macdonald was now sadly diminished. CVFT's diary in late August recorded his anger and frustration. He and his men faced as much danger on this march from the blistering heat and lack of water as if they had been under fire, so it is to Townshend's credit that he was able to exercise his pronounced leadership skills and experience in getting his battalion through the trial. Nevertheless, several men died of heatstroke and others succumbed to exhaustion. On arrival, Macdonald ordered Townshend to send 180 men to labour on fatigues and a further thirty to build huts for the Brigadier's headquarters. This order was almost the final straw and Townshend commented: 'I would not have had any hut made for myself till the men's were made.'

The Brigade lost 463 men in the desert who had to be recovered, but despite Townshend sending every mule and camel he had it was too late and many of these trusting soldiers perished. Little wonder that Townshend questioned why on earth Macdonald had ordered them to march during the day. It got worse when, on 5 September, in the hottest of weather, Macdonald ordered his brigade on a route march for no other purpose than training.

At the end of August 1896, everything was in place and the river had risen, but then two massive and destructive storms washed away miles of the vital railway line and, overnight, did the enemy's work for him. It took a week to get the line running and by 18 September three gunboats had found their way above the third cataract. Kitchener moved on and occupied Dongola with not a shot fired in opposition – much to the disappointment of Townshend.

There was now a lengthy lull in offensive operations as Kitchener had no instructions to proceed further. The force sat and waited for something to happen. This stagnation was to last from September 1896 until April 1898, during which time there was an unreal atmosphere. The force was encamped at the end of a lengthy supply line and was achieving nothing but costing a great deal of public money to maintain.

Townshend did not waste his time and in a remarkably disciplined way he continued with his self-education. His routine was that on Mondays, Wednesdays and Fridays he spent two hours in the morning dealing with private correspondence and three hours in the afternoon on French exercises and French reading. On Tuesdays, Thursdays and Saturdays he followed a similar pattern but substituted Arabic for French. Sundays were devoted to yet more private correspondence and military history. He filled in any spare time studying the drill book. Anyone who spends upwards of twelve hours a week on 'private correspondence' must have a wide circle of acquaintances and a great deal to say to them.

Townshend heard, on 18 November 1896, that he had been made Brevet Lieutenant Colonel. This was yet another mark of official favour and an event to be celebrated. It drew admiring letters of congratulations 'from all his lady friends at home'[8] and, no doubt, a prompt response to them all. F.C. Younghusband, the famous explorer, wrote in the most generous terms, going so far as to say to Charles Townshend: 'I reckon you to be among my real pals.' Townshend was still only thirty-five and, by the standards of the day, he was positively racing up the promotion ladder. Townshend had come to the notice of Kitchener, one of the leading military figures of the time, a man of international renown and, ere long, a man who was to become Minister for War. That is just the sort of supporter a thrusting officer dreams of having. He also had E.F. Knight, the war correspondent, and his erstwhile subordinate in the Hunza-Nagar campaign. He and Knight got on well and Townshend described him warmly in his diary. Knight's despatches did Townshend no harm either.

Townshend was granted leave from 15 February 1897 and made his way to Debbeh to take passage in a boat to Cairo. At Luxor, during this voyage, he was introduced to the Comtesse Cahen D'Anvers and her daughter Alice. He pronounced them both to be 'charming' and contrived to take his meals in their company. The voyage was much enlivened by their presence and that of Alice who, in particular, had taken his fancy. The ardent young man did not overplay his hand and devoted himself to both ladies, riding into the desert with them after they eventually reached Cairo on 26 February. Restrictions on leave spent in Cairo imposed by the Sirdar required Townshend to return to his battalion on 28 March after six weeks absence.

The Comtesse and her daughter went on to Paris where they both narrowly escaped being burnt to death in a fire that destroyed their building and killed 146 other residents. Townshend heard about the fire and sent off telegrams enquiring about their safety. A flow of increasingly warm and intimate correspondence followed and on 22 June, Townshend noted: 'The letter of the Comtesse D'Anvers is the sweetest I have ever had in my life. She writes as a mother to me. Never have I been touched like this. She and her daughter Alice are the best of friends I have, and I look forward only to the time when I can get home and see them again.'

The weeks ticked by, but Kitchener would not be hurried and waited patiently for the railway line to be completely overhauled and functional. He was not going to commit his troops until he had sufficient assets in place to be absolutely assured of victory. The final advance to Khartoum was to be a foregone conclusion and Kitchener would not settle for less. On 10 September there is a rather different entry in Townshend's diary which reads:

> This evening I gave an entertainment for the Battalion. This is a sort of show called by the Sudanese a 'Darluka'. Much 'boosa' or Sudanese beer is given out, and everyone turned up at the 12th Sudanese quarters at 6.30. Colonel Lewis and I paid a visit after mess. All the tribes danced to the music of tom-toms and the accompaniment of singing in perfect time. The black women, naked to the waist, danced frantically face to face with the Sudanese troopers shaking their breasts and swaying big hips and diffusing all around with a strong odour of fille du Sudan. The men twirled around them with gestures at once amusing but obscene. At the end they all got very drunk and abandoned themselves to fiercer orgies, but it is no affair of mine. I was discreet and left the scene early. Poor devils why should they not amuse themselves in their own fashion? And, after all, as Sir Richard Burton said, 'morality is largely a question of geography!'

Townshend reveals a very human face in this entry and sound judgment. He must have learned as a young officer the golden rule that an officer should never have dealings with a drunken soldier. To try to reason with a drunk is to open the door for that soldier, perhaps, to commit an offence that cannot be ignored.

On 20 December, 12th Sudanese received orders that are difficult to fathom. The Battalion was despatched to Berber and embarked on the steamship *Abu Klea*. Townshend dined with the Sirdar whilst in Halfa and was told that there was a rumour that the Dervishes intended to attack Berber. Whilst Townshend socialized, those of his men with local wives had the chance for a conjugal visit, but to the credit of the Battalion they all reported back on time, we can safely presume, with smiles on their faces.

Responding to no more than a rumour, the Battalion entrained on the newly constructed railway line back *north* to a point about 12 miles beyond Abu Hamed. This extraordinary exercise seems to have been a political ploy by the Sirdar to extract another £50,000 from the Government to allow him to extend the railway to Atbara. However, the political niceties were lost on the soldiers who merely thought that the General had lost his reason.

On 7 January 1898, Townshend's 12th Battalion marched back into Berber unopposed. Once again the Battalion marked time and for three months energetic inactivity was the order of the day. In the first week of April 1898, the railway reached Berber where 12th Sudanese now formed part of the garrison. Kitchener was content that he was now fully prepared and when he finally issued his orders, the protracted Sudanese Campaign was restarted. Townshend was joyfully in the thick of the fighting and described it in graphic terms soon afterwards:

> We advanced with bayonets fixed, drums beating and colours flying: it was a grand sight! Then the Dervish riflemen opened a biting fire from the trenches. The ground was perfectly open and descended in a gentle slope towards the Dervish position, putting us up against the skyline, as it were. I soon opened fire in return, using independent fire instead of volleys, as I do not believe in volleys at short ranges. After a short fire I advanced again, myself leading the centre, Lieutenant Harley leading the right wing, and Captain Hon. C.E. Walsh the left wing. Captain Ford-Hutchinson, my Second-in-Command, was in charge of the two companies in reserve, in rear of the centre. My orders to him were to keep the two companies in hand at all costs, for I knew that when we rushed the zariba the confusion would be very bad.
>
> Alternately firing and rushing forward, I rapidly approached the Dervish position. The men were dropping fairly fast. Walsh had been shot and the fire got very hot. I led each rush myself, sounding the 'cease fire' on my whistle, which the men obeyed very well. Then I dashed through the ranks, leading the Battalion about thirty yards ahead, the men following excellently. General Hunter was riding along with me in the front rank of the Battalion for he accompanied

the 12th Sudanese in the assault, cheering them on . . . A lot of men
were firing as I called on the 12th to charge, waving them on. They
broke into a rush with cheers and we swept into the position through
the zariba. How it was I wasn't hit I don't know for the Dervishes must
have been firing at me and the bullets were cutting the ground all
about me. They did not run till we were about thirty yards from them.
Harley was shot just behind me, just as I started the charge. I did not
see him fall, and only heard of it when we had reached the river bank
– victors!

The disorder was great when we had got through the zariba; a
bickering fire was being kept up on us from the interior trenches. All
companics were mixed up except the two reserve companies. Sergeant
Hilton, my drill instructor, was hit in the arm but went on all the same.
It was a splendid charge. We were in first by a long way. The day
before I had determined, in my own mind, to be first in and to show
everyone that the 12th were second to none. I had the chance (as I had
had at Chitrál) and I took advantage of it.

This was an officer who had every chance of being spitted on a Dervish
spear but who, nevertheless, viewed the exercise as no more than a career
opportunity. Townshend's ambition seems to transcend a natural emotion
such as apprehension or, God forbid, fear. He continued:

When we entered the zariba, my Scrgeant-Major heard General
Hunter order Kincaird to ride to the Sirdar, and tell him the 12th was
in the enemy's position. I now collected a crowd and rushed the
second line of trenches, after keeping up a short hot fire on them. Two
or three mines exploded on us: one of our men had the top of his head
blown off: this makes me think that they must have been a sort of
fougasse loaded with stones.

A fougasse is an improvised mine constructed by making a hollow in the
ground or rock and filling this with explosives. Originally, black powder was
used – crude perhaps, but effective nevertheless.

We kept on surging through the crowd, carrying two or three lines of
trenches by by rushes and arrived on the river bank. The men were
drunk with excitement and fight. The men crowded round shaking
and kissing my hand and said that I should be a Pasha, and now lead
them to Omdurman! . . . The scene in the trenches was awful: dead

and dying Dervishes, all black riflemen, like our own men. No quarter
was given, and they did not ask it. They fought heroically, but they
could not stand against our splendid Sudanese. In the trenches, I saw
a dead girl lying beside a dead Dervish. The losses of the Dervishes
were computed at 3,000 killed and many crawled away to die in the
bush. In the trenches they lay as thick as blackberries. General Hunter
warmly congratulated me on the 12th Sudanese, and on the way in
which I had led them.

Out of the 13,000 men of Mahmoud's army, only the 8,000 Jehadia
had stood: as usual, the scoundrelly Bagaras had bolted and got off scot
free. On reaching the high ground, the Sirdar with his staff rode up
and said, 'Townshend, I congratulate you.' He addressed the
Battalion, telling them that he was proud of them. He called for
the Sergeant-Major and promoted him to be Second-Lieutenant
on the spot. I have never had a prouder day, nor felt more elated in
my life. It had been a proud day for me when the Queen pinned on
my C.B. at Osborne. To-day was prouder, for I had been congratulated by the Commander-in-Chief on the field of battle.

Townshend won his fifth 'Mention'[9] and his reputation continued to
blossom.G.W. Steevens, the war correspondent, who was present at the
battle, also wrote about it afterwards and having dwelt at some length on
British losses in his book,[10] he went on to say:

The Egyptian loss was heavier. They had advanced more quickly, and
by reason of their line formation had got to work in the trenches sooner
than the British; but they had not kept down the enemy's fire with
such splendid success. The 11th Sudanese, which had the honour of
having been one of the first inside the zariba (thorn fence) lost very
heavily – 108 killed and wounded out of less than 700. The total casualties were 57 killed, and 4 British and 16 native officers, 2 British
non-commissioned officers, and 365 non-commissioned officers and
men wounded. The white officers were Walter Bey and Shekleton
Bey, commanding the 9th and 14th Sudanese respectively, and
Bimbashis (officers) Walsh and Harley[11] of the 12th Sudanese. The
former lost his leg. The instructors were Sergeants Handley of the 9th
and Hilton of the 12th. Thus, out of five white men, the 12th had three
hit. Townshend's battalion was in the thick of the fight and he was one
of only two British officers to survive the battle unscathed.

Mahmud himself said that his strength on the 8th was 12,000 infantry and 4000 cavalry, with 10 guns. Some days afterwards he asserted that his cavalry had left him the day before, but that was the brag of returning confidence. We all saw his cavalry. To be sure, the cavalry did get away; and Osman Digna, who never fights to a finish, got away with them. The cavalry did nothing and behaved badly, which is significant. On the other hand, the Jehadia, the enlisted black infantry, fought most nobly. If their fire seemed bad to us, what hell must ours have been to them! First an hour and a half of shell and shrapnel – the best ammunition, perfectly aimed and timed, from some of the deadliest field-pieces in the world; then volley after volley of blunted Lee-Metford and of Martini bullets, delivered coolly at 300 yards and less, with case and Maxim fire almost point-blank. The guns fired altogether 1500 rounds, mostly shrapnel; the Camerons averaged 34 rounds per man. A black private, asked by his Bimbashi how many rounds he fired, replied,

'Only 15.'

'Why, you're not much of a man,' said his officer.

'Ah, but then, Effendi,' he eagerly excused himself, 'I had to carry a stretcher besides.'

If the black bearer-parties fired 15 rounds, what must the firing-line have done! Mahmud said that his people had only laughed at the shrapnel, but that the infantry fire was '*Sheitun tamam*' – the very devil . . . I saw scores and hundreds of dead goats and sheep, donkeys and camels, lying in pits in the part of the zariba stormed by the British. Now Thomas Atkins does not kill animals needlessly, even when his blood is hottest. The beasts therefore must have been killed by shrapnel; and if so many beasts, we may presume that many men, no better protected, were killed too. And so, I am afraid, unavoidably, were many women, for the zariba was full of them.

Yet the black Jehadia stood firm in their trenches through the infernal minutes and never moved till those devilish white Turks and their black cousins came surging, yelling, shooting, and bayoneting right on top of them. Many stayed where they were to die, only praying that they might kill one first. Those who ran, ran slowly, turning doggedly to fire. The wounded, as usual took no quarter; they had to be killed lest they should kill. For an example of their ferocious heroism, I cite a little, black, pot-bellied boy of ten or so. He was standing by his dead father, and when the attackers came up, he picked up an elephant-gun and fired. He missed, and the kicking monster half-killed him; but he had done what he could.

In the zariba itself Bimbashi Watson, ADC to the Sirdar, counted over 2000 dead before he was sick of it. There were others left: trench after trench was found filled with them. A few were killed outside the zariba; a great many were shot down in crossing the river-bed. Altogether 3000 men must have been killed on the spot; among them were nearly all the Emirs, including Wad Bishara, who was Governor of Dongola in 1896. . . . Now you began to comprehend the perfection of the Sirdar's strategy. If he had waited for Mahmud on the Nile, fugitives could have escaped up-stream. If he had waited low down by the Atbara river, they could still have got across to the Nile. But by . . . giving battle at the confluence . . . he gave the escaping Dervish thirty miles of desert to struggle across before he could reach water and such safety as the patrolling gunboats would allow him. A few may have got back to Omdurman – if they dared; some certainly were afterwards picked off by the gunboats in the attempt. Others fled up the Atbara; many were picked up by the cavalry through the afternoon: some got as far as Adarama or even near Kassala, and were killed by the friendly levies there. For the wounded the desert was certain death.

Mahmoud had been captured and Townshend saw him splashed with blood, but dignified and defiant in defeat. He was a handsome young man of about twenty-seven and 'well built and good looking'.[12] Leaving Mahmoud to his fate,[13] Townshend found his two subordinates Walsh and Harley lying under a tree, their wounds had been dressed and the hope was that those wounds were not infected. The Battalion could not linger with them and Townshend had to muster his troops at 1540 hrs for the march back to Umdabeah Camp from whence they had started at about 0600 hrs that morning. The 12th Battalion led the force and Townshend, still brimming with pride, had his ideals dented as he recorded that:

It was a strange sight at sunset, the flags and spears which the men were carrying, the singing of the men, and now and then men dashing out of the ranks, wildly brandishing their rifles in the air, many Dervish women accompanied us, having become the willing prey to our blacks though their own husbands were hardly cold in the trenches. We all felt disgust as we gazed on the picture that would have made the fortune of any artist who could have painted it just as it was.

The poet McGonagall offered up one of his extraordinary pieces to mark the victory. It is not great poetry but it gives a flavour of his day, toenail-curling though it is. A brief extract is below, but readers of weak disposition should swiftly move on.

The Battle of Atbara

Ye Sons of Great Britain, pray list to me,
And I'll tell ye of a great victory.
Where the British defeated the Dervishes, without delay,
At the Battle of Atbara, without dismay.

The attack took place, 'twas on the 8th of April, in the early morning dawn,
And the British behaved manfully to a man;
And Mahmud's front was raked fearfully, before the assault began,
By the disposition of the force under Colonel Long:
Because the cannonading of their guns was very strong.

The main attack was made by General Gatacre's British Brigade,
And a heroic display they really made;
And General Macdonald's and General Maxwell's Brigade looked very fine,
And the Cameron Highlanders were extended along the line.

And behind them came the Lincolnshire Regiment, on the right,
And the Seaforth Highlanders in the centre, 'twas a most gorgeous sight,
And the Warwickshire Regiment were on the left,
And many of the Dervishes' heads by them were cleft.

General Macdonald's Brigade was on the right centre in similar formation,
And the 9th Battalion also in line in front rotation;
Then the whole force arrived about four o'clock,
And each man's courage was as firm as the rock.

At first the march was over a ridge of gravel,
But it didn't impede the noble heroes' travel;
No, they were as steady as when marching in the valley below,
And each man was eager to attack the foe.

There is a great deal more in this vein and the epic concludes with the following verses:

Captain Urquhart's last words were 'never mind me my lads, fight on,'
While, no doubt, the Cameron Highlanders felt woebegone
For the loss of their brave captain, who was foremost in the field,
Death or glory was his motto, rather than yield.

There have been 4,000 prisoners taken, including Mahmud himself,
Who is very fond of dancing girls, likewise drink and pelf;
Besides 3,000 of his followers have been found dead,
And the living are scattered o'er the desert with their hearts full of dread.

Long life and prosperity to the British army,
May they always be able to conquer their enemies by land and by sea,
May God enable them to put their enemies to flight,
And to annihilate barbarity, and to establish what is right.

The poet was writing for a Victorian readership and he probably captured public sentiment at the time. The fact that he burst into print is indication of the importance of the battle and the pride that that society had in its Army.

In the twenty-first century it would be most unreasonable to apply modern 'standards' to Victorian actions. In 1896 there were no sophisticated means of bringing an adversary to the negotiating table and, given that the political aims of the two parties were diametrically opposed and that on one side uncompromising religious zeal was the prime motivator there really was nothing to talk about anyway. The matter had to be settled on the battle-field and, that being the case, the better-armed, better-prepared and better-disciplined force would prevail.

War is not like golf, there is no handicap system to even out the ability of the two protagonists and Kitchener, once committed to battle, was obliged to win with least cost to his army – he succeeded magnificently. Townshend's battalion had performed well in this overwhelming victory and, as is usually the case, the commanding officer was accorded much of the glory.

Atbara was not the end of the campaign. The final objective was Khartoum and the Sirdar continued in his painstaking way to prepare for the final confrontation. The railway was extended to Atbara in June and fortunately the river from Atbara to Shabluka, (the position of the 5th and final cataract) was open and British gunboats moved upriver in support of the ground troops. The logistic plan was in full flow and stores of all descriptions were steadily stockpiled by rail and river at Shellal, Fort Atbara and at Nasri Island. As the Nile continued to rise, so resupply became a matter of routine. Four months' preparations catered for every eventuality and during this lull Townshend took the chance to take leave, making straight for Paris.

On 12 May a very determined Townshend proposed to Alice Cahen D'Anvers and was accepted at once. Inevitably he recorded the moment:

> At last we were alone together. I had long loved Alice Cahen D'Anvers and she loves me. Before luncheon, while we stood looking at a log fire in the library, I told her that whether I left the Sudan directly after Khartoum depended on her. If she would marry me I would leave directly we had taken Khartoum; then she said, 'If it depends on me you will not stay in the Sudan very long . . .'

The next step was to raise the matter with the Count and here Townshend got a very positive and welcome reaction. The Count thoroughly approved of his prospective son-in-law and he said so in warm terms. It had been a happy and productive leave and six weeks later the young Colonel returned to his battalion. He was very anxious to get on with the unfinished business at Khartoum because he now had urgent calls on his time in Paris.

July gave way to September. Finally, Kitchener was ready and, with the desert pacified, he called forward troops from Suakin who advanced almost due west straight to Berber. On 1 September, Kitchener and his force of 8,200 British troops and 17,600 Sudanese and Egyptians navigated around the Shabluka gorge and bivouacked on the left bank of the Nile. The multitude of men, horses and mules then spent an uncomfortable, wet, cold night. The prospect of very serious fighting on the morrow would have caused apprehension in some, excitement in others, and an element of calculation in a very few others. Townshend was among this latter group and he envisaged not a painful death but the chance to win even greater personal glory. The Dervish army was well placed to attack Kitchener whilst he was in bivouac but failed to do so. They left the initiative in Kitchener's capable hands – and they made a mistake.

Kitchener ordered his force into an arc with its rear backing onto the Nile. The force was supported in this position by a number of anchored gunboats. Brigadier General Hector Macdonald's brigade was posted in the centre of the arc. Townshend made a very lengthy entry in his diary after the event and here, in his words, is how he saw the battle unfold.

2 September. The bombardment of Omdurman by the gunboats began at 5.45am. After about an hour, the Dervish army came into sight, dense columns marching due north as if to cut off our line of retreat, a vast number of red, green and white standards, cavalry and Emirs on horseback. One saw that there were at least thirty thousand Dervishes opposed to us, and one realized that it would be a good fight, as we were about twenty-two thousand, I believe, of whom about seven thousand were picked British soldiers.

Our guns then got to work on these columns but they never broke; they kept steadily on. I thought that when they had got far enough to overlap us towards the north that they would 'right form into line' and come straight down on us to sweep us into the river, for we were drawn in position with our backs to the Nile. The two British brigades faced south, on the river bank. Our brigade (Maxwell's Sudanese Brigade) faced west towards the desert, and on us the whole brunt of the first Dervish attack fell. Macdonald's Sudanese Brigade and Lewis's Egyptian Brigade faced north and Collinson's Egyptian Brigade were in support behind Maxwell's Brigade in the centre. It turned out, as I thought, the Dervish hosts stopped and faced towards us, and slowly advanced, our guns keeping up a biting shell fire all the time.

At the same time clouds of men appeared over the high ridge and hill to the south-west and opened a heavy musketry fusillade on us. The bullets began to sing overhead as these new forces of the enemy got nearer. I got the men to lie close down in the trench with which I had strengthened our front, and I felt glad that we had done so. The British Brigade had got some zariba thorn from the village near us, and had placed it in front of them, and owing to this they lost more than we did from the enemy's rifle fire, which now got annoying.

This last remark is confusing because the zariba was a defensive device that gave limited cover from view but no protection from fire – this should have been perfectly well understood by the British Brigade.

One heard the beautiful volleys of the British with their long-ranging Lee-Metford rifles, and the Maxims making a noise like fire engines, and their 15-pounder field batteries, all busy on this force of the enemy who had appeared from the south and west. They came on with the greatest pertinacity, and shells literally smoked among them, but they seemed to forge slowly on.

Then I turned my glasses to the mass of enemy coming straight down on my front. On they came, running now and firing from the hip as they came. I was walking up and down behind the regiment, the men all lay in their trench, the rifles all ready to fire, only waiting for my order, but I determined that not a trigger should be pulled until they were 400 yards from us. Many of the men kept looking round at me as much as to say, 'let us fire now . . .'

The masses of the enemy began rushing and cheering, the Emirs leading them with flags, just as one sees with the Pathans on the north-west Frontier of India. I now began to think that it would not do to wait until this mass got much closer, so I sang out the order for sights to be put at six hundred yards, and then opened with a heavy independent fire, and in a short while our line was all smoke and a ceaseless rattle of Martini rifles. The enemy came on till they reached about four hundred yards, and then they seemed to enter a rain of bullets. Struck by a leaden tempest, they bundled over in heaps, and soon they stood huddled in groups under the retaining power of the Martini-Henry. I saw a brave man leading them on with a large flag (I have his flag); I have never seen a braver. Alone he came on and on, until about one hundred and fifty yards from us, and then he and his flag fell like a piece of crumpled white paper on the ground and lay motionless.

The Dervishes were now retiring, not running, but skulking away. Some of them walked off as if they were the victors. Our men were cheering now and I got them up in the trench and we kept up our close and searching fire. No troops in the world could have lived under that fire; no Europeans would have faced it. The valour of those poor half starved Dervishes in their patched jibbahs would have 'graced Thermopylae' as Napier would have put it.

I thought the battle was over, so did everyone, but we were mistaken.

A large force now appeared to the north, streaming over Kerreri Hill in swarms, like ants, and cutting off our line of retreat. Our guns were soon busy on the north front of our position; one of our new class gunboats also went down stream at full speed, and soon the shells were searching Kerreri Hill, and the mass of Dervishes broke up and fairly fled off the hill down on to the desert side. I could see them all running as hard as they could, through my glasses, and we were very much interested in the way the shells kept bursting about a large, green flag that was hurrying and bobbing up and down. This force was apparently defeated, as the others had been, and we again thought that the battle was over, but again we were mistaken.

Townshend was not alone in thinking that it was all over. Kitchener thought so too and he was guilty of a serious error of judgment when he ordered his army into 'column of route'. In this formation the army was deployed in a long line with unprotected flanks. It was in this non-tactical configuration that Kitchener prepared to occupy Omdurman.

The enemy, although blooded, had 52,000 men in the field on 2 September 1898 and they were far from finished. Brigadier General Hector Macdonald's Brigade was now in reserve and it was about a mile north of the main body of Kitchener's Army. Macdonald's Brigade, about 3,000 strong, was composed of Sudanese and Egyptian troops, and was not expecting to see any further action. However, a message reached Macdonald that the enemy, estimated to be of the order of 20,000 strong, was advancing on Kitchener's exposed rear. Macdonald's brigade was the only obstacle between the oncoming Dervish mass and Kitchener's rear. In the most masterly manner, Macdonald redeployed his units to face the incoming assault in which the brigade was all that stood between Kitchener and annihilation. It was very heavily outnumbered but it had to block the Dervish advance for long enough for Kitchener to redeploy his forces. The Dervishes fell upon Macdonald's brigade and it, inadvertently and unwillingly, fought one of the most famous actions in the history of the British Army. In the most carefully controlled and calm manner, Macdonald redistributed his units to face the incoming assault. The fighting was desperate and in many cases hand to hand. But the Brigade hung on until Kitchener was able to respond effectively to this new and unexpected battle.

Winston Churchill, who was present at the battle and rode in the famous charge of the 21st Lancers, said of this situation when speaking of the native soldiers, 'The valiant blacks prepared themselves with delight to meet the shock, notwithstanding the overwhelming numbers of the enemy.' Macdonald was in complete control of the situation, desperate as it was. Winston Churchill, commenting on Macdonald, said, 'Amid the roar of the firing and the dust, smoke and confusion of the charge of front, the General [Macdonald] found time to summon the officers of 9th Sudanese Battalion around him, rebuked them for having wheeled into line in anticipation of his order, and requested them to drill more steadily in brigade.'

Townshend takes up the story again at this point and gives an eyewitness account, although he had no idea of the 'big picture' and the gravity of the situation:

There was a very large force coming steadily on from the north- west. Orders came to march on to Omdurman, and the British brigades started, our brigade being on their right and very soon these two brigades were heavily engaged with an enormous force of Dervishes with whom was the great, black flag of the Khalifa. The Khalifa was not with it, however; he was near the famous ridge to the south-west above mentioned, standing by the Krupp gun of the Dervishes which was shelling us.

We, that is to say, the British, and Maxwell's Brigade, had topped this ridge; and I remember being much struck with the few men killed by our artillery fire, which had made splendid practice. I am certain that not more than two hundred dead lay on this ridge. When we heard a tremendous fire from our right rear, Maxwell's Brigade hastily changed direction from south to west, to relieve the pressure on Macdonald's and Lewis's brigades. As we drew near them the fight was practically over, and the Dervishes were beginning to stream off under a fierce fire from Macdonald and Lewis. They had charged our people, and came on in crowds to within fifty yards of Macdonald's Sudanese, only to fall in heaps under our withering fire. A crowd of fanatics surrounded the large, black flag of the Khalifa; and as each standard bearer was killed, another sprang to the flag. At last the flag lay on the ground, and as the brigades advanced it was picked up and taken to the Sirdar.

In the meantime, we were hurrying across to the assistance of Macdonald and Lewis, who were very seriously pressed, and it looked at one time as if the Dervishes would have succeeded in getting hand to hand, in which case their numbers would have swept our people over. I saw that if I took my regiment more to the south than due west, I should get on some high ground above the Dervishes, from which we could do tremendous execution. I went trotting along on my horse at the head of the battalion, the men doubling after me. Maxwell came up and said he wished I would not try and work independently, and ordered me to continue due west, in the old direction. I did so, only at the end of it to be ordered to change and go back to where I was making for in the first instance! It was rather a pity, as we should have shot many more. But of course Maxwell was right, as he said at the time: 'What you are doing may be the best thing, but I have to obey the Sirdar's order.' The battle was now over in reality, and we all marched on due south for Omdurman.

The plain was covered with Dervishes, keeping a long way out in the desert, and all in a disorderly flight. The cavalry did not dare to molest them, but the field batteries fired at them, as they moved along parallel to us ... Osman Azrak, who used to be the scourge of the frontier at Wadi Halfa up to Aswan even, lay dead with his camel close to him and all his baggage. Right and left the Dervish wounded were getting up and firing at us as we passed, and our men were shooting them dead.

At Khor Shumbat the whole force halted, and as there was water in the khor we refilled. It was about one o'clock, the heat was awful and the men quite done. I there heard of the charge of the 21st Lancers. They charged some Dervish horsemen and suddenly came on a concealed khor (a narrow ravine, what we call a nullah in India). They could not check their speed and all came full gallop bang down among the rocks of this khor. Numbers of horses came over, about sixty men were killed and wounded, for there were about two thousand Dervishes in the khor, one officer killed and five wounded. Poor Grenfell of the Life Guards, who was attached to the 21st, was cut to pieces, his head split in two by a sword cut. The Lancers struggled through to the other side, and then when they could re-form, began firing. I heard that Yakoob, the brother of the Khalifa, had been killed and that, as I expected, Osman Digna, the famous bolter of the Atbara, was romping into Omdurman an easy winner at the head of all the fugitives.

The well-disciplined fire of the British force throughout the engagement had had a devastating effect and the Dervish attacks had each lost momentum, withered and died, as did about 10,000 of the attackers. A further 16,000 wounded and 5,000 prisoners meant that 50 per cent of the original enemy force had been eliminated. The British Army lost forty-eight men killed and 382 wounded – a derisory number given the size of the engagement. It is a compelling footnote that Macdonald's men had on average only two rounds per man left when the attack upon them petered out. It had been too close for comfort, much too close.

Townshend's account continues:

Maxwell's Brigade and a British field battery were told that they would have the honour of first entering the citadel of Omdurman, and accordingly we marched on, the heat very bad. Rumours reached us that the Khalifa had gone to the sur (the great wall forming the redoubt or citadel of Omdurman), that he was praying in the mosque, that one thousand of his blacks were with him, and that all meant to die together.

The three regiments, 12th (mine), 13th and 14th Sudanese, kept well spread out on as broad a frontage as possible. But as the houses began to grow closer together, and regular streets formed, we had to march in fours. At last we reached the outside of the sur, or great wall. It is about fourteen feet high and three feet thick. However, in my opinion the Khalifa was never there at all and that is what the natives tell me in Omdurman now. They say that he rode straight back from the battle, drank at his house, and started off at once on fresh camels, with his favourite women, for the south, en route to the Kordofan. We camped outside Omdurman to the west of the Great Mosque, at the Khalifa's house on the parade ground called 'El Ardar', where the Khalifa used to review his troops, and where he kept many of his wives. It is a very large house – my quarters now, and I am writing there.

Several shots were fired during the night at us by fugitive Dervishes, and a few men were hit. The Dervish killed amount, I am told, to ten thousand! The wounded must be much more – hundreds of them the next day were crawling down to the Nile – some fearfully wounded. Imagine their suffering! Imagine the thirst through the night! Our losses are just over five hundred killed and wounded, I hear, about the same as at the Atbara.

I think Gordon has been avenged now.

Kitchener was vengeful in victory; his first act in Omdurman was to desecrate the Mahdi's tomb as a means of preventing its becoming a focus of pilgrimage. The war in the Sudan was not yet over, but Townshend had had enough and, on 12 September 1898, he abruptly resigned his commission in the Egyptian Army. This resignation seems to have been effected with the minimum of fuss and just a month later he was unemployed but still, nominally at least, an officer of the Indian Army.

He had just fought in two major battles with his 12th Sudanese and confided in his diary:

I am sad to at leaving my blacks . . . they know me; they know that I am strict on matters of discipline, and slack on all points concerning their beloved women! And lenient on their petty faults. They like this; and they know that [when] I lead them in a fight that I say 'Come on' not 'Go on' and in that lies the whole secret of making not only native but European troops fight. When things are warm you must be prepared to lead the way' [Townshend's punctuation].

His British officers 'dined him out' and one of them called Ford-Hutchison spoke after dinner, and made some very agreeable remarks about CVFT which were much appreciated. Indeed, he confessed to being 'touched' by the remarks. After the event Townshend reflected in his diary that he was aware that his appointment to command 12th Sudanese had not been universally popular and, 'there must have been a lot of jealousy and bad feeling about it among the older men who had been passed over for me.' He was almost certainly correct because an officer in any army does not discover who his real friends are until he is promoted over them and then 'friends' and close companions suddenly become distant acquaintances. It is the way of the world. Townshend would, in due course, see the other side of the coin.

For Charles Townshend there were more important fish to fry and, characteristically, he focused on his personal affairs. One month later he was steaming into the Gare de Lyon to be met by the Countess Cahen D'Anvers and her daughter Alice and, if 3 March 1895 was the turning point of his professional career, then 22 November 1898, the date of his marriage to Alice Cahen D'Anvers was certainly the greatest day in his private life. The gilt on the gingerbread followed just a week later when he was decorated by the Queen with the DSO. 'It would be pleasant if it were possible to conclude at this point by saying that everybody lived happily afterwards.'

It was not to be.[14]

Notes

1. Prince George, Duke of Cambridge (George William Frederick Charles (1819- 1904) was a member of the British Royal Family and a grandson of King George III. The Duke was an army officer and served as Commander-in-Chief of the British Army from 1856 to 1895. This was an unprecedented tenure in command; it was far too long and inhibited much-needed modernization.
2. The Sirdar, or Commander-in-Chief of the Egyptian Army.
3. The famous explorer famed for his travels on the North-West Frontier.

4. He was a junior minister in 1895 and eventually promoted to be Paymaster General in 1902.
5. The famous actor of his day.
6. CVFT diary.
7. CVFT's diary, as reported by Sherson, is very specific about the destination. But having taken Ferkeh it seems strange that Macdonald's brigade should then retrace its steps. Barker ignores this anomaly entirely. One can only speculate that Sherson's account has transposed or corrupted the dairy entry. However, notwithstanding the ultimate destination, the events deserve to be recorded.
8. Sherson.
9. *London Gazette*, 24 May 1898.
10. Steevens, *With Kitchener to Khartoum*.
11. Lieutenant Harley DSO, of Chitrál fame, who had obviously followed Townshend's rising star.
12. CVFT.
13. Kitchener paraded his captive through the streets of Berber. G.H. Steevens commented that the display of the captive had a powerful effect on the local people and said, 'You may call the show barbaric if you like: It was meant for barbarians.' From *With Kitchener to Khartoum*.
14. A.J. Barker.

Chapter 7

1899–1900
India and South Africa

Townshend was granted three months' leave and, now married, he turned his mind to the perennial issue of 'transfer'. His cousin Erroll Sherson, who made every allowance for CVFT's foibles, commented, rather sadly, in 1928, 'It must be confessed that he was one of the most restless individuals in the whole Army. As soon as he obtained one appointment by the incessant wire-pulling among influential friends, he thirsted for a change . . . more than once, however, he nearly spoiled his chances by an ineradicable habit of grumbling, added to perhaps pardonable vanity.' His detractors, and by now he had created a few, were a lot less forgiving.

Townshend had had aspirations to attend the Staff College and win the prized post-nominal *psc*. In Gupis, five years before, he had started working for the entrance examination. Nothing came of it and by 1899 Charles Townshend was thirty-eight and too old. He was keenly aware that he had missed a trick and although *psc* was not yet an absolute prerequisite for a general officer (colonel and above) it would have helped.

Perhaps it was this perceived deficiency on his part that fuelled his all-consuming drive for yet another transfer, although he found nothing contradictory in applying for a six-month extension to his leave – and this was with pay. It is just as extraordinary that his application was granted. This freedom of action gave him ample chance to catch up with his theatrical friends, especially Arthur Roberts, the actor. It also allowed him time to lick his wounds after an undisguised and well-deserved snub from Lord Wolseley, who comprehensively rejected his approach when CVFT had presumed to press his suit with the Great Man. This latter setback had the effect of causing him to abandon his quest to transfer into a line regiment and instead he regrouped and decided that an appointment on the Staff was, perhaps, best suited to his ample talents.

His diary entry for 8 April 1899 reads as follows: 'I have made up my mind to start for India . . . getting my leave converted into Indian leave and going straight up to Simla. This I do because I am trying for a staff appointment on the Army Headquarters Staff at Simla.'

Charles Townshend, for all his personal gallantry, was hopelessly insensitive to the effect his career machinations had on others and the damage he did to himself in the process.

At this time the Townshend family's financial affairs were in shreds. Balls Park, one of the properties, had been in the family since 1723, it had not been sold and was rented out to Sir G. Faudel Phillips who now made an offer of £40,000 for the property. The difficulty was that this estate and also Raynham Hall carried crippling mortgages. Raynham Hall was the family seat and its ownership went as far back as Henry III (1207–1272). The retention of Raynham was Charles Townshend's priority because he still entertained aspirations of one day being Lord Townshend and living in the house. The 5th Marquess, John Villiers Stuart Townshend, was now in his late sixties and in failing health; his heir, John James Dudley Stuart Townshend, who was born in 1866, remained unmarried. What is more, he showed no signs of even looking for a wife.

The family affairs were very complicated and quite how Charles was able to dabble in them when he was not in direct line is unclear; characteristically he was not inhibited by such niceties. The likelihood being that he knew he had the backing of a wealthy father-in-law as his diary entry for 9 April 1899 states: 'I wrote to Lord St Levan saying that I would cross from Paris to London as I wished to see him about doing something towards paying off the mortgages on the estates.' This was a gesture well beyond an officer living on his pay. Nevertheless, the upshot was that eventually Balls Park was sold to Phillips and the sale helped to stave off the family's financial meltdown for the time being.

Passage had been booked on a P&O ship from Marseilles to India departing on 20 April, but now Townshend altered his plans and decided to put off his move 'until the autumn'. Instead, in early May, he and Alice went to Raynham Hall as Charles had decided to write a biography of his illustrious forebear, the 1st Marquess.[1] The great man's letters and a positive stack of documents relating to his life had been sitting gathering dust in the attic of Raynham Hall for over a century. It was a literary goldmine and a by-product was that on reading his way through all these documents Charles Townshend became a subject matter expert on the Townshend estate and the structure of its indebtedness. He speculated in his diary: 'I propose to buy Raynham and 5000 acres around it, and let them sell all the rest of the 18,000 acres. In this way the mortgage will be paid off.'

Armed with all of the family documents, Townshend started the lengthy process of writing the biography of George, and whilst busily engaged on the exercise he received a letter from Winston Churchill who was himself a new entry into the authorship stakes. Churchill was writing his book *The River War*, an account of the campaign in the Sudan, and he asked if Townshend would consent to read the manuscript. Churchill, aged twenty-five and thirteen years younger than Townshend, was still a subaltern and hence much the junior officer. Townshend acquiesced and his somewhat patronizing reply reflected their relative status in 1899. He replied as follows:

Dear Churchill,

I think it would be best if you would let me have a look at the work you are writing, some morning before lunch and I would, perhaps on points you are doubtful about, clear up the situation . . . It has struck me since I wrote that you might possibly think I was discontented perhaps with the Sirdar by my writing as I did, but not for a moment! Few men in the Army have had such rapid advancement as I have. Buller gave me to understand that it was the first time a captain had received the C.B. and I have now had six campaigns (counting Atbara and Omdurman as one). So it is not likely that I am discontented and wanting to (as a matelot might put it) 'shove my oar in'. The British Public have made over a job well done and well rewarded – not to say over-rewarded and the consequence is that the Sirdar, Hunter, Macdonald and Co. get a reputation – perhaps greater than they can uphold. The self-advertisement of some people in 'The River War' as you call it (a very good name) also appeals to me . . . Perhaps you would let me know some day next week when we can meet. I go to France in ten days' time, as I am tired of London. As regards the development of the Sudan, I confess one needs 'faith'. I suppose you remember the definition the Charity Boy gave of faith when asked by the school examiners to describe it? 'Faith,' he said, 'is a firm belief in something which you know to be perfectly untrue.' I don't know whether he was sent to the top or the bottom of the class for his answer, but he might of course, have been thinking of women, wine, or the Indian Turf.

Yours sincerely,
Charles Townshend

In this letter, Townshend is referring to Kitchener, 'the Sirdar' who had been his great supporter, Major General Sir Archibald Hunter, Kitchener's second-in-command and Major General Hector Macdonald – all of them vastly more experienced soldiers and his previous commanders. The letter, written by a lieutenant colonel to a subaltern, is disloyal, inappropriately phrased and reflects no credit on the writer.

Townshend, himself a master of self-advertisement, was clearly unaware of the irony of his criticism of others that he judged to have the same characteristic.

Townshend's relationship with Churchill would alter radically over the next eighteen years as the younger man entered politics and romped up through the ranks of government, while Townshend remained in the relative backwater of the Army. In national life the Army is a long way down the organization chart and, today, the Chief of the Defence Staff, head of all three Services, is without any discernible political influence – that is, if the management of the Armed Forces since the mid 1980s is any yardstick.

The situation in South Africa was worsening by the day and Townshend had a rethink. He started to doubt the wisdom of seeking a staff job in India and so, on 11 July 1899, he yet again opened correspondence with General Sir Redvers Buller asking him to arrange a transfer into a line regiment. The General had just taken command in South Africa and had many more important things on his plate to worry about than CVFT's career. The following day the supplicant burst into print again with a further appeal to Buller, and for good measure he also wrote to General Sir Evelyn Wood VC GCB GCMG (1838–1919, later field marshal), asking both to provide him with employment 'should active operations be undertaken against the Boers'.[2] This flurry of self-interest was overtaken by events because on 13 July a telegram was sent in the name of the Commander-in-Chief, India offering Townshend the post of Deputy Assistant Adjutant General (DAAG), Punjabi Army. The incumbent in this job had wide responsibility for personnel issues, whilst working under a more senior officer, the Assistant Adjutant General (AAG). It was a prestigious appointment. CVFT accepted the post, not waiting for any response to his appeals to Buller and Wood, and confided to his diary: 'This going to the staff will suit me very well. I can effect my exchange to a line regiment and join the next regiment at the expiration of my staff appointment.'

It had been a busy week on the career front. Buller wrote to congratulate him and apparently discussed his ambitious kinsman with Lord St Levan.[3] Townshend recorded on 1 August: 'Sir Redvers Buller told Lord St Levan that he was glad I had been given this staff appointment. It put my foot in the stirrup and I now had a big career ahead of me.'

Notwithstanding the new appointment that awaited him, and the manipulations that had acquired it, Townshend was in no hurry to take it up
because he was immersed in his biography of George Townshend. To this
end he and his wife set off to stay with her family at Bad Gastein, from
whence he was able to sally forth to view the ground over which his forebear had acquired his military reputation. He visited the battlefields of
Dettingen and Fontenoy and these excursions provided useful grist to his
literary mill.

On 5 October, he paid a visit to the 5th Marquess who was in France but
clearly very unwell. Townshend remarked that the Marquess broke down
and wept when he told the younger man that the doctors had warned him
of his impending death. He furnished Townshend with some 'notes' for him
to peruse on his journey to India, but their content was not revealed and it
must be presumed that the notes referred to family matters.

It was 23 October before Charles made his belated appearance on the
Indian military stage. He had had the company of his former brigade
commander, Hector Macdonald, as a travelling companion aboard the P&O
ship *Egypt* – the man he had damned with faint praise to Churchill – and
they discussed amicably, and at length, the tactics that Buller might employ
in South Africa now that hostilities had broken out and Ladysmith,
Mafeking and Kimberley were invested. The Second Boer War was to
last from October 1899 until the signing of the treaty of Vereeniging in
1902.

On his arrival in India, CVFT was greeted by a telegram from the Military
Secretary to the Commander-in-Chief which said, starkly, that the appoint-
ment of DAAG had been filled as it could not be kept vacant awaiting
Townshend's availability. It instructed, 'You should re-join your regiment.
Your claims (to be considered for a staff appointment) will however not be
overlooked when opportunities offer.'

The Military Secretary was naive if he thought that he could resolve his
manning problem and at the same time brush off Charles Townshend in
such a peremptory manner. The monumentally aggrieved Townshend
went straight to the top – he went to plead his case with no less a person
than the Viceroy of India, Lord Curzon. The only individual who ranked
above Curzon in the entire British Empire, in 1899, was a little old lady
called Queen Victoria. One might speculate that Townshend might even
have considered a direct approach to the Sovereign, for any acquaintance
he ever made was always a potential pawn in his career plan. Townshend
commented in his diary on the meeting with Curzon:

He was quite glad to see me, and Lady Curzon was also very nice to me. We had a long chat and much laughter, the Viceroy referring to the famous supper I stood him at the Savoy in '95 when he was on one side of Arthur Roberts and Kitchener on the other. He asked me where Alice was. He told me that Sandbach had told him they had filled up my Punjab appointment while I was at home, saying nothing to me, and I also told him how I had lost my opportunity of going to the Cape with Buller, as I thought I was doing the correct thing in not making a cat's paw of the appointment and taking another one. We went in Sandbach's carriage, and he showed me a wire to the Military Secretary of the Commander-in-Chief, which said I had seen the Viceroy, and that his Excellency hoped the matter would be put right for me. Lady Curzon is looking just as pretty as she was in '95, when I first met her.

Incredibly, Curzon had supported his appellant, given him comfort, and fed his ego. If Townshend had an inflated idea of his own importance then the Bullers, Curzons, St Levan, Woods et al. bear some responsibility for according CVFT's undoubted talent disproportionate attention.

On arriving at Simla, he was met by two further telegrams. One was from Alice, his wife, and the other from a solicitor, both giving him the news of the death of the 5th Marquess Townshend. It was not unexpected and the demise of John Townshend had the effect of making Charles Vere Ferrers Townshend the heir to the title and the estates. The health of the new 6th Marquess, a man of Townshend's generation, was now an unspoken but compelling topic of interest. The succession allegedly raised several questions in Townshend's mind and, although he had yet to unpack his bags, he made immediate application for more leave. He believed that, with the affairs of the family estate being in the greatest disorder, he was the man to restore stability. This was a position he advertised as widely as was advantageous.

The application for further leave was not well received, and little wonder, as by now he had been absent from duty for almost a year. The Military Secretary and his staff were predictably and cordially obstructive. However, Townshend's persistence and string-pulling eventually succeeded and he took passage in the *Arabia* back to France where he met his wife before moving on to Britain. His final act, during this lightning visit to India, was to write a 'long letter of complaint to Lord Curzon'.[4] This was presumably about his difficulty in getting immediate clearance for his leave and no doubt he hoped that, having loaded the gun, the Viceroy would fire the bullets at the Military Secretary. It was a very foolish and petulant act and, apart from achieving nothing, it added to the unenviable reputation he was building as a prima donna.

He presented himself at the India Office in the required manner, but only after first stopping off in Paris for a few days. The object of all his dealings with the India Office and the Headquarters of the Indian Army was to start the process of getting out of the Indian Army and into a command appointment in South Africa. It was fortuitous that he was at home because on 21 January 1900, his daughter, Audrey, was born. She was to be a much-loved daughter upon whom Charles Townshend doted. He was also able to give some time to family estate matters.

So far he had not immersed himself in the wider affairs of the Townshend family because there were more important matters to deal with. Top of the list was his career and to further that Townshend was very busy tugging at all the same old strings. But, in doing so, he irritated the Indian Army which wrote to him saying: 'Major and Brevet Lieutenant Colonel Townshend may not go to South Africa. By Indian Army Regulations, Volume XXII, paragraph 743, an officer of the Indian Army may NOT volunteer for service outside India.'

Townshend was not in the least bit phased by this bureaucratic answer and he responded by saying: 'I respectfully beg to be allowed to transfer from the Indian service to a British Line Regiment.'

The rejoinder said: 'By Indian Army Regulations, Volume XXIV paragraph 1065 you are not allowed to transfer . . . '

Townshend realized belatedly that he had overplayed his hand and that he had precious few friends in the Military Secretary's office. Uncharacteristically, Townshend humbled himself, at least publicly, and phrased his next communication rather differently. He murmured: 'Request loan to the War Office for special service in South Africa pending exchange to the British Line.'

This formal and, on the face of it, reasonable request was his official approach but, behind the scenes, Townshend was sending personal telegrams to everyone he knew who could influence the outcome. The whole episode is rather distasteful but it worked, and by 8 February 1900 Townshend sailed from Southampton in the *Armenian* bound for Cape Town. Safely in his pocket was a letter signed by General Sir Evelyn Wood recommending his appointment as Assistant Adjutant General (AAG), in the rank of colonel, to the South African Field Force. The fires of war were burning brightly now and Charles Townshend was determined to be in the very thick of them.

Charles Townshend, who had not earned a penny of his pay since November 1898, had travelled around the world at public expense, had claimed extra leave for unfulfilled family business, had dallied in France and manipulated the system entirely to his advantage and satisfaction, was for the moment – but only briefly – content.

There had been a revealing little incident when Townshend joined the troopship *Armenian*. A Lieutenant Colonel Lowe, commanding the 7th Dragoon Guards, was appointed 'Officer Commanding Troops'. Townshend, who must have consulted an *Army List* to obtain the facts, complained to the staff officer responsible for the embarkation of all the passengers that he was senior to Lowe and thus he, Townshend, should be OC Troops. The officer explained patiently that as Townshend was going as a passenger he was in the same position as a general and that, in these cases, it was entirely normal for a more junior officer to be designated OC Troops – because it was an unenviable post that involved a host of daily administrative tasks. Townshend was mollified but reserved his position and commented darkly in his diary: 'I said, "Very good": but if any case of emergency arose I should take command. And he said, "Of course, in case of emergency you would do so."'

Townshend was now thirty-nine years of age, wearing the badges of a full colonel, yet still displayed astonishing ignorance of a long-established custom of the Service whilst at the same time revealing how rank conscious he was.

The journey to Cape Town took over a month, there were no emergencies aboard the *Armenian* and so Charles Townshend was not called upon to exercise his capacity for command. When the ship dropped her hook in Table Bay on 1 March 1900, it was clear that there was something to celebrate as the ships in harbour were dressed overall. HMS *Majestic* signalled by flag that Ladysmith had been relieved and that Cronje and 4,000 prisoners had been taken. What was more, General French had lifted the siege of Kimberley. The news was all good and that made a welcome change, as hitherto the campaign had been a series of disasters for the British Army as it faced its first white adversaries since the Crimean War (1853–1856). For almost half a century it had defeated brave, poorly equipped, ill-organized and unsophisticated opponents. This time it was different – horribly different – and the body count was vastly in favour of the Boers.

Townshend's orders required that he go to the Orange River, there to get further instruction from the Headquarters of Lord Roberts. But confusion reigned and there were no instructions. An acerbic Colonel Townshend did not bandy words with the Staff, instead he signalled Lord Methuen who was in command of the 1st Division located around Kimberley, suggesting that the noble Lord apply for his services. Once again, he stepped outside the chain of command and, once again, it worked. By happy chance Methuen, who knew Townshend, signalled back telling him to join him, but was apologetic when Townshend arrived because there was no appointment for him to fill.

It got worse when Townshend's very presence in South Africa came into question. Lord Roberts's staff questioned by whose authority Townshend was touring this theatre of war. It all took time to sort out and the issue got to the upper level of command involving Kitchener, by now the Chief of Staff to Roberts. Kitchener was a Townshend fan and, with his help, the situation was regularized.

Townshend was directed to Bloemfontein by way of the headquarters of the 7th Division commanded by the irascible Lieutenant General Charles Tucker. Unbidden, Townshend took charge of a convoy that was headed for the 7th Division. The five days on the road were uneventful until 14 March when a messenger came out to meet the convoy and told Townshend that the GOC 'was surprised I had not communicated my whereabouts and composition of my convoy and that I was to send the information back by bearer'.

The meeting between an irritated general whose dinner was disturbed, by an officer he not only did not know but who gave every indication of being an officer he did not want to know, did have most of the elements of farce. The dignity of the meeting was not enhanced by the GOC. His torso was garbed in his uniform jacket complete with medal ribbons, badges of rank and red tabs, but his lower half was covered in pyjama trousers. Initially, the meeting was explosive but eventually reason found its way to the party and the result was that Tucker offered him either a place in the 7th Division or an escort to Bloemfontein.

Townshend opted for the latter but it was a long ride, Bloemfontein hove into view on 16 March 1900 and here there was yet more bad news and more disappointment when Colonel Neville Chamberlain,[5] the Private Secretary to Lord Roberts, explained that Townshend was too senior to fit into the headquarters. He said that Townshend was so senior as a lieutenant colonel that he was senior to most of the colonels on the staff. Then he wafted an opportunity in front of Townshend as a fisherman tempts a hungry trout with a succulent fly. 'Would you,' he asked, 'care to undertake a mission of particular interest to Lord Roberts?' Townshend fleshed out the offer in his diary saying: 'The mission was to visit Wepener on the Basutoland border, and also Maseru, just inside Basutoland, where it was reported that large bodies of Boers were inclined to surrender to the British if an officer of rank were sent. I accepted.'

Chamberlain was a member of Townshend's current regiment and they had met at Fort Gupis on the North-West Frontier about seven years before. He promised every assistance and Townshend would not have been human if he had not relished the opportunities that Roberts's mission offered. Here was a chance to get his name in lights. He was whisked in to see the great 'Bobs', who was actually quite a small man. All seemed to be in place and Charles Townshend was ready to set out the very next morning. He was disappointed not to have been given command of a fighting unit but then, for CVFT, life never did quite deliver the prizes he really deserved.

Up, dressed and breakfasted, the day started well, but thunderclouds moved in when Chamberlain told him that Roberts had changed his mind and was not going to accept all those publicity worthy surrenders.

Why Roberts changed his mind, history does not tell us.

Had Charles overplayed his hand?

This seems to be unlikely as Roberts had made the offer after their meeting. The upshot was that Townshend was diverted to work as Assistant Adjutant General (AAG) on the staff of Major General G.T. Pretyman CB, the Military Governor of Bloemfontein. Pretyman was a martinet who had little doubt that he had a God-given monopoly on wisdom. Serving under this man promised to be a difficult period in Townshend's life. This was to be his first experience of working as a staff officer, he had no staff background and he had never even been an adjutant or an ADC when a captain.

The successful general is one who understands how a complex organization like an army works. He has to understand the systems and the limitations of those systems, and the people in them. He has to have an appreciation of all the arms and services and the manner in which they combine to make a cohesive whole. The secret is to understand that the mastery of detail is the secret of success. Staff work can be time-consuming and tedious. No one has ever claimed that it is fun, but it can be rewarding. Townshend will have noted that the winning of medals is difficult for a staff officer. There was hard work in abundance but precious little glory to be had.

Townshend took up the appointment of AAG, HQ Bloemfontein Area on 19 March. Initially, for a couple of weeks or so, he found the new employment interesting, but it took barely a month before the rose-tinted spectacles fell off with a resounding tinkle. Extracts from the diary illustrate his growing disillusionment:

<u>19 March</u>. I have been quill–driving from 9am to 6pm with one hour for lunch. General Pretyman took me into his office and discussed the work to be done, and it is a very big job indeed. The Military Governor is to be Governor of the whole Free State, as well as Bloemfontein, which will become a large arsenal and magazine and depot of provisions with at least a brigade of troops to hold it. The General told me that all the troops will be in my command, also the civil part of the Government of the country, customs, schools, trade, etc. The General asked me to work out some scheme to submit to him. I am afraid I shall not see any fighting, but my work will be the most important I have ever done and gives me a great responsibility.

<u>21 March</u>. I went round all the public buildings in Bloemfontein with the Military Governor, including barracks, jails, powder magazines, schools and a museum. £120,000 has been found in one bank and £140,000 in the other, and securities to the value of half a million. We have taken over all of it! They were in such a hurry to bolt that they left all that Government money behind to fall into our hands.

<u>22 March</u>. I dined with Gwynne of Reuters [Author's note: Gwynne was to reappear later in CVFT's life with dramatic news. See Chapter 16]. Saw Burleigh of *The Daily Telegraph*, Ralph of *The Daily Mail*, and London of *The Times*. Gwynne told me that the German military attaché with our army here told him that he thought our infantry the finest in the world. In his opinion they were far beyond his own and the Turks: their advance under the fire they had to sustain was magnificent. There is a lot of anti–British feeling here and I expect the place is a hotbed of intrigue. I have ordered to–day the arrest of an Irish Fenian, O'Carroll, who had the impudence to advertise in the Express calling on all Irish Fenians in South Africa to concentrate, and that orders would soon come from him! I also hear of a tobacconist who openly wears Boer colours, and him I am going to muzzle also.

<u>3 April.</u> I find this office work very wearisome, I am at it all day. Not a moment even to write a private letter; and it is very difficult to get through any real work as the office is crowded all day with people wanting to see me on all sorts of subjects.

That is why staff officers were invented!

By 16 April he had had enough. His cousin, supporter and biographer, Erroll Sherson, who fell over backwards not to criticize his kinsman, was moved to remark that, 'he had become very disgruntled and his diary is full of strictures on other people.' This was a characteristic of Townshend and he went as far as making an acid commentary upon his friend 'Bean' St Aubyn. He wrote: 'Fancy Bean St Aubyn being made a DAAG to Buller! But perhaps the excellent training he has received at the Bachelors Club fitted him for the post of DAAG to the General commanding the forces in Natal.'

Perhaps there is a hint of jealousy in this remark as both men were linked to Buller through his marriage and hitherto Charles Townshend had considered Buller to be his 'area of influence'. Townshend, by now very jaundiced about the lifestyle of a staff officer, went to some pains to list the extraordinary number of entirely superfluous aides-de-camp who had no operational part to play, and were clearly along for the ride and the social aura that surrounded Lord Roberts. CVFT's angst, as a professional soldier, is understandable and he remarked that: 'it makes very pretty reading, a sort of extract from the peerage, with a few names of untitled officers thrown in here and there.' Townshend was quite correct – the plethora of minor aristocrats and other well-connected young men cluttering up the place and posing as soldiers added little to the conduct of the war, and just added to the administrative burden.

By the late spring of 1900 there were high hopes that the war would soon be over. Charles thought it expedient to make a start on sorting out his next appointment, post war, and to that end he started to cast his net wide. Having bent all of the rules and called in lots of favours to get to South Africa on 'special service', he nevertheless remained an officer of the CIH and the Indian Army. His return to India would have been the expected consequence of the ending of the war. But he had already registered his ambition to transfer to a British Line regiment, preferably in command. He set this to one side and approached Lord Chermside to ask him for a post on his staff if his Lordship were given the administration of the Transvaal after the war.

In a nutshell, he wanted a transfer out of the Indian Army, a command in Britain or a job in South Africa. Whilst he devoted some time to his career, he was making arrangements for his wife and her mother to visit South Africa. They arrived on the *Tantallon Castle* on 29 May 1900 and not unnaturally he was delighted to be reunited with Alice.

Only days later, Charles heard that his transfer to a British line regiment had been approved and a place had been found for him in the Bedfordshire Regiment. Remarkably, Charles Townshend then dashed off a letter to Henry Charles Keith Petty-Fitzmaurice, 5th Marquess Lansdowne KG GCSI GCMG GCIE PC (1845–1927). In his letter he said that what he would really,

really like was a transfer to the Irish Guards, without the boring inconvenience of having to join the slightly downmarket Bedfordshire Regiment first.

In 1900, Lansdowne was no less than the Secretary of State for War. Townshend's impertinence in taking his career concerns to this level and, particularly, during wartime is utterly breathtaking. What is all the more remarkable is that Lansdowne actually took on the matter and duly replied.

The Military Secretary at the War Office in London was probably unaware of the feelers for the Irish Guards and sent a telegram to Townshend asking if a major's appointment in the Royal Fusiliers would better meet his needs. Townshend immediately abandoned any ambitions for a post under Chermside and replied accepting the transfer to the more upmarket Royal Fusiliers. At the same time Lord Lansdowne closed out the Irish Guards option by saying there were 'insuperable difficulties in transferring to the Irish Guards in the rank of captain'. He confirmed the majority in the Royal Fusiliers. This is all rather confusing and CVFT's file got thicker as a result.

The Townshends got down to some serious entertaining and socializing. When he could spare the time Charles Townshend addressed the affairs of General Pretyman. By August, the end of the war could be seen over the horizon and on 19 August Townshend received a posting order that freed him from tedious staff work, boring visitors and the strictures of his general.

The Boer War, which had appeared to offer a thruster like Charles Townshend ample opportunities to shine, proved to be a disappointment for him. He had bent or broken all the rules to get to South Africa in the first place, but once there had been bogged down in paper serving the requirements of a demanding master, albeit for only five short months. He had not enjoyed working on the Staff even when wearing the badges of a colonel. He heard that his next unit was earmarked for service in Cairo and so, with no regrets at leaving Pretyman and all his works, Charles packed his kit and moved on.

Notes
1. Field Marshal George Townshend, 1st Marquess Townshend PC (1724–1807), known as the Viscount Townshend from 1764 to 1787. He served as a brigadier in Quebec, under General James Wolfe; when Wolfe was killed and his second-in-command was wounded, Townshend took command of the British forces. He saw to its finale, the siege of Quebec. George Townshend received Quebec City's surrender on 18 September 1759. He shared with his descendant,

Charles Townshend, a readiness to criticize his superiors. In this case George attacked a man who, in the judgment of the public, was a hero and a dead hero at that. He held General Wolfe in sufficient contempt that he published a most unflattering caricature of the General and was harshly criticized upon his return to Great Britain for that reason.

He was promoted major general on 6 March 1761 and fought at the Battle of Villinghausen. He served as Lord Lieutenant of Ireland from 1767 to 1772. On 2 February 1773, he fought a duel with Charles Coote, 1st Earl of Bellomont, badly wounding the Earl with a bullet in the groin. Townshend was promoted to general in 1782, and elevated to the Marquessate in 1787. He became a field marshal on 30 July 1796. On 19 December 1751, Townshend had married the daughter of James Compton, 5th Earl of Northampton. They had eight children.

George and CVFT seem to have shared some unfortunate family traits.

2. Sherson.
3. John St Aubyn, 1st Baron St Levan (1829–1908), married Lady Elizabeth Clementina, daughter of John Townshend, 4th Marquess. This association by marriage was the link between the three men.
4. Sherson.
5. Later Sir N.F.F. Chamberlain KCB KCVO KPM (1856–1944), late CIH. The inventor of snooker in India in 1875 and NOT to be confused with Arthur Neville Chamberlain (1869–1940), Prime Minister.

Chapter 8

1900–1903

Service in the United Kingdom and the Canadian Expedition

The Townshends had travelled back to the United Kingdom together on the *Kildonan Castle* which docked on 5 October 1900. Charles called at the War Office and then paid a brief visit to his new regiment. The 2nd Battalion, The Royal Fusiliers was stationed in Dover and Townshend was not impressed with Dover at all. He was even less impressed to discover that the rumour that the 2nd Battalion was going to Cairo was just that – a rumour. Like it or lump it, Dover was going to be home for some time.

He met his new commanding officer and then applied for and was granted a month's leave. Whilst on leave, later in October, he had to purchase all of his new Royal Fusilier finery and found himself back in 'a red coat again which I had not worn since I left the Marines for the Indian Staff Corps in January 1886'.

Hitherto, Townshend had been used to getting his own way. He had been sporting the badges of a full colonel and, as an AAG, had been at the very centre of things in a war theatre. It therefore came as a shock to the system when, notwithstanding his brevet rank, he reverted to the status and duties of a major. He also found that his commanding officer was not likely to be compliant. Far from it – Lieutenant Colonel A.C. Annesley had all the makings of another Pretyman as far as Townshend was concerned. His first act was to recall Townshend to duty before the expiration of his leave, and then to reject, out of hand, Townshend's optimistic request for 'a few days off to visit the Paris exhibition'. Annesley took the view that his new arrival and company commander had had ample leave in the recent past and it was high time he started to earn his pay. This was the practical manifestation of how the mighty had fallen and an indictment of the absurd brevet system.

Townshend was outraged.

He was used to dealing only with the Viceroy, commanders-in-chief, lesser generals, the Military Secretary, peers of the Realm, the Secretary of State for War, and others of similar standing, all of whom played in the first XI. Now he had to bandy words with a mere lieutenant colonel. It was all very irritating because Annesley evidently did not appreciate what a gem he had been given. As far as Townshend was concerned, 'The work in a line regiment in an English town like Dover is pure *Opéra-comique*.'

It did not take more than a few weeks for Townshend to decide that the Royal Fusiliers, Colonel Annesley and Dover were really not his style. The routine of a battalion in barracks he judged to consist of: 'Inspecting [the] kit of recruits, in fact keeping them clean and listening to the tirades of a terrible CO in the orderly room. One lives on courts martial and on boards; and I never saw such a place as Dover for rain.'

It should be explained that CVFT's reference to the parade held daily 'at the orderly room' refers to the procedure when the CO would summon soldiers to his office to congratulate, promote or punish those who had committed military offences under the Army Act. The CO also dealt summarily with minor civil offences. The process, amended to accommodate changes in society over the last hundred years, continues to this day. Townshend might not have liked it but the system worked and it still does.

It was as soon as December 1900, and without the least trace of embarrassment, that the unhappy major rejected service with a line regiment and started to manoeuvre for a job back on the Staff.

It was a manoeuvre too far and much too soon.

His supporters had had enough and, to a man, they were not prepared to take further steps on his behalf so soon after his return to the UK to a regiment of his choosing.

But Charles Townshend did not pick up 'the vibes' and wrote to the Adjutant General, Sir Evelyn Wood, asking for a post, any post, in South Africa. He got a very dusty answer. Not a man to take 'No' for an answer he merely shifted his sights to the Military Secretary, but met a brick wall there too. The perfectly reasonable War Office position was that Major Charles Townshend had to complete the regimental tour that he had so actively pursued.

Townshend did not believe that the normal career profile for an officer should apply to him. Accordingly, he wrote to Sir Francis Wingate, the successor to Kitchener as the Sirdar of the Egyptian Army, asking him to find an appointment in his army. Using the shotgun approach under which he thought he would hit a target, any target, somewhere, he also applied to the War Office for a regimental command in South Africa. This request was doomed because it would have been directed to the staff of the

Military Secretary. Wingate expressed scant regrets while the War Office once more rejected his application and said that his name was 'noted'.

The name of Charles Vere Ferrers Townshend certainly had been 'noted' and all of these machinations had added yet more paper to his personal file. The formidable collection of requests, complaints, appeals and applications all combined to give even the most neutral reader of the file a negative impression of Major Charles Townshend CB DSO. Townshend did not seem to appreciate the impression he gave; perhaps he did not care.

But, he should have.

In December 1900, he was constantly acting outside the chain of command and in doing so he by-passed his commanding officer in the most disloyal manner. Annesley had every right to be 'in the loop' and when he discovered that Townshend was making every effort, behind his back, to leave 2nd Battalion, Royal Fusiliers his reaction would have been a combination of anger, irritation and exasperation. No commanding officer would ever wish to retain the services of an officer with Townshend's attitude, but until the matter was resolved the relationship was likely to be very cool, at best. Commanding officers were then, and are now, sensitive souls; they tend to take any criticism of their unit, in whatever form that takes, as a personal affront. To affront one's commanding officer is career inhibiting and is not recommended.

Townshend might not have enjoyed garrison service. He said so publicly, loudly and often but it was the job which he had sought, was selected for and was paid to do. This did not prevent him from getting actively involved in family affairs. He was still working on the biography of the 1st Marquess and now he addressed the parlous financial state of the, current, 6th Marquess. This latter had only succeeded to the title about fifteen months earlier and was living in penury. All of the family property was rented out and the family seat, Raynham Hall, was the subject of a 21-year lease.

By now Balls Park had been sold and Stiffkey Hall was let. The family was in very bad order and Townshend was identified as a possible saviour. However, he was a 39-year-old major, living on his pay and the only card he had to play was a very wealthy father-in-law. Townshend opted to buy back Balls Park, although this was in the face of stern opposition from his solicitor and the Count, his father-in-law. The 6th Marquess was not in good health and, given his likely demise at an early age, Charles was seen to be the man to restore the family fortunes. In the event he was not able to raise the funds for Balls Park and it was duly sold to the tenant.

When Queen Victoria, in whose name he had served for twenty years, died on 22 January 1901, he promptly asked Colonel Annesley if he could command the Guard of Honour to be found by the Battalion as he had twice been decorated by the Queen. [Author's note: the British Army has 'Guards of Honour'. The United States Army (no relation) has 'Honor guards'.] Annesley said that CVFT had commanded the guard recently mounted for the King of Portugal and accordingly Major Townshend was to take his place, at the head of his company, with the remainder of the Battalion when it lined the route.

In these early weeks of 1901 Townshend was the recipient of a deal of gratuitous advice and his friends all urged him to keep his head down and get on with his job. No less a person than Lord Lansdowne told him to stick fast, but Townshend could not recognize good advice if it poked him in the eye. It was at this time that he received the most pointed rejection yet when the Military Secretary to the Commander-in-Chief wrote to him to say: 'It is not considered desirable for officers to urge their own advancement in the manner in which you have continued to do for some time past in private letters to the Military Secretary, and such claims should be put forward by an officer on full pay through the usual channels of communication.'

Someone once said that, 'a nod is as good as a wink to a blind horse', and most officers would have been mortified to receive a letter couched in these terms. They would have immediately modified their style, but Charles Townshend was not 'most officers'. Colonel Annesley had clearly been briefed on his recalcitrant subordinate and his covert career operations. The Colonel tightened the screw and gave Townshend responsibility for the regimental workshop accounts and the company account. These are jobs that are very boring but they require detailed attention. The sums of money involved were not large but Townshend knew that the path to professional failure is a discrepancy in a regimental account. He could not 'dodge the column' here and had to apply himself.

It was not for long.

Annesley had seen enough of Townshend and what he had seen was not to his liking. After employing him for only six months as a company commander, Annesley arranged for him to be transferred to command the Regimental Depot at Hounslow Barracks, just west of London. This was an independent command, a major's appointment, but it was a second division job. Alice went back to France until a suitable house could be found.

It is a custom of the Service for a commanding officer serving 'unac-companied' *not* to live in the Mess if at all possible. This is because his presence inhibits the normal social intercourse of the junior officers and because the commander is never separated from his job. The wisdom of very many years urges a CO to 'live out' as it is the best solution for all concerned

Townshend ignored the conventional wisdom and, to the discomfort of his officers, he 'lived in'. The man who had found Pretyman difficult and Annesley demanding, but now with an independent command, he was every bit as demanding as his two former commanders.

General Buller was under a darkening cloud, he would soon lose his job and in October 1901 he was forced to resign his commission – this of course reduced to nil his ability to help Townshend any further.

It was a boost to morale for CVFT when his book, *The Military Life of the First Marquess Townshend*, was published and it received some appreciative reviews. It drew him once more into the public eye and, as a published author, it added a plus to his curriculum vitae. Townshend had hoped to draw on General Wolfe's Order Book in writing the book, but he had not been able to find it, nor had he been able to find other key docu-ments. He was quite understandably furious to discover, after publication of his book, that the agent at Raynham Hall, a man called Day, had, of his own volition, lent some of the important documents relating to the career of the 1st Marquess to the Historical Commission – they had retained these vital documents for ten years. What happened to Mr Day is not recorded but Charles Townshend was not a forgiving man.

Townshend had been in command at Hounslow for just a year when he thought of another strategy that would serve keep him in the public eye.

He would go to Canada.

Townshend's file was decorated by yet another letter of request when he asked for two months 'special leave' in order to make a survey of the routes that the United States Army would take if it were to invade Canada – the most unlikely war zone ever. Although his outline plan to examine roads, blocking positions, logistic storage and the myriad other elements to be considered in rejecting a cross-border incursion found lukewarm support in Horse Guards, the leave was granted but on the proviso that the exer-cise was at Townshend's expense. On 12 June, he sailed, unaccompanied, for Quebec with an official letter of introduction to the Governor General. Sherson[1] commented on his cousin's expedition saying: 'He most certainly felt that he would be a person of considerable importance in the eyes of Canadians (he was never lacking in a sense of his own importance).'

Townshend was an ardent student of military history and had read sufficiently widely on the subject to be an expert. His interest in the defence of Canada might be judged, on a superficial level, to be the concern of a patriot with the national good as his prime motivation.

The reality is that it was not like this at all.

The trip to Canada was an opportunity for him to tread in the footsteps of the 1st Marquess and see for himself the ground over which he had fought. He spent a disproportionate amount of his time in Quebec and Montreal. In both places he was generously entertained and his extrovert personality went down well. In passing, he submitted several reports to Lieutenanty General Sir William Nicholson, the Director of Mobilisation and Military Intelligence, and to Lord Lansdowne, by now the Foreign Secretary. These documents included, *Report on the Niagara Peninsula*, *Political notes on Canada*, *Strategical Essay on Canada*, and a *Sketch of the Military History of Canada*. It is unlikely that Townshend was able to provide the British Government with any background on Canadian affairs that was not readily available to the Governor General. The cynic might suppose that these reports were designed to justify the leave – which had now been extended.

In the interests of balance, and to be fair to Townshend, it must be recorded that he was told that his reports were to be printed and read to the Committee of Defence,[2] although history does not tell us if this actually happened.

The United States of America has not invaded Canada in the 108 years since Townshend's survey, which is presumably gathering dust somewhere. It will probably continue to do so for at least another 108 years.

After his contrived and well-engineered mission, Townshend might have been expected to be back in command at Hounslow by, say, 1 August 1901. In fact he did not reassume command until January 1902. The reason for the gap in his duties is not fully explained by his diaries. He went to France to see his wife, spent time with the 31st Regiment of Infantry, an elite French regiment, and was entertained by the officers. This hospitality did not prevent Townshend criticizing his hosts – the only good word he could spare for the 31st was to say that the band played well during lunch.

Inexplicably, the War Office was very indulgent and a commanding officer absent from his unit for six months would normally expect to be replaced. Not in this case – Townshend merely sailed on and set his own priorities, one of which was the family finances; the other was, of course, his career. He addressed both issues assiduously and in the meantime the Regimental Depot got by without him.

The Count Cahen D'Anvers was very supportive and, in principle, was prepared to buy Raynham Hall, but he was not willing to pay what he thought was an extortionate sum for house and grounds. These unsuccessful negotiations were time consuming, delicate and ultimately very frustrating.

Failure on the family front was matched by professional difficulties. Townshend's unfortunate relationship with Major General Pretyman was the subject of gossip, none of which was to Townshend's credit. Pretyman held Townshend in low regard and said so, not least to his close friend Lord Roberts. Roberts was left in no doubt that Townshend was a pushy and arrogant upstart – it will be remembered that it was Roberts who had found an assignment for Charles Townshend in South Africa, but then changed his mind overnight. This incident preceded the judgment of Pretyman, but Roberts had had this earlier brief meeting with Townshend and so he could put a face to this ill-favoured person. To some extent General Sir William Nicholson was able to ameliorate the situation by speaking very positively of Townshend's Canadian reports to Lord Roberts.

Still in France in mid-October 1902, Townshend met up with Lord Kitchener of Khartoum, who was en route to take up his appointment as Commander-in-Chief, India. The meeting bore fruit and by year's end Kitchener had found a job for Townshend in India.

In the opinion of Charles Townshend history had been unfair to George, the 1st Marquess, and his book had been designed to redress the balance. He was only too delighted when a Mr Doughty, a resident of Quebec and a historian, wrote to him to say that he agreed that George had been short-changed and he proposed to write a guide book to Quebec entitled *Quebec under two flags*. He explained that in his view George deserved at least fifty pages of text on the siege and the part he had played in it. Charles swelled with pride and Sherson commented: 'Townshend, whose vanity was as much concerned with the doings of his family in the past as with his own, prided himself that his visit to Quebec had put the historians on the side of his ancestor.' He was quite right; the Quebec trip had achieved all that he had hoped for and more.

Morale was on the up and in December, Major Townshend took the decision to seek an audience with Lord Roberts. If he knew of the gossip, his diary does not acknowledge it. The meeting went tolerably well and Townshend came away convinced that Roberts was going to do what he could to get him a brevet Lieutenant Colonelcy for 'war service'. The brevet did not materialize and only a few weeks later Roberts denied knowing anything about such arrangements.

Christmas 1902 was spent in France with the family and Townshend was obviously entranced by his little daughter, Audrey. The festivities over, Charles Townshend returned to the UK and, on New Year's Day 1903, he returned to take up command once again in Hounslow. He took a flat in Piccadilly which would have pleased the officers 'living in' the Mess. The idea was that, from his flat, he would be able to take full advantage of the theatrical scene in central London. Thus, it must have come as an unexpected surprise on 7 January, when he received a posting order from the Depot to the 1st Battalion, The Royal Fusiliers. The Battalion was serving in India and the move was just what Townshend wanted, although he intended to do whatever it took to wriggle out of a regimental appointment just as soon as he got back to the sub-continent.

There were several immediate priorities, the first of which was to obtain leave until he was due to embark on a ship for India; this was granted. The next two months were yet more leave and he departed from Hounslow without a backward glance. He was probably not missed and had left no mark on his most recent command.

The next issue to be addressed was the manner in which he had been shamefully disadvantaged and his career damaged. He wrote personally to Major General Horace Smith-Dorrien, the Adjutant General (AG) in India. For the General's consideration, he explained that although a brevet lieutenant colonel for six years he was still a junior major in his regiment. He commented on the iniquity that in the 1st Battalion he was to join in Mandalay, he would find himself five years senior to his commanding officer. The AG would have been well aware that it was possible for a regimental major to hold a brevet lieutenant colonelcy with seniority over his own commanding officer, a regimental lieutenant colonel, and the brevet could, in some circumstances, even be given command of a brigade that might include his own regiment.

The brevet system really was nonsense and seems to have created many more problems than it ever solved. In the case of C.V.F. Townshend it fuelled his driving ambition, and added to his impatience and frustration.

He briefed the AG on his recent meeting with Lord Roberts, said that it had come to naught but asked by way of compensation to be recommended to Lord Kitchener as an Assistant Adjutant General (AAG).

Townshend and the AG both knew that an officer serving on the Staff could use his brevet rank, and perhaps this was seen as a way of keeping

Townshend quiet.

Thus Major Townshend was asking for an appointment as a full colonel. He should have been sent packing but Smith-Dorrien became the most recent in a long line of senior officers who indulged Townshend and fed his ego. This being the case, it is little wonder that he had a wildly distorted view of his value to the Service.

Notes
1.   Sherson, *Townshend of Chitrál and Kut*, p. 203.
2.   Ibid., p. 205.

Chapter 9

1903–1908

India

It was on 6 March 1903 that Major Charles and Mrs Alice Townshend embarked on the *Assaye* headed once more for India. When the ship reached Aden a brusque letter from Smith-Dorrien reached Townshend telling him that Lord Kitchener had 'taken note' of his wishes for an appointment on the Staff.

Townshend had no intention of serving in a regimental appointment and he was prepared to pull any strings that came to hand to free himself from the drudgery of garrison life. AG's letter gave him every cause for optimism but this optimism, experienced in Aden, was dashed when he reached Bombay, because the latest news was that there were no vacancies for him and he would have to go to join his battalion, which had by now moved to Burma.

The stop in Rangoon drew from Charles Townshend some appreciative remarks on Burmese women and he noted: 'I like the look of the Burmans, pretty well-built girls, many of them decidedly handsome and beautifully made, with glossy black hair.' Charles Townshend had been an admirer of the female form from his youth and nothing had changed. In this aspect of his life he was refreshingly normal.

Mandalay did not please Charles Townshend. There were no officers' married quarters and the only accommodation suitable for his wife was an 'awful hotel'. On arrival he was given command of the Mandalay garrison, but although it was an exciting and exotic scene far removed from dreary Hounslow, there was no one to fight and only the day-to-day routine of a peacetime garrison to occupy his time.

The Battalion was commanded by Lieutenant Colonel Cooper and he too was a contrast comparing more than favourably with Colonel Annesley. Cooper might have been slightly wary of his much-decorated subordinate but, whatever his motivation, he was agreeable and Townshend should have been happy with his lot.

But he was not.

At once he took up his pen to harass the authorities and to cajole them into recognizing his worth. His lack of humility and grace were matched by his insensitivity and arrogance. He appeared to have no concept of the effect his voluminous self-serving writings had and, in the case of Smith–Dorrien, he wrote one letter too many.

General Smith-Dorrien replied in sharp and very robust terms saying that there were many other officers in the theatre who had claims for advancement that were superior to his own. He added that Townshend had insisted on leaving India in 1899 of his own volition and, in the face of official objections, to serve in South Africa, but now he had come back to 'take the bread out of other peoples' mouths'. Incredibly, Townshend did not get the message and continued his campaign of self-aggrandisement unabated. Smith-Dorrien wrote again, this time in even more unvarnished terms, saying that Lord Kitchener was irritated at the receipt of so many personal letters from Townshend, all of them about himself and his employment. It was a very blunt letter and a crushing 'put down', one that was long overdue and thoroughly deserved. Some of those in the know thought that it could not have happened to a nicer chap.

Today, one would say that, Townshend finally 'logged on'. He buckled down to his job and was fortunate to have such a supportive CO who found him a command of 200 soldiers at Thayetmyo. Initially, he gave every impression of enjoying the opportunities the job offered, and wrote enthusiastically about the quality of his soldiers and the area in which he was stationed. He was meticulous in preparing the defence of the fort and the opportunity to have an independent command was something he relished, albeit he had no doubt that his should be a battalion command and not just a reinforced company.

Alice was a great supporter and she acted just as her military sisters of countless generations before and after her. She served in a hot, hostile climate, with a small child and a difficult, discontented husband who was isolated in command. Army wives have to be special people and, on the face of it, Alice made the transition from French aristocrat with a life in the smart salons of Paris, to the steamy jungle-wrapped and very limited social life of a garrison in Burma, with aplomb. Alice was an accomplished hostess and her social skills allied to Townshend's extrovert personality and his willingness to entertain on the banjo made them a formidable pair. Barker remarks that 'Townshend was a "ladies' man" and Alice must have had to exert considerable patience and tact on many occasions.'[1] This is the only reference to Townshend's roving eye in any source document, but from the tone of his diaries it is evident that 'ladies man' describes him well. There is no evidence that he was an unfaithful husband but he spent long periods unaccompanied and he had ample opportunity to be so. Given that he was selfish he was unlikely to deny himself any sexual opportunity that arose. However, he was prudent enough not to refer to any affair of the heart, if indeed he had any, in his diary.

The tour in Thayetmyo extended to five months and then the Battalion had a unit move to Bengal. In November 1903, Alice and her maid went on ahead and Charles sailed on the trooper with his soldiers. On arrival in Calcutta he was given the appointment of 'President of the Defence Committee', which required him to plan, in detail, the arrangements to safeguard the city in the event of civil unrest. Memories of the Indian mutiny were now fading but they had not yet disappeared. Quite why it was necessary to make these plans is not clear and one wonders why such plans to support the civil power were not already in place and practised regularly. He was stimulated by the task and completed it within a month, having been allocated three. This was very Charles Townshend and a further indication, if any is needed, of his professional skill. As it happens, events overtook him and in January 1904 he was told of his award of a brevet colonelcy. In short order he contrived an interview with Lord Kitchener.

Kitchener was a capable man and a shrewd judge of character. By now he would have had no illusions about Charles Townshend. He recognized that the younger man was a competent, gallant and resourceful leader, and that those soldierly characteristics went to balance his disagreeable and unattractive ambition. The meeting, on 7 January, went well. There were the usual social exchanges that gave Townshend the chance to sing the praises of the Royal Fusiliers and the quality of the soldiers. When the conversation 'cut to the chase' Kitchener said that he knew that Townshend wanted a staff job and that he had earmarked him for something suitable. Townshend had just been offered the Holy Grail, the object of all his earlier manipulations. Without batting an eye he retorted that what he would really like was the command of a regiment.

If Kitchener had kept a diary it would be interesting to read his account of this meeting.

Things moved quickly and on 30 January 1904 he took over as AAG in Calcutta; this was only in an 'acting' capacity to fill in whilst the incumbent was on leave. Having got the very job that he had been lobbying for he grumbled to his diary about: 'All uninteresting, moves, cantonments, volunteers, camps, medical pensions, accounts etc. From 7am every morning, the work is very heavy; if one does all that one should do oneself.'

This job lasted only two weeks and perhaps his attitude would have been more positive had he been posted into the job and not just used as a stop-gap. As it was he was then sent off to Lucknow to act as AAG there, again to fill in for the incumbent. This was rather more agreeable and he was able to exercise his interest in military history, immersing himself in the detail of the Indian Mutiny. Socially it was more fun and he dined with the Gloucestershire Regiment in which the 1st Marquess had served.

Charles Townshend dealt with similar issues in Lucknow as he had in Calcutta, but at least here he had a chance to get his teeth into the job and he appeared to be at ease. There is no doubt that his natural aptitude for hard work (when not on leave) and his unerring eye for detail made him a successful, self-taught staff officer. Wearing the badges of a colonel again would have been a fillip to his morale and Charles enjoyed not only the job but the domestic and social setting. If he had to endure peacetime soldiering then this was about as good as it got.

Townshend was not only blessed with a charming wife but a very supportive father-in-law. Count Cahen D'Anvers telegrammed to say that he had had the opportunity to buy all manner of Townshend family treasures at a recent public auction. Pictures and other family memorabilia were rescued by the Count and, in due course, were restored to family ownership. This was a very satisfactory outcome and Townshend was touched by his father-in-law's generous act in buying articles he did not need. In the fairly recent past Charles Townshend had disputed the right of the 6th Marquess to sell off family heirlooms, but had been defeated in court. Now he commented: 'I have no reason to regret that Lord Townshend was successful in the action between him and me as to whether he had the right to sell the heirlooms.'

The tour in Lucknow was a happy time but all good things come to an end and in November 1904 he had another interview with the Commander-in-Chief. Sherson quoted an extract from Townshend's diary which is a little obscure. The text is:

I told him that I had been up for the examination for tactical fitness and believed that I had passed. He jokingly said that he, for his part, always got out of examinations when he could. He then told me that he was most anxious to keep me on the Staff, but there were many difficulties and few vacancies. He said that General Archie Hunter[2] had spoken very highly of me, and that General Elliott had also praised my work. Towards the end of the interview I said it was hard to go back to the regiment as a major.

Hamilton[3] retorted, 'I don't see any grievance in that. Others have to do it.' It ended by Kitchener saying that he would do what he could to get me command of a regiment.

General Hunter and Townshend knew each other well and they probably corresponded about the interview because a letter found in Townshend's papers was from Hunter who wrote:

> You have evidently written too many reminders about yourself, and have somewhat wearied Lord Kitchener's staff with matters concerning yourself. But Lord Kitchener said to me that you need not write any more, and that he would not forget you and that your interests were more likely to be furthered than forgotten by silence on your part. He added that he quite knew your value, but that he could not always find a billet everyone required at a minute's notice.

This was but the latest rebuke to Townshend and, in the manner of the times, it was delivered in gentle, courteous and euphemistic tones. Charles Townshend had a month to digest the implications of failing to heed this quite clear direction to shut up and get on with his job when he was at sea returning, with his battalion, to the UK. The family arrived on 18 January 1905 and Alice and Audrey went straight to Paris, leaving Townshend in London to take up with his theatrical friends and spend time in the fashionable watering holes where his gregarious bonhomie was welcomed.

A visit to Paris during which he was able to view family pictures hanging in the elegant home of the Count took only a few days, and by 26 January he was back in London. Totally ignoring General Hunter's advice, Charles Townshend once more started to lobby anyone who would listen. He absolutely did not want to stay with the Battalion which was now stationed at Parkhurst on the Isle of Wight, a military and social desert as far as Townshend was concerned. He wrote, called upon and telephoned any of those who he thought might further his cause.

He failed in his machinations and had no option but to rejoin his battalion. He took leave in Paris in April and spent every evening at the theatre. Sherson commented that 'he never missed a night . . . unless something official stopped the way.' His leave over, the future started to look bleak when he heard that he was to be sent back to Hounslow to reassume command of the Depot. This was an extraordinary way to manage any officer and it was a serious 'career foul'. Townshend had a very strong case for redress but uncharacteristically he did not complain, at least not publicly.

*   *   *

In late April 1905, luck was on Townshend's side when he heard that a Colonel Barham, who had just been appointed the Military Attaché in Paris, was ill and could not take up his post. A Colonel Lowther was nominated to replace him but was unavailable. Charles Townshend seized his chance and once more pulled every possible string, this time even more vigorously than normal. The process took time and, whilst the cogs in the War Office slowly turned, Charles escaped the environs of Hounslow by squeezing in yet more leave. All the pieces in the manning jigsaw somehow fell into place and on 24 June Townshend crossed the Channel for the umpteenth time to take up the post of Military Attaché on a temporary basis.

He was the attaché for Paris and Berne and was for once delighted with his situation. His wife and daughter were close to her parents and their house in Rue de Basano, and close enough to their other residence in Champs sur Marne. The theatre was on offer every evening, the social life was glittering and, as the military representative of the greatest military power in the world, Townshend was lionized.

Life was very sweet indeed, other than that, at forty-four years of age, Charles Townshend was still a regimental major.

He was invited to attend manoeuvres of the French Army as an observer, something he knew he would relish. He attended the reception arranged by the American Embassy to mark the removal of the remains of John Paul Jones to the United States. Townshend was jaundiced by these particular celebrations as he viewed Jones as a pirate and the American style full of 'too much sloppy sentiment'.

Family matters briefly intruded when he heard of the thoroughly unexpected marriage of his cousin, the 6th Marquess, to the daughter of a Mr Sutherst, an unsuccessful barrister. Mr Sutherst was an undischarged bankrupt and was later drowned when a German U-boat sank the *Lusitania*.

In August 1905, Charles was still heir presumptive and, on the face of it, a late marriage such as this was unlikely to produce any offspring. He did not feel threatened but he was surprised.

The French Army manoeuvres were a high spot. The French artillery, generally recognized as the best in Europe, lived up to its reputation. The entire exercise was a credit to the diligent staff officers who had stage-managed the event from first to last. CVFT's short term as Military Attaché came to a close on 1 October, but it had been a stimulating and enjoyable three months and during this time Townshend had established a new network of useful acquaintances, one of whom was the Austrian Military Attaché.

With considerable aplomb, considering that he had spent three months eating, drinking and theatre-going, CVFT applied for and was granted two months leave. The arrangement was that, thereafter, he would return to the battalion at Parkhurst.

Meanwhile, the recently married 6th Marquess now embarked on the surreptitious sale of further family artifacts, and when this came to the notice of Townshend and other senior family members swift and draconian steps were taken to restrain him. He was declared to be unfit to manage his own affairs and a committee of trustees was appointed to take over estate matters on his behalf.

This was to sour family relationships for years to come and it fell to Sir Redvers Buller, now of course unemployed, to take on the unenviable task of chairing the Trust and trying to stabilize family affairs in order to protect the assets for future generations. Buller, a charming, gracious and caring man, might have been a poor general but he did his level best to manage family matters in an equable way right up to his untimely death in 1908. The Trustees were ultimately successful and Sherson, writing in 1928, said that 'owing to the firm management of the appointed trustees the Raynham estate was saved for the holder of the title except the pictures and practically anything of artistic value in the house, although Stiffkey Hall and other family places had to be sacrificed, as Balls Park had been before.'

Townshend, doggedly commanding his company on the Isle of Wight, must have been bored rigid. By the very nature of the island the training opportunities were very limited and the restrictions of living on a small island were irksome. 'The theatre' did not thrive here and shows on the end of the pier in summer were not to the liking of a man with sophisticated tastes better catered for in Paris and London.

The new year, 1906, got off to a good start when on 23 February Townshend was posted to be second-in-command of the King's Shropshire Light Infantry stationed at Fyzabad in India. This presumably meant yet another cap badge change and the process by which he was selected for the appointment is unclear. Be that as it may, Townshend did what he always did in these circumstances – he went on leave.

He joined the Regiment in mid-April and Alice followed him out to India in June. Together they called on Lord Kitchener, who must have been the most forgiving of men. He received them with his customary courtesy but enjoined Charles to 'stick to the regiment and not to try for a staff appointment at present'. The vagaries of the brevet system were again in evidence when in July 1906, Major C.V.F. Townshend CB DSO was appointed to command the Allahabad Brigade during the absence of Brigadier General Woolcombe. He launched himself at the job and recorded his very positive impressions of a visit to the Staffordshire Regiment. He was much taken with the amenities on offer to the rank and file which, by his account, would please the soldiers' modern-day counterparts. Sherson, who tried loyally to present Townshend as a caring officer, selected this visit and Townshend's comments as indicators of his concern for his soldiers.

This period as a brigade commander was a brief three months, but it whetted Townshend's appetite for the command of a major formation. It was with regret that he returned to the mundane duties of a second-in-command on 17 October, a job that he filled until July 1907 when a posting order arrived appointing him to the long-awaited staff job.

He went to be AAG to the 9th Division under the command of Major General Sir James Wolfe Murray KCB. This new commander was no hard charger. He was a charming but rather ineffectual officer who was, for the early months of the First World War, the Chief of the Imperial General Staff as a lieutenant general, being the most junior in rank ever to be so appointed. He was quite unlike Pretyman, and life under him was conducted at a well ordered and sedate pace.

Wolfe Murray became an important supporter of Townshend and played a role in the passage of CVFT from major to colonel, which was swift and unmarked by any unusual incident. Townshend held the rank of lieutenant colonel only briefly.

Substantive promotion to colonel was promulgated in February 1908, just before Charles's forty-seventh birthday. 'Substantive promotion' is the name of the game and only death or dishonour can remove it. This rock-solid status was all the motivation Townshend needed to start lobbying for his next job. He wrote to Kitchener saying that as there was some unrest on the North-West Frontier he was the man to take command there. The civil disturbance quietened down, however, and so nothing came of his appeal other than to add yet another folio on his file.

Redvers Buller, over-promoted soldier, patriot, family friend and patron, died in June 1908. His death came hard on the heels of Lord St Levan of St Michael's Mount, also a loyal and supportive friend. Townshend mourned both men and had good cause to do so.

Life with the 9th Division was tranquil and Townshend had, by now, firmly established himself, not only in the Headquarters, but also in the local area where his generous and entertaining hospitality was notable. Alice, as ever, charmed all those who entered her aegis. We can speculate with some assurance that her English, spoken with a marked French accent, was enchanting; she was by now an experienced army wife and a significant asset to her husband.

It was not until February 1909 that Townshend slowly started to emerge from the pack and this was when he was offered command of the Orange River Colony District in the rank of brigadier general. Brigadier general (with or without the hyphen) was a rank that only applied to officers commanding brigades or their equivalent. On that basis it was a temporary rank. Commodore in the Royal Navy was similar. Today, brigadier is a properly established rank between colonel and major general.

Charles Townshend immediately accepted but, as he had not been home for three years, he asked for three months leave. The request was firmly denied and he was told to shift himself and his household to South Africa – as soon as possible.

Notes
1. Barker, *Townshend of Kut*, p. 121.
2. Major General (later General) Sir Archibald Hunter (1856–1936).
3. This reference to Hamilton, who apparently sat in on the interview, is confusing; it might refer to Lieutenant General Sir Ian Hamilton (1853–1947) who had been AA&QMG in the Chitrál Relief Force in 1895. He was serving in India in 1904, but in a quasi-diplomatic role that would have put him outside Townshend's chain of command. The tone of the remark indicates that, whoever this 'Hamilton' was, he was senior to CVFT and not one of his supporters.

Chapter 10

1909–1911

South Africa

'It is singular how a man loses or gains caste with his comrades from his behaviour in the field. The officers too are commented upon and closely observed . . . I know from experience that in our Army the men like best to be officered by gentlemen.'

Rifleman Harris, Peninsular, 1808

There was a sense of irony when Townshend took up his new job in Bloemfontein in that he found himself living in the residence formally occupied by General Pretyman. He took up the reins of command on 14 May 1909 at the age of forty-eight.

Townshend was certainly not in the career fast lane. His promotion to brigadier at his age was, at best, an average performance. To what extent he had damaged and slowed his advancement by his incessant letter-writing and appealing cannot be measured. However, his eventual promotion was a measure of the regard in which he was held in the Army. He was viewed as a competent staff officer, a skilful leader and a courageous man – but then the British Army of 1909 was filled with officers who had the same qualities. The judgment was that Charles Vere Ferrers Townshend was nothing special. Charles Townshend, himself, did not share that view and had other ideas.

The Orange River Colony and Bloemfontein district was hit by a new commander determined to get everything and everybody 'shipshape.' It was a big command and it took until September to impose his standards on all he surveyed. After only five months in post, on 19 October, he departed South Africa on three months leave to deal with 'urgent private affairs'. Soon after his arrival in London he formed up to see General Sir William Nicholson at the War Office.[1] The great man asked him how the job was going in the manner that superiors always question their subordinates. The expected answer is an enthusiastic response that assures the leader of the establishment that all is well. It is the military equivalent of saying to someone, 'How are you?' The question does not invite a detailed rundown on the individual's state of health.

Unfortunately, Townshend did not know the rules – he said with marked lack of enthusiasm that he liked his command 'fairly well' but what he really wanted was a command in the Mediterranean or at home. That was his heart's desire. He took the chance to point out that he had had more than his share of foreign service, but nevertheless command in Cairo was his absolute dream posting. 'It would be,' responded Nicholson dryly, adding, 'Cairo is a major general's job,' making it clear that it was not available to a substantive colonel, acting brigadier general.

Quite what Nicholson made of Townshend is not recorded but Charles once again probably did himself more damage than good by the exchange in which he appeared not to have a clue as to what he really wanted. It was a bizarre performance.

Townshend was politically aware and he went to pains to be amicable to the Boers who, although defeated some seven years before, still nursed deep wounds. Between 1909 and 1911 the Townshends went about the King's business in Bloemfontein with style. Alice added grace and charm and Audrey was growing into a confident and attractive young woman. Professionally the job was not demanding and there were only three significant events. The first of these was the death of King Edward VII on 6 May 1910. This was a matter of international significance and a memorial service was held on 20 May. Townshend sent an embarrassingly obsequious telegram to Lord Crewe, Secretary of State for the Colonies.

It is difficult to describe the deep loyalty and devotion manifested by all classes of the Orange River Colony population, represented by the great crowds assembled at Bloemfontein, together with all the troops in garrison, for the strikingly impressive memorial service to our late King today.

There was more, much more, of the same. Reading the telegram one hundred years later, even allowing for the more informal syntax that would be used today, the impression is that the message is unctuous and self-serving on Townshend's part. It begs the question 'Who was the organiser of this wonderful display of loyalty?' In later life, as we will see, Townshend thought that he had a flair for the written word and that he expected, nay demanded, to be quoted later and widely.

The following month the Union of South Africa was formed and

Townshend's role as the administrator of the Orange River Colony came to an end. That was of no great concern because he was heavily engaged with the manoeuvres planned for August. Lord Methuen attended the exercise and then participated in the 'staff ride'[2] to some of the battlefields of the Boer War; he was delighted with what he saw and commented on it in glowing terms. Townshend reported his Lordship as saying: 'He thought I should be promoted very soon now, that he would be sorry to lose me and so would everyone, as no one could be more popular with the troops than I was. I understand that he had been cracking me up to the War Office over the manoeuvres.'

There is ample evidence that Townshend was popular with soldiers. His forthright manner and strong personality left a vivid impression and he was able to capitalize on the natural willingness of soldiers to like their officers.

In October 1910 the Duke and Duchess of Connaught sailed into Cape Town for the celebrations for the formation of the Union of South Africa and the Townshends had a part to play, not least at the great review in Bloemfontein which he staged particularly well. The Union Medal was widely distributed and Townshend was a recipient. But he was aggrieved that Alice, who had entertained ceaselessly during the protracted celebrations, did not get one. He wrote to Lord Lansdowne to complain about the omission, explaining that Alice had succeeded in bringing the disparate elements in the Colony together. He opined that the medal given to Lady Gladstone, wife of the first Governor General, should more correctly have gone to Alice.

This was just another in a long line of ill-considered and intemperate letters directed to the wrong person at the wrong level. He did not seem to learn and Alice still did not get a medal.

Townshend's scholarship as a student of military strategy and, by definition, military history, is not to be questioned. He thought deeply about his profession and his expertise was by now being broadly recognized. A Commandant Mardacq consulted Townshend who then translated the Frenchman's book into English. Mardacq was anxious that Townshend make the acquaintance of a General Foch who was at this time the Commandant of the *Ecole de Guerre*. Foch is a name the reader will be familiar with but in 1911 he was not yet in the public eye.

Townshend took leave, went to France and the two men met on 4 May 1911. Foch was well aware of Townshend and knew him to be a military philosopher with whom it was worth debating. They had a long and detailed discussion. Foch had not the least doubt that, ere long, the French, Belgian and British Armies would have to confront an aggressive Germany and, what was more, he had already calculated the strength and disposition of the invading force.

For CVFT promotion to major general was firmly on the cards and he hoped that he would be advised, formally, whilst he was home on leave. However, by 31 May there had only been silence from the War Office. He heard nothing and, for once, seems not to have tried to manage events. Accordingly, he embarked on the *Edinburgh Castle* for his journey back to South Africa and his responsibilities there. He had only been back at his desk for a month when on 21 July 1911 he was notified of his promotion to major general. There were letters and telegrams of congratulation and there were many who seemed genuinely pleased for him and sorry to see him leave. Charles Townshend was fifty years of age and he had achieved an important goal. There was now no longer any need to push himself to the fore. The opposition in the promotion stakes at major general level was stronger but there was less of it. With reasonable luck he could expect at least one more step up the ladder and a 'K' (knighthood) to go with it. There was even an outside chance of making full general. That would bring four stars and a Knight Grand Cross. Life really was very good indeed.

Charles and Alice left South Africa on 20 September on the *Briton*. His long-serving soldier-servant, Whitmore, came too bringing up the rear.

Notes
1.   General Sir William Nicholson GCB (1845–1918) was appointed Chief of the General Staff, soon to be Imperial General Staff, in 1908. He was thus, in 1909, the professional head of the Army. He had had dealings with Townshend before when he had been Adjutant General, India in 1898–9 at the time Townshend was angling for a move to South Africa. He was the recipient of Townshend's intelligence reports from Canada and defended Townshend to Lord Roberts (see page 138). Nicholson was promoted field marshal in 1911.
2.   A staff ride was an exercise for officers only in which various tactical situations were examined on the ground. Once the horse became redundant the expression 'staff ride' was dropped and 'Tactical Exercise without Troops' (TEWT) was substituted. It had the same function.

Chapter 11

1911–1914

Major General's Command,
the Territorial Army and India

Townshend reached the UK in early October 1911 and was soon given notice of his selection to command one of the new Territorial Army (TA) divisions that had resulted from the reforms recently instituted by Richard Haldane,[1] the Secretary of State for War.

This was not what Charles Townshend wanted one little bit. He wanted a Regular division, not least because he deserved it. He was sufficiently dissatisfied to consider rejecting the appointment, but his advisors all warned him that such a step could have a very deleterious effect on his future. He was told in no uncertain terms that Haldane had ruled that, as a matter of policy, newly promoted major generals were to command TA divisions as a first appointment. He was left in no doubt that he had been promoted over the heads of other officers more senior than him and that if he refused the job then he would have no case if he, in turn, was passed over. That was an argument to which he could relate, as being 'passed over' was his blackest nightmare, a fate difficult to contemplate.

With poor grace he accepted command of the Home Counties Division of the TA but, as the job would not be vacant until April – he went on leave.

Command of volunteer soldiers has always been difficult. They would then, and still today, only respond to an enlightened leader who was able to empathize with their domestic situation. They had full-time jobs and 'soldiered' as a hobby, or a social and physical outlet. They did not respond to heavy handed discipline and, unlike the Regular soldier, they could simply walk away. Their training had to be hard but only hard enough to be enjoyable. It had to be as authentic as the trainer could arrange and it usually had to be accomplished in short time frames with inadequate equipment. This was the situation in April 1912. Some of those matters have not changed in a hundred years.

Townshend was probably not the ideal officer to command a TA division but he recognized that it was a rite of passage if he was to move ever onwards and upwards. He applied himself but did not enjoy the job. Only three months after taking command he wrote to his French friend, Colonel Mardacq:

> 14 Hill Street
> Berkeley Square
> London
> 27 July 1912

My dear Mardacq,

You will have perhaps wondered why I have not written, but if you had to train a Division of some 18,000 territorial troops, comprised of three brigades in the areas of Kent, Surrey and Middlesex, with some scattered detachments in Sussex, and get in four hours' study of strategy and haute tactique daily, you would well understand why I have not written.

I wonder if I can go with General Foch and his Division to the manoeuvres? Could I be useful to you in this way? I must come and see General Foch at Chaumont before the manoeuvres begin. I was very angry the other day when I went to the War Office, and was told I had applied too late to be granted one of the passes to the French manoeuvres. I suppose a lot of junior officers who do not know French, and have no real sympathy with France, and who do not know some of her leading soldiers as I do, have been selected to go. I want to write a good account of the French Grand Manoeuvres from a haute tactique point of view. I think Brigadier-General Wilson had a good deal to do with who should go from the British Service and as I am much senior to him I do not suppose he was over anxious for me to go.

The dissatisfied tone of this letter is revealing. It is petulant, undignified and his remarks about the unfortunate Wilson, although they might be accurate, are not appropriate. In late September 1912, after a scant five months in command of the Home Counties Division, he was moved to the East Anglian Division – home country for Charles Townshend and he was delighted, if not with his new job, at least with its location.

He was able to spend some time on domestic matters and soon made it his business to visit Vere Lodge which was adjacent to Raynham Hall. Charles Townshend still entertained high hopes of succeeding to the title and his ambition was to own the Hall – no longer in the family's ownership but in the meantime he bought Vere Lodge and started to adapt it to his needs. He was in regular contact with Foch who held Townshend in high regard, and the British infantry in even higher regard. Theirs was a corre-spondence that gave Townshend great pleasure.

Townshend now experienced the frustration of all regular officers serving with the TA. In the Home Counties he had arranged local camps to make best use of time and money, and he sought to implement the same arrangement in East Anglia but was defeated by rampant apathy. He commented:

> I could have trained them at Thetford, but am given to understand that the want of amusement (cinemas, theatres, etc.) in the locality caused it to be so unpopular with the Territorials when General Byng trained there before, it lessened the number of recruits. Lots of them would leave. Everyone, in short, seemed to be in collusion to arrange a 'good time' when out from training!

Townshend is deserving of some sympathy. His motives were pure – he wanted to produce an efficient, battle-ready division. Sadly, his priorities did not accord with those of the local population from which he drew his soldier recruits, and for that matter his officers as well. Not surprisingly Townshend decided that he had 'done' the TA, got in touch with the War Office and said that he would be happy to accept a command in India – anything, but anything to get away from the Territorial Army.

It did not take long for him to be offered command of the Jhansi Brigade and on 6 June 1913 he took passage to India accompanied by Whitmore. His first tour as a major general had been for a scant two years and it had not been either very successful or great fun. However, there is no record of him bombarding the War Office with complaints and appeals, and perhaps this is why the move to India came through so quickly.

It was quite normal at this time for brigades to be commanded by major generals and his new command was relatively small. He launched himself at the job with typical enthusiasm and quickly identified the priorities. He set out a comprehensive and progressive training programme, and paid particular attention to the Non-Commissioned Officers (NCOs) who he recognized, in war, might well have to act in the place of an officer casualty. It was all going swimmingly when he was subjected to a douche of very cold water. He received a letter from Lieutenant General Sir Percy Lake KCB, who was the Chief of the Indian General Staff, and in effect, the second-in-command to the Commander-in-Chief, the professional head of the Indian Army. Lake wrote:

Dear Townshend,

General Peyton has shown me a circular entitled the 'Necessity of a Doctrine', recently issued to your Brigade. In private life there is every scope for 'Tot homines tot sententiae'; but where in soldiering, you substitute 'duces' for 'homines', there is every objection, and his Excellency the Commander-in-Chief has expressed his view on this subject very fully in the Memorandum on Army Training in India 1911- 1912, and later in his speech at the Inter-Divisional Manoeuvres December last.

Owing to your only lately having arrived in India, you may not have had an opportunity of reading His Excellency's speeches, so I am enclosing a copy. I feel sure that you will thoroughly agree with H.E.'s remarks as to 'adherence to regulations', with which the second speech concludes. I know that H.E. has strong objections to officers in command issuing training memoranda of their own, and so I am sending you this note privately.

Yours sincerely,

Percy Lake

Townshend ate the token slice of humble pie expected of him, but took the opportunity to complain about the small cash grant for training and obviously related this to his frustrating time with the TA. Lake replied saying that he found Townshend's account of his time with the Territorial Force 'interesting – and depressing'.

Townshend was good at his job – when his brigade exercised with other formations it excelled and the commander was quite correctly the recipient of congratulations on the quality of his training, not least from Lieutenant General Sir John Nixon of whom we shall hear a great deal more. Flushed with success Townshend resumed his letter writing, the object of the exercise being to get him 'upgraded' from command of a brigade to that of a division. As part of his campaign to keep himself in the public eye and as grist to his mill he produced a lengthy paper which he entitled *Wanted: a doctrine. Re – Politics and Strategy in the Afghan Question 1913*. The document was clearly aimed at the parochial question of Afghanistan but Townshend indulged himself by discussing and contrasting the preparedness for war of Germany and Britain. In the preparation of the paper he drew on the wisdom of General Foch and distributed the final document widely to senior officers around the world. It was well received. General Nixon wrote to tell him that he had recommended him for command of a division. Sherson says ambiguously in his book: 'and he immediately wrote to Kitchener, French, Frankleyn and others to tell them so!' The exclamation mark indicates that the 'he' was Townshend – certainly it would have been in character. He had any number of supporters and one of these was General Sir James Willcocks GCB GCMG KCSI DSO who was commanding the Northern Army. He wrote warmly:

> Dear Townshend
>
> I am very glad Nixon was pleased with your Brigade. I was sure he would be, for you are a keen soldier and do your duty. I met one of your COs the other day, and he was loud in praise of your lectures, and said he had learned a lot from them. French is our best soldier, and would, I am sure, do well in war. I like his looks. It goes a long way on service. Repington talked vaguely of coming out to India, but men in his billet find it difficult to get away for long, and I am sure he has no intention of coming out really . . . I go in October, and have no idea of what I shall do then – perhaps go and help the Turks if they will have me! A happy 1914 to you.
>
> Yours sincerely,
James Willcocks

In February 1914, Charles Townshend was surprised to be offered the command of the Rawal Pindi Brigade in the 2nd Division; this division was currently commanded by the difficult, irascible Major General Sir George Kitson KCVO CB CMG, whose demeanour was thought to be the result of a protracted period of poor health. But it was his subordinates who paid the price. The situation was fully appreciated in official circles and sufficiently so for the Military Secretary to suggest to Townshend that he might have a rough ride with Kitson. Townshend commented in his diary: 'Lady Kitson does not appear to be very popular with the Indian Army officers, as there is too much of "none but Rifles need apply", and that sort of thing.'

Townshend took the job on the basis that, as and when Kitson resigned, was removed or died, he would be on the spot to replace him. It did not work like that and Kitson remained in command until 1916, by which time Townshend had more serious matters on his mind.

The situation in Europe was becoming tenser and although he had only just taken up a new job, Townshend telegraphed General French asking him to find him a command in France when the balloon went up. On 28 June, Archduke Francis Ferdinand of Austria-Hungary and his wife were assassinated in Sarajevo (in what is now Bosnia) by Gavrilo Princip. Charles Townshend, not unreasonably, wrote a letter of condolence to an Austrian officer who, like him, had been a military attaché in Paris back in 1905. They knew each other quite well and it seemed to be a comradely thing to do at the time – the letter turned out to be a time bomb with a long fuse.

Elsewhere the balloon duly went up on 4 August 1914.

The declaration of war pushed Townshend into overdrive. He sent a telegram to Kitchener and enlisted the aid of his supportive wife, living in London. She, too, approached French but with no success. Townshend would not take any answer except 'yes' and to this end thereafter he made contact with anyone who was anyone – pleading, begging or demanding command of a division in France. Alice eventually sent a message saying, 'Know on authority waiting for opportunity, caution and patience vital.'

Patience and caution were strangers to Charles Townshend and his continued verbal, worldwide, assaults were highly counter-productive. Sherson[2] asserts that in the War Office he was being described as a 'mad fanatic' and had only himself to blame for this damning assessment.

Alice was devoted to him and her letters were little gems of military intelligence. She gleaned what she could from rumour in the smarter salons in London, distilled it and passed it on. CVFT was, of course, unaware of the bigger picture. By keeping him in India the Establishment was ensuring the presence of an officer who was very experienced in campaigning on the North-West Frontier, where some tribes were, in Sherson's word, 'unsettled.'

The early defeats suffered by the British emboldened their potential foes and on the North-West Frontier a weakened Britain was seen as being ripe for easy pickings. Townshend took his time but recognized the danger and grasped the nettle by suggesting a 'demonstration' of military power and resolve. This was mounted, Townshend was involved and the 'demonstration' had the desired effect, for by 15 January 1915 all was 'sweetness and light' once more – almost. However close at hand, in Rawal Pindi the 35th Sikhs were on the edge of mutiny and the Commanding Officer was seriously worried as he described his men as 'surly, discontented and semi-insolent in their manner'. Townshend went to the heart of the matter and sent for all the native officers of the Regiment. His 'chat' was something of a tour de force and by a mixture of badinage, good humour and thinly veiled threats he carried the day.

Elsewhere in the Far East it was much more serious. In Singapore, on 15 February 1915, the 5th Native Light Infantry mutinied and killed forty-seven British soldiers and civilians. In Rangoon, on 19 February, a planned insurrection by the 130th Baluch Regiment was foiled by the police, acting on intelligence obtained from within the Regiment, and retribution followed. The 12th Pioneers at Quetta were unstable and a possible hot spot in the making.

These were dangerous times but Townshend revelled in the tension and detailed the 35th Sikhs to provide the guard over his quarters at night as a demonstration of the trust he had in them. He confided in his dairy: 'I did not trust them one little bit, but by putting my life in their hands I bluffed them and established confidence all round.' This was an act of cold and calculated courage. He put his very life on the line and no soldier could have done more. It worked and he rose to eat a hearty breakfast next morning.

Whilst Charles Townshend was growing to manhood, Admiral of the Fleet Lord Jackie Fisher had revitalized the Royal Navy and had overseen the transition from sail to steam in the latter part of the nineteenth century. He built new classes of ships and had left, as his legacy, a modern, well-found fleet. It was the greatest fleet on earth and Britannia truly did rule the waves. Fisher had also taken the crucial and very brave decision to abandon coal as the motive power for these ships. Britain had incalculable stocks of coal but, nevertheless, Fisher opted for oil – of which Britain had not a single drop. It was a very bold decision that, in large part, triggered the ill-fated British expedition to Mesopotamia in 1915.

The British Government had had a long and friendly relationship with the Ottoman Empire, and Germany not only wanted the same but had been working hard for fifty years to develop that which the British took for granted. In Gladstone's view, Tsarist Russia was a much more important ally and, as Russia and the Ottoman Empire were incompatible, one would have to be gently shelved. Germany watched with incredulity as Britain quietly rejected its long-term ally and then rushed in to fill the vacuum Britain had left behind. Loans were granted, railways constructed, bridges built and military instructors were attached to the Turkish Army, which was fitted out with German equipment. The Turkish Navy was supplemented with German ships and treaties of mutual defence entered into. Imperceptibly, at first, Britain and Russia were seen increasingly by the Turks as potential foes and no longer as old friends.

When war was declared in August 1914 it became imperative that the oilfields that centred on Abadan were secured. Two Cadmus class sloops, HMS *Espiègle* and HMS *Odin*, were sent up the Shatt-al-Arab waterway as a demonstration of British power. The ploy did not work and both ships had to beat a hasty and ignominious retreat when Turkey, which bordered the Shatt, entered the war on Germany's side.

The British Government delegated the military issues in that vast area, known as Mesopotamia, to the Indian Government, as it was fully occupied with events close to home. The name 'Mesopotamia' is taken from the Greek and means 'between two rivers' – the Tigris and the Euphrates. It covered an area now identified as Iraq, north-east Syria, south-east Turkey and parts of south-west Iran. It had no recognized international boundaries and it has one of the most hostile environments in the world.

The Indian Government was told to raise and equip four expeditionary forces, one of which was to be earmarked for deployment to Mesopotamia. The Indian Army had long been starved of funds and was undermanned. However, on instructions from Whitehall, the 6th Division (known as Indian Expeditionary Force D or IEFD) was despatched to advance up the Shatt-al-Arab and occupy the strategically important town of Basra about 50 miles north of Abadan.

Charles Townshend was bursting to get into the fight, any fight, and things could have been so very different. Had he been sent to Flanders, the chances are that, like his contemporaries, he would have been unable to break the deadlock of trench warfare and his war would have been unique only in the number of his soldiers who were killed.

On 12 April 1915, he was ecstatic when he received notification that it was he that was to command the 6th Division. Sherson, not the most objective of biographers, had this to say: 'His final act at Pindi was to issue an order to the troops in garrison in which he thanked them all, "for their fine soldierly conduct and discipline in a most trying time". He loved his men and was grateful for their support and they loved him too, as few Commanders have been loved.'

Sherson's view was almost certainly coloured by a letter written by a Gunner Grant to an unknown recipient. Gunner Grant was one of the soldiers selected to accompany Townshend and he was offered £10 for his place on the draft (an enormous sum at the time), so anxious were some men to serve under Townshend. Grant wrote and said:

The day before our General left Rawal Pindi he gave a farewell speech to us in the garrison theatre. It was packed to suffocation. His words were, 'Well, comrades, to-morrow I leave you: I go to Mesopotamia.' There was a great silence in that great gathering of his soldiers. He asked why we were silent. One old soldier said: 'We want to come with you.' Cheer upon cheer greeted this remark. They shouted. They cried out. Our gallant General saluted us and said, 'I tried hard to take you to France, and now I have received orders to go to Mesopotamia.

I wish I could take you with me but I cannot do so. Perhaps we may meet again. Good-bye, my men, good-bye!' . . . The whole Brigade turned out to wish us farewell. Some of the boys in their excitement even kissed me good-bye (I think they were drunk). Crowds of them marched with us to the station . . . on the steamer was 'Our Charlie' as Sir Charles Townshend was always known to his troops, and in a very short time I was having a chat with him. It was a very frequent thing to see 'Our General' laughing and talking with a private. That is one of the reasons every man worshipped him.

Sherson's view is ingenuous.

There was, in 1915, and to a lesser extent today, a considerable gap between officers and other ranks. That is the result of four factors: social, educational, economic and professional, and in that latter category, discipline is an important part.

Officers in 1915 were drawn from different strata of society to their men. It may be politically incorrect now but it was the norm then – it was the unspoken 'class system' that predominated in the early part of the twentieth century. This was an unwritten arrangement that 'pigeon-holed' people. And the criteria for this pigeon-holing was the birth, residence, education, employment and in some cases religion, of the individual. It was an arrangement that served the society that created it. There were exceptions and some officers, relatively few, were commissioned on merit, from the ranks and by definition from a lower social class. Similarly, some young men, who might have been considered by their 'class' to be 'officer material', chose to serve in the ranks.

Officers were invariably better educated than their men. Education was the first criteria in the selection of an officer and, logically, so it should be. Knowledge is power and an officer's education had, as a by-product, a degree of worldliness that most of his soldiers, and particularly conscripts, did not have.

A sound education led either naturally to a successful civilian career or subsequent commissioning after conscription, or to Sandhurst or Woolwich and a regular commission. Either way the officer had more money in his pockets. Officers' pay scales have always reflected their responsibility and been far in excess of that of soldiers; it is the way of the world and the reality was that officers could afford different pastimes, conducted in different places, and so there was no social interaction between Thomas Atkins and his officer. Finally, the Army Act passed by Parliament was and is the basis of all Army discipline. It commands a soldier (of any rank) to obey his superior. It enshrines in law the authority of a commissioned officer and makes provision for a host of acts deemed to be counter to the Army Act which are punishable. Often that punishment is meted out by an officer whom the soldier knows well. No officer invokes a section of the Army Act unless he has no other choice, but the unquestioned authority it bestows acts as an invisible but powerful barrier between commissioned and non-commissioned soldiers.

All of these factors combine to create a social and professional divide and the more senior the officer the more evident that divide becomes. It is human nature to like someone who is agreeable and so it was vastly flattering to a young soldier if his colonel stopped to chat and, even more so, if his general, covered in campaign ribbons, does the same. Townshend, along with countless officers before and since, knew that being approachable on a superficial level to his soldiers had a disproportionate effect to the effort involved and, here, it worked in his favour.

The best judges of an officer are his peers and his batman. Later in this book the words of Townshend's soldier servant are quoted. The evidence of Private (later Lance Corporal) John Boggis of the Royal Norfolk Regiment, provides some balance.

Townshend's men did not *love* him because they did not know him. They admired an outgoing, affable personality who was good at what he did and who made an effort to communicate with them. Their response would make any officer very proud and there can be no serious doubt that to the majority of soldiers Townshend was seen as a charismatic and a popular leader.

Notes

1. Richard Burden Haldane (1856–1928). Later Viscount Haldane of Cloane. Haldane assumed office in 1905 and, with commendable energy and foresight, made lasting reforms to the Army after the debacles of the Boer War. He established a peacetime army of 160,000 (almost twice the size of the Army 100 years later), established the General Staff and made the key appointments of Nicholson to be CGS and Haig to be Director of Training. It was Haldane who produced the highly professional 'Contemptible Little Army' that acquitted itself so very well in 1914.

2. Sherson, *Townshend of Chitral and Kut*, p. 242.

Chapter 12

1915–1916

The Campaign in Mesopotamia

'When Allah made Hell, he did not find it bad enough, so he made Mesopotamia – and then, he added flies.'

An Arab proverb

It was a remarkable state of affairs that the Indian Empire should be administered by individuals appointed by HMG in Whitehall but who, after their appointment, were then in a position to ignore the strictures of their government thousands of miles away. It was an anomalous situation. It was also the foundation for the tragic events that took place in Mesopotamia during 1915–1916, in which Charles Townshend played a major role. A global war was wreaking havoc, Britain was sorely pressed and needed the unqualified support of its empire, not least that of India.

The British Government personified by the Indian Secretary, Sir Joseph Chamberlain, had appointed and was obliged to deal with the Viceroy, Lord Hardinge,[1] and his Commander-in-Chief, General Sir Beauchamp Duff.[2] These latter two men did not offer unqualified support. Quite the reverse, rather they were blinkered and obstructive at every turn. Apparently they did not appreciate the global nature of the war and were entirely focused on the maintenance of India's borders. They resisted sending Indian troops to fight overseas because they saw such a step as being deleterious to their parochial needs. The unsparing generosity of Australia, Canada and New Zealand, all countries with small populations, was not matched by India, one of the most populous nations on earth.

The Indian Army at the outbreak of war was composed of 76,000 British and 159,000 Indian troops. It did not have the benefit of any munitions factories or any associated defence industry assets. It had virtually no transport as most of its operations were conducted away from paved surfaces. Its military hospital services were poor and this particular deficiency was to be critical. The Indian Army in 1915 was capable of subduing unsophisticated

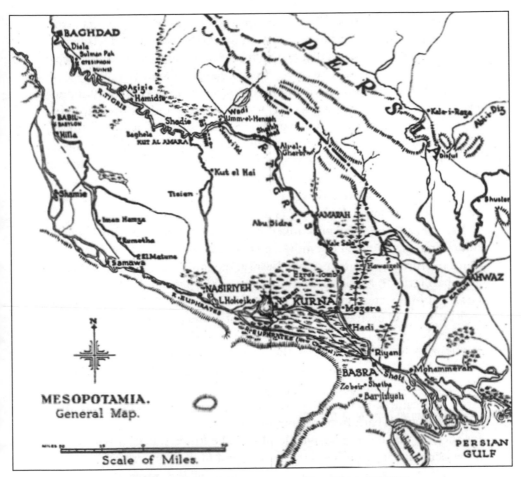

Fig 7. Map of Mesopotamia and the River Tigris. (CVFT)

tribal opponents but was completely untested against a well-equipped and well-led adversary.

This was the unpromising background under which the 6th Division went to war, albeit piecemeal, and initially under the command of Lieutenant General Sir Arthur Barrett. The Division was told, at the outset, that its mission was 'to protect British oil interests on the Shatt al Arab waterway'. This was to ensure that the Royal Navy would have un-interrupted access to oil and that the greatest fleet in the world could continue to function.

16 Brigade led the way under Brigadier General Delamain with orders to occupy Abadan Island at the head of the Persian Gulf, to protect the oil

refineries there and, if possible, to occupy the city of Basra. As a precursor to the ineptitude that was to be the norm for these operations, Delamain's brigade embarked in ships that had no means of landing troops and equipment on a hostile shore. The convoy anchored off Bahrain Island.

16 Brigade could see that the Fort of Fao was under fire from the Cadmus class sloop *Odin* which was shelling it to good effect and, as they steamed past *Odin,* a Turkish flag was run up in front of the Customs House. Delamain sent a party of Dorsets to investigate and they found the place deserted. HMS *Espiègle*, a ship that looked more like a yacht than a warship, engaged the Turkish guns opposite Abadan Island and silenced them. 16 Brigade moved slowly upriver heading for Basra and past the refinery with its seven distinctive chimneys.

Basra was taken after only token resistance and Barrett's 18 Brigade under Brigadier General Fry moved on to threaten and then take Kurna (or Qurna), a further 35 miles north of Basra at the confluence of the Euphrates and the Tigris. In his book *My Campaign in Mesopotamia* CVFT makes it clear that in his view any advance beyond Kurna was folly until a strong logistic base had been established and a light railway had been constructed between Kurna and the sea.

He made his judgment after the event but nevertheless he was quite correct. 17 Brigade, commanded by Brigadier General Dobbie, had now rejoined the Division and it brought the force up to 15,000 combatants, with 1,600 pack camels. General Barrett did his appreciation and promptly sent half of his camels back from whence they had come as there was no grazing for them in this bleak inhospitable place. The Force was now beset with other administrative difficulties. Not the least of these was that Basra was not built to act as a staging port, it had none of the infrastructure that was needed and it had insufficient wharves. All stores had to be double-handled from the ship onto bellums. These were flat-bottomed, ungainly craft with a low freeboard that had been employed on these rivers for thousands of years. They were propelled by punting 'à la Thames' or by the use of paddles. The movement of stores and personnel from ship to shore using these bellums was a laborious business.

To compound the problem, command of the Mesopotamian Expedition was divided between London and Delhi, with no clear line of demarcation. When the War Office asked that reinforcements be sent to the theatre it was quite unaware of local conditions, whereupon Hardinge and Duff, who were both equally unaware of the situation, refused outright. After an unedifying political spat, conducted by telegram, London ordered that two further brigades be sent to Basra. Hardinge and Duff reacted petulantly and, without further reference to London, elements of the 12th Division under Major General Gorringe moved into the theatre. This formation was incomplete, not least because it was bereft of artillery.

A two-division force is the minimum complement for an army corps, and Lieutenant General Sir John Nixon was appointed by the Viceroy to travel from India to take command of what was now termed Indian Expeditionary Force 'D'. Nixon had been born in 1857 and was described as 'a dashing cavalry officer . . . a secretive, thrusting man with a thick moustache, a beaky nose and a strong but ungainly physique.' He was fifty-seven years of age and committed to a lengthy campaign in one of the most demanding climates in the world. It was to be Townshend's very bad luck to serve under this over-promoted incompetent.

Nixon's direction from the Viceroy was at odds with the wishes of the British Government, which put the protection of the oilfields firmly as its top priority. Indeed Lord Crewe had made it clear that Britain's main theatre of war in Asia Minor was the Dardanelles, while the defence of Suez also ranked above Mesopotamia. In his words, 'Mesopotamia was where a safe game must be played.'[3] However, Nixon arrived in the theatre with a much wider brief from the Viceroy – 'the subjugation of as much of Mesopotamia as possible' about sums it up. This latter aim was patently impossible unless there were sufficient military assets in place to occupy and hold vast swathes of hostile territory. His 1½ weak divisions, with no demonstrable logistic system behind them, were grossly insufficient. But common sense was not to be allowed to inhibit Nixon's ambition, which flourished in a situation where there was no single, agreed, strategic aim for Mesopotamia.

Soon after Nixon's arrival Suleiman Askeri, with a mixed force of about 30,000 Arabs, Turks and Kurds, attacked the British encampment, an event that became known as the Battle of Shaiba. It was a bloody affair and very closely contested. The Turks were calculated to have lost 3,000 killed and wounded, as well as 800 prisoners – something of an embarrassment in the circumstances as they had to be fed, watered and guarded. British losses were 1,000 killed and wounded, including eighteen officers killed and forty-two wounded. Even at this early stage the deficiency in the medical support was glaringly obvious. The failure of the Indian Government to provision sufficient doctors, medical orderlies and medical equipment was to develop into a public scandal as casualties mounted and men died of neglect. The system to evacuate the wounded was inadequate and dependent upon absolute control of the Shatt-al-Arab waterway. Major General Mellis VC, a fire-eating leader of the first water, who had been with his brigade in the thick of the action, commented afterwards that was 'a real soldier's battle'. The Turks recognized that in Mellis they had had a redoubtable adversary, well worthy of the appellation 'Pasha'.

The aftermath of the battle was to fill the rudimentary hospitals with men who had suffered wounds quite unlike those previously experienced when fighting dissident tribesmen. Turkish shells inflicted injuries that tore men apart and then the injured were subjected to the intolerable heat and flies.

Survival rates were not good after the Battle of Shaiba.

At this point General Barrett fell sick and was evacuated;[4] Townshend arrived to replace Barrett on 23 April 1915. He was met by Nixon, at his Corps Headquarters in Basra and briefed. Nixon had specifically asked for Townshend to command the 6th Division because his aggressive style mirrored his own. At the briefing, Nixon told his new subordinate that his orders were 'not only to drive the enemy from his present positions between Pear Drop Bend (see Fig 8 on Page 171) and Kurna and capture his guns but also to push up river and occupy Amara – the operation to be continuous.' Kurna had first to be taken and Amara was a further 87 miles up the Tigris. The river was the only viable axis and the only means of reaching Amara. The factor that does not seem to have been considered in any detail by either general was the availability or not of shallow-draft, high-capacity vessels able to navigate the unpredictable waters of the river.

Excited by the wide canvas spread out before him and the opportunities on offer, Townshend went off to inspect his brigades. He was impressed with the Dorsets and the Norfolks but less so with his Indian troops.

He decided that he needed an additional orderly and he enquired of the Commanding Officer of the Norfolks if there was anyone in the battalion who might like to take the job on. A young man called Private John Boggis put himself forward and, having gone through the normal military processes required, he was eventually called to be interviewed. Boggis was twenty-three, slightly built and of less than average height. He was, in turn, surprised that the General was so short but this first meeting was very brief.

'Ah' said the General, 'I see that you are from Raynham.'

'Yes, Sir. I worked in the Hall as a boy.'

'Just what I want,' rejoined Townshend.[5]

Boggis got the job and it probably saved his life, enabling him to reminisce about Charles Townshend when he met Russell Braddon fifty-one years later. They say that no man is a God to his valet and certainly Boggis had no illusions about his erstwhile boss.

Domestic issues resolved, Townshend went forward to make a personal reconnaissance of his first objective, Kurna, the alleged 'Garden of Eden'.

He made his way upriver in a launch and when he mounted a rickety observation tower he did not like what he saw.

All he could see was water – lots and lots of water. There were many square miles of brown, muddy water of uncertain depth.

Then there were the flies – countless billions of flies.

The area ahead of him was Bahran, a small settlement, located alongside the river about 10 miles to the north and sited on a patch of higher ground. In the spring of 1915, the snow had started to melt in the mountains and the small rivers had filled and flowed down to the plain to join the mighty Tigris, which was now in spate. It had broken its banks, as it did every year, and had submerged all the low-lying land from Baghdad to Basra. Any advance that the 6th Division was to make would be across a vast flooded plain. All normal military tactics were rendered null and void because they simply did not apply in this situation.

At intervals patches of higher ground rose from the muddy water and of these some appeared to be fortified. They were astride the river and its relatively deep navigable water. The islands were about 3,500 yards away and, beyond them, further Turkish redoubts of varying strength were located on a line of sandhills. The deep defensive position blocked the way to Amara and could not be bypassed.

It was an extraordinary situation that called for an extraordinary solution and an extraordinary man to put that solution into effect.

Intelligence sources estimated the enemy strength at six battalions of Turks, or about 5,500 trained soldiers, with an additional 600 Arab soldiers and 1,200 marsh Arabs of questionable quality, ten field guns and a gunboat – the *Marmarice*. Townshend had no illusions of the difficulties he faced and asked Nixon to come to see for himself. This was little more than a device to ensure that the 12th Division would also be fully committed to the battle, but Charles Townshend's manipulation failed and Nixon would have none of it. Certainly not, if such a decision would involve Gorringe breaching Persian sovereignty by crossing its borders in order to outflank the enemy.

Townshend had only one option and that was frontal assault across two miles of water of varying depth. Although he was a general not an admiral, there was no doubt that boats and many of them were going to be needed. For a man so versed in the theory of war it was galling to have to conduct his first major operation in such bizarre circumstances. The circumstances called for an unorthodox plan – a very unorthodox plan.

Townshend did not have his entire division to hand, quickly discovering that many of his soldiers had been hived off by Corps Headquarters to act as batmen, drivers, clerks, signalmen and a host of other jobs in the line of communication for which the Indian Government had made no provision. He protested vigorously to Nixon but with little success.

Townshend's study of military history had given him an insight into the challenges faced by the great captains and, not lacking in self-esteem, he felt that in particular he related to Napoleon Bonaparte. Nixon's obstinate refusal to release 'bayonets' back to their units was a set-back but, more significant, was his withdrawal of 18 Brigade from Townshend and its re-deployment to a defensive position around Basra. Townshend noted that Napoleon did not have to deal with such obstacles and he bore Nixon's decisions stoically – he contented himself by criticizing Nixon privately, whilst planning to fight and win an inland battle in which all the troops were water-borne, with command exercised from a warship.

First he had to assemble sufficient bellums to carry a full brigade and he set his staff to work to requisition 328 of these craft. He ordered that as many as possible be fitted with rudimentary armour to give the passengers protection against small-arms fire. Some of the bellums, most of which were between 30 and 40 feet in length, had to be equipped to carry machine guns and the guns of a mountain battery. The infantry were allocated ten men to a bellum and of these two were to be trained in punting! One of these was a reserve punter to be used if the first was shot. Each bellum had to carry picks, shovels, ammunition, paddles, caulking material (to plug bullet holes), water bottles and the personal kit of each soldier.

The matter would be funny if men's lives were not at stake. The soldiers were only too aware of how very vulnerable they would be as they were slowly propelled through the reeds and across two miles of open water into the face of Turkish fire. Absolutely all the usual elements for a military disaster, as well as some entirely new ones, were in place.

The bellums were obtained, armoured where possible, the punters were trained and the operation order was written by Townshend. Unlikely as it may seem, but by his account, even the General was filled with doubt and expressed those doubts to his soldier servant, Whitmore. Whitmore, who had been at his side for fourteen years, brushed the General's fears aside saying, 'It's alright, Sir, you'll have the Townshend luck.'[6] For Whitmore, however, luck was running out and he was already a sick man. The climate and the poor food had not helped.

The success of the attack would depend upon the support of the Royal Navy which had on the river HMS *Espiègle*, *Odin*, *Comet* and *Clio*, the minesweepers *Shaitan*, *Lawrence*, *Miner* and *Lewis Pelly*. *Mejidieh*, *Blosse Lynch*, the sparsely named *P-1* and, in addition, four armed launches, two

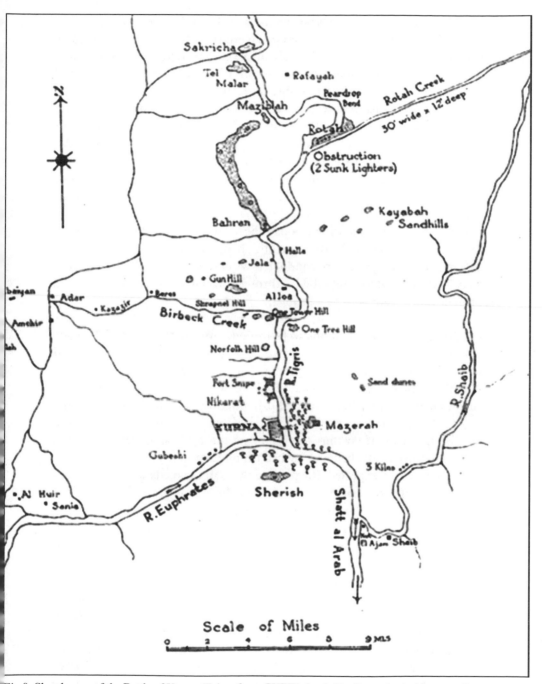

Fig 8. Sketch map of the Battle of Kurna. Taken from CVFT's book *My Campaign in Mesopotamia*.

naval horse boats (odd vessels but armed with 4.7" guns) and several smaller craft. This colourful and extraordinary riverboat flotilla was commanded by Captain Wilfred Nunn RN. Townshend asked Nixon for, and was granted, command of the naval assets. Nunn took his direction from the General and he and Townshend worked amicably thereafter.

These small ships were severely at risk from the mines sown in the river by the retreating Turks and Townshend offered a reward of 400 rupees for every mine hauled out of the river. This galvanized the local Arab population which habitually fished the river and they went looking for a different – and lethal – alternative. It also served to occupy a large group of people who might otherwise have been harassing Townshend and his division on behalf of the Turks.

On 28 May, the assaulting troops rehearsed their roles and what had at first seemed to be an absurd idea now had a semblance of practicality, although the rehearsals were conducted without shot or shell. Some issues were resolved but the reed beds, through which the bellums had to be propelled, were going to be a problem.

On 30 May 1915, the bellums were loaded with the troops of 17 Brigade who were briefed, the punters were well practised and every mine that could be found had been lifted. Everything that could be done had been done. Then, at the last minute, Brigadier Dobbie, the commander of 17 Brigade, succumbed to an earlier injury and handed over command to Colonel Climo. Townshend moved to HMS *Espiègle*, and established his command post on the ship. At 0600hrs the following morning, as *Espiègle*'s engines started to turn, so the bellums pushed off on their journey.

Initially, and as expected, the passage through the reeds was difficult and it was found that the armour plates that had been hung over the sides of the boats snagged in the reeds and made progress very slow. It was very hard work poling a bellum and even enthusiastic paddling by some of the passengers did not help very much. The temperature was rising, minute by minute, and another brutally hot day of around 110°F was in prospect. The high humidity caused the soldiers to sweat and that attracted myriad insects all of which seemed to be carnivorous. The men all knew that anyone who was wounded and fell in the water would drown. Any bellum that was sunk would consign ten men into water that might be three feet or even thirty feet deep.

The principal player in the battle was to be the artillery. There were now guns positioned at Kurna and on all the naval ships. Together they had to suppress the Turks' defensive fire from the small islands that dotted the flooded plain as they were the first objectives. The islands were known as

One Tree Hill, Shrapnel Hill, Tower Hill, Gun Hill and Norfolk Hill.

The engagement fought on 31 May 1916 is known as the Battle of Kurna, however, to those who were present it was always referred to as 'Townshend's Regatta'.

The bellums made slow progress and the naval force led by the launches *Shaitan* and *Sumana* idled along in the river keeping pace with them. Mines were still a hazard but, by happy chance, the Turkish naval officer who had sown them had been captured and was installed in the leading launch. He cheerfully , and with remarkably good grace, pointed out where his mines were located. They were to have been fired electrically, but long immersion in the river had affected the connections and, as it happened, none of them exploded.

The river was ill-defined because the flood water had covered everything in an anonymous shimmering sheet so that great care had to be taken by the helmsmen to stay in the middle of the stream. Fire was opened on Norfolk, Two Gun and One Tower Hills. At such short range the gunfire was shattering and Townshend had an excellent view as the battle unfolded as he was relatively high up in a cockpit rigged on the mast of *Espiègle*. There was some return fire and shrapnel bursts near *Espiègle* were sufficiently wide to do no damage, but then she was hit twice – the ship, built in 1880, was not designed to absorb much of the punishment meted out by twentieth-century guns.

The 22nd Punjabis, commanded by Lieutenant Colonel Blois-Johnson, leapt from their bellums as they grounded in the shallows of One Tree Island on the right flank, and with bayonets to the fore, fell upon the Turkish positions. At the same time the Ox and Bucks (Oxfordshire and Buckinghamshire Light Infantry) stormed Norfolk Hill; Captain Brooke at the head of his company was the first man in the redoubt – he was also the first to die.

The other strongpoints were assaulted in turn and, in each case, it was found that the artillery barrage had obliterated any defence works. There was no natural material on the islands; no stone for building sangars or timber for re-inforcing trench systems. The islands were barren and the defenders could only shelter behind inadequate 'berms', man-made defence work constructed only of sand, that were no protection against modern artillery. Many of the defenders were already dead when 17 Brigade launched its assault. Resistance was slight and losses were very modest – far less than Townshend had feared.

The first line of objectives had been taken and Townshend's fleet of bellums had performed far beyond his hopes, but the day was not yet done for 6,000 yards ahead lay the next target, a crescent-shaped line of sandhills supported in turn by strongpoints to their rear. Townshend ordered his troops to bivouac and they gratefully took the chance to consolidate, treat the wounded, eat and clean weapons. They spent the night among the former occupants who, although dead, still made their presence obvious by the stench that rose from their quickly putrefying corpses. It was a smell that was to become very familiar to those who served in this theatre.

It was clear that Bahran and the area around it were strongly fortified and Townshend resumed hostilities at daybreak. He ordered 17 Brigade to move out to the west and his flotilla to move upriver and around the bend between One Tower Hill and One Tree Hill. The progress of the bellums was painfully slow, the reeds were still a major factor and the rate of progress made the occupants very vulnerable to Turkish fire. However, 103rd Mahratta Light Infantry heading for Gun Hill met only token resistance and then saw white flags being waved about thirty minutes before they made landfall in the late afternoon. 300 prisoners were taken and Townshend commented that it was as well there was not a stern fight as Gun Hill was out of range of his guns.

The day ended with Townshend's force in possession of all the 'high' ground (although 'dry' ground would be more accurate) north of Kurna, leaving him poised to assault Bahran and Maziblah. Another hard day's poling lay ahead and the Turks were expected to contest possession of the Bahran ridge vigourously – they did not.

An aeroplane, recently arrived in the theatre, flew over the enemy position and the pilot dropped a message to *Espiègle* to say that the enemy had abandoned Bahran. Not a shot was fired as the 6th Division, in its curious transport, celebrated a bloodless victory.

General Nixon arrived in his steamer to savour a victory to which he had contributed nothing. Since his arrival in Mesopotamia and the establishment of his headquarters in Basra, he had been dilatory to the point of culpability. The medical support for his soldiers was almost non-existent and the resupply system hopelessly inadequate. Nixon's headquarters acted as little more than a post office and he was well out of his depth, even as a postmaster.

At their meeting Townshend told Nixon that he was going to press on upriver with a small element of his flotilla, as far as he was able. Immediately *Shaitan*, *Espiègle*, *Clio*, *Odin*, *Lewis Pelly* and *Samana* set off in pursuit of the Turks. The river had been blocked at Ruta but, as the British flotilla approached, it could be seen that the Tigris was not to be denied for it had breached the barrier and developed a gap just wide enough to allow a passage. *Espiègle* was able to bring her bow guns to bear on the Turkish ships

Mosul and *Marmarice* which were fleeing for Amara and were about 8,000 yards ahead. Several hits were not enough to stop either ship and as darkness intervened Townshend's tiny force, with only a handful of bayonets, was 20 miles north of the morning's action. They were getting close to Ezra's Tomb[7] and here they captured three large barges filled with munitions, mines, three field guns and 200–300 enemy soldiers who were made prisoner. These prisoners added to the logistic burden but CVFT makes no specific mention of them being a problem in his diary.

Colonel Gamble, the GSO 1, and all the staff officers were disembarked and told to reassemble the Division at Ezra's Tomb before sending it on to Amara by brigades.

As soon as the moon gave enough light Townshend pressed on upriver, accompanied by only a token force of thirty or forty soldiers and his ADC, a Captain Peel. It could be argued that Townshend's action in pressing on, unsupported, was reckless in the extreme and that he wantonly put at risk the most important ships on the river. These were ships that were absolutely vital for all future operations. By any yardstick it was an extraordinary state of affairs – a general officer, in command of a division, almost unaccompanied, was driving deep into occupied enemy territory, up an entirely predictable route, thereby obviously exposing himself to death or capture – neither alternative was in the best interests of his country.

Townshend was not stupid.

In military matters he was, in fact, highly perceptive and well informed. His actions can only have been motivated by some desire to steal the limelight and win fame and glory. Incidentally, he did, of course, put at risk the lives of everyone else in those small ships.

But, 'Fortune favours the brave', they say. 'Lady Luck' was certainly with Townshend's small and vulnerable force and, as the river narrowed and shelved, progress was slow and potentially hazardous. The captain of each vessel had to feel his way gingerly around each bend – where it could be identified. *Espiègle* was about 180ft long, drew about 10 feet and had particular difficulty in making the turns. The skills of Captain Nunn were sorely tested. Several times the ship ran aground, albeit very slowly, and either into the soft sand of the bank or a sand bar in the stream. Each time judicious use of the engines freed her. *Odin* and *Clio* were also substantial vessels and 'with their rigging and spars they must have looked more like full-rigged sailing ships than steamers. They must have made a great impression on the Arabs.'[8]

The sun beat down on the flotilla and despite the modest slipstream the crews were plagued by flies. The pursuit was long and tiring but the British flotilla was faster than the Turkish vessels ahead and, at day's end, the Turkish ships *Marmariss* and *Mosul* could be seen towing barges laden with soldiers. The two steamships were accompanied by a fleet of 'mahailas'. These mahailas are similar to the Arab dhow in that they carry lateen sails and have forward-sloping masts. They have the capacity to carry a burden of 50–100 tons. The mahailas accompanying the two Turkish ships were also laden with troops and equipment – they presented an excellent target and as fire was opened, the two Turkish steamships cast off their tows and headed north into the gathering dusk, leaving the powerless barges and wind-driven mahailas to their fate.

Odin was detached to take the boats and the men and equipment therein prisoner, whilst Townshend continued to press on upriver in hot pursuit. Darkness fell and Townshend called a brief halt but, by 0200hrs, the moon provided enough illumination to allow for more cautious navigation. The British ships passed Ezra's Tomb but about seven miles further on, at 0415hrs, *Espiègle* grounded yet again. She was a sea-going ship but by now she was more than 200 miles from her natural element. Her grounding was particularly frustrating as *Marmariss* could be seen a little way ahead. *Espiègle* opened fire but there was no response. Captain Nunn called away a ship's boat for a boarding party and when this pulled up to the Turkish ship they found that she had been abandoned. Little wonder as the gunnery of *Espiègle* and her cohorts had reduced the vessel's upper works to matchwood, although her hull was intact and so she was still of value. Moving forward slowly the British reconnaissance group discovered that *Mosul* was around the next bend and what was more she was showing a white flag.

The boarding party found a few wounded Turks in occupation. They spoke of the demoralization of their comrades and made the prospect of pressing on a very attractive option. However, *Espiègle* and her guns could go no further and it would have been prudent to stop and wait for Delamain's brigade to come upriver to consolidate the British position. Townshend did not know how far behind him the brigade was.

Was it a day? Two days? A week?

Despite the lack of any information and against all the rules of prudence, Charles Townshend decided to move his 'headquarters' – a grandiose name for the General and his ADC, to the armed steamer *Comet*. He took Captain Nunn RN with him. That raised the total complement of *Comet* to about eighteen. *Shaitan* had a complement of ten. *Samana* and *Lewis Pelly* were armed tugs towing horse barges in which there were three 4.7" guns, each served by a crew of four men. Each tug had a complement of about four. The major town of Amara lay about 50 miles further upriver and clearly this was a prize, but was it within the capacity of about forty-eight men (author's calculation) to take and hold? The size of this small force is open to speculation and CVFT makes several references to 'twenty-five men' and once to' twenty–two', but his sums are incorrect unless he did not include officers – and himself. He was notoriously slack with numbers and often adjusted them to suit his circumstances. This might be the case here.

The tiny force sailed on and met no opposition. Along both banks of the river, Arab villages flew white flags and the occupants came out to line the banks and salaam as the flotilla passed. It was midday when, at Qalat Salih, a nondescript settlement about halfway to Amara, there was a brief flurry of activity. A small force of mixed Turkish cavalry and infantry was sighted but it was dissuaded from taking any hostile action by several well aimed 12-pounder shells from *Comet* and it quickly headed for the distant horizon.

At this point a local sheikh came aboard *Comet* and submitted to Townshend. It was an unasked-for gesture but indicative of the impact Townshend's incursion was having, not only on the Turks, but also on the indigenous Arabs. It was at this point that Charles Townshend played his finest cards.

'Fifteen thousand men are coming up behind me,'[9] he announced authoritively. Exuding confidence and with characteristic bluster he then ordered the sheikh to arrange the collection of food for the 15,000 for which he offered to pay. Townshend knew he might not get the food but had no doubts that the Arab would rapidly pass the news of the, soon to arrive, 15,000 men further upriver. As it happened events were to prove him absolutely right. There are many examples of bluff being used successfully in warfare and this is a superb example of that genre.

The journey continued until nightfall and then *Comet* and *Shaitan* tied up. These two small ships, anchored in the river deep in enemy territory, were horribly vulnerable, but the Turks made no move against them and as dawn broke at 0500hrs they were free to continue their remarkable excursion.

Shaitan moved on to lead the other three vessels and was first into Amara. When *Comet*, following on, tied up at Amara on 3 June, Townshend was greeted by 'Halim Bey, the defeated Turkish commander at Kurna, Aziz Bey the Governor of Amara and some 30 or 40 Turkish officers including three or four colonels who came on board to surrender.'[10] The situation now almost descended into farce, but Townshend played his bluff with conviction and recorded that when a whole 'fire brigade battalion' of Turkish soldiers wanted to surrender he sent a naval lieutenant and a private soldier from the Dorsets in a small boat. The coxswain of the boat raised the strength of the party to three – they accepted the surrender of the Battalion, about 600 men, and marched their captives down to the quay, onto a big iron lighter which was then moved to midstream for security. The fire brigade battalion was one of two similar battalions that had been sent from Constantinople to reinforce Halim Bey in the 38th Division at Kurna. They were indeed firemen and their prowess as soldiers was to be proved.

Townshend hectored the Governor about supplies for the 15,000 men 'close on my heels' and insisted on sheep being collected at once.

That evening two Turkish engineer officers dined with Townshend and Nunn aboard *Comet*. The general conversation was in French but Townshend confided in Nunn the absolute necessity of keeping all the POWs under the guns of the British vessels as, if they guessed that rein-forcement was some way off, they might break out. Later in the evening one of the Turks revealed a working knowledge of English and an understanding of the true state of affairs. Townshend made doubly sure that that officer was secured for the night.

The following day the Arabs started on a maelstrom of looting. They sacked the Turkish offices and barracks and were dispersed with machine guns but by now it was starting to dawn on everyone that these 15,000 were more than somewhat overdue. Townshend and his small group had 700–800 prisoners to secure and he could not possibly mount any sort of sally away from his ships. He noted that it was 'on the evening of the 5th or 6th June that I had united all my troops at Amara'.

General Nixon and his staff arrived as soon as it was safe and 'congratu-lated Townshend warmly'.[11] Nevertheless Townshend complained that 'no one . . . seems to have recognised the difficulty of the operation and the possibility of disaster.' Obviously Nixon was not loud enough in his praises.

Nixon was a very relieved and lucky man. He had exceeded his brief when, without reference to London, he had permitted Townshend's advance to Amara. He had suffered a well-deserved and severe rebuke from Lord Crewe and had been obliged to accept complete responsibility for Townshend's activities. Nixon held the Turks in such complete contempt that, not only had he sent Townshend further up the Tigris, he had denuded Townshend of most of his artillery, one of his brigades and had failed to supply any sort of logistic support. There was no doubt that Townshend had pulled Nixon's chestnuts out of the fire.

Townshend had achieved a remarkable feat of arms. He had made a major advance, captured a modern, garrison town, and imprisoned that garrison all without a single lost life. He had taken terrible risks but the proof of the pudding was his occupancy of Amara, the most important town south of

Baghdad. Thus far he had every cause to be proud of his achievements in Mesopotamia, having enjoyed unbridled success at modest cost.

Nixon was not chastened by Lord Crewe's earlier rocket and it became clear that he was intent on taking Nasariyeh and, that being the case, he intended to reinforce Gorringe and 12th Division at Townshend's expense. He refused to return Townshend's assets, contradicted Townshend's plans for the defence of Amara and rejected, out of hand, Townshend's request for six months reserve of supplies – quoting Indian Army authorization as his reason.

The atmosphere between the two generals cooled noticeably.

Townshend, who was physically brave, was somewhat short on moral courage and, unusually for him, he now took a strong position. He said that, on his own authority, he would purchase the required stores and hold them in Amara. He immediately started to implement, what turned out to be, a wise decision with important consequences.

It would be of assistance to the reader who is confused about the geography of Mesopotamia, without the added confusion of military and political strategy, to do the following: place the right-hand palm downwards, fingers extended, and there is a guide to the various operations of IEF 'D' in 1915, as described by Russell Braddon:

> The wrist is the Persian Gulf; the vein running up the back of the hand is the Shatt al Arab   running up past Abadan to Basra; the little finger is the Karun River – at its tip, Ahwaz and oil; the thumb is the Euphrates – at its tip, Nasariyeh; the junction of the thumb and first finger is Kurna; the first finger is the Tigris – at its first joint, Amara; at its tip, Kut el Amara; and running sluggishly down from the tip of that first finger to Nasariyeh at the tip of the thumb, is the shallow Shatt al Hai.

By June 1915, Nixon controlled the wrist and the back of the hand (Abadan and Basra), the little finger (Ahwaz, with its oil), the junction of first finger and thumb (Kurna) and the first finger as far as the first joint (Amara). The Turks held the tip of the first finger (Kut-al-Amara) and the tip of the thumb (Nasariyeh). It was Nixon's contention that the Turks – denied access down the first finger to Kurna and Basra, because he held the first joint – would march and sail from Kut-al-Amara, the first fingertip, down the Shatt-al-Hai to Nasariyeh, the thumb tip, then along the thumb itself (the Euphrates) to Kuna, and so threaten the hand under which Force 'D' held most of Basra province. To protect the hand, he argued, he must seize the entire thumb and all of the first finger – the second and third fingers being unimportant since they pointed only into desert and marshes, and not even the Arabs wanted them.

This was the case, he argued and, in typical Nixon manner, he conveniently ignored the fact that the Shatt-al-Hai is quite unnavigable for a full seven months each year, and navigable only by the shallowest draught vesseis with ...e utmost difficulty during the other five. His argument attracted no dissent from Duff, his military commander, or Hardinge his political superior, neither of whom had any local knowledge.

Thus it was that India approved.

But, Whitehall did not.

On 14 June, Chamberlain cabled Hardinge saying so. The Viceroy countered with a cable saying that, in India's opinion, the advance on Nasariyeh must be made; and when, by 21 June, no reply had been received from Chamberlain, he ordered Nixon to commence, as soon as possible, the operation that Whitehall had vetoed once already.'[12] Townshend had already served in some of the most disagreeable places on the planet – Hunza, Chitrál and Suakin, spring to mind. Basra was awful and Kurna was no better, but Amara was seriously grim. Like Suakin it had looked so much better from a distance – close up it lost its appeal. It was unbearably hot with the glare oi ше sun uncomfortable in the extreme. There was no sanitation system and the evidence was underfoot. The smell turned the stomach and only the myriad flies and mosquitoes seemed to thrive. Mr E.J. Mant, who recalled his service there fifty years before said, 'Amara was a thief-ridden incubator of dysentery, sunstroke, malaria and paratyphoid.'

This unattractive environment was exacerbated by the dearth of medical personnel, equipment and drugs. There was little or nothing that could be done for the soldier who succumbed to illness. The only medical advice on offer was to 'stay out of the sun from 0900hrs until 1800hrs daily'. Sunglasses were sent for but, when they arrived, they were of the cheapest variety from the bazaars of India, and the sepoys were so disgusted with them that they threw them in the river. No doubt the bed of the Tigris is still paved with them.

Cooped up in unsanitary billets, bored, poorly fed, with no water purification system in place and subject to a cocktail of ailments, the men of the 6th Division started to die. Ten days after Amara was taken there were 1,200 men on the sick list many of whom died because Lieutenant General Sir John Nixon had done nothing at all to provide for their fundamental needs, not even the most basic of medical cover. He had failed to supplement his artillery, had failed to build the railway line from Basra, had no system in place for battle casualty replacements and he was content with his five aeroplanes. His force was deficient in wire-cutters, Very pistols, mosquito nets, sun helmets, periscopes, telescopes, hand grenades, blankets and replacement clothing. The two divisions with the misfortune to serve under him had what they wore and what they carried, but little else. Nixon's neglect of these soldiers is one of the most culpable examples of dereliction of duty in the history of the British Army. All the ghastly lessons learned at great cost during the Boer War were wantonly disregarded and thousands of men were to die as a consequence.

Whilst Nixon made his grandiose plans to conquer the remainder of Mesopotamia, Townshend was taken ill and within three days he had deteriorated into a life-threatening condition. Unlike his soldiers he was immediately evacuated downriver and despatched via Bombay to recover in Simla. Townshend had the best possible care but, as he modestly recorded in his diary, 'it was only my splendid constitution that pulled me through.' He spent time in Simla at the house of his friend, Sir James Roberts, and whilst there he wrote to his wife as follows:

This is the first day, my darling, I am up and dressed and am now rapidly getting strong. After the business was over at Amara, I was on a long reconnaissance all day along the road to Baghdad and no one looked after me to see that I had any food and I was too much taken up with my work to think of food, and so I went empty all day under a blazing sun. When I got back my head was on fire and I vomited everything I touched. The sun had taken me and thrown me down and, strong as I am, I was a helpless weak child in two days. To save my life they sent me down in a gunboat to catch the hospital ship leaving Basra for Bombay and Sir John Nixon himself helped to carry me aboard. I nearly died on the voyage.

They say such a rapid hard-hitting pursuit after a victory has hardly a parallel. Eighty miles without stopping and I was so excited and never going to sleep and so determined to destroy all the Turks that I ate nothing. They used to bring me a biscuit or a cup of tea. I took all their guns but two. My constant watchword was 'smite them hip and thigh – the sword of the Lord and Gideon!' I am sure no bloodhound ever followed up his man fugitive with more tenacity.

I told you, darling that I only wanted my chance! You should have seen the British and Indian soldiers cheering me as I stood on the *Comet*. I must have a gift of making men (I mean soldier men) love me and follow me. I have only known the 6th Division for six months and they'd storm the gates of hell if I told them to.

This letter is revealing on two fronts. First his remark about 'not being looked after' is a pathetic statement for any soldier to make. His recce party will have stopped to eat and water their horses at regular intervals and if he had wanted food or water he had only to ask.

Secondly, not even Townshend's greatest detractors would ever accuse him of being anything other than highly heterosexual. It is odd that he has to make this point and to his wife, of all people, when referring to his men.

Sherson commented on this letter describing it as 'rather incoherent, and not wanting in a little trumpet-blowing'. He goes on to add: 'but how natural, the first letter he had written to his wife for a long time'. Townshend, prodigious letter writer that he was, has left enough written evidence upon which to assess him. In this case he would have served his memory better if he had not put that last paragraph to paper. He wrote to his wife in the same letter about Whitmore his soldier servant:

> Whitmore has hopelessly broken down. He knocked up directly we got to Basra. Could do nothing in the heat and, at Kurna, before the battle, he utterly collapsed but persisted in joining me at Amara. He was not much use, but did his best seeing me so ill. He attended me down to the river on the hospital ship, would not leave the door of my cabin . . . the doctors and nurses said it was quite pathetic, he was like a faithful dog but a skeleton himself, like I was, and he had frightful diarrhoea. He is now in the civil hospital in Simla and recovering but I think it is time I pensioned him off home.

This extract is very much to Whitmore's credit. He was a devoted servant and the reference to 'a faithful dog', although not originally Townshend's, is nevertheless a form of words he would have done better to rephrase. What happened to Whitmore is not known. A Private B.S. Whitmore of the Norfolks died in France in August 1918 and is buried in Bagneux Military Cemetery at Gezaincourt, France. It is possible that Whitmore rejoined his regiment and was sent to France where he was killed, or it may be that Whitmore survived the war and died in his bed. However, there is no further reference to him in Townshend's diary and Braddon could not trace him.

During his convalescence Townshend made the best use of time and got down to some serious politicking. He met with the Viceroy and was duly congratulated on his now famous 'regatta' and his taking of Amara. He caught up with his correspondence and wrote again to his wife:,

Gen Redvers Buller VC GCB GCMG (1839-1908). Following the war in South Africa he was, briefly, a publicly acclaimed hero. However, later he was held to be responsible for the deficiencies of the Army in that campaign and sacked. Photographed here in about 1900. (*WWW Crediton*)

EF Knight, the war correspondent, who interrupted his golf to fight with the Hunza-Nagar Field force. Photographed here as an old man. (*Source not known*)

Lieut F Aylmer RE. (Later Lieut Gen Sir Fenton Aylmer VC KCB (1862-1935)). He was seriously misled by Townshend in 1916 and his career was ruined as a result. (*Wikipedia*)

Col Durand CB CI. (*Durand*)

This is the only known image of the gallant sepoy, Nagdu. (*Knight*)

Capt CP Campbell CIH. (*Robertson*)

Sher Afzul and friends – wearing, what looks like, a British Army great coat. (*Robertson*)

Amir-ul-Mulk under close guard and facing an unhappy future. (*National Army Museum*)

The very young Shuja-ul-Mulk 'Sugar and milk' installed as Mehtar by Robertson. (*Robertson*)

Surgeon–Capt HF Whitchurch VC. (*Robertson*)

Chitrál fort looking north. The roof of the water tower is in the centre. The oblique and opposite view today is on the next page. There were enemy sangars on that opposite bank throughout the siege. (*Robertson*)

Chitrál fort viewed from the north and showing the battlefield of 3 March 1895 at the top of the photograph. (*Robertson*)

LOWER ROAD	HAMLET ATTACKED MARCH 3RD	THE BAZAAR-SERAI	OLD MISSION HOUSE	WHERE BAIRD FELL

The enemy view of Chitrál fort showing the north-eastern aspect. The vital Water Tower is centre above the marble rock with rubble from Campbell's covered way between the two. The Stables, the latrine area are front left. (*Robertson*)

A photograph taken in 2008 of the very much changed fort. The marble rock is in the centre of the picture and the base of the old water tower is just behind it where a door is visible. The walls have been reduced in height. (*Col Amir Ali*)

View of the beach and the water tower. The over hanging trees that could have provided access for the attackers can be seen on the right. (*National Army Museum*)

The remains of the sap from the Summer House destroyed by Harley and his party. The wood and stone construction of the fort can be seen in the wall behind. (*Robertson*)

Lieut Col JG Kelly (centre with white beard) and his officers, 'The Saviours of Chitrál.'
(*National Army Museum*)

Lieut HK Harley, Lieut BEM Gurdon, Capt CVF Townshend. Seated. Surg Maj GS Robertson with his wounded left arm in a sling. (*Robertson*)

Mrs. Alice Townshend in 1920.
(*Countess Audrey de Borchgrave-Townsend*)

The re-interment of Capt J McD Baird was on the south bank of the river. The water tower is behind and to the right. There are a high proportion of officers present; judging by the swords and Sam Browne belts. The headstone and grave surround suggest that this ceremony took place some time after the relief. The probability is that Capt Baird rests in this spot to this very day. (*National Army Museum*)

Maj CVF Townshend CB CIH photographed in about 1896. His uniform differs from that of Capt Campbell CIH on page 2 and he could be wearing the dress of his parent regiment, the Indian Staff Corps. (*Sherson*)

Maj Gen GT Pretyman CB, not a man to trifle with and he and CVFT did not blend. Later Maj Gen Sir George Pretyman KCMG CB (1845 – 1917). (*Source not known*)

Marshal of France, Ferdinand Foch (1851-1929). An outstanding military theorist, he was appointed Supreme Commander in March 1918 and his well coordinated attacks in September 1918 led to the final collapse of the German Army and the end of WWI. He was a confidant and good acquaintance of CVFT. (*Source not known*)

Maj Gen Sir Archibald Hunter KCB (1856-1936). He knew CVFT well and was the purveyor of good advice – not always taken. He and Townshend had served together in the Sudan in 1884-85 and again in 1896. He was later Gen Sir Archibald Hunter. (*Maj Gen HH Rich*)

Vere Lodge, Raynham, Norfolk in about 1920 – the home of Sir Charles and Lady Townshend for the latter part of his life. (*Barker*)

Lieut Gen (later Gen) Sir Percy Lake KCB KCMG (1855-1940). He was the first Chief of the Canadian General Staff. In 1916 he replaced Lieut Gen Nixon and assumed command of Indian Expeditionary Force 'D'. (*The Mansell Collection*)

Lord Hardinge (1858-1944), Viceroy of India, 1910-1916. (*National Portrait Gallery*)

Sir Joseph Chamberlain (1863-1937). Secretary of State for India 1915-1917. (*National Portrait Gallery*)

Lieut Gen Sir John Nixon, Commander of Expeditionary Force 'D' in Mesopotamia, 1915-1916. (*Source not known*)

Maj Gen Sir Charles Mellis VC KCB KCMG.
(*Radio Times Hulton Picture Library*)

Maj Gen GF Gorringe, GOC 12th Division. Later
Maj Gen Sir George Gorringe KCB KCMG DSO.
(*The Mansell Collection*)

One of the Tigris steamers upon which operations in Mesopotamia were completely dependant.
(*Source not known*)

HMS *Espiègle*, an elegant ship, photographed in action during the advance up the Tigris from Kurna to Amara on 31 May 1915. CVFT can just be seen in the forward look-out, where he was very exposed. (*Lt Col HG Thompson*)

Water-borne artillery on a Tigris steamer. The gunners have scant protection and the vulnerability of the ship to incoming fire is evident. (*Imperial War Museum*)

Nur-Ud-Din, Defeated by Townshend at Kurna, Amara, Kut and Ctesiphon. (*Turkish General Staff Department of War History*)

Khalil Pasha, Nur-Ud-Din's aggressive second-in-command, who was appointed after the battle of Ctesiphon to replace him. Khalil was the victor at the siege of Kut. (*Turkish General Staff Department of War History*)

Left to right: LCpl J Boggis, CVFT's Turkish ADC Tewfik Bey, CVFT, his ADC Capt Morland Ox & Bucks LI. The soldier on the right, judging by his Light Infantry cap badge, is Morland's batman. His name is not known. (*J Boggis*)

The great arch of Ctesiphon – which survived the battle that bears its name and still stands today. (*Wikipedia*)

The river steamer *Méjidieh*. This unlikely and very unwarlike craft was Chitrál Charlie's accommodation and headquarters during the battle of Ctesiphon. (*AJ Barker*)

Field Marshal von de Goltz (1843-1916), Military Governor of Belgium 1914, where he established a well-deserved reputation for ruthlessness by the expedient of shooting hostages. He was sufficiently unpleasant to draw favourable comments from Adolf Hitler 25 years later. Nevertheless, he proved to be a formidable opponent. (*Source not known*)

Spot, the object of Townshend's affection. (*Sherson*)

The GOC 6th Division with his divisional staff, September 1915. Left to right Capt Clinton (ADC) Maj EE Forbes (DAD Tpt) Col Annesley (AD S&T) Col UW Evans (GSO 1) Col P Hehir (ADMS) CVFT (GOC 6th Div) Capt WFC Gilchrist (DAQMG) Col WW Chitty (AA & QMG) Lieut Col NS Maule (Acting CRA) Lieut Col HO Parr Lieut Col FA Wilson (DCRE).
(Countess Audrey de Borchgrave-Townshend)

The Villa Hampson on the island of Prinkipo which was to be Charles Townshend's 'prison' for over two years.

This Indian soldier, who survived imprisonment and forced labour under the Turks, shows only too graphically the extent of his neglect. Images such as this inflamed public opinion in Great Britain.
(Major EWC Sandes)

The grave of Chitrál Charlie in East Raynham's churchyard. (*Author*)

CVFT on the roof of his headquarters in Kut in 1916. (*Sherson*)

Elected as MP for The Wrekin, CVFT sat as an Independent Conservative from November 1920 until 1923. (*Countess Audrey de Borchgrave-Townshend*)

I passed the medical board yesterday and am sailing from Karachi on August 15th to resume my command in Mesopotamia. I have been very ill but made a rapid recovery owing, the doctors say, to my good constitution . . . I believe I am to advance from Amara to Kut el Amara directly I get to my division. The question is where are we going to stop in Mesopotamia? . . . I stayed with the Viceroy last month but could get nothing out of him as regards his policy. We have certainly not got enough troops to make certain of taking Baghdad, which I hear is being fortified and gun positions installed. We can take no risks of defeat in the east. Imagine a retreat from Baghdad and the consequent instant rising of the Arabs of the whole country behind us, to say nothing of the Persians and the Afghans, for the Amir only keeps his country out of the war with difficulty. You may afford to have reverses and retreats in France, perhaps, but not in the east and keep any prestige. Of our two divisions in Mesopotamia mine is complete but Gorringe's has no guns or divisional troops, and whenever Nixon wants them for himself he takes them from me if Gorringe has to go anywhere. I consider we should hold what we have got and not advance any more so long as we are held up in the Dardanelles.

A friend in the Foreign and Political Department at Simla, who knew of Townshend's views, wrote to him on 9 August 1915 and commented that moving further north to take Kut-al-Amara doubtless had military attractions and there would not be any political objections to such a move. He went on to say that 'I do not think that there is any idea, at present, of an advance to Baghdad, unless the forces at our disposal were more than adequate for the purpose.'

Townshend had a meeting with General Sir Beauchamp Duff, the Commander-in-Chief, who allegedly said to him, 'I quite agree with you. Not one inch shall you go unless I make you up to 30,000 men.' 30,000 men is the complement of an Army Corps and a lieutenant general's command – what is more, that prized third star was usually accompanied by a 'K'. Townshend returned to the fray much refreshed and immeasurably cheered by Duff's words. His prospects looked quite bright but those of his men in Amara were demonstrably worse.

Whilst Townshend had been away the Viceroy had ordered Nixon to take Nasariyeh and to this end one of the 6th Divisions brigades, commanded by Brigadier General Delamain, had moved upstream to Ali Garbi. He left two brigades in the hell-hole of Amara and a fourth brigade was sent to

12th Division to reinforce Gorringe as he advanced up the 'thumb'. The 12th Division was in bad order having been involved in heavy fighting over to the east when it attacked the 'tip of the little finger' and the town of Ahwaz. Gorringe had suffered 50 per cent casualties in this action and once again the lack of medical cover became, literally, painfully obvious.

The survivors of the Battle of Ahwaz had pursued their defeated enemy to the north-west and the general direction of Amara for six bone-wearying weeks, existing on water of the lowest quality and, eventually, on no water at all. It was only when the 6th Division dragged barges filled with potable water down canals to meet them that the depleted 12th Division was able to drink and rest.

These were the men that Nixon now charged with taking Nasariyeh. It was as well that he had a man like Gorringe in command.

In 1911, at the age of forty-three, Gorringe was one of the youngest and most promising major generals in the Aarmy. He is described as 'A big man, highly coloured, deeply tanned, officious and utterly without tact, he reminded those more sensitive than himself of an enormous he-goat and he allowed nothing – not Turks, Nur-Ud-Din (the Turkish commander), counter attacks, casualties, swamps, marsh Arabs or deeply entrenched redoubts – to stop him.'[13] Gorringe was a disagreeable person and a bully. He was, however, a tenacious commander who was able to kept a cool head under pressure. His senior staff officer later, in 1918, when he commanded the 47th Division, was Bernard Montgomery. Montgomery always spoke well of Gorringe and attributed the success of his own 'Chief of Staff system' in the Second World War to the lessons taught by Gorringe.

In contrast, Townshend was referred to and known as 'Charlie' throughout his division and he was held in a measure of affection, certainly by his soldiers, although the view of his officers, as recorded by Braddon, was rather more objective.

'A bit frenchified,' was one opinion.

'A bit of a ladies' man,' was, without doubt, an accurate summation.

'A thruster, you know, the sort of feller that will ride too far ahead and destroy the scent for the hounds and drive the Master mad,' is less complimentary.

'A man who'd rather go to the theatre than a shooting party,' is almost damning.

Finally, 'the only real general in the Indian army; but not exactly a gentleman,' would have cut Townshend to the quick because there was absolutely no doubt at all about his aspirations to gentility.

Despite Townshend's very human deficiencies, he was not all bad.

Gorringe was quite the opposite. He really did not care what his officers and soldiers thought of him, and this lack of a normal human response made him a dangerous, callous and very ruthless man.

Gorringe advanced and took Nasariyeh on 24 July and, with Townshend ensconced in Amara, the ambition of the strategically illiterate Nixon was re-fuelled. The object of Nixon's expedition to Mesopotamia, which had been to secure for the Royal Navy the supply of oil that emanated from the oilfields in the Basra area, was forgotten. The capture of Baghdad, if one ignored the practicalities, looked to be an achievable and attractive new aim. Nixon was encouraged in his plans by his superiors in Simla, who accepted that the first stepping stone would have to be the occupation of Kut-al-Amara.

Whitehall and Chamberlain, in particular, were not enthused. The object of the expedition had already been exceeded and London made it plain that there were no additional troops available to supplement further adventures in this sun-baked and merciless land. It followed that any further movement north would have to depend on the use of the troops already in the theatre, or on reinforcement from India. The Viceroy, Lord Hardinge, doubtless advised by Duff, his commander-in-chief, cabled Chamberlain to say: 'Now that Nasariyeh has been occupied the occupation of Kut-al-Amara is considered, by us, to be a strategic necessity.' Significantly and weakly, London did not forbid a further advance, probably quite unaware that General Sir Beauchamp Duff had yet to visit the theatre of operations (and indeed he never did). Despite his ignorance Duff was not in the least inhibited from advising his political master on military issues of which he had no personal knowledge whatsoever.

This toxic combination of Hardinge, Duff and Nixon was eventually to cost thousands of lives.

To revert briefly to the right-hand analogy: Ahwaz, at the centre of the oilfields and at the tip of the little finger, was secure. Nasariyeh at the tip of the thumb was in the hands of Gorringe. The index finger is the line of the Tigris, and Amara, at the first joint of that finger, had recently been taken by Townshend in his amazing race upriver. Kut-al-Amara the likely next objective lay 90 miles north-west of Amara at the tip of the index finger but twice that distance by way of the sinuous river. The river was the lifeline, the only effective means of moving men and materiel in either direction. The alternative was for troops to move on foot in this forbidding and unforgiving environment.

The Turkish general Nur-Ur-Din had withdrawn all the remnants of his army that had been defeated by Townshend at Kurna and Amara, and by Gorringe at Nasariyeh, to a position astride the Tigris about eight miles south of Kut where he had absorbed the garrison of that town. He had dug in and presented a formidable obstacle to Nixon's ambitions which, notwithstanding the difficulties, had gained lukewarm support from London. London's caveat was that any support was limited to an advance to Kut.

On 23 August, Townshend received his formal orders from Nixon. The stated aim was 'the destruction and dispersal of the enemy who, according to the intelligence already furnished you, are prepared to dispute your advance, and the occupation of Kut-al-Amara, thereby consolidating our control of the Basra Vilayet' (Province).

Townshend was to have at his disposal his own 6th Division plus the 7th Lancers, some additional artillery, the armed steamer *Comet*, the launch *Sumana*, two aeroplanes and two pack wireless sets. Nixon did not deem it necessary to provide additional river craft – he judged that eleven paddle steamers, two tugs and twenty-three lighters were ample to sustain his soldiers, maintain his logistic chain all the way to Kut and evacuate any wounded from engagements fought in that area. The small craft enumerated had barely sufficed for the 140 miles voyage from Basra to Amara. Notwithstanding that, Nixon saw no need to supplement his river assets which would now be required to service a division fighting 290 miles upriver from Basra. Surgeon General Hathaway had diffidently requested that one hospital ship be added to the flotilla to supplement the ad hoc medical arrangements made on one of the paddle steamers.

HQ India ignored the request.

There were no more river craft available and Nixon made no attempt to obtain more. All manner of other war material was deficient; more importantly there were no ambulances. The wounded were to be evacuated in some of the 330 unsprung carts pulled by mules or horses of which he had 740. The lack of any sort of practical evacuation plan for his wounded disgraced every one of the officers responsible. It is to Townshend's shame that he did not make an issue of the dearth of medical cover for his 10,275 combatants (later amended by CVFT to 11,103) and hundreds of supporting coolies. The combatant strength of the Division had been bolstered by an assiduous sift through the sick list and several hundred men were judged to be fit enough to take their place back in the ranks.

Charles Townshend had a heady vision and suddenly, out of the blue, he opined that he would first rout Nur-Ur-Din at Essinn outside Kut, then again at Ctesiphon outside Baghdad, and might also pursue him into Baghdad.' This was a change in his position and he made no caveat about needing 30,000 troops.

Previously, and in the most professional and perceptive manner, Townshend had made quite clear what folly it would be to move north up the line of the Tigris with insufficient force and inadequate support. Now, inexplicably, he abandoned military common sense and, not only did he accept Nixon's order to take Amara, but, quite unprompted, went so far as to suggest enthusiastically that, having taken his objective, he would willingly pursue his enemy a further 190 river miles to Baghdad.

This was madness.

On 29 August 1915, the Major General General Staff (MGGS), Nixon's senior staff officer, enquired how Townshend would take Baghdad, with what troops and with what aim. Charles replied: 'I would carry out a pursuit with my naval flotilla, as I did after the battle of Kurna . . . Act according to circumstances to rescue the European women prisoners there. I should take perhaps a battalion and machine guns with me on the flotilla.'

Well, that all seems to be pretty straightforward – but, in fact, quite divorced from reality.

It will already be evident that Townshend was driven by a degree of ambition that was sufficient to make him unstable. Duff had allegedly said that he would give Townshend 30,000 men and perhaps it was the thought of commanding a corps, putting up a third star and reigning as Lieutenant General Sir Charles Townshend, the Governor of Baghdad, that caused the aberrational change in his position.

Townshend was physically a very brave man but he was not morally brave and, when confronted by his seniors, he was loath to take a minority position. He had displayed just this weak characteristic in Chitrál back in 1895, when he walked on eggshells with the dominating George Robertson. This was a time to demonstrate moral courage and say 'No'. Nixon's ambitions were clear and the easy option was to go along with Nixon's half-baked plans. Sir Percy Scott, Nixon's Political Officer, put the cap on the issue when he remarked to Townshend, 'If you were to go to Baghdad it would have almost the same political significance as if you were to enter Constantinople.' No one expressed any qualms about the expedition that Townshend was about to lead, not even the man who was fully aware that he had insufficient transport to do the job.

Amara, in August, was hot, very hot and the temperature hovered between 110° and 117° F. The troops camped outside the town on the edge of the desert were still beset by flies and endured poor food, but they were spared the olfactory horrors of an Arab settlement.

In 2007, ninety-two years later, very little had changed and Major Chris Hunter RLC wrote recently of Al-Amara (modern spelling) as follows:

> As I climb out of the Warrior, I'm blinded by the brilliant sun. The stench of rotting garbage and crap is all too familiar now, but it still makes me want to puke. It's just like being back on the streets of Basra. I'm beginning to wonder whether every city in this country smells of shit or if they just saved the best ones for us. Among the two-storey flat-roofed buildings and palm-lined boulevards I can feel the simmering tension. It's as if somebody's about to light the blue touch paper and the whole place is going to explode any second. This is supposed to be the location of the Garden of Eden and to those that live there I'm sure al-Amara is the most wonderful place on earth. But as far as I am concerned, this collection of fly-blown hovels in the middle of nowhere is one of the most violent shit-reeking slums I've ever visited . . . Burnt-out cars, festering rubbish and piles of brick and rubble litter every street. Centuries-old buildings have been destroyed by insurgent mortar and RPG fire. Al-Amara is a city in ruins, and the people who live here don't give a damn.[14]

Charles Townshend wrote to Nixon on 2 September and complained about the resources that he had been given. He said:

> I feel very hurt at being told that I am to base my plans on the river and land transport allotted to me. I have cut down my units to the minimum and I have more troops under my command than Lord Wolseley had in the Nile Expedition of 1885. You have given me the most serious and important operation to carry out – the most important and serious one I know of for the last 30 years . . . as for your MGGS saying that I have delayed operations for a fortnight by my demands for transport! I must suppose that he is not serious.

There was more in a similar vein, all from a general who only days before had welcomed his difficult brief, and had offered to expand it and take on greater difficulties. It was a very contradictory posture to strike at this late stage.

Townshend was served by five capable brigade commanders. They were Delamain CB DSO (16 Brigade), Hoghton (17 Brigade), Fry CB (18

Brigade), Smith (Commander RA) and Climo (30 Brigade). The latter of these was a colonel and although he was much the junior of the others he was, nevertheless, their equal in skill and determination. The twelve regular battalions of infantry were eight of the Indian Army and four of the British Army. Two Indian regiments of cavalry completed the teeth of the 6th Division.

Intelligence reports indicated that Nur-Ur-Din had 7,000–8000 infantry and about 3,000 irregular Arab horsemen. He had eighteen guns all sited in well-prepared gun pits. The Turkish leader had been preparing for the British attack since June and had used the time available to good effect. Railway sleepers and steel plate had been moved down from Baghdad and incorporated into his defences. Townshend commented in his diary on the enemy position saying, 'On the right bank there were three lines of trenches, one behind the other with transverse trenches etc. On the left bank there was only one line of entrenchments and the flank was open to the desert.'

The river, which of course flowed through the position, was blocked by two mahailas and eight barges, all filled with sand and rocks. These floating obstacles, low in the water, were linked by heavy duty chains, presenting a barrier that would not be easy to breach. Nur-Ur-Din had a boat bridge well to his rear and beyond artillery range.

Townshend embarked his headquarters in the steamer *Mejidieh* and moved upriver to Ali-al-Gharbi on 11 September where he concentrated his division. He transferred to *Comet* and made a personal reconnaissance up the river as far as Sheikh Saad. Of inestimable value at this juncture was the use of an aeroplane piloted by a Major Reilly, who provided detailed intelligence upon the Turkish dispositions. On 15 September, the Division moved cautiously forward to Abu Rummanah about eight miles short of the Turkish position at Essinn. The stage was now set for the Battle of Kut-al-Amara.

Townshend resolved to attack the Turkish stronger left flank but first to feint at the right flank. He believed that Nur-Ur-Din would respond to the feint allowing the 'Principal Mass' of the 6th Division to launch a determined assault on the left.

'A picture is worth a thousand words' as some sage once remarked, and the sketch map (produced after the war at Townshend's behest) that follows on Page 191 illustrates the movements made by the two adversaries. The Turkish left flank lay behind 2,000 yards of two impenetrable, brackish, mosquito-ridden swamps. These were the Suwada marsh and the Ataba marsh. There was a gap between the two and this gap was to prove to be significant.

Townshend, great student of military history and tactics that he was, viewed the forthcoming battle almost as an intellectual exercise. He had a clear vision, was completely self-confident and issued a communiqué to his men saying:

> Major General Townshend wishes to say that the 6th Division has fought five engagements in the last eleven months and has gained in the Empire a reputation second to none . . . There is no need for him to remind the troops of what their King and Country expect of them and he hopes that a good blow struck now may well end their Mesopotamian labours.

This was a curiously phrased message in the third person and it did not have the highly personalized tone of his later communiqués. The less welcome news was that Nixon wanted to be present at the battle and he sailed upstream to join Townshend.

On the night of 26 September, Brigadier Fry's 18 Brigade was positioned alongside the river and confronting the Turkish element that lay between the Suwada marsh and the Tigris. The following morning the two British generals climbed up into an observation tower that had been constructed during the night and through their glasses were able to follow the early stages of the drama. The desert was almost flat, it had minor undulations but, nevertheless, it was a lethal piece of country for heavily laden assaulting infantry.

Townshend saw, over to his left, several thousand of his men making a great show of advancing and then digging in, in front of the Turkish lines. They had with them as many carts as they could find, and at a distance and with the dust they created the enemy was deceived into thinking that they were artillery. Nur-Ur-Din responded by moving his reserves across the river to counter the anticipated general assault just as 'Chitrál Charlie' had hoped.

In the meantime his 'main force'[15] had crossed the river and headed six miles into the desert. This would allow part of it to outflank the enemy beyond the Ataba marsh and the remainder to drive a wedge into the enemy front between the two marshes. The plan had been compromised by the desertion of a small group of Punjabis during the evening prior to the attack and Townshend feared that they would reveal his plan.

They duly did just that.

Nur-Ur-Din did not believe them.

Fry's 18 Brigade added to the feint by advancing up the river line with

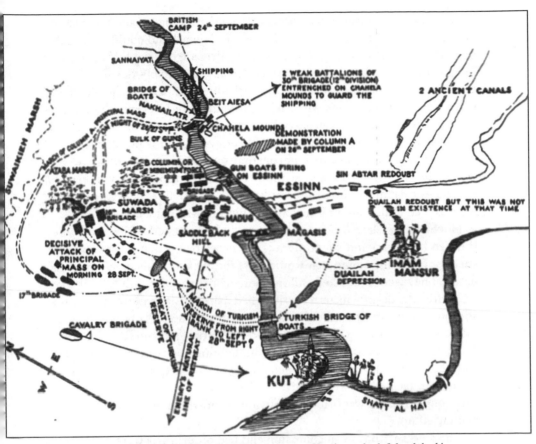

Fig 9. Sketch map of the Battle of Kut-al-Amara. Kut is on the left bank looking downstream; the river flows to the top in this sketch map, that is broadly east. Many accounts refer to either the left or right bank. Aylmer faced the same defensive positions in January–March 1916. (CVFT)

the maximum amount of dust. The Brigadier deployed his machine-gun crews to best advantage but their mortality rate was high as the Turks perceived this to be the main assault. Fry was supported by the guns of the naval flotilla and Nur-Ur-Din had every reason to suppose that the main attack was now in progress along the river line. In their tower Townshend and Nixon waited anxiously for an indication that, over to their far right, 17 Brigade was finding a route between the Suwaikieh and Ataba marshes, while close to hand 16 Brigade was exploiting the gap between the Ataba and Suwada marshes. It was a tense time as Fry's 18 Brigade was being incessantly hammered by the entrenched Turks.

Delamain (17 Brigade) telephoned to say that he had made the passage on the far right of the British line. However, Townshend could see no sign of Hoghton (16 Brigade). Unfortunately 16 Brigade had got lost during the long, dark, outflanking march across a terrain completely devoid of landmarks. He was unable to advise of his difficulties because his signallers had exhausted their telephone wire. When daylight would eventually dawn it would bring the usual heat haze that precluded any sort of visual signal. Hoghton had no radio, a deficiency that compounded his problems.

Regardless of Hoghton's peregrinations Delamain's brigade was committed to the attack and without adequate supporting artillery. 17 Brigade was launched into the assault and the front-line Turkish trenches were carried at the point of the bayonet but not without a cost.

Hoghton was late but eventually, having 'marched miles and miles through that grim and silent night – the order being that no man should speak or make any sound that would alert the enemy',[16] his men joined the battle. They were exhausted and foot sore before they fired their first shot.

16 Brigade, despite its tardy arrival, had marched around the enemy line and now found itself in the Turkish rear area. It was a situation that the soldiers, tired as they were, all knew had to be exploited and they fell on the enemy's communication trenches and his administrative areas. They killed countless surprised Turks and when they reached the front line found their opponents facing the wrong way. A bloodbath ensued and although the close-quarter battle was brutal, before it had ended the two British brigades had linked up.

The Turks withdrew in confusion and bad order, their trenches heaped with dead and dying. In a perfect world they would have been pursued, but the British troops were at the end of their tether and many men of 16 and 17 Brigades simply stopped and rested among the Turkish dead.

For 18 Brigade the day was not yet done and as they pressed forward to join 16 and 17 Brigades they were silhouetted against the late afternoon sun sinking in the west. They presented an easy target and in the face of withering fire had no option but to stop, go to ground and scrape some sort of cover in the sand.

Townshend had devised the plan, Nixon had endorsed it but, with Fry's 18 Brigade burrowing for its life, their influence was slight. Townshend was out of touch with his formations and ordered Major Reilly to fly to Delamain to obtain a situation report. When the report was delivered by the intrepid Reilly, the bones of it were that 17 Brigade was utterly spent. The protracted exertion, the stress of hand-to-hand action and the all-pervading heat temporarily combined to stop the Brigade in its tracks. The men slept among the Turkish dead in the trenches. It was late afternoon before they were in a fit state to continue operations and when they did it was to repulse and shatter the Turkish reserve which had mounted a counter-attack.

Townshend ordered his flotilla to move upstream to seize the enemy shipping which he anticipated that Nur-Ur-Din would use to withdraw his surviving troops. The river, however, was blocked by a heavy iron barge anchored with heavy chains. An attempt to cut the chains from a small boat failed and a most gallant naval officer was killed in the process.

Night fell and Fry was ordered to cease fire with his guns as there was a chance of inflicting damage on 17 Brigade who were now established behind the Turkish line that confronted Fry. 17 Brigade was very well placed to assault the Turkish rear and join up with 18 Brigade and, had they been able to so, would have carried the day. However, the men of 17 Brigade were totally exhausted; they dug scrapes in the sand and slept as and when they could.

Townshend turned to Nixon and said, 'The battle is won; they'll go in the night.' Once again he was correct and at dawn the Turks had gone to pastures (well, desert) new leaving behind only their masses of wounded and thirteen guns.

Townshend had estimated that he would suffer 6 per cent losses; in fact the butcher's bill was 12 per cent. Now the indigenous Arabs fell upon the dead of both sides, plundering and stripping the bodies as they lay. They treated the wounded with merciless ferocity during that long, very cold night. The British and Indian wounded who were fortunate enough to survive were put upon unsprung carts and carried, bumping at every turn of the wheels, across broken ground to the river bank where, in blinding sunshine, tormented by flies and with only the minimum of medical assistance, they were loaded onto iron lighters. The lighters were towed slowly downriver to Amara. There were no sanitary arrangements on these lighters and, by journey's end, the men were lying in a ghastly stew of blood, excrement and soiled clothing. The measure of the culpable lack of preparedness was that whisky crates had to be broken up to provide splints, men died on this ghastly journey and many of those deaths were avoidable. Had all of this been a single isolated case it would have been reprehensible. Sadly, it was to be repeated.

In the battlefield trenches the dead were already starting to putrefy.

The two sides had been fairly evenly matched and there can be no doubt that it was Townshend's generalship that made the difference. The Turks lost 1,289 killed and wounded (CVFT claimed 1,700) and 700 prisoners. British and Indian losses were 1,229 killed and wounded. Nevertheless, the

6th Division held the ground, Nur-Ur-Din had retreated and the world was Townshend's oyster. This was arguably the high water mark in Townshend's life and career.

Little did he know that, from here on, his star would wane.

Notes
1. Lord Hardinge of Penshurst (1858–1944). Said to be one of the most distinguished diplomats of his day but his reputation was damaged by the campaign in Mesopotamia.
2. General Sir Beauchamp Duff GCB, GCSI, KCVO, CIE, KstJ (1850–1918), Commander-in-Chief India, 1914–1916.
3. The Mesopotamia Commission. 1917.
4. Time would show that Barrett's illness was fortuitous. It saved him from the blight that affected the future of every other general engaged in the campaign of 1915–16 and he went on to greater things, becoming Field Marshal Sir Arthur Barrett GCB GCSI KCVO ADC. He died in 1926 aged sixty-nine.
5. Mr J. Boggis, 1967, quoted in Braddon, op cit.
6. CVFT.
7. The shrine of Ezra, the Jewish prophet, is located on the plain of the Tigris River. It was Ezra who returned to Jerusalem at the end of the Babylonian exile. According to biblical scholars, Ezra died years later at this spot in Mesopotamia, called Uzair, at age 120. Locals believe Ezra died while roaming through the area. His shrine survives in this predominantly Shiite district of Amara province. Baghdad is 268 miles distant
8. CVFT.
9. CVFT.
10. Ibid.
11. Braddon, op cit.
12. The Mesopotamia Commission, 1917.
13. Braddon, op cit.
14. Hunter, *Eight Lives Down*.
15. CVFT always used terms such as 'main force' or 'principal mass' and rarely referred to formations such as 18 Brigade.
16. Diary of Mr D.R. Holzmeyer. Later estimated to have been 20 miles.

Chapter 13

October–November 1915
Advance to Ctesiphon and the
Retreat to Kut

'Success in battle comes from a combination of the skill and daring of the leader and the skill and confidence of the led.

Field Marshal the Lord Harding of Petherton

Townshend commented that:

> The battle of Kut-al-Amara can be said to have been one of the most important in the history of the British Army in India. There had been nothing of its magnitude either in the Afghan war or the Indian mutiny. For it was fought against troops equally well armed and of equal numbers to ourselves. In addition we ejected them from a very strong and up-to-date position, commanding ground as flat and open as a billiard table.

The soldiers of the 6th Division held their general in the very highest regard. He had won every battle whilst in command with apparent ease and, as a result, 'Chitral Charlie' was the toast of Mesopotamia. He had imbued the Division with some of his own burgeoning self-confidence. The Turks were in awe of him and wondered if he was irresistible. Turkish prisoners treated Townshend with an attitude of out-and-out reverence – which he probably found most agreeable.

Although he was not a person 'to hide his light,' there is no doubt that Townshend had indeed won yet another superb victory and his comment above had not overstated the case. But, and this is the big 'but' . . . he had failed to destroy Nur-Ur-Din's forces, which had successfully withdrawn to fight another day.

War is beset with unknowns and Townshend could not know that Hoghton's brigade would get lost in the desert, could not have anticipated the complete exhaustion of Delamain's Brigade, nor would he have anticipated that his indifferently mounted cavalry would refuse to pursue retreating Turks because they had not carried with them their clearly marked cooking vessels. They absolutely would not use Arab cooking pots. As a result, this might just be the only instance in military history that an overwhelming victory was denied by the absence of . . . cooking pots!

General Sir Beauchamp Duff cabled his congratulations to the commander of the 6th Division, in his message saying that he was 'deeply aggrieved to hear of your unavoidable losses . . . trusting that the wounded are doing well'.[1] This was high-end hypocrisy because Duff had been instrumental in denying those soldiers adequate medical cover. They went into action without ambulances, a field hospital or a properly equipped hospital ship to back them up. The men who died of neglect after the battle went to their graves not knowing that Duff was responsible for their demise.

King George V, the sailor King, could teach his admirals and generals a thing or two about caring for their men and during the war there were several examples of his concern. He wrote to Lieutenant General Sir John Nixon offering congratulation on the success at Kut-al-Amara but enquiring as to the welfare of the wounded.

Nixon, when replying to his sovereign, deliberately lied. For a senior officer to mislead the King deliberately is off the scale of dishonourable conduct. Nixon said: 'sick and wounded are well and it is hoped that many will be back in [the] ranks shortly. Spirit of troops splendid.'[2] In fact nothing could have been further from the truth because the medical situation was dire. This misleading action of Nixon's was compounded when he sent a similarly worded message to the Viceroy, who too had expressed a concern for the well-being of the men.

Townshend occupied Kut but assembled the bulk of the Division at Aziziyah a few miles upriver from Kut. Here the river was narrower and shallower so that progress by boat above Kut was very slow, even small vessels being constantly grounded. Early October 1915 was the time to consolidate, rest, take stock, reinforce and consider carefully the strategic aim of the campaign – which, to reiterate, was to secure the oilfields way to the south of Kut-al-Amara. That original aim became 'incidental' because Hardinge, Duff and Nixon had by now set a new goal quite unrelated to the national needs. Townshend and his division were to be the tools to achieve that goal. It was nothing less than the capture and occupation of Baghdad.

It became clear from aerial reconnaissance that Nur-Ur-Din had retired in good order and was now building his defences at Ctesiphon. He was establishing a formidable position and had been reinforced with further reinforcements on the way. His troops were not the disorganized rabble defeated earlier in the south – many of his force now were experienced and seasoned soldiers. A decision had to be taken by the British as to what to do next. Townshend, as a student of military history, was aware that his line of operations and his line of communications were one and the same, and that the River Tigris was central to any activity. The 6th Division, now in possession of Kut, was at the end of a very vulnerable line of communication. Townshend had no desire to extend this line and exacerbate his position by proceeding further, but he was about to be hoist with his own petard.

He had made clear to Nixon before the Battle of Kurna that he faced a vastly difficult and daunting task and had indeed asked for the support of the 12th Division to do the job. As it was, his 'regatta' carried the day with little more than one brigade and that had taken small losses. He had gone on to take Amara at no cost at all. He had explained to Nixon that capturing Kut would present an enormous challenge and success was not assured. Once again he had carried the day. Little wonder then that Nixon had every confidence in Townshend and believed that, in him, he had an instrument that would continue to enhance the reputation of the Indian Army . . . and himself. The minarets of Baghdad now beckoned invitingly and Nixon was not going to stop at Kut. If he had to lie to ensure a further advance then so be it. He was pushing against an open door because the compliant General Sir Beauchamp Duff and Hardinge, the Viceroy, were quite content to ignore completely the firm direction from London, received on 14 October, that the 6th Division was to stand fast at Kut until the reinforcement issues had been resolved.

Townshend started to get cold feet.

He had previously waxed and waned on the degree to which he could and should advance, and, in large measure he had fed Nixon's ambition. Now that it looked increasingly likely that he was to be asked to 'put his money where his mouth was' and crack on to the north, he thought it prudent to get some defensive words on paper and into the public domain. He was now firmly against any movement north of Kut and said so. Later generations would say, indelicately, that he was 'covering his arse' and that would be an accurate summation.

On 3 October 1915, Townshend remarked: 'I sent the famous telegram which has been so much discussed in both Houses of Parliament and in the Press.' The telegram said:

By the aviator's report attached, you will see that the chance of breaking up the retreating Turkish forces, which by now have taken up a position at Salman Pak (Ctesiphon) no longer exists. The position is astride the Baghdad road and the Tigris and it is estimated to be six miles of entrenchments . . . my opinion, if I may be allowed to express one,[3] is that up to the battle of Kut our object has been to occupy the strategical position of Kut and to consolidate ourselves in the Vilayet (province) of Basra. Ctesiphon is now held by the defeated Turkish forces. Should it not be considered politically advisable by the Government to occupy Baghdad at present on account of the doubtful situation at the Dardanelles, and the possibility of our small force being driven out of Baghdad by strong forces from Anatolia, which would compel us to retire down a long line of communications (Baghdad to the sea is 400 miles), teeming with Arabs, at present more or less hostile, whose hostility would become active on hearing of our retreat, then I consider that on all military grounds we should consolidate our position at Kut. The sudden fall of water, which made the advance of our ships most difficult and toilsome, upset our plans of entering Baghdad on the heels of the Turks while they were retreating in disorder.[4] If on the other hand, it is the desire of the Government to occupy Baghdad, then unless great risk is to be run, it is, in my opinion, absolutely necessary that the advance from Kut by road should be carried out methodically by two divisions or one Army Corps or by one division supported closely by another complete division, exclusive of the garrisons of the important places of Nasariyeh, Ahwaz and Amara.

Townshend's telegram attracted enormous attention and projected him right into the public eye as his views were discussed in both Houses of Parliament. Although slanted and somewhat self-serving as he angled once again for command of a corps, it nevertheless did make several perfectly valid and blindingly obvious points. The parlous condition of the river was one, the length of the line of communication a second and the need for adequate resources a third. He remarked that: 'It is not discipline to *protest* [CVFT's italics]. My long experience of the army, and, in particular, my acquaintance with military history, told me that if I considered that the mission I was given might entail disaster to my country, my duty was to warn my superior.'

In passing and, in a display of erudition, he went on to compare himself with Wellington who, in 1808, had been placed in a similar situation. He observed, quite correctly, that when Napoleon entered Moscow in 1812 he was 570 miles from Nieman. The Emperor had 213,000 men but had 600,000 men guarding his line of communications.

Nevertheless, Napoleon failed.

In this case, IEFD of only 25,000 men was committed to the defence of a line of communications already 320 miles long and totally dependent upon the Tigris. There were lessons to be learned here. Charles Townshend had many skills and, not least of them was to compare himself and his situation, usually favourably, with those faced by the great generals of the past. He knew that military history repeats itself, generation upon generation, and mistakes are invariably replicated. His new, much more pragmatic, position was no more than an expression of his military education, combined with his instinctive judgment of all the factors.

Townshend waited with his division at Azizieh and promptly received a rebuke from Nixon's Chief-of-Staff for presuming to disagree with Nixon's 'appreciation of the situation'. The Army Commander had determined that the Turks had only 4,000 bayonets, 500 sabres and twenty guns, and, on this basis, Townshend would have a superiority of better than 2:1. Nixon was not in the least swayed by Chitrál Charlie's view and promised 'jam tomorrow' in the shape of a reinforcing division from France. This was cynically and dishonestly misleading, although Nixon and his MGGS, significantly, did not indicate when this additional division would arrive. However, whenever, if ever, it did arrive it would not be in a position to participate in operations for months, and Nixon knew that. Nevertheless, he ordered Townshend to submit to him plans for the defeat of Nur-Ud-Din at Ctesiphon and the capture of Baghdad.

Townshend, having had his say, accepted both the rebuke and the decision. He set about preparing for the stern test that lay ahead.

In the meantime, battle casualty replacements to make good the losses in the previous engagement were filtering into the Division, and the commander was singularly unimpressed by their quality. Hitherto his success had owed much to the professionalism and tenacity of his British battalions, the Norfolks, Dorsets and Ox & Bucks, but because they had been in the thick of the action their numbers were now sorely depleted and they were at half strength or less. More reliance would have to be placed on the Indian units in the future and it was to these battalions that the low-grade, inexperienced replacements were sent. Many of them were Muslims and there was a marked and stated reluctance to attack Ctesiphon as it was the holy place of Salman Pak, a saintly follower of

Mohammed. He was said to have been the prophet's barber and was buried there.

One entire battalion of Indian soldiers deserted in such numbers that the remainder were returned to India. This attrition alone reduced the 6th Division to 8,600 bayonets, albeit it was 14,000 strong – to put that into context a division serving on the Western Front had an establishment of just over 19,000. Townshend recorded: 'it was on the infantry that I relied to win battles.' He never had enough and the infantry he did have bore a very heavy burden.

Delamain warned Townshend that the morale of his Indian troops was low and he went as far as to say that he was convinced that if they had to assault solidly held trenches again they would not succeed. This galvanized Townshend. By 11 October, he had ascertained that not only did Nur-Ud-Din's force match his own numerically, but that the Anizeh and Shammar Arab tribes, with thousands of fighting men, had joined with the enemy. The balance was changing quickly and clearly every last man would count. So from Azizieh, Townshend harried Basra for the return of the hundreds of British soldiers employed on domestic duties as clerks, batmen drivers, bodyguards, marines on river launches et al. A few were grudgingly released back to him but not all.

Very much in character, Townshend wrote to the Viceroy, privately, commenting that his troops 'had their tails down' and were not pleased at approaching the sacred precincts of Salman Pak[5] . . . 'troops not confident'. There was more in a negative tone and much of the message sent to Hardinge in this letter was untrue. In fact, some Indian units were low but generally the force was confident that it could take on and beat anything Nur-Ud-Din had to offer. The greater majority of the Indian soldiers were *nimak hilal* or 'true to their salt' (to quote Braddon), and what was more they had no doubt that 'Chitrál Charlie', now referred to by some as the 'Man of Mesopotamia', would see them through. This latter appellation would soon be quietly dropped until later re-attributed to General Maude, the officer who eventually captured Baghdad.

Townshend frequently, and throughout his career, strayed outside the chain of command – his private letter to the Viceroy was just the latest example and there was an inferred criticism of Nixon contained therein. He then took considerable offence when he discovered that Nixon's staff was dealing directly with units of the 6th Division and by-passing his divisional headquarters. He would have none of that and took up the issue with the Chief-of-Staff saying: 'Will you kindly inform me if the Army commander is commanding this operation in person, or if he intends me to command as

I did in the Kut operations?' A contrite Nixon conceded that Townshend had a point, agreed that he was in command and there was no more direct interference.

Hardinge and Duff had been warned that IEFD was very deficient in water transport. This lack of capacity was the weakest link in a very weak chain as events would soon prove. Hardinge, sitting in all his vice-regal glory in Simla, did not pass on this vital information to London. In blissful ignorance the Cabinet took comfort that IEFD was well equipped for its water-borne activities and considered the possibility of reinforcing Nixon as Hardinge had categorically stated that India could provide no further support. The Western Front and the Dardanelles were swallowing thousands of men on a daily basis and the Cabinet's options were very limited. Reinforcement, only ever a 'definite maybe', was now just a myth.

Almost incidentally, a programme to build river boats was put in place, but it was far too late. The boats took time to be designed, built and delivered. Then they were found to have too deep a draught and to be too wide in the beam – but that particular nonsense still lay in the future.

The 6th Division waited at Azizieh for five weeks in the mind-sapping sun, which generated 110°–120°F each and every day without respite. The heat was accompanied by hosts of flies and slowly the sick list started to grow. There were no fresh vegetables and beriberi became an increasing problem. The force had no Very pistols, telescopic sights or wire-cutters but it did have hundreds of sporting rifles which had taken up valuable shipping space. Now they provided the means for officers to slaughter and reduce the number of sand grouse in the area which, until then, had been mere spectators to the war. The soldiers did not get fat on the product of the shooting.

Officers and men who were employed on garrison duties in Nasariyeh, Basra and Amara were all anxious to be in Baghdad and prepared for shooting of a different sort. They wanted to be in at the kill and there was no shortage of people wanting to join 'Charlie' in his next conquest. For Charlie himself it was rather different – he had no illusions and his plan catered as much for the withdrawal of his survivors as it did for the occupation of Baghdad. He entertained very serious doubts about the enterprise and it was unfortunate that he was almost alone in holding this view.

London finally agreed that, at some unspecified time in the future, it would provision two divisions and suggested that on a temporary basis India might find a division from its resources. Hardinge replied, predictably and negatively, 'in no case could I undertake to supply from India, even temporarily, a further force of the strength of one division'.[6] Hardinge then had the brass neck to say that, given the offer of two divisions in the future, and unless London advised him to the contrary, he intended to order Nixon to march on Baghdad immediately. Chamberlain replied: 'If Nixon is satisfied that the force he has is sufficient for the operation, he may march on Baghdad. Two divisions will be sent as soon as possible, but . . . will take time to dispatch.'

Thus by inept, long-distance management, with none of the principals having any accurate information about the situation and without any personal knowledge of the issues that Townshend faced, IEFD, and the 6th Division in particular, were committed to an operation that had little or no chance of success.

On 15 October, Townshend received a 'fizzer' from Nixon who wanted 'to know what on earth your engineers are doing' in demanding defence materials. Nixon viewed this as indicative of a defensive attitude in the 6th Division. Azizieh was less than 50 miles by road from Baghdad but it was 90 miles north of Kut by river and Nixon's rebuke was not only ill-timed but was further poor judgment on his behalf. It was also an irritant for Townshend who considered that Azizieh was sufficiently close to the enemy to warrant his defensive actions. In defensive terms there was also the question of the security of the convoys of mahailas making their laborious way upriver in the face of hostile Arabs on the right bank of the Tigris, usually at close range.

This hostility was exemplified by the attack by about forty Arabs upon Frazer's Post an encampment (on the right bank) of the 110th Mahrattas, about four miles below Azizieh. Ten Indian soldiers were killed and a dozen rifles were lost. Much more important were the facts: first, that a group of irregular Arabs felt confident enough to attack a defended military position; second, that they were successful; and third, that the sepoys panicked under the attack. It was only the personal bravery and leadership of the Commanding Officer, Colonel Frazer, which saved the day. Townshend was sufficiently concerned that he made a personal investigation of the incident. Two Indian officers were tried by court martial and 'broken for cowardice, together with three or four sepoys'.[7]

On 12 November, *Firefly*, a new, fast and well-armed gunboat was sent south to meet a convoy beating upriver, under sail, and long overdue. It was just one example that underscored the complete dependence of 6th Division upon the river for resupply. The vessels allocated to the Division for the assault on Ctesiphon and which were absolutely critical were: HMS *Firefly*, *Samana* (an old armoured tug), *Comet* (an old paddle-wheel steamer),

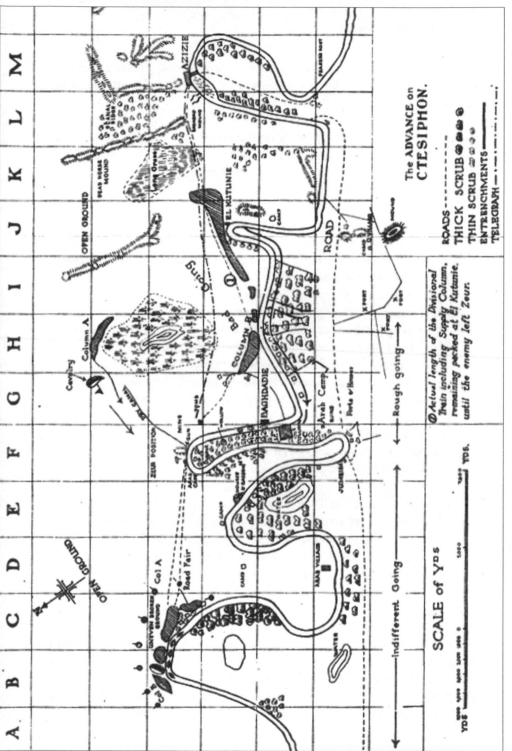

Fig 10. Sketch map of the Advance to Ctesiphon. (CVFT)

Shaitan (armoured tug), *Mejidieh*, *Blosse Lynch*, *Mosul*, *Julnar* and *Salimi* (all river steamers). Of this group *Blosse Lync*h and *Mosul* were designated 'Hospital Clearing Ships'.

Several weeks later, and four days after the assault on Ctesiphon had started, Sir Mark Sykes MP, writing in *The Daily Telegraph* of 22 November 1915, commented with chilling accuracy upon the disparate flotilla of vessels upon which the very survival of IEFD depended. He wrote:

> There are paddle-steamers which once plied with passengers, and now waddle along with a barge on either side, one perhaps containing a portable wireless station and the other bullocks for heavy guns ashore; there are once-respectable tugs which stagger along under a weight of boiler plating, and are armed with guns of varying calibre; there is a launch which pants indignantly between batteries of 4.7"s, looking like a sardine between two cigarette boxes; there is a steamer with a Christmas tree growing amidships, in the branches of which its officers fondly imagine they are invisible to friend or foe. There is also a ship which is said to have started life as an aeroplane in Singapore, shed its wings but kept its aerial propeller, took to water and became a hospital. . . *And this fleet is the cavalry screen, advance guard, rear guard, flank guard, railway, general headquarters, heavy artillery, line of communications, supply depot, police force, field ambulance, aerial hanger and base of supply of the Mesopotamia Expedition* [author's italics].

The sketch map at Fig 10 on Page 203 illustrates the sinuous nature of the Tigris and the character of the ground that had to be traversed.

General Nixon accompanied by Sir Percy Scott, the Political Officer, took passage from Basra in the *Malamir* and arrived in Azizieh on 13 November. Nixon wanted to enter Baghdad as a conqueror and to do so he had to be on hand – his presence will have taken up Townshend's valuable time as the junior was bound to defer to Nixon's needs, both domestic and professional. Charles Townshend ordered the construction of a pontoon bridge in order to allow a column of his troops to advance up the opposite bank, and the Sapper Major charged with the job was obliged to improvise with local boats as he had insufficient pontoons. Nixon decided to inspect the bridge and the following exchange was reported.[8] Nixon asked if the boats were satisfactory and was surprised to be told that they were not enough.

Nixon enquired, 'Why don't you use pontoons?'

'Only eighteen pontoons authorized, Sir,' replied the harassed Major.

'Wire India for more,' commanded Nixon to one of his staff officers. Then, turning back to the Sapper, the General continued, 'How many do you want?'

Pontoons were expensive and the Major wondered if he dare ask for twenty but, before he could respond Nixon offered, 'A hundred?'

The Major was speechless; this was riches beyond his wildest dreams. His silence caused Nixon to up the ante. 'Two hundred?' he suggested.

'Fifty, Sir,' replied the Major.

Nixon gave instructions for a demand to be placed on India for fifty pontoons at once. It was no more than a futile gesture because the pontoons simply did not exist either in Mesopotamia or India.

On 15 November Townshend marched the Division to El Kutunie, a distance of about seven miles, where it joined up with the advance guard commanded by Hamilton, who had occupied it on 11 November. Three days later the much-delayed ships caught up and brought with them very welcome supplies.

The Turks came from behind their defences and advanced down the river line to threaten Zeur. They were in considerable strength, 5,000–6,000 strong. Townshend responded at once, formed his force into two columns about three miles apart and went to meet the threat. The Turks withdrew and Townshend and his division bivouacked 14 miles upriver from Azizieh at Zeur. The battle for Ctesiphon could not be delayed much longer and the portents were not good.

The Turks were established in two well-constructed trench lines, each about two miles long, on the left-hand side of the river, looking downstream; the trenches ran all the way to the river. On the right-hand side of the river the ground was very broken and difficult to cross. There were dried water courses and canals in various states of repair, each one providing comfort to the enemy. The ground was impassable for cavalry and wheeled vehicles such as guns and ammunition limbers. Attacking on the right-hand bank was not a viable option for Townshend, and Nur–Ud–Din, secure in his command post, knew it. The Turks were well prepared for the coming attack which they expected to come on the left and were comforted to know that massive reinforcement from the north was due at any time. The historic arch of Ctesiphon[9] was located in the middle of the Turkish position. There were boat bridges in place behind Nur–Ud–Din's lines which would enable him to move his forces across the river at will.

The sketch map at Fig 11 illustrates the layout of the battlefield and

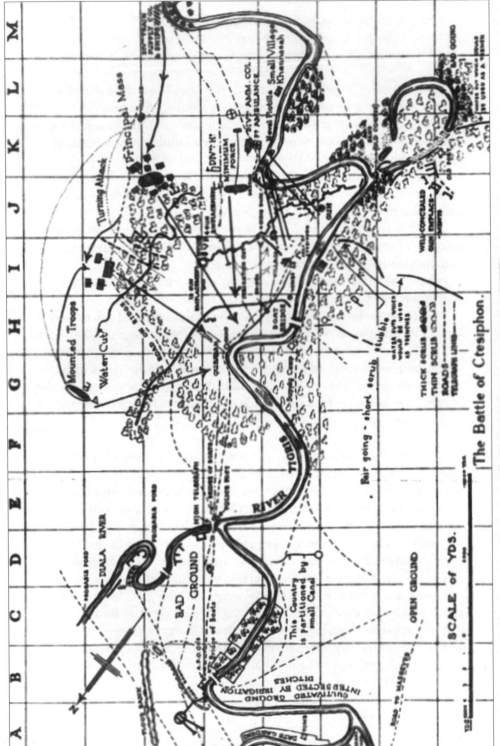

Fig 11. The Battle of Ctesiphon. (CVFT)

shows the sequence of events as Townshend planned them. He explained
the plan as follows:

At Kut-al-Amara I divided my force in to two portions – a minimum
force, Column 'B', and a Principal Mass or maximum force, Column
'A.' Whilst I held onto the enemy with Column 'B' I gave the round
arm swing and punch with Column 'A'. The cavalry co-operated with
the attack of the offensive wing of manoeuvre working on its exterior
flank which is the accepted position for the bulk of the cavalry in battle
in both the French and German armies. It will be observed that in the
coming battle I have added another portion or rather divided my force
into three portions.
    The Minimum Force or Preparatory Attack.
    The Turning Attack with which mounted troops co-operate.
    The Principal Mass or Decisive Attack.
    The reason for this is that the enemy will expect me now to repeat
the distribution of troops in deployment as was made at Kut-al-
Amara, and will endeavour to meet the turning attack with his reserve
of 3000–4000 men, placed back as far as Qusabah (centre of Fig. 11).
I hope to surprise him at a time when the Turning Attack is hotly
engaged, with a powerful blow of the Principal Mass delivered on the
spot marked V P (see sketch map). That is the Vital Point.
    If during the attack of the Principal Mass, the enemy counter-
attacks any other portion of my force, all the threatened troops have
to do is to hold on and the vigour of the Decisive Attack will be
increased. The success of the Principal Mass at the Vital Point means
ultimate success at all points.
    In addition, I trust to Column 'C' (mounted troops) to paralyse all
action of the enemy's general reserve by attacking him in the rear.
    Though the three attacks (in reality four counting the attack of the
mounted troops as being distinct from the 18th Brigade's turning
attack) appear to be separated, they are not so in reality, for I shall place
them at distances apart, not beyond effective field artillery range, i.e.
a distance of from 4000 to 2500 yards.
    Role of Preparatory Attack:-
    If I attack on the left bank, in all probability the Preparatory Attack
under General Hoghton will move frontally against the enemy on a
front of, say, 1000 yards with his right resting on the telegraph line.
The Divisional Artillery will be with the Preparatory Attack so as to
aid it. Thus General Hoghton's role will be to attack the left wing of

the enemy which is furthest from his line of retreat. His role is characterized by a defensive attitude and is analogous with our Second or Defensive Field in strategy . . . he will work his way forward aided by the artillery to within long range of the enemy. Not only is his role to hold the enemy by the collar in his position, but, by making a great display and fight, he should induce him to use up his reserves. He will utilize all natural obstacles in the way of dry canals, water cuts and the accidents of the ground. He will not make his attack a decisive one until it is seen that the Principal Mass is moving forward to the attack. This will be the signal for every able-bodied man in the force to move resolutely toward the enemy.

The role of the Turning Attack:-

After the battle has been well commenced by the Minimum Force the turning attack – 18th Brigade and Divisional cavalry (one squadron) under Brigadier General Hamilton – will attack the enemy's left flank (on the British right) and rear, which is a direct menace to his natural line of retreat. This attack must be pushed with vigour; nothing must stop it.

Column 'C' mounted troops, compromising the Cavalry Brigade, 'S' Battery RHA and 48th Pioneers, under Major General Sir Charles Mellis, will co-operate by working on the exterior sweep (north of 18th Brigade), in a wide sweep of some eighteen miles, so as to attack the enemy in rear with its H.A. guns in the neighbourhood of Qusabah and take his second line of trenches in enfilade, thus seriously menacing his line of retreat. Its attack should be vigorously pushed and the sound of its guns will cause the Turkish Forces to the south to look over their shoulders with a feeling of fear.

Role of the Principal Mass

On principle I shall order the Principal Mass forward as soon as the enemy seriously feels the Turning Attack. This attack will be launched straight forward against the spot marked VP on the map. The advance of the Principal Mass will be the signal for the whole force to move forward against the enemy; and every effort will be made by the Divisional Artillery Commander to bring converging fire on the VP. Even the guns of the Turning Attack will direct their fire if possible on VP so that a clear avenue of approach may be swept by the Principal Mass under General Delamain.

In his book, *My Campaign in Mesopotamia*, Charles Townshend made it clear that his plan for this battle would have won the approval of not only his hero Napoleon Bonaparte, but also his pupil, Moltke. All his preparations made, operations commenced on 21 November 1915 when the village of Lajj (Llaj) was occupied unopposed and the 6th Division was now in striking distance of its objective. The great arch of Ctesiphon could be clearly seen but between it and the British force there were Turkish redoubts and trenches festooned with wire. Townshend and his men knew that Kut was behind them 90 miles to the south and Basra a further 210 miles beyond that. Baghdad however was little more than two day's march away. 'A spirit of intense optimism animated the headquarters and the administrative staffs,' alleged the Mesopotamia Commission after the event, but Townshend observed sourly that he 'knew nothing about intense optimism'. Quite the reverse, and he confided in his diary that 'all my study indicated disaster to me.'

General Nixon questioned Townshend and asked anxiously, 'Are you confident of winning?'

'Yes,' Townshend replied, 'I shall win alright.'

He was right, but in reviewing the battle today it could be compared to that of Bunker Hill because it was to be a Pyrrhic victory at best.

The aeroplane which had made its debut on the military scene only recently had already been of great use in obtaining intelligence, and now one of the first generation of pilots offered to land behind the Turkish lines and cut all the telegraph lines, at a stroke cutting communications with Baghdad. It was an offer too good to miss The pilot, a man named Yeates-Brown, flew his grossly overburdened aeroplane loaded with explosives to a point between the Diyala River and the Turkish second line. It was a brave venture that came to naught when Yeates Brown was unable to bring his aeroplane to a halt once he had landed; he hit one of the very telegraph poles he had come to destroy but unfortunately lost a wing in the process. He and his observer were captured and subsequently paraded in Baghdad.

Before the battle Townshend was ensconced on the river boat *Méjidieh* and he was living in some comfort, his needs attended to by Boggis, his soldier servant. Boggis was good at his job and he made it his business to see that Townshend had clean water to drink and plum cake to eat if he was peckish between meals.

The night before the assault Boggis slept under a thin blanket on deck outside the General's cabin. It was particularly cold and Townshend's dog 'Spot' lay down with John Boggis; they snuggled up together to sleep. Boggis woke to hear the dog yelping and in the dim light of dawn saw Chitrál Charlie thrashing Spot.

'Why are you doing that, Sir?' enquired a bemused Boggis

'He was sleeping with you,' growled Townshend as he continued to beat the small animal. 'He's my dog and he's got to learn.'

Boggis was puzzled as he knew full well that Townshend was devoted to his horse and to Spot. He concluded that Townshend was 'a hard bastard'.[10] This episode, remembered by Boggis and recounted fifty years later, gives a small insight into the curious personality of the much-respected Chitrál Charlie.

Townshend certainly had some nagging concern about the performance of his Muslim troops. They did not know that they would be asked to fight over the sacred precincts of Salman Pak and the significance of Great Arch was lost upon them. The General had gone to some pains only to refer to the area as Ctesiphon, and accordingly the name Salman Pak was proscribed. The British soldiers, with typical irreverence, called it 'Pissedupon.'

Hoghton's column started the ball rolling at 1400 hrs on 22 November 1915, when, with every last available bayonet, he departed from Lajj. His mission was to preoccupy the Turks facing the British left and his advance was across difficult broken ground. There was nothing covert about this advance as the object was to convince Nur-Ud-Din that this was a serious attack. The advance drew no response and at 2000hrs Hoghton halted, short of his objective.

The sun had long set and the Mesopotamian desert was shrouded by night when Hamilton, commanding 18 Brigade, and part of the 'Turning Attack', followed in the hoofprints of Mellis who was in command of the cavalry. Mellis and his men had a very long ride, well out into the desert on the British right and they too would be an element of the 'Turning Attack'. Delamain and Climo, each leading a component of the 'Principal Mass', moved forward in complete silence with wheels, harnesses and equipment all muffled. Each column took post at their assigned places on the start line and their soldiers slept fitfully waiting for the dawn and Hoghton's 'Minimum Force' diversionary attack on the left of the British line.

Nixon and Townshend spent the night on the river where they received a message that 30,000 enemy reinforcements were en route to Baghdad and thence to Ctesiphon. Their commander was a man called Khalil but much more worrying was the added intelligence that the German Field Marshal von de Goltz had assumed command of all Turkish operations in Mesopotamia. Nixon, with extraordinary sangfroid, decided, on a whim, that the information was untrue. He ignored it and ordered the operation to proceed.

Came the long-awaited dawn and Hoghton's 'column', looking nothing like a column, was now arrayed in open order and covering a front of about one thousand yards. The soldiers moved steadily forward and, to their surprise and relief, received no welcoming fire. The sun started to rise higher in the sky and the long shadows disappeared. On they plodded, noting scorched patches of earth and small craters, clear evidence that Turkish artillery had been registering ranges. Despite this, the Turks continued to hold their fire – it was oddly disquieting but they had the flies for company. Behind them and to their right the waiting troops could see that their cover from view was being swept away by the sun as it rose higher. It was clear that any hope of surprise had been lost and surprise had been a key ingredient of Townshend's plan.

Hamilton asked his commander if, despite all, he could engage the enemy – when Townshend agreed Delamain wheeled his horse and rode up to his battalion of Dorsets. He roared from the saddle, 'There you are Dorsets – it's all yours.'[11] It was just then that the first gunfire was heard from the direction of Hoghton.[12]

The artillery that had opened fire had the range of Hoghton's Brigade to a yard but, unfortunately and inexplicably, it was the fire from British gunboats. The guns were damaging but there was some cover in the broken ground and the seasoned troops were well spread. The Turkish artillery joined in. It was only then that the gunboats switched their sights onto the Turks. Despite this 'blue on blue' incident, the advance of Hoghton on the left had had the desired effect. It had drawn attention from the outflanking sweep on the British right which now enjoyed enormous early success.

On the British right the Turks found themselves fighting an enemy coming at them from the rear – their trenches, with fire steps facing forward, were less effective against an enemy coming from the 'wrong' direction. The Turks vacated their first-line trenches to meet the rush but it was inexorable. Most of those who survived decamped toward their second line but remnants hung on tenaciously and gave a good account of themselves. Hamilton sent a message to say 'The enemy is in full retreat. May I advance on VP with the Principal Mass?'[13] Townshend immediately agreed and he too thought that the day was won. He expected that there would be a general Turkish withdrawal to the Diala River.

Climo, commanding 30 Brigade, took VP 'after a short and very fierce fire and bayonet fight in the most brilliant manner'[14] Townshend galloped across the desert to join him – and became an artillery target. Later he owned that the Turks 'pitched some shells fairly close'.

Hamilton and Delamain's formations moved swiftly towards the enemy second line, brimming with confidence. It was 3,500 yards further on than VP and when the British troops fell upon this second line they found that they might just have bitten off rather more than they could chew. The Turks held their ground and displayed a quality of tenacity that came as an unwelcome surprise.

It was an absolute bloodbath that extended throughout the day and, in the process, much of the 45th Turkish Division was annihilated but British losses were also unacceptably high.[15]

Townshend wanted to get to Delamain but the action was so close that he was prudent enough to dismount and make his way on foot. His passage was through a charnel house of the dead, the ground carpeted thickly with hundreds of Turks, but Punjabi, Gurkha and British too. Lieutenant Colonel Raynor remarked later that the General seemed to be unperturbed by the ghastly scene and 'in one place, eleven Gurkhas lying dead surrounded by their Turkish victims – each with his head split open, or cut off, by Gurkha kukris – Townshend watched the course of the battle. Binoculars to his eyes, he missed nothing; nor was he afraid to expose himself in order to peer over the top of the trench to gain a panoramic view.'

John Boggis recalled an incident at some stage in this fierce battle when the following exchange took place.

'Boggis!'

'Sir.'

'A change of clothes.'

'Now, Sir?'

At this point a stunned Private Boggis set off through shot and shell a couple miles to the river and the waiting *Méjidieh*. Here he collected a complete change of fresh clothes for Chitrál Charlie and set off on the hazardous journey back to the line. When a breathless Boggis arrived Townshend took his burden, stripped naked and, as if he were in his private changing room in the Mess, he dressed. All about him were dead and dying men. Putting his pith helmet back on and swinging his binoculars in one hand, he accepted a piece of plum cake passed to him by a young staff officer.[16]

He resumed his survey of the battlefield with studied insouciance.

This is an interesting anecdote, vouched for by two witnesses, that speaks volumes for his complete lack of care for Boggis, his soldier servant. A young soldier was sent on an asinine and hazardous journey merely to bring him fresh clothes. Perhaps it was a little piece of theatre put on to impress all present with his imperturbability? Perhaps he saw his order to Boggis as normal? Whatever his motivation, for better or worse, the story has added to the legend of Chitrál Charlie

Delamain and Townshend conferred behind a small sandhill which gave cover from the fire of a group of Turks who had been cut off, but were still installed in a redoubt some 700 yards away. Delamain explained the disposition of his brigade and told the GOC that he had sent two companies of Dorsets towards the great Arch to attract attention away from Hoghton who was still actively involved over on the left. As the Dorsets advanced so groups of Turks retreated towards the Arch. Townshend commented in his book: 'If only the gunboats would now appear by the Arch! But they were held up and could not advance beyond Bustan.'

Townshend moved his headquarters to VP and was joined there by General Nixon and his staff at about the time that 30 Brigade pierced the Turkish second line led by the Gurkhas, Punjabis and Dorsets. The Dorsets were not part of that brigade and their presence was an indicator of how intermingled the formations were by this stage.

Then the tide of battle started to turn against the attackers. The cavalry column under Mellis had met with serious difficulties and was unable to deliver the crushing blow envisaged by Townshend. The men had dismounted and attacked the Turkish second line on foot but made no progress as part of the Turkish reserve had by now been deployed to Qusabah. This part of the battle ebbed and flowed, but the 76th Punjabis, who were in support of the cavalry, distinguished themselves and carried several objectives in 'fine style'.

The loss of their officers caused some Indian battalions to falter, not from lack of courage but lack of firm direction. The second Turkish line had been hotly contested and at one time the British had the upper hand, holding it for more than an hour,[17] but then Nur-Ud-Din was reinforced by the advance guard of those 30,000 reinforcements, under the command of General Khalil. This was the reinforcement that Nixon had airily dismissed only twenty-four hours earlier. The Turkish counter-attack was savage, with fresh troops pitted against men who had been fighting for hours, and the results were inevitable. The withdrawal of the gallant West Kents, Norfolks, Gurkhas and Punjabis back to VP and the Turkish first line, which they had taken with such élan earlier in the day, was a bitter pill.

The day was not going well for the 6th Division which was now outnumbered, had suffered a grievous number of casualties and was on the brink of defeat. This was when Townshend was at his magnificent best, riding slowly along the British line showing himself to his men. This demonstration of courage, foolish perhaps, was not enough. The wounded were struggling to the rear, among them Colonel Climo, a most gallant officer, but now wounded in three places. The British abandoned any aspirations of holding the Turkish second line. Townshend had no reserves and had no way of plugging holes in his front.

Then the ammunition ran out.

Volunteers ran across the exposed desert to the mules to take boxes of ammunition from their panniers and, despite the weight, ran back to the grasping hands that awaited them. 'Pass 'em along my lucky lads. Who'll say no to a bunch of fives?'[18] (Rifle ammunition was packed in clips of five rounds.) The British infantry stood firm and with cool, well-aimed shooting slowed the Turks.

However, it was not enough.

At first just a few and then a flood of Indian troops fled to the rear. Panic had taken hold and their NCOs were powerless to restore order. The men withdrew, although 'retreated' is more accurate, in bad order. The system had started to break down as the officer casualties rose. There was no cohesion and although there were numerous individual acts of great bravery the Turkish advance could not be stemmed

'Cowardly bastards!' the British troops shrieked at the fleeing Indians, but rude words were not enough to halt what had now become a rout. The British troops started to follow the Indians. Townshend and as many officers as he could muster drew their revolvers. Shouting, striking, bullying and threatening with death on the spot, they managed to slow and then stop the rabble which had once been the proud 6th Division. The men who fought on might just have given some thought to their likely fate if they had fled into the desert and into the realm of the Arabs. Better to be killed by a Turk than by an Arab, or worse still his woman.[19]

An ad hoc defensive line was formed around VP and Townshend resolved to stand here. The day was well advanced and by 1800hrs some semblance of order was being restored as individuals and small groups sought to find the remainder of their battalion, with the darkness and artillery fire to contend with.

Townshend took stock. Hoghton's brigade was only 700 strong, Delamain's brigade numbered barely 1,000 and Hamilton's was at best 900 men. Very first calculations showed that, of an opening strength of 8,500 bayonets, about 4,000 had been killed or wounded. The Mesopotamia Commission made the following judgment:

> Over 3,500 wounded had to be removed from the battlefield to the river bank, in some cases a distance of ten miles, without proper ambu-

lance transport, and with an insufficiency of medical personnel, of food and of comforts, so that a large proportion had to make their way on foot in spite of their injured condition. When they arrived at the river, the available steamer accommodation was gravely inadequate. The wounded and weary men had to be crowded into steamers and barges without sufficient medical attention, appliances, or conveniences. Some of the wounded were disembarked at Amarah (alternative spelling), but the majority went on down to Basra, a journey from the battlefield, which, in some cases, took as much as fourteen days, and the discomforts of which were aggravated for the wounded by the presence on board of many cases of dysentery and other sickness. Thus the sick and wounded were put to great sufferings during the evacuation from the battlefield to the river bank at Lajj, and also during the protracted journey down the river. Though the successful evacuation of the wounded in the face of a superior and pursuing enemy was a fine military performance, it was carried out in a manner which involved for the sick and wounded conditions of neglect, misery, and suffering, which were lamentable. Not a hint of this regrettable breakdown is to be found in the official report sent to England after the battle.

Edmund Candler, an eyewitness, had this observation:

At Basra we met men who had been at Ctesiphon. We heard of wounded who had been carried nine miles from the battlefield to the ship in these carts. They are springless, made of wood and iron bars with a grid iron bottom ordinarily employed for the carriage of equipment or supplies. Every jolt in them over this broken ground was like a deliberate blow; men with broken arms and legs were condemned to them in prolonged agony. Generally there were no mattresses. To a twice-wounded man, who had made the journey before, they must have seemed like the tumbrels of the Revolution. To be consigned to one after hemorrhage or with a wound in the stomach or about the spine meant death. Every doctor who packed such a case in the A.T. carts knew the man's fate as certainly as if he had signed his death warrant. Yet these carts were tolerated in Mesopotamia as the normal ambulance conveyance for nearly two years.

The number of deaths caused by these carts is far, far greater but official acquiescence to their use has a parallel with the protracted employment of 'snatch' Land Rovers in Iraq and Afghanistan 2003–8 which, in turn, cost too many lives.

Major Carter IMS, who was in medical charge of the hospital ship *Varela* at Basra, waiting for the wounded from Ctesiphon, gave evidence to the Mesopotamia Commission and described, to the Commission, the arrival of one of the river convoys:

> I was standing on the bridge in the evening when the *Méjidieh* arrived . . . As the ship, with two barges, came up to us I saw that she was absolutely packed and the barges were too, with men . . . there was no protection from the rain. The barges were slipped and the *Méjidieh* was brought alongside. When she was about three or four hundred yards off it looked as if she was festooned with ropes. The stench when she was close was quite definite, and I found that, what I mistook for ropes, were dried stalactites of human faeces. The patients were so crowded and huddled together on this ship that they could not perform the offices of nature clear of the ship's edge and the whole of the ship's side was covered. This is then what I saw. A certain number of men were standing and kneeling on the immediate perimeter of the ship. Then we found a mass of men huddled up anyhow, some with blankets and some without. With regard to the first man I examined . . . he was covered with dysentery, his thigh was fractured, perforated in five or six places. He had been apparently writhing about the deck of the ship. Many cases were almost as bad. There were . . . cases of terribly bad bed sores. In my report I described mercilessly to the Government of India how I found men with their limbs splinted with wood strips from Johnny Walker whisky boxes, bhoosa (compressed hay), wire and that sort of thing.

The whisky case splints had achieved a degree of notoriety much earlier in the campaign but, clearly, they still remained one of a poor set of options. The suffering of the evacuated wounded was grim but others were not so lucky and died of their wounds on the battlefield.

The night of 22/23 November was marked by a series of forays against the British lines but the Turks did not realize how close they were to success and did not press home their numerical advantage. On the morning of 23 November 1915 Townshend was confident that the Turks would withdraw. It was a forlorn hope and during the day there was renewed and savage fighting. The Turks were repulsed but, at one point, they got close enough for Townshend to feel it necessary to unbutton the flap on his revolver holster. The next day was a long, hard one and by now ammunition was generally running short in the face of continuous Turkish pressure. Darkness fell for the second time and the attacks showed little sign of ceasing.

The 6th Division was beleaguered, weak and on the edge of collapse. Despite this Townshend sent a message to his formations which commanding officers must have read with utter incredulity – he said that he intended to resume the offensive the next day. Then, later that night, a more rationale and sober appreciation of the situation caused him to reconsider. He knew that Nur-Ud-Din had been, or was about to be, massively reinforced and air reconnaissance quickly confirmed the bad news. It was now clear that the tattered remains of 6th Division were hopelessly outnumbered, that he had a very long, undefended line of communication and that his logistic support was minimal. He concluded correctly that if he had had two divisions or even just one more brigade he would have won an overwhelming victory. But then war, like life, is full of 'ifs'. Regretfully, and not a moment too soon, he also concluded that his offensive days were over.

He now had to preserve the lives of as many of his men as possible and to this end he prepared to withdraw. The question, where to? Kut was 90 painful miles to the south. The closest safe haven was Amara, 130 miles away as a mosquito flies, but 250 miles by way of the sinuous Tigris. The 130-mile route was impractical because he had to have access to water and had to offer protection to his flotilla of assorted vessels.

At about 0200hrs on 24 November, the incoming fire died away and then stopped. The desert was quiet, very quiet. When it was light it could be seen that the Turks had gone. Townshend was in possession of the field and, if that is the measurement of success, he had won the day. There was no time to spare and Townshend made arrangements for the withdrawal of his force starting at about 2100hrs that evening.

A disappointed Lieutenant General Sir John Nixon, who had seen himself as conqueror of Baghdad, had made a hasty exit from the scene and left behind his Chief-of-Staff, Major General Kemball – presumably to act as a sounding board for, or as a check on, Townshend. The protection of river craft was put into focus almost immediately, and especially for Nixon.

On his passage as he headed downstream, south to Basra and absolute safety, Nixon's unescorted paddle steamer came under attack from Arabs on both sides of the river and ran aground. It was a sitting target, casualties mounted until the Commander-in-Chief, Mesopotamia ran up a white flag and invited his attackers to parley. The Arabs had seen the writing on the wall and had changed sides as the tide of war had turned the Turks' way. They struck a hard bargain and Nixon had the ignominy of paying an undisclosed, but very large sum of money before he was allowed to continue to Basra. Everyone on board the steamer was sworn to secrecy on pain of death.

This incident is, even today, cloaked in mystery. Albert Maynard was an eyewitness to this event and this account of his is to be found on the Internet. No corroboration of his story has been found. It is alleged that Mr Maynard, aged eighty-five, believed that by telling his story sixty years later he was still liable to be shot.

Townshend had his faults but he was a consummately skilled soldier and the withdrawal of the 6th Division from Ctesiphon was a model of its kind. Silently the force, either on foot or on the water, slipped into the night leaving only the dead and the detritus of battle behind. Townshend rode his charger with the rearguard and 'those who watched him were reminded irresistibly of his hero Napoleon on his retreat from Moscow as doubtless he intended they should be.'[20]

Notes
1. CVFT.
2. CVFT.
3. An unnecessary piece of shallow servility – of course CVFT could express a view, he was a general commanding a division on active service. It was his job to 'express a view'. It was the job of his superiors to respect that view.
4. The Turks withdrew in good order. The exhaustion of 6th Division was an important factor that militated against hot pursuit but is not mentioned.
5. This was deliberately misleading. The troops knew nothing of Salman Pak and the area was always referred to as Ctesiphon.
6. The Mesopotamia Commission, 1917.
7. CVFT.
8. Sandes, *In Kut and Captivity*.
9. Ctesiphon is approximately 20 miles south-east of Baghdad, alongside the River Tigris. The city of Ctesiphon originally measured 20 square miles, but the only visible remains are the great arch located in what is now the Iraqi town of Salman Pak. This arch was built in AD 400 by the Persians to be the largest single-span vault of unreinforced brickwork in the world. The arch is considered to be among the greatest architectural sights of Mesopotamia.
10. Mr J. Boggis, 1967. Quoted by Braddon.

11. Maj. F. Castaldini. Quoted by Braddon.
12. Col. W.S. Spackman. Quoted by Braddon.
13. CVFT.
14. CVFT.
15. A.J. Barker.
16. Lieutenant Colonel C.A. Raynor. Quoted by Braddon.
17. Braddon.
18. Mr H. Eato. Quoted by Braddon
19. Mr D.R. Holzmeyer. Quoted by Braddon.
20. Lieutenant Colonel H.G. Thomson DSO. Quoted by Braddon.

Chapter 14

November 1915 to April 1916
Besieged

'I would say without hesitation that lack of food constitutes the single biggest assault upon morale.'

Brigadier Bernard Fergusson, *The Wild Green Earth*

The 6th Poona Division, or what remained of it, started to make its way to Kut in well-disciplined order. The column halted every hour, water discipline was as strictly observed as the shroud of darkness allowed. The rearguard screened the main body and, at first, it seemed that they were clear away.

Townshend, once clinically observant in tactical matters, now seemed to lose a grip on reality. It was not the first time. He had once talked about taking Baghdad as no more than an afternoon jaunt, but later was to warn strongly against the advance to Ctesiphon. Now he telegraphed Nixon and told him that his objective was Lajj where he intended to stop and 'consume his supplies'. This is a very strange motivation for a general to halt his force and was completely at variance with what he told his soldiers in two communiqués. In these he said that they were moving back to Lajj because they were short of food and in order to secure his river craft, which were very vulnerable until they got below Bustan. He had added that many troops, who are coming from France, would reach Basra 'in a week or ten days time and will join this force to take Baghdad'.

This was complete 'pie in the sky'. Not to put too fine a point on it, he willfully misled his soldiers. He knew that there was not the means to transport a division upriver to Azizieh – even if that division were in the theatre. Braddon speculated that at this point Townshend was a sick man and had been so since his evacuation to India in July 1915. His argument was that Chitrál Charlie:

in July after a long chase from Kurna to Amara, during which he had eaten too little and stood in the sun too long . . . fallen suddenly ill –

so ill that he believed himself lucky to have survived. In August, still complaining of weakness and exhaustion, he found himself back in Amara, in temperatures as high as 125°, required immediately to plan and lead an operation he believed to be fraught with danger . . . So after three sapping months of planning, fear and frustration, he had fought at Ctesiphon and spent two gruelling days in the sun and two nerve-wracked nights in the cold. It was the sun, Townshend thought, that had struck him down at Amara in July. The sun at Ctesiphon – in addition to too short a convalescence in India and too much work, anxiety and disappointment since that time – could well have done it again. From the age of twenty-three to fifty-four, Townshend's diaries, letters and cables had revealed a man of ruthless consistency but from the moment his convalescence had begun in India, consistency had vanished.

This relatively sympathetic explanation of Townshend's conduct is of great value because the source, Russell Braddon, was a very stern critic of Townshend and, in the main, wrote of him in a negative tone. A close examination of Townshend's actions does support Braddon's hypothesis. It is true that Charles Townshend had vacillated about the taking of Baghdad and the means by which that could be achieved. He had fortified Azizieh, consumed 30 miles of wire and caused even the unresponsive Nixon to question his actions. Then he de-fortified Azizich, a decision that, in late November 1915, he was starting to regret. He had thrashed his dog in a curiously emotional outburst. Unforgivably, he had put John Boggis in harm's way for the sake of a clean shirt and underwear. After this recent engagement at Ctesiphon he had initially said that he would resume the offensive with about 4,000 men against an enemy perhaps six or even ten times that number. Whether Townshend was mentally sick or just plain exhausted, he was still, nevertheless, the GOC 6th Division and there was a job to do.

Turkish troops were within three miles when the column moved out but not a shot was fired by either side. The Division marched into Lajj early on the morning of 26 November 1915 and from here the commander sent another telegram to Nixon in which he said:

I consider that with 4500 casualties . . . and where the brigades are reduced to little more than a full strength British battalion it would have been madness to stay at Ctesiphon a moment longer than I did . . . At 4pm yesterday three large Turkish columns estimated . . . 5000 each were advancing . . . There is no question of my engaging such a force in my present state. I am entrenching (at Lajj) and am going to make myself comfortable.

CVFT had by now established a reputation for poor accounting and here about 4,000 had been promoted to 4,500. Major J.J. O'Connor USAF estimates the 'butcher's bill' at Ctesiphon as: Turkish 9,600 killed and wounded and 1,000 taken prisoner; he gives British casualties as 4,200 killed and wounded.

Charles Townshend then went on to make sure that Nixon understood fully the difficulty of the withdrawal he had just accomplished with such skill. The following day CVFT sent yet another telegram and this time he said that his fortifications at Lajj were 'light entrenchments merely to give camp security'. That is a curious description and if he was expecting to be attacked one wonders why his defensive arrangements were 'light', especially as in the same telegram he observed that 'the enemy would never permit me to remain at Lajj unmolested.' He said that he intended to move back to Azizieh 'as soon as I have eaten up my supplies'. He said that he had ten days supplies for British troops and seven day's worth for his Indian soldiers. In a contradictory or very optimistic phrase he said that he 'intended to base himself at Azizieh as I desire to concentrate our force there for the advance on Baghdad'.

What advance on Baghdad? With what forces? And when? This was yet more pie in the sky.

Not twenty-four hours later he conceded that it would take nearly three months to assemble sufficient ships, boats, launches and barges to move a new division upriver to Azizieh and pointed out that, by then, the winter rains would have come and Lajj and Azizieh would both be under water. Quite without a blink he finished: 'Thus every reason indicated Kut as my final halt.'

Perhaps Braddon was right.

The Turks were advancing on the busily masticating 6th Division with an advance guard of 12,000 men of the Turkish Sixth Army. A hasty move to Azizieh was prudent. The 22 miles were covered in a single march, the column by-passing Zeur and El Kutunie on the way. The Division rested on 28 and 29 November at Azizieh, where they had good news from the MGGS, who signalled to say that 28 Indian Brigade would join the Division by 15 December and that 24 and 25 Brigades would follow on.

This news was just what Townshend needed and he now promulgated his decision to fall back to Kut, 'a strategical point we are bound to hold'.

That he had previously described Kut as 'a position undesirably remote from Basra' was ignored. He now took the view that 'If the enemy should follow to Kut, so much the better, we ought to destroy him in that case . . . the further we get him from Baghdad the more chance, in our next battle of knocking him out altogether.'

Chitrál Charlie was talking here about a weak division composed of survivors and fresh, untried troops, 'destroying' an army that was probably at least four or more times his size. It was nonsense.

Azizieh was where the Division had left all of its heavy baggage and there was a chance for the troops to find their kit for the onward march. Chaos reigned as thousands of men hunted through a mountain of kitbags and regimental property in a haphazard and ill-disciplined manner. They could only take that which they could carry and all manner of treasures were left for the Arabs who had been in constant attendance as they trailed the Division down the line of the Tigris. There was going to be no use for ceremonial uniforms or mess silver from here on and so these were abandoned.

Now Townshend was reinforced by half a battalion of the Royal West Kents and the 14th Hussars. However, the men of the Royal West Kents and the 14th Hussars were more than a little disenchanted to discover that having hurried north to join 'Our Charlie', they were now going to have to retrace their steps.[1] Their morale was not raised by the derision that greeted their arrival. The attitude of many of their countrymen was along the lines of 'where the hell have you lot been?' Asked how many of them they were, the reply was 'half the West Kents'. The response was 'That's no bloody good, we need half the British Army.'

Other reinforcements were making their way north and among them were the Anglo–Indian gunners from Amara, anxious to eradicate the derisive appellation 'Bombay fizzers'. Their journey had been halted at Kut because of the shortage of river craft, most of which were making their laborious and putrid passage south with the suffering wounded. Given Nixon's earlier and embarrassing brush with local Arabs, he was understandably concerned about his line of communication which was under daily threat from the increasingly emboldened Arabs. This concern of Nixon's had come a little late in the piece and it was a shame that it did not manifest itself some months earlier. Nixon asked Townshend to help secure the river line, and Mellis, commanding 30 Brigade, hurried south to assist.

The next morning, 30 November 1915, Townshend's force departed from Azizieh, burdened with as much as it could carry. Food, souvenirs, personal possessions and the possessions of men long dead adorned the person of every soldier as they struck out into the desert. Azizieh, once a well-defended location, was abandoned and put to the torch. Unusable ordnance such as Ariel bombs joined the pyre and black smoke stained the crystal-blue sky. Nur-Ud-Din was about six miles behind and the smoke told him that Townshend had opted out of an engagement. The Turk had not only a numerical supremacy but now he held the moral advantage of a pursuer.

It was winter in the Mesopotamian desert but as the sun rose so the over-laden soldiers started to wilt and soon the trail that they left in the sand was littered with the booty that they had so rapaciously gathered the day before. After only four miles Townshend ordered a brief halt. Most of the stragglers caught up, grateful not to be in the hands of the unmerciful Arabs who were trailing the column like so many wolves. Some did not catch up and that was because they had given up the struggle. They were dependent on their friends, an example of which was recorded by Arthur Kingsmill in his book, *The Silver Badge*. He wrote:

> He was lying on the ground, and when I told him to get up he said he was finished. I took his rifle, grabbed him by the collar, pulled him to his feet and kicked him. 'Now come,' I said. He hung onto me and as luck would have it, we caught up. 'Any more tricks and you get your throat cut,' I said, giving him half a biscuit and a piece of bully.

Whoever that soldier was he should have been very grateful to Kingsmill who, without question, saved his life. The column pressed on and reached Umm-al-Tubul at about midday. The river craft had shadowed the progress of the marching men and provided mutual protection. There was then an important misunderstanding between Townshend and the admirable Captain Nunn RN, the Senior Naval Officer. Nunn thought that the halt was because the men were exhausted and were able to march no further, on the basis of which he told Townshend that his ships would not proceed. Unfortunately Townshend interpreted 'would not' to mean 'could not', believing that Nunn was unable to take his ships any further.

Townshend had resolved not to engage Nur-Ud-Din but in these unfortunate circumstances he decided to stay in Umm-al-Tubul and take his chances if he was attacked. He called his commanders together and gave outline orders that would be executed on the morrow if the situation was appropriate. He called for volunteers to ride to Mellis to ask him to return and when Captain C. Trench and Lieutenant W.J. Coventry offered to ride through the desert teeming with hostile Arabs, he assured them that he would recommend them both for the VC. The two officers were to be escorted by six Indian soldiers who got no such promise. In the event both officers were awarded the DSO – at the time the next best thing to a VC.

Nunn was told to send a similar message to Mellis downriver in one of the launches. For Lieutenant Wood RNR, who was to bear the message, it was always going to be a long shot. His little vessel was predictably attacked by Arabs and stopped after two members of his small crew were wounded.

The orders for Mellis, if he ever got them, were to return but to stay well away from the river so that he could outflank any Turkish force threatening 6th Division. Townshend's force bivouacked for the night, which was cold. An uneasy night it was too. Townshend did not sleep and when he could not sleep, no one else did either. He woke Boggis, who recalled the following exchanges:

'Boggis.'

'Sir.'

'Can you hear wheels?'

'No, Sir.'

'Well, I can. Go and get Colonel Evans and we'll see if he can hear anything.'

Boggis said that he found and woke Colonel Evans, the GSO1 and senior staff officer. Evans was a short, red-faced man with a bristling moustache who was alleged to be the most profane officer east of Suez. Evans was not best pleased.

'Evans,' said the GOC, 'can you hear wheels?'

'No, Sir.'

'I can. There are Turks on the move out there. Why haven't the outposts reported it? See to it.'

Evans returned to his own tent and one of the occupants of that tent recalled[2] being woken by the irascible Evans who ordered, 'I want you to listen and tell me if you hear anything.'

The officers listened intently. They heard the wind in the guy ropes and the jingle of the harnesses in the horse lines. No one spoke until one ventured bravely, 'I think it's only the mules, Sir.'

'I know that's only the mules, you pissbegotten bugger; but what else can you hear?'

'Nothing, Sir.'

'Well, the General can!'

That was good enough – every man 'stood to', put on his equipment, went to his defence position and, through sleep-dulled eyes, peered into the stygian desert night. The early glimmerings of dawn when they came brought an unwelcome surprise – a few miles to the rear, on a line of low dunes, lights began to show. The opinion was that it was a group of Arabs who were ripe and ready to be attacked. However, as the sun made its lazy way over the horizon the British could see a veritable tented city.

These were no Arabs, this was the Turkish Army.

The Turks were as surprised at the view as were their adversaries. The British gunners were the first to react and open fire, finding the range at once and effectively shelling the now, rapidly advancing, Turks. Townshend commented: 'I have never seen artillery shoot with the precision of 10th Brigade RFA which opened a rapid fire. This was most deadly. One saw the Turkish lines of men dissolve in a regular cloud of our shells. What a splendid gun is our 18-pounder field-gun!'

Townshend was his usual crisp self. He ordered Major General W.S. Delamain, commanding 16 Brigade, and Brigadier W.H. Hamilton, commanding 18 Brigade, without any further formal orders to attack the Turks head on. This was daunting stuff because the Turks were estimated at 12,000 strong. This battle, albeit a brief one, saw the usual anonymous acts of bravery. Lieutenant Colonel J. McConville reported: 'a Norfolk, with both legs broken, ignored his injuries. Spreading his ammunition carefully around him, he continued his deliberate fire, round after round.' The two infantry brigades were heading into the teeth of a storm but, as in all the best westerns, and unlikely as it seems, the cavalry rides over the hill in the nick of time to win the day. Something very like that happened on the early morning of 1 December 1915.

Townshend's cavalry, with the famous 'S' Battery in support, appeared on the enemy flank and occupied some dominating high ground. Heavily lathered horses now strained to bring the guns into action; when a horse was hit it was quickly cut from its harness and the team moved on. The cavalry dismounted and added to the fire of 'S' Battery. Engaged on two sides, the Turkish attack started to falter. They began to fall back but as they did so, so their artillery came into action. Their counter-battery fire was accurate and Townshend commented how close he and his staff were to being hit as they had positioned themselves near the guns. Townshend prudently decided to break off the engagement having had very much the better of the encounter. He recalled Delamain and Hamilton, and both brigades fell back. Townshend observed:

We were under very severe shell fire; but I have never seen – even in peacetime manoeuvres – a retirement carried out better, both as regards steadiness and suppleness in manoeuvre than was executed by 6th Division at this critical moment. The sight of the brigades falling back steadily in echelon, with the precision of clockwork, and the gradual development into one steady flow of retreat in perfect order – guns everything in their proper place – filled me with pride. Shall I ever have such a command again, I thought?

These words were actually penned in 1919 when Townshend knew full well that he would not.

The Turkish gunners had by now hit the old wooden paddle steamer *Comet*, which was disabled and in flames. Townshend felt a twinge of regret for it was on this quaint old vessel that he received the surrender of Amara. *Firefly* took a shell in her boiler room and was completely disabled – her loss was important for she was a new ship, well armed with a 4.7" gun and, hitherto, had been a major asset.

It was about 0730hrs when the retreat began with 6th Division having lost 500 men killed and wounded. Turkish losses had been much heavier and a Turkish officer who had been present at the battle said, 'Turkish losses were terrible . . . artillery fire had paralysed all movement.'[3] However, the British had not lost a gun, or a prisoner (of whom there were now 1,500 marching with the divisional train and supply column). At about 0900hrs General Mellis and his 30 Brigade met the Division on the march and joined the column. He had returned at his best speed and he and Townshend shared regrets that he had not been able to play a part at Umm-al-Tubul.

In his book,[4] Chitrál Charlie takes every opportunity to exonerate himself for anything for which he might be criticized, and to draw attention to his consummate tactical skill whenever that is possible. For example, on pages 195 & 196 of the book he lectures rather pompously on his conduct at Umm-al-Tubul, quoting from the careers of three obscure generals (MacMahon, Pelle and Chanzy) and their even more obscure battles to justify his tactics. It is quite unnecessary because the adept way he extracted the Division is proof enough of his ability. The book was written in 1919 and at that stage in his life Townshend was justifying all of his actions. However, when reading his account of the battles, it feels uncomfortable to be invited to bask in the glow of Charlie's brilliance.

The column was anxious to get under way, a fierce battle had just been fought against a numerically superior enemy and now, although an ordered retreat was required, panic was not too far away. Delamain, as always a rock of calm, good order and common sense, was fully aware and, pointing at three Dorsets, he detailed them to 'go with the 66th Punjabis. Don't let them run.' The three British soldiers shrugged on their packs and took their place in the Punjabi ranks, ready to march alongside the Indian officers and if necessary 'order' them not to run.[5] Despite the best efforts of the three Dorsets, the Punjabis set off at such a cracking pace that the column quickly started to straggle. It took Townshend himself to spur his horse to the front of the column to call a halt and restore order. John Boggis commented to Braddon that Townshend's ambivalence about his Indian soldiers was fed by incidents such as this. Order restored, Townshend marched his men remorselessly; the sun rose to its winter zenith and as it dropped in the sky so the men of 6th Division started to drop.

The sun set and Townshend rode on – the men marched. Delamain could see that the men were spent and suggested that they might halt, if only to fill their water bottles. But Townshend was unsympathetic, saying, 'Once these men get down to the river bank we shan't collect them for hours. They'll lie by the water, drink, and fall asleep like logs.'

Delamain protested further, which was something new for Townshend who usually got unquestioning obedience. He rejected Delamain's appeal out of hand.

'How do I know that the Turks aren't only a mile or so behind?' he snarled.[6]

The column kept on marching through the early hours of darkness until 2100hrs, by which time it had reached Shadie. The march had been 36 miles long for the majority; however, 30 Brigade had probably marched at least five miles further as a result of its excursion earlier in the day. The, oh so welcome, halt brought precious little comfort to anyone as it transpired that some of the smaller vessels in the flotilla were lost, including a barge filled with wounded that had run aground hours before, just after leaving Umm-al-Tubul. These wounded were cruelly butchered by the Arabs.

Townshend was mortified to hear that his invaluable bridging pontoons had all been lost. This was because the launches towing the equipment had come under attack from the river bank so frequently that the locally employed Arab skippers had panicked and cut the pontoons free in order to make their escape. And that was not all. Townshend knew that any stragglers had been despatched by the predatory Arabs and, to add to his woes, there was no food and not a single form of comfort. The men slept where they had halted in the column despite the now very cold desert night.

Townshend steeled himself and went aboard the *Mejidieh* to visit his casualties. It was not a pretty sight and the ship still had a long way to go before the men, who were already lying in their own excrement, would find any form of succour. Townshend did not know at this stage how the Turks cared for British/Indian POWs, which was perhaps as well because 'care' is not quite the right word. Their medical arrangements were even more inadequate than those of the British and Mr E.H. Firman, who survived imprisonment by the Turks, recalled a lieutenant of the Dorsets who, having been wounded at Ctesiphon, was neglected and when, belatedly, the Turks amputated his leg it was too late. The young man died of gangrene. It was a life wasted and one of far too many.

The morning of 2 December was greeted with mixed feelings by the soldiers of 6th Division. Daylight was welcomed by men with empty stomachs but the consensus was: 'I expect that bloody Charlie will resume this sodding march.' How right they were. The column moved on and Townshend observed clinically from the back of his horse that 'The troops seemed to be very tired and fagged after their thirty-six mile march with no food. But I hoped they would warm up as the day progressed – they were naturally very stiff at first. The march was a very painful one and towards midday the men fell out in scores.'

CVFT's comment that 'the men seemed to be tired and fagged' must surely rank as one of the most blindingly obvious understatements ever – on a par with Robertson's comment at Chitrál (see Page 64).

No halts were called until 1300hrs, by which time the carts at the rear of the column were full of exhausted men. Just behind, and kept at bay by the rearguard, were the ever-present Arabs. At 1300hrs, when the column halted, the divisional train and supply column continued on to Kut. It took with it orders to send out food to the next proposed bivouac, six miles short of Kut at Shumran bend. By now the men of the 6th Division were desperately, ravenously hungry.

Brigadier General Rimington, a sapper officer, rode out to meet Townshend and brought with him two telegrams from Nixon with news of further reinforcement – 800 of whom were 'convalescents capable of using a rifle'.[7] Shumran was reached at dusk on 2 December but the rearguard of 17 Brigade, under Brigadier General F.A. Hoghton, which had had a most difficult job, did not arrive until well after nightfall. Sweeping up the stragglers had been onerous and demanding work but, as far as could be ascertained, no one was missing.

Townshend commented later that a German artillery colonel who had been with the Turkish advance guard told him that they saw 'bodies of Indians killed by the Arabs; in one case half a dozen English soldiers had been stripped naked and their throats cut by these Arabs.'[8] These poor fellows were among the sick being evacuated in a barge that had run aground and was captured. Some of the men managed to get ashore to make a run for it – they failed and paid a high price. The unqualified contempt for the jackal-like Arabs that the fighting soldiers on both sides felt is understandable. The Arabs killed stragglers from both sides indiscriminately and were cordially loathed for it.

The column, now fed, watered and rested, marched into Kut on the morning of 3 December 1915. It had high hopes of char and wads, a cooked breakfast, pretty nurses, mail from home, newspapers, a decent bed raised off the desert floor, a bath and a shave in hot water. Soldiers ask for very little. It was just as well because there was very little in Kut, which was a most unattractive place to spend a protracted stay. It was a squalid, stinking town and home to about 6,000 totally untrustworthy Arabs, whose brothers and cousins were just outside the walls baying for British blood. Kut was deficient in many ways, not least of which was the fact that despite it being contained in a bend in the Tigris on three sides, it had an open front to the north and west of over 1½ miles. The exhausted troops of the 6th Division were going to have to dig a multiple trench line to defend this gap.

Townshend sent a telegram to Nixon to say that he intended to entrench at and hold Kut which, in Townshend's latest thinking, was a pivotal point in the defence of the lower Tigris, Basra and the oilfields. In the same telegram he said that he had sufficient rations to feed British troops for a month, and enough for two months for the Indians. He added that he had ample ammunition. Townshend saw his occupation of Kut as being strategically important in that it held up any Turkish attack further downriver towards Basra. It is true that he could impede river traffic but it was patent nonsense to suggest that his position at Kut formed any sort of serious obstacle to Turkish movement to the south. Goltz could easily contain Kut and bypass it, which was what he duly did, in order to block the progress of the forces intent on lifting the siege of Kut.

The first entry in Townshend's diary after he occupied Kut is revealing. It read: 'I mean to defend Kut as I did Chitrál.' Charlie had made his name at Chitrál and, to some extent, had continued to reap the benefits for the previous twenty years. Since then he had examined Khartoum, Ladysmith and Mafeking in great depth – the fact was that CVFT was a self-confessed expert, not only on sieges but on all the conditions of war. The historian might speculate that not having taken Baghdad, then a siege at Kut was an alternative path to glory. However, Townshend presumably knew of the dictum of Frederick the Great, who said, 'To make war is to attack.' Withdrawing into the confines of Kut was, logically, to be attacked and Townshend acknowledged, without equivocation, that 'a force should not shut itself up in an entrenched camp unless the commander can reckon with certainty on approaching reinforcements.'

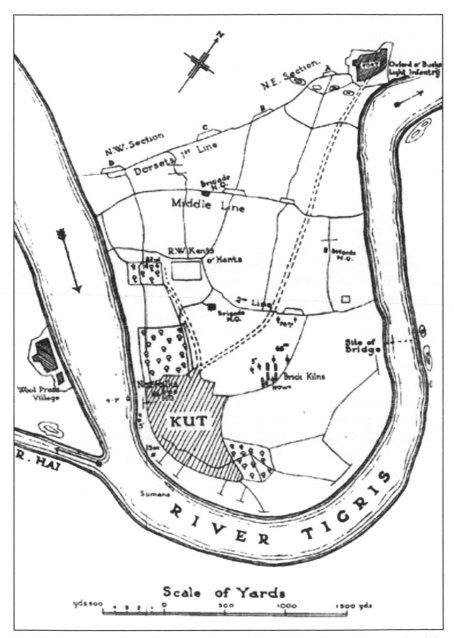

Fig 12. Sketch map of Kut. Note the isolated position of Wool Press Village on the right bank and the Fort, top right, both of which were the scene of much heavy fighting, but Townshend never visited his soldiers there. (CVFT)

The situations in Chitrál and Kut were completely unalike. At Chitrál Townshend had faced a disparate group of uncoordinated tribesmen armed, in the main, with unsophisticated weapons. They had no artillery and their only effective tools, apart from small arms, were fire and mining. Chitrál Charlie had to secure a small perimeter with ample riflemen and, what is more, he could be confident of eventual relief.

Kut was not like that. This was to be a serious siege.

Here the enemy was a modern army equipped with artillery, machine guns and aeroplanes. The Turks were led by the redoubtable German Field Marshal von de Goltz, who was operating on a different planet to Sher Afzul and the like. The Turks had a massive numerical superiority *and very importantly* (author's italics) sufficiently so as to be able to take on any relief force with equanimity.

The greatest enemy faced by a besieged force is starvation. Goltz knew that he had all the time in the world and, as time passed, he judged that Townshend and his men would eventually dig their graves with their teeth. 'Our Charlie' busied himself with his preparations, his energy and expertise as invaluable now as they had been back in 1895, when H.C. Thomson had commented with a degree of admiration on Townshend's particular skills.

However, the General had been riding a horse whilst his men had covered about 80 miles on their feet, over two days, carrying heavy loads. Now, and despite their commander's acknowledged expertise and sense of urgency, they lay down and slept. It was only later in the day and just as the Turks appeared on the horizon that the soldiers turned to the preparation of their defences. Kut was not a fortified town. It was a warren of evil-smelling, narrow streets lined with two-storey houses that afforded cover from view, but little protection from artillery fire. There were three or four blockhouses and a mud-walled enclosure, termed 'The Fort', about 2,000 yards from the town to the north-east of the river. There was a lot to do but an early priority for Townshend was the issue of the first of his written communiqués. In the cold light of peace, these were later subjected to detailed analysis and treated rather unfairly by his sternest critics. The document that was circulated on his behalf said, quite reasonably:

> I intend to defend Kut el Amara and not to retire any further. Reinforcements are being sent at once to relieve us. The honour of our Mother Country and the Empire demands that we all work, heart and soul in the defence of this place. We must dig in deep and dig quickly, and then the enemy's shells will do little damage. We have ample food and ammunition, but commanding officers must husband the ammu-

nition and not throw it away uselessly. The way you have managed to retire some eighty or ninety miles under the very noses of the Turks is nothing short of splendid and speaks eloquently for the courage and discipline of this force.

On 4 December, the parade state showed that within Kut there were 10,398 combatants, of which 1,505 were the Cavalry Brigade which could play no useful part in the events to come. Two days later Townshend sent them back to Basra. At the commencement of the siege Kut had 9,980 defenders 7,411 of which were infantry. With this force, 2,700 yards of front had to be defended and, taking Townshend's criteria of 'three to five men per running yard of trench', it was clear that he did not think he had sufficient manpower to defend his land frontage alone. A defending force had to be provided for the village known as 'Wool Press' (see Fig 12 on Page 231) on the right bank of the river (looking downstream) and that absorbed one battalion; in addition, the town of Kut had to be garrisoned in order to exercise some control over the indigenous population.

Townshend had no illusions about the hostile civilian Arabs he now unwillingly had under his aegis. He realized that they were a fifth column and had no doubt that there were concealed weapons in the town. His first instinct was to expel the entire population but he was constrained in this by Sir Percy Scott, the Political Agent, who pointed out that the women and children would certainly perish in the desert, either from hunger or at the hands of the vicious desert Arabs. The political ramifications of such an expulsion would in any case be enormous, with an impact all over the Arab world. Townshend took the advice and so limited his action to the ejection of all Arabs who were not householders (about 700); he also took twenty hostages from the balance of the population (between 5,000 and 6,000) as surety for the good behaviour of the rest.

This latter act, which would no doubt be condemned today, was mild compared with his action against looters. He said in his diary: 'In order to put a stop to looting by the Arabs at the commencement of the siege, I had caused twelve men who had been caught in the act to be tried by a military commission and shot – *pour encourager les autres*.'[9]

Townshend drew up comprehensive plans for the defence of Kut in his usual painstaking way and the reader of this volume, having come this far, will accept that all that could be done was done. On the morning of 5 December, a message was received from Nixon to say that he expected to relieve Kut 'within two months'. This would not do for Charles and he responded robustly and at length, helpfully pointing out both the military and political consequences should Kut fall. He said that in two months he would be invested by a whole Turkish army of six divisions – relief of Kut in the opposition of such a powerful force was unlikely. Applying another lever, he said that he only had sufficient rations for a month. Then he enquired if the Russians were moving on Baghdad because, if they were, it would oblige von de Goltz to thin out his troops at Kut.

The bad news was that they were not.

A boat bridge was constructed almost abreast of the brick kilns and this was used by the Cavalry Brigade as it withdrew on the morning of 6 December. That same day all shipping and spare transport was ordered south, better to assist the relieving force now being assembled. For all of Townshend's curious personality quirks he was not an ungenerous man. He wrote in the most handsome term of his subordinate generals at the Battle of Umm-al-Tubul. In his words: 'What would have happened if I had not had those perfect Brigade Commanders? There is no doubt that the most severe selection should be exercised for promotion to Brigadier General.'

He sent a despatch seeking recognition for a number of officers who had performed with distinction, not least those very brigadiers. Among those listed were Generals Mellis, Delamain, Hamilton, Hoghton, Roberts and G.B. Smith RA. It was on this list that he submitted the names of Trench and Coventry for the VC. Nevertheless, the list was not comprehensive and he said that more names would follow. He knew from personal experience that all a soldier can really hope for is a medal or a 'mention', but that when awarded (at little cost to anyone) they are a morale booster.

In early December 1915, the Turks invested Kut by a converging movement on both banks north and south of the Kut peninsular. They advanced and dug in as close as they were able on Townshend's northern front. Soon a veritable warren of fire and communication trenches was in place and the topography started to look like the Western Front in France, with the addition of sun, smells and flies – millions, nay billions, of flies. Townshend flew a public kite by suggesting a further withdrawal to Ali Garbi south of Kut but north of Amara. It was too late in the day for this and fortunately Nixon did not support the idea. Townshend and Nixon corresponded frequently, with Townshend constantly and irritatingly patronizing his boss and by semantic gymnastics confusing most of the issues at hand.

Nur-Ud-Din sent a message to Townshend saying that the British position was hopeless and, in order to save lives, he should surrender. He also complained that the British were exposing the peaceful citizens of Kut to the horrors of war. Townshend replied in courteous terms rejecting the offer to surrender but commenting that the Turkish Army was now led by Germans who were particularly adept at occupying towns in a manner quite peculiar to themselves. Von de Goltz knew all about the shooting of innocent civilians.

On 10 December, Lieutenant General Fenton Aylmer VC, a man CVFT had known from his youth, signalled to say: 'Have assumed command Tigris line. Have utmost confidence in the defender of Chitrál and his gallant troops to keep the flag flying until we can relieve them. Heartiest congratulations on brilliant deed of yourself and your command.'

Townshend's cousin, Sherson, remarked that this message must have been balm, especially the reference to Chitrál some twenty years before. Aylmer had been given a poisoned chalice. He was an officer of the Royal Engineers who expected to find the technology of the day available to him but was disquieted, on taking up his command, to find a dearth of bridging and signalling equipment. Then he found that he had to cope with Nixon's curious reinforcement policy, which involved sending each draft of reinforcements on foot on the fourteen-day march to the north, with their equipment following after them. Their second-line transport which included such trifles as blankets and medical supplies, came on last. Under this extraordinary arrangement the men, quite unnecessarily, spent fourteen very cold nights in the desert. Inevitably the cold and the rigours of the march contributed to some of the reinforcements being medical cases before battle was joined.

CVFT's consistent pressure on Nixon to hasten to his aid was effective and it was promptly transmitted straight to Aylmer, which meant that his disparate, ill-equipped force, one that had never trained as a formation, was to be committed at the very earliest opportunity.[10] It did not auger well.

HM Government belatedly woke up to the potentially disastrous situation at Kut and Chamberlain signalled direct to Townshend asking for information, ignoring the chain of command and adding thereby to the difficulties. He asked about the calibre and effectiveness of the Turkish artillery, how many barges had been lost and what had they contained? How long could he hold out and what was the condition of his troops? Chamberlain, in London, could do nothing about any of these matters but the signal gave Townshend an opportunity in his reply 'to increase the pressure on Nixon, and his reply was a characteristic mixture of optimism, fact, disloyalty and deceit'. This is the opinion of Braddon and the effect of CVFT's reference to 'ten or fifteen days' cannot be ignored. Townshend's response first dealt with the matters of fact concerning the artillery and the loss of stores and equipment. He then went on to say:

My view of the situation is that our strategic offensive has received the usual check, common enough in history when the offensive has not got sufficient troops nor a constant flow of reinforcements to keep the offensive up to its high water mark (Hannibal, Charles XII and Napoleon all failed for the same reason); . . .

This situation can be quickly remedied by rapid concentration of forces and the relief of my beleaguered force, uniting all forces at Kut for a final advance on Baghdad; example, Wellington's resumption of the offensive after his retreat from Burgos . . . The fighting value of my troops has naturally much decreased since Ctesiphon, and although discipline maintains, I am very anxious as to the result if enemy makes a determined onslaught with very superior numbers. We are constantly shelled all day and I am anxious to be relieved in, say, ten or fifteen days.

He now admitted to Nixon that he had rations sufficient for two months and by doing so made clear that the urgency that he had imposed on Aylmer was artificial. For three days – 10, 11 and 12 December – the Turks, by now with about 12,000 men ringing the town, laid a heavy bombardment on Kut which they followed up with successive infantry assaults. It was expensive, quite unnecessary and they suffered an estimated 2,000 casualties. The Turkish wounded could expect little in the way of sophisticated medical aid because there was none available. To be wounded was life-threatening.

The bridge of boats that the cavalry had used for their evacuation from Kut was now a double-edged sword and Townshend could see that it was more of an asset to the Turks than to himself. He ordered that it should be blown up and to this end once more the call went out for volunteers. Lieutenant Sweet 7GR and Lieutenant Mathews RE agreed to lead a mixed party of Gurkhas, sappers and miners to carry out the demolition on the night of 9/10 December. Townshend reported that:

It was a most gallant affair, the two officers going to the enemy's side of the river, across the bridge, which had sagged in places under the swift running current owing to waterlogged pontoons, and laying the saucisson, while the others stood by to cut the anchor cables. [Author's note: in 1915 a 'saucisson' was the French name for a type of fuse made with a long tube of cloth or leather resembling a sausage.]

With the explosion the bridge blew up . . . I recommended both officers for the VC and the men for the Indian Order of Merit.

Townshend failed again to break his duck with recommendations for the VC. Both officers received the DSO which was probably about right at the time. Today, the likelihood is that they would have received the MC. CVFT asserts that, in the period 4–25 December, his losses were 1,625.

The attrition among his soldiers started to rise. He lost 199 men on 9 December, 202 on the 11th, another 88 on the 12th, and a further 122 on the 13th. However, it seemed that the Turks losses were sufficiently greater that they decided there was little profit in frontal assaults on an entrenched enemy with abundant ammunition, and resorted to very efficient sniping instead. A counter-sniping team was formed under a Major Booth of the Signal Company, and he and his team proved to be efficacious. Townshend encouraged frequent trench raids as he considered that 'offensive defence' was an aid to morale. These small-scale raids were successful and the product of one raid was the eleven prisoners that were taken, who incidentally were eleven more mouths to feed. The prisoners were all from 39th Division but they volunteered the information that the 35th, 38th, 45th and 51st Divisions were all besieging Kut, and added the highly unwelcome news that the 52nd and 26th Divisions were on their way. This now all added up to 40,000 or more Turks on the doorstep.

The apparent lull came to a bloody end on Christmas Eve when von de Goltz launched a night attack that culminated at 0200hrs with the Turks forcing their way into one of the strongpoints near 'The Fort', where there was unrestrained, savage, hand-to-hand fighting. The defenders lost 315 killed and wounded but Turkish losses were immeasurably greater and a figure of 2,000 was later confirmed by a Turkish medical officer who was taken prisoner. The defenders had taken 926 casualties in the first three weeks of the siege and the probability is that, of these, 200–300 were killed. The remainder were to be an ongoing problem for the medical officers.

Von de Goltz, having failed in his Christmas Day exercise, left the scene and returned to Baghdad. Enemy dead were strewn in front of the British lines and by 29 December the familiar stench of putrefaction assailed the nostrils of the defenders. An approach under a white flag of truce was made by the Turks who asked if they could bury their dead. This initiative was naturally welcomed but, nevertheless, Townshend warned that, if the tactic previously used dishonourably by the Turks at Gallipoli – that is to say to use the white flag as a means of inserting fresh troops into the forward trenches – was repeated he would open immediate and heavy fire upon them. The Turks did not take up the offer and the conclusion drawn is that they had indeed intended to use the white flag as a ruse. The smell turned the stomachs of the defenders and the Turkish bodies were not moved for three months. By the end of March 1916, exposure to burning sun, cold nights, driving rain and the close attention of the insect population of the Middle East had caused the Turkish corpses to decompose – to the point that they could only be moved into prepared graves by dragging them with long poles fitted with iron hooks. Many bodies fell apart in the process.[11]

It was a grisly sight – these poor men were all some mothers' son.

The trenches got deeper, but only as deep as the water table would allow and the flood season was soon to make digging a very unproductive pastime. Those manning these wet holes in the ground came to have a healthy respect for the Turkish artillery and their expert snipers. Mr H.V. Plumb, when reminiscing with Russell Braddon, said that at first the British troops had been disinclined to believe that they could be hit at 600 yards range. That, after all, would take a very skilled marksman and Kut was not Bisley Common (nor was it Chitrál). However, when an officer was shot dead by a sniper concealed in a sandhill 1,000 yards away it was time for a rethink. Another sniper on the far bank of the river achieved the 700-yard kill of an unwary sergeant. It was clear that if you could be seen then you could be killed. A 'Kut crouch' was developed by the denizens of the garrison.

Mr Plumb went on to say that a hand waved across a loophole or to the side of a protective sandbag would bring a response. Enough hands waved often enough would eventually allow an observer to spot the sniper who would be targeted as he reloaded. The role of the sniper is as important today as it has ever been and in recent years in both Iraq and Afghanistan sniper teams have consistently 'punched above their weight' in that a three-man team can achieve a disproportionately high body count.

The parapets of the trenches were reinforced with anything that came to hand and which could be filled with sand: oil drums, jam tins and window-sills from houses in the town were all turned to good use. Doors and window frames were commandeered to revet the trenches and in the town, houses were requisitioned for military use. The whine of shrapnel was so common-place that it no longer attracted attention and the young unblooded reinforcements soon abandoned any thoughts that they might have had about war being in the least bit 'glorious'. There were unsung heroes in this drab trench war and they came from an unlikely group. The Bhistis were camp followers and water carriers, as was the famous Gunga Din of literary fame. They were small, dark-skinned men in stained turbans and grubby loinclothes whose job it was to keep the garrison supplied with water. They daily ran the risk of sniper fire in order to fill goatskin bags. A quart of water per man was the aim for him to drink and shave in. Brave men, all of them, but not all evaded the snipers.

Major General Sir Charles Mellis vc strode the scene like a human dynamo. He was a remarkable man, as brave as a lion and as profane as a three-badge stoker. He had two dogs with him and he roamed around the perimeter displaying his quite unique personality that raised the morale of all who came within earshot. 'Where the hell is that bugger Delamain?' he roared to the vast amusement of the soldiers and the discomfort of Major General Delamain, a man of a more moderate turn of phrase and, recently promoted, junior to Mellis.

On New Year's Day 1916, a sepoy on sentry in the second line of trenches levelled his rifle and shot at one of his officers – he missed but, undaunted, he then mounted the firestep, lifted himself over the parapet and headed forward in the direction of the British first line. He was en route to join the Turks but it was a forlorn hope and he never got there. He was caught, tried by court martial later that day and was shot at sunset.

Meanwhile, Lieutenant General Sir Fenton Aylmer was assembling his relief force at Ali-al-Gharbi, about 56 miles south of Kut, and Townshend expressed the view that Aylmer should start his move north on 3 January 1916. It was about this time that Townshend's impatience, compounded by his lack of veracity, would lead to another series of disasters. It is tedious to dwell on the accounting accuracy of a general under siege and great mental pressure but, as the siege wore on, the quality of Townshend's accounting became an issue.

As an early example, and using Townshend's own numbers, on 4 December, he claimed a combatant strength of 8,893. He had suffered between 926 and 1,625 casualties, leaving a balance of between 7,967 and 7,268. To those could be added men who were recovering from wounds but who could still fire their personal weapon. In answer to an enquiry from Aylmer he said that he had 'no more than 5000 rifles fit to cooperate' with Aylmer when he arrived. To be generous, part of the apparent discrepancy could be the sick or wounded – some but not all. A further explanation could be that he had disregarded 2,500 men needed for the ongoing defence of Kut and thus they too were unavailable. If either or both of these two speculative suggestions do not fit the case then Charles Townshend had deliberately understated his strength to the man charged to save him – and that begs the question, why?

The daily casualty rate had now dropped to 26–36 per day, most of whom were the result of the incessant shelling which, although random at first, did start to concentrate on Townshend's headquarters. Someone, an Arab one presumes, must have supplied the gunners with the intelligence that allowed them to lay their guns so accurately. Several men were killed in the headquai ᵤᵣs area and more when the hospital was hit. It would have been simple enough for an intrepid Arab to slip out, swim the river and deliver information, and no doubt some did. The Turks did not encourage the local population to decamp because their consumption of food within the forti-fied town was to the Turks' advantage and hastened the impending starvation of the garrison.

Aylmer signalled to say that he had two divisions in his corps. They were the 3rd Lahore Division commanded by Major General Keary and the 7th Meerut Division under Major General Younghusband. Major General Kemball, hitherto the MGGS to Nixon, was now commanding a brigade. A brigade of cavalry had also been allocated to Aylmer who then asked for the details of Kut's forward defences. This was an encouragingly optimistic question but as he faced about 30,000 obstacles with eighty guns between him and Kut, some difficult days lay ahead.

Townshend had concerns about his personal future and, in particular, his promotion to lieutenant general. Any promotion in this theatre was going to go to an officer with two divisions under command but in early January 1916, Townshend was not a likely candidate – he had a horror that perhaps Gorringe, his junior, might be promoted over his head. To be 'passed over' would be difficult to bear. He consoled himself and kept himself in the public eye by his complete domination of the two wirelesses that he had well protected near the town bazaar. The wireless operators were fully employed sending streams of messages to Nixon and to his friends in London, many of whom were of theatrical bent and female. This facility could have provided a comfort to countless families had short personal messages been allowed to his soldiers. They were not and 'Our Charlie' kept the sound waves to himself. The wireless operators who passed all these messages judged him correctly to be 'a bit of a ladies' man' as they noted the names of the recipients.[12] The soldiers had no aspirations to send messages and they looked no further than a cup of hot tea when on sentry. Townshend might have been the subject of mixed emotions among the officers but the respect, bordering on adulation, he enjoyed from his soldiers was unabated.

Whilst Charles Townshend mused on his career prospects, *Firefly*, which had been disabled during the battle at Umm-al-Tubul, reappeared on the river obviously repaired, but now unfortunately in Turkish hands. Townshend had to suffer the ignominy of being shelled by her 4.7" gun from around the Shumran Bend. Two enemy divisions were seen marching eastwards downriver, out of range but clearly moving to a blocking position between Aylmer and Townshend, at which Chitrál Charlie took it upon himself to patronize Aylmer by advising him to initiate a 'turning attack'. This was because, as Charlie put it, 'I very much feared the usual frontal attack, which so many of our generals favour and which I looked on as doomed to failure.' Aylmer probably ground his teeth at this gratuitous advice.

On 7 January, General Gorringe, still in command of 12th Division, made a 'demonstration' up the Shatt-al-Hai. There was some inconclusive fighting but nothing was achieved other than to refill the lamentably inadequate hospitals once more. Aylmer, meanwhile, was striving to turn his corps into a cohesive force whilst in action against a tenacious foe. The 7th Division engaged the Turks about 2½ miles below Sheikh Saad, took losses and could not advance further. The guns of Aylmer's corps could be heard but they never came closer and, at this point, Townshend once again floated the idea to Aylmer of either making a sortie in force or even 'to attempt to cut my way out'. He then argued against his own idea by saying he would have to abandon his wounded and his guns. The following day Nixon cabled to say he was 'not to resort to the expedient of cutting your way out except in desperate extremity. We have plenty of reinforcements here, which are being sent up river as empty shipping is returned, and also daily by road.'

Townshend had never entertained any serious ambitions for a breakout but he had kept Nixon on the back foot by making the offer and in the coming weeks raised the issue again, but the reality was that he had no intention of leaving his lines. He argued, after the event, that to make a foray from Kut would inevitably end in a withdrawal back to the town and that act of withdrawal would be bad for morale. Probably true but it would have been of inestimable help to Aylmer as the Turks, facing an enemy approaching from their rear, would have been somewhat discommoded.

Aylmer sent a message to say that, notwithstanding Townshend's suggestions and advice, he would concentrate his corps at Sheikh Saad prior to an advance on 9 January. Townshend was in no position to do anything but agree. Soon after, two Turkish divisions were seen in the distance, by-passing Kut and heading south to strengthen the force opposing Aylmer. When intelligence reports told Aylmer that he was faced by 30,000 men and eighty-three guns, he asked Townshend to voice an opinion and 'Our Charlie' was only too happy to oblige. He replied saying, '20,000 and 32 guns was more like it' and added that '4000–5000 had been lost since the siege had begun.'[13]

It was curious that Townshend should so comprehensively downgrade the opposition facing Aylmer, based on no concrete information. It served the interests of no one. It may have been to persuade Aylmer to hasten his advance but, if that was the case, the misleading information would compound Aylmer's problems and lead to his defeat. Was it no more than a further symptom of Townshend's mental instability?

Aylmer intended that he would use Sannaiyat, a point about 15 miles downriver from Essinn, as the launch pad for his attack. He selected part of his force to take Sannaiyat and viewed it as likely to be no more than an opening skirmish. However, first it was necessary to take on Sheikh Saad where he had been repulsed before. History repeated itself because a determined Turkish rearguard fought to defend Sheikh Saad with great tenacity and denied Aylmer access even to his launch pad. The fighting was savage and the British and Indian soldiers lost heavily. The wounded, if recovered, were subject to similar privations as the survivors of Ctesiphon just a month earlier. The medical arrangements remained dire, although two weeks before Whitehall had contacted the Viceroy and asked: 'Can the British Red Cross help in any way with hospital supplies for your force?' Hardinge replied: 'Nothing required at present. If anything needed in future, will not hesitate to ask you.'[14] The conduct of Hardinge in this matter amounts to nothing short of criminal neglect.

Nur-Ud-Din's intentions were to fight a delaying action to provide sufficient time for even more reinforcements to reach him. He was preparing to withdraw but von de Goltz countermanded his orders and peremptorily appointed the implacable Khalil Pasha in his place.

On 16 January, von de Goltz visited the Kut front with his entourage to inspect the Turkish lines and the body of mounted observers could be seen from the British lines. They presented an attractive target and there are several versions of what happened next. Townshend reported that:

> One of our guns fired on the group which took refuge in a trench. I was very annoyed with the officer who ordered this gun to be trained on the Field Marshal and fired without my orders for I had great respect for the man whom I considered to be the leading strategist in Europe; I ordered the fire to cease at once.

Townshend was told later that the single round fired at Goltz very nearly killed him. However, Major General G.O. de R. Channer, who was present, said three batteries of guns opened fire. To confuse the matter completely

Braddon asserts, on the evidence of Captain H.S.D. MacNeal, that Goltz was not actually present but that the target was Khalil.

Whatever the facts, Townshend's response to order 'cease fire' was bizarre. This was an extraordinarily 'chivalrous' gesture on Townshend's part and he at once compared the situation with that of Massena reconnoitring the British position at Torres Vedras when British guns merely fired warning shots to deter him. The reality is that to spare the life of the man dedicated to the killing or capture of Townshend and his soldiers was absurd, and it contrasts sharply with an incident that took place at about the same time.

LCpl John Boggis recalled that he was with the GOC on his rooftop observation platform and both were peering through slits in the steel plates that offered some protection from small-arms fire. They looked out over the Turkish lines which now ringed Kut with about 30 miles of trenches. In the far distance a solitary Turkish soldier was at the river bank drawing water.

'Boggis,' called Townshend.

'Sir,' replied his orderly.

'Rifles! See that man over there.' The General pointed out the distant figure. 'We'll have a go at him.'

Both of them aimed, Townshend with a borrowed and unzeroed rifle. The GOC fired first and the man dropped. His can of water, no further use to him in this life, fell unheeded to the desert floor.

'Mine,' exclaimed Townshend exultantly and Boggis was disinclined to argue the toss.

The General was a good shot and now, as he left the roof top, he was in high spirits, singing a music hall hit of the day, 'When I was single my pockets would jingle, I long to be single again.'[15]

Townshend had quite happily killed an anonymous soldier who could have no influence on the outcome of the siege, but had spared the architect of his misfortunes who he knew of, albeit only by repute.

On 26 January, CVFT issued another lengthy communiqué. The issue of starvation had to be faced. Townshend was confident that he could resist a conventional attack but as a student of military history he was painfully aware of the historical precedents that pointed out his vulnerability the longer it took Aylmer to reach him. Bazain had fatally locked up France's best army in Metz and there he had starved. Mach had done no better at Ulm and Cornwallis had been defeated at Yorktown by hunger. Time was not on Townshend's side. Well knowing his vulnerability, he had inexplicably made no arrangements to restrict the consumption of food, having indicated that he had rations sufficient to last until early February. Perhaps it was because he was quite confident that he would be relieved before then, but as Aylmer continued to batter his corps against the unyielding Turkish redoubts to his south, Townshend decided, on 20 January, that a reassessment was called for and put his force onto half rations. When he belatedly instituted a search for foodstuffs in the town, he was gratified to find considerable stocks of grain concealed by the Arab population.

1916 had not brought any comfort as the weather turned for the worse and torrential driving rain propelled by gale-force winds made life misery for the men in the trenches as they started to fill with water. This weather was another factor that Aylmer had to contend with as his men too were wet, cold and dispirited. Nevertheless, Fenton Aylmer battered away at the Turkish block until by late-January he had suffered almost 50 per cent casualties and was running out of steam. Despite the fact that he had no new hard intelligence, locked up as he was in Kut, Townshend continued to share his thoughts with Aylmer and with Nixon as to how they might want to proceed in effecting his salvation.

Aylmer's protracted, costly and abortive attempts to break through to Kut are a saga, worth a book in its own right. This most gallant of officers knew that he faced a strong and implacable enemy and, after a series of rebuffs, he could see no alternative but for Townshend to cross the river and march round the enemy flank on the right bank to assist. He made the suggestion again, for the fourth time, on 21 January. What is more, he explained that his engineers proposed that 'they run a cable to the far bank of the Tigris, loop it over a pulley, bring it back to the Kut bank and attach it to the bow of a mahaila. The Kut end of the cable being attached to the stern.' A flying bridge it was called.[16] It would speed the transit of troops from one bank to another and would contribute to the rapid build-up of a bridgehead on the far bank.

There was no doubting the practicality of the idea but Townshend was not enthused and, whilst invariably paying lip service to the break-out philosophy, did nothing practical to implement it. Aylmer was left to fight his own battles. As it happened, Nixon, on his last day in command, and from his sick bed, countermanded that suggestion, producing some inventive figures to support his judgment. It was the last decision he took in this campaign and it was almost certainly the wrong one. Lieutenant General Sir John Nixon, who had been ailing for some time, was invalided back to India and would have the rest of his life to think about the suffering that had directly resulted from his heroic incompetence, conducted on a titanic scale.

*   *   *

Lieutenant General Sir Percy Lake arrived from India to take command. For the purpose of this narrative, the reader is spared the heart-rending detail of Aylmer's dreadful losses and the manner that they were incurred. Suffice to say that Townshend, who was no more than a passive, very long-range observer and critic did nothing to assist in any material form.

In the town of Kut, exuding confidence and authority, he patrolled his parish accompanied by the faithful 'Spot'. He seemed to be impervious to the constant shelling and by his very presence he imbued his men with confidence.[17] He looked like a general and he acted like one. The men had food, water and well-constructed defences. They had started with ample ammunition – about 800 rounds per rifle – and there was plenty left. Life was uncomfortable; it was hot and sweaty during the day and very cold at night but, as generations of soldiers have said, 'If you can't take a joke you shouldn't have joined.' The garrison at Kut was well ordered, organized and in good heart.

In Basra it was very different. Here, the dreadful legacy of Nixon was evident and General Lake was horrified at what he found. Hitherto, he had been Chief-of-Staff to General Duff, the Commander–in-Chief. In that appointment he had seen all the telegrams, read all the letters and thought he had a handle on the situation in Mesopotamia. Now he found out how deeply he had been misled and realized how severe the problems were. Nothing of any significance had been achieved in terms of port facilities since IEFD had arrived on this barren shore over a year before. Ships still arrived with war stores and could not be unloaded for days, and then, when unloading started, there was the double handling in and out of mahailas. The dockside was still chaotic and, as reinforcements arrived, they could see with a sense of foreboding that the hospital system had broken down. Having disembarked, there was no transport to move them up–country and in any case their equipment might well be on another ship, idling its time in mid-stream and waiting to be unloaded. The man responsible for this utter shambles was now home in India.

It was down to Lake to pick up the pieces.

On 23 January, Townshend produced yet another of his 'appreciations of the situation'. In summary, he said he had three options and these were: (A) to break out with as many able-bodied men as possible; (B) to defend Kut to the last round; or (C) to negotiate with the enemy and give up Kut in exchange for free passage for his garrison. Townshend recommended plan 'A', with his tongue firmly in his cheek, because his staff had already proved that they did not have the means to meet the logistic effort of crossing the river at night undetected. All the principal players acknowledged that a crossing, if detected, would be a catastrophe. Notwithstanding this, Townshend had proposed a solution that he knew full well was quite impractical. He disregarded the suggestion made by the engineers of Aylmer's corps about a flying bridge, but the idea refused to die. In a response that must have caused Townshend consternation, Lake said that thought that the breakout was a good idea and told him to start to plan the operation, but to take no action until he, Lake, had visited Aylmer in the field.

Option 'C' had obviously been in Charlie's mind and his anger at the shelling of Goltz a few days earlier starts to make sense. This was the man with whom he hoped to negotiate his way to freedom, and throwing high explosive at the other party is no way to win friends and influence people.

Townshend returned to the subject of food and provided an inventory of his stocks which amounted to a further thirty-four days' worth of rations with the addition of 80 tons of barley and ample horse meat – still sadly on the hoof and starving. On 26 January, Townshend issued the following communiqué to his beleaguered men:

> The Relief Force under General Aylmer has been unsuccessful in its efforts to dislodge the Turks entrenched on the left bank of the river, some fourteen miles below the position at Essinn, where we defeated the Turks in September last when their strength was greater than it is now. Our relieving force suffered severe loss and had very bad weather to contend against. They are entrenched close to the Turkish position. More reinforcements are on their way up river and I confidently expect to be relieved some day during the first half of the month of February.
>
> I desire all ranks to know why I decided to make a stand at Kut during our retirement from Ctesiphon. It was because so long as we hold Kut the Turks cannot get their ships, barges, stores and munitions past this place, and so cannot move down to attack Amarah. Thus we are holding up the whole of the Turkish advance. It also gives time for our reinforcements to come up river from Basra and so restore success to our arms; it gives time for our allies, the Russians, who are now overrunning Persia, to move towards Baghdad. I had a personal message from General Baratoff, commanding the Russian Expeditionary Force in Persia, the other day, telling me of his admiration of what you men of the 6th Division and troops attached have done in the past few months, and telling me of his own progress on the road from Kirmanshah, towards Baghdad.

By standing at Kut I maintain the territory we have won in the past year at the expense of much blood, commencing with our glorious victory at Shaiba, and thus we maintain the campaign as a glorious one instead of letting disaster pursue its course down to Amarah and perhaps beyond. I have ample food for 84 days, and that is not counting 3000 animals which can be eaten. When I defended Chitral some twenty years ago, we lived well on atta and horse-flesh, but, I repeat, I expect confidently to be relieved in the first half of the month of February.

Our duty stands out plain and simple. It is our duty to our Empire, to our beloved King and Country, to stand here and hold up the Turkish advance as we are doing now, and with the help of all, heart and soul with me together, we will make this defence to be remembered in history as a glorious one. All in England and India are watching us now and are proud of the splendid courage and devotion you have shown. Let all remember the glorious defence of Plevna,[18] for that is what is in my mind.

I am absolutely calm and confident as to the result. The Turk, although good behind a trench, is of little value in the attack. They have tried it once, and their losses in one night in their attempt on the Fort were 2,000 alone. They have also had very heavy losses from General Aylmer's musketry and guns. I have no doubt they have had enough. I want to tell you now that, when I was ordered to advance on Ctesiphon I officially demanded an army corps, or at least two divisions, to perform the task successfully. Having pointed out the grave danger of attempting to do this, God knows I felt our heavy losses, and the sufferings of my poor brave wounded, and I shall remember it as long as I may live. I may truly say that no General I know of has been more obeyed and served than I have been in command of the Sixth Division. These words are long, I am afraid, but I speak straight from the heart, and you see I have thrown all officialdom overboard. We will succeed; mark my word. Save your ammunition as if it were gold.

CHARLES TOWNSHEND
Kut-al-Amarah.
Major-General Commanding 6th Division

Closer examination of the communiqué does not show the GOC in an attractive light. His opening remark denigrates Aylmer and his men and his final paragraph is drafted in disloyal terms, unfitting for a general officer.

'Our Charlie' knew his audience and, although the communiqué attracted adverse comment from people who were not fighting for their lives, the brigade commanders reported that the message was very well received by the 'Kuttites' as they now called themselves. The Commanding Officer of 7th Rajputs, Colonel Parr, was asked to write to the GOC on behalf of the Indian officers of the Battalion and, in his letter, the Colonel assured Townshend that his officers were 'with him to the last breath'.[19]

Sherson, that most sympathetic of biographers, draws attention to Townshend's frequent visits to the hospital and his generosity in giving small gifts to the wounded. There is no doubt that they were appreciated and 'Our Charlie's stock, at least with his British soldiers, was undiminished. Unfortunately, CVFT's hospital visits were concentrated on the British soldiers and he ignored his wounded Indians. Similarly, he rarely visited the firing line to see for himself the conditions under which his men were living and fighting. He never went to Wool Press village.

It is interesting that his ration reserves had been subject to regular upward revision. On 3 December, he had announced that he only had rations for a month but on 6 December, having been told that relief would come within two months, he updated his assessment to sixty days. On 20 January, he had complained that he now only had rations for ten more days but, later that day, and presumably to negate the need for a sortie, he revised his provision state to twenty-seven days. On 24 January, he announced that by killing his horses and mules he had sufficient food for fifty-six days, this figure being further enhanced in his communiqué to eighty-four days. His credibility in Basra and in Aylmer's Corps Headquarters must have been very low, and justifiably so, because Aylmer's frantic efforts to get to Kut were all based on the supposition that the garrison was short of food. He and the entire system had been cynically and comprehensively misled by Townshend. The only interpretation that can be put on this is that Townshend lied in order to manipulate Aylmer. This manipulation cost lives and, one day, Townshend would be called to account. The GOC took stock at the end of January and noted that on 27 January he had:

> 8356 effectives of whom 6430 were infantry. If I include combatants in hospital, men of the Field Ambulance, Medical establishments and Supply and Transport Corps the total was 10,513 men; in addition we had 2908 native followers and so a total of 13,421 moths to feed. The casualties up to 27 January were 2240. There were 756 rounds for each of 7100 rifles.

The town under siege wrestled with the practical problem of turning raw materials into palatable food. Wood was virtually all gone, either to revet the trenches or to burn in the ovens. Millstones had to be found to grind the available grain and those that were available were so smooth that they had to be recut by a Dorset who had the requisite skills.[20] The sheer size of the grinding operation could not depend on just two plodding donkeys, and so a pump was rigged up to force water from the Tigris to supplement their labours, and presumably this also relieved the Bhistis of the hazardous task of filling water containers at the water's edge. Soon 960 lb of flour a day was being produced. The dearth of wood was a problem, but a barge full of oil tied up on the river provided the solution and the ovens became oil-fired. It is so easy for a latter-day author to summarize these activities as routine and cover them in a few glib words. However, for the Kuttites life was getting difficult and even simple problems required inventiveness and initiative if they were to be solved.

The food was not attractive but it sustained life. Major General H.H. Rich commented that 'horse-meat was pleasant enough; mule-meat was sinewy; ox-meat was jaw breaking. The diet was supplemented by the meagre bodies of the starlings shot in Kut and sparrows in Wool Press Village to which starling and generals never came.'

Mr T.A. Lloyd, in commenting on the diet, recalled an incident in the hospital where a Dorset soldier, who had been the victim of a sniper, called out to a boyhood friend, now a gunner, as he passed by.

'Tom?'

'What happened to you?'

'Sniper.'

'How are you getting on?'

'Ah, we're not getting much here.'

The gunner returned to his billet by the brick kilns and made a collection; he raised eight rupees and, armed with the cash, walked into town. He entered into negotiations with an Arab over a can of condensed milk, paid the money and returned to the hospital. His friend's bed space was empty.

'Sorry,' sympathized an orderly, 'you're too late.'

There were innumerable incidents of similar poignancy as this, as soldiers did their best for friends who were wounded or sick. Without exception men sought to avoid the hospital and, although life in the trenches was miserable, it was at least as active a life as one could hope for. In the trenches it was a cold, muddy existence – there were no newspapers, precious little to eat and drink, and no form of entertainment other than the conversation of comrades. Football matches, long played, were rehashed and debated at length. As January gave way to February, at the very top of the Kuttites' 'wish list' were a hot bath, roast beef, a welcoming kiss and a warm hearth. The list had not changed since Ctesiphon.

There were 35,000 well-entrenched, well-fed, confident Turkish troops between Aylmer and Townshend and, to make matters much worse, after the evacuation from the Dardanelles by the Allies, which started on 8 January 1916, several Turkish formations were freed up for employment elsewhere. The very bad news was that a further 36,000 Turks were on their way to Mesopotamia. Lake had about 40,000 men but he was inhibited by his deeply flawed administrative arrangements in Basra that were going to take months to sort out.

In Mesopotamia, the weather is a constant factor for the soldier to consider. The flood in January that had driven the Kuttites from their trenches and which was now receding would be as nothing when the snow on the mountains melted in March. The snow melt fed innumerable small streams and they all flowed to the Tigris. The annual inundation that would come in March would make any opposed advance on Kut impossible. Lake's appreciation was that, come what may, Kut had to be relieved in February 1916.

There was a lull before the storm as the level of the Tigris dropped, and the trenches dried out a little. Major General Rich recalled a game played by both sides. It appears that as either side was digging and the blade of a shovel appeared above the parapet of the trench, it would at once attract fire, thus becoming a non-lethal game. One of the Turks, something of a sport, entered into the spirit of the contest and exposed his shovel every few seconds. The shovel moved its position and the length of its exposures also varied – it was all just like 'snap' practice on Bisley common. After one exposure the shovel disappeared and several hundred British soldiers squinted over their sights at the Turkish parapet waiting for the next one. There was a lengthy pause and, as shooting men know under these conditions, the eyes water, the muscles tighten and the foresight starts to waver. Suddenly the Turkish shovel reappeared – sporting a white bandage.

Life in Kut had other lighter moments and one such was when the GOC paid a forewarned and unusual visit to a section of the line. He arrived as the officer responsible was bathing naked from a bucket assisted by his orderly. The naked officer saw the GOC and hastily reached for his clothes. 'No, No,' said Townshend, 'come as you are and show me everything. Your men will enjoy seeing you like that.'[21]

*   *   *

The 13th Division was en route to Mesopotamia, but was going to arrive far too late for a February offensive. The importance of this new division to be added to the order of battle of IEFD was that it would generate the formation of a new corps in addition to that of Aylmer's. Remarkably, and whilst in the middle of a siege, Townshend thought it important enough to signal General Lake asking that his name be put to General Duff as the commander of the new corps and, by implication, promotion to lieutenant general. This was another piece of extraordinary self-advertisement from an officer physically unable to exercise command anywhere but within the confines of Kut.

The intrepid RFC pilots in their canvas and string aeroplanes flew missions to Kut and free-dropped whatever they could carry. The base organization had curious priorities and caused these men to risk their lives by delivering newspapers and correspondence for Townshend and Townshend alone. On one occasion the package was opened eagerly to find that it contained rifle pull-throughs.[22]

At no time during the siege of Kut did Townshend make any attempt to get mail for his troops in, or messages from them out, both measures that would have been easy to initiate and would have brought great comfort to many.

The horses and mules were being progressively slaughtered and provided meat of a sort, but horsemeat was unacceptable to the Sikhs, Dogras and Raputs on religious grounds. To eat horsemeat would be to invite social death. No such man would be welcomed as a husband or son-in-law; a family would spurn a son who had transgressed. Townshend needed these soldiers – all 7,000 of them. If they were to be effective soldiers, they had to eat what was available and that was horse. Rather than offend against their beliefs they would starve. In the opinion of one Kuttite, Colonel R.O. Chamier, Townshend could have given an order to his Indian troops to eat horsemeat and they would have complied. As it was, the GOC sought the help of Simla to obtain dispensation from the spiritual leaders of those concerned. It was duly given, albeit rather late in the day, and on the understanding that the beasts were killed in accordance with religious custom that their throats were cut.

It was a source of some irritation to the Kuttites that the Turks would perform their daily defecation in the river that provided both sides with water in the Kut area and a much larger population downstream. Inexplicably, some of them chose to perform in sight of the garrison and within rifle shot. Townshend would invite officers to join him at daybreak and together they would snipe the squatting Turks. 'Shooting a sitting Turk was,' in the judgment of some, 'unsporting.'[23] That said, Townshend's prowess was admired.

There was now a trickle of desertions from the ranks of the Indian units. The sepoys slipped into the river and hoped that the current would take them to the Turkish lines but, to get there, they had to float past the British picquets on the bank. If seen they were shot. Similarly, any who were captured in the act of deserting were also summarily shot. Those few who did get through to the Turkish lines were not assured of a particularly warm welcome and were clothed in a special black uniform so that they could be readily identified.

The Tigris was central to life in Kut, indeed to life in Mesopotamia, and was summed up admirably and almost poetically as follows:

> The muddy, orange-coloured Tigris was many things to the men of Kut. She slaked their thirst, and was therefore blessed. She succoured their enemy, and was therefore cursed. She was their link with freedom, and was therefore friendly. She was a barrier against freedom, and was therefore hostile. She was their moat and therefore protective. She was the spy's route to the enemy, and therefore threatening. She was their own escape route, and therefore kindly. She flooded and drowned them, and was therefore malignant.[24]

The days passed, one much like another. The sniping and shelling produced a consistent harvest of dead and wounded; most of those who fell to snipers were head shots and beyond medical help, but the shelling casualties suffered a miscellany of injuries that shattered limbs and torsos. The filth, diet, flies and cold generated sickness. Inexorably, men lost weight and the health of the Kuttites started to deteriorate. The hospital was filled as the doctors and their staff worked ceaselessly to alleviate the suffering, but not always with success as medical stores started to run out.

When Lake assumed command in the theatre, in mid–February 1916, the War Office took over direction of the campaign. This was in response to the public outcry that developed when it was finally revealed to the public in Great Britain that, far from Townshend merely 'returning to a coaling station on the Tigris', he and his 6th Division were in fact under siege. What is more, the scandalous manner in which the Indian Government had managed affairs had leaked out and this had added to the widespread anger.

The Sailor King, who had an empathy with the Services, sent a signal of encouragement on 17 February, in itself an indication of the gravity of the situation. After Townshend had responded by saying 'the knowledge that we have gained the praise of our beloved Sovereign and our fellow-countrymen will be our sheet anchor in this defence', he then promptly fired off another signal to Lake, this time advising him, gratuitously, to emulate himself by defending his lines of communication with soldiers convalescing from hospital, and pointing out that he, Townshend, had adopted a similar policy to release fit men for the more arduous tasks with great success. General Lake had been a supporter of the GOC 6th Division whilst both were serving in India, but by now, and after only a brief and geographically distant relationship on Active Service, Lake's attitude towards Townshend started to change.

Townshend cabled the Russian General Baratoff who had recently taken the Turkish fortress of Erzroum, congratulating him and allying himself with the Russian's tactics, commenting that they both 'believed in the economy of force'.[25] The exchange of messages would have been seen by Lake and he would have noted the implied and, again, gratuitous advice.

It had always been highly unlikely that the 13th Division was ever going to arrive in time to influence events and by mid-February any faint hopes that beat in optimistic breasts were finally stilled – 13th Division would most definitely not participate in any relief of Kut for several weeks. Aylmer had no choice but to assault the Turks with the limited assets he had on the ground. He therefore launched the last of four abortive attacks but could not budge his tenacious adversary. The casualty lists lengthened and the hospitals in Basra and Amara were refilled. In the distance, and out of sight, the Kuttites could hear Aylmer's guns and their answering Turkish opposite numbers. They were prepared to launch themselves from their trenches, into the mahailas and undertake a contested crossing of the river, if the opportunity presented itself. But it did not.

It was probably just as well that that opportunity did not arise because to cross under fire would have been disastrous. The Turks well realized that a breakout was an option and, to deter such thoughts, they brought their artillery to bear on Wool Press Village. They supplemented the artillery with energetic sniping and made it abundantly clear that any move from the trenches would be hazardous in the extreme. Mr A. Hayden, when speaking about this phase of the siege, said that, as always, Major General Mellis was in the thick of the action and was very often in the front-line trenches. One day, as he made his way down the trenches offering his uniquely profane advice and support, one of his soldiers let out a cry of rage. It appeared that by some chance of, perhaps, trillions to one, a Turkish sniper had fired a round straight down the soldier's rifle barrel. It had done the weapon a power of no good and frightened the man who protested to Mellis.

'Look what that bastard's done to my rifle,' he complained. 'He bloody nearly killed me.'

Mellis enjoyed the moment, patted the soldier on the arm and said, 'Give it to 'im, my boy.' Then he moved on chuckling, old warhorse that he was, relishing the situation about him. Mellis was not the intellectual or tactical equal of Townshend but he was a practical soldier to his boot straps. He was held in deep affection by his men because they knew, and had seen ample evidence, that they were his first and overriding priority.

Morale started to drop by the middle of February, especially among the Indian troops, and on 22 February, Charles Townshend's diary noted soberly:

> A Mohammedan sepoy of the 119th Infantry, who shot the Jemadar Adjutant of the battalion dead yesterday, was tried by court martial and sentenced to death. I confirmed it and ordered sentence to be carried out at the fort at sunset. Another Mohammedan sepoy, of the 66th Punjab Infantry, deserted, and also a third of the 120th Infantry quartered in the Liquorice village on the right bank . . . two Mohammedans of the 78th Punjabis also deserted.

The solid citizens of the British county regiments, however, remained stoically at their posts. The desertion of just a single British soldier, anywhere, was extremely serious, but in these circumstances it would have had a catastrophic effect on morale.

On 22 February, Aylmer tried again, even though he was facing a force of 32,000 in well-prepared defensive positions. The attack was on the right bank and towards and directed at Essinn and the Dejailah depression (see Fig 9 on Page 191). The Turks had established themselves, in force, at Hannah on the left bank, and had constructed a bridge over the Hai River to their rear and on the right bank. The Essinn redoubt was a formidable obstacle, much more so than when 6th Division had taken it, just a few months earlier. Aylmer's hope that Chitrál Charlie's men would rise from their trenches, cross the river and attack the Turkish rear at Essinn, or indeed advance to Hannah, went unfulfilled and the attack failed. More men were killed and the hospitals were replenished with shattered bodies. Aylmer's series of attacks petered out, having achieved nothing.

Meanwhile, in the mountains, it was getting just a little warmer and the first of the snow melt trickled down to the Tigris.

On 26 February, a battered Aylmer signalled Townshend to say that he intended to advance and make a flank attack on a position known as the Dejailah Redoubt on the right bank. Once again the matter of Townshend and his Kuttites leaving their positions and contributing to the action as soon as the flanking attack was having an effect was suggested, despite it being tactically desirable but practical nonsense. It would take Townshend eight hours to get a viable force across the river, and then only if it all went like clockwork. Should the sortie fail then that element of his force across the river would be annihilated as it would have no means of withdrawing quickly back into Kut.

Aylmer's insistence that the sortie be attempted was, surprisingly, not disputed by Townshend, for he of all people was painfully aware of the desperate folly of such an expedition. Nevertheless, he made plans to cross the river with two brigades and two four-gun batteries. He commented: 'General Aylmer knew all the difficulties and delays of my crossing, which were so great as to make my co-operation of little practical use.' He went on to say: 'I was much concerned at my means of crossing the river. Two flying-bridges, two or three rafts, the *Sumana*, and a barge made it a most difficult problem to cross with any rapidity. I could not begin the flying-bridge preparations till Aylmer was engaged in battle, or it would show the enemy what was intended.'

In a message to Aylmer he did not reject the crossing out of hand but he drenched it with very cold water by explaining:

> If I cross at night there is no concealment in the terrain on the right bank (even if I could cross unobserved) and I should be overwhelmed on that bank before you could arrive. My engineers declare it will take three hours to fix up the flying-bridge, and a further two hours for a small mahaila flying-bridge. Commander RE says that not more than 150 men an hour could be crossed by the flying-bridges.

One hundred and fifty men an hour does seem to be a very small, conveniently impractical number. A cynic might speculate that the figure is Townshend's and not that of his Commander, Royal Engineers (CRE)`.

Aylmer's attack failed and the Kuttites were not required to vacate their uncomfortable trenches for the hazards of the right bank. German aeroplanes started to fly over the besieged town and perversely made the clearly marked hospital their target. The anti-aircraft defences were rudimentary in the extreme – Lewis guns mounted on tripods. This most dependable of weapons was designed to be fired from the horizontal position and, when fired almost vertically, feeding the weapon with ammunition was difficult and it was prone to jam. On 1 March 1916, three German planes dropped about forty bombs on the town and nine men were killed, twenty-eight wounded. The civilians suffered too – six were killed, four were wounded and sixteen were buried in debris. Townshend remarked: 'If one of the German pilots had fallen into the hands of my troops he would have been torn to pieces . . . the victims were often women and children and our poor wounded in hospital.'

There was a rumour that the Turks were about to use poison gas supplied by their German friends, the same product that was being used on the Western Front. Townshend, ruthless as he sometimes was, nevertheless described the use of gas as 'cowardly barbarism worthy of Chinese pirates'. He responded by issuing gas masks to his troops in the trench line. As it happens gas was never deployed and one wonders how the rumour originally started. The soldiers were unimpressed and responded in their normal cynical and negative manner. 'Fancy this place having respirators. Respirators being a bit of flannel you had to piss on and then wrapped around your mouth and nostrils. No bloody food but respirators you pissed on. Typical bloody army.'[26]

In the trenches the conversation was desultory because in this, the fourth month of the siege, anything of importance had already been said.

'You know the worst thing about this place?'

'Yes, no smokes.'

'The worst thing is the scrawny cats.'

'Wonder what cat tastes like?'[27]

The Turks were not living in the lap of luxury either. Their logistic chain was unhindered, but nevertheless the food was indifferent, medical support was inadequate and overlaying it all was a code of discipline that was draconian in the extreme. They cleaned their weapons and braced themselves for Aylmer's next approach.

In Kut the sappers laboured to construct the elements of the flying-bridge and were closely observed by three recalcitrant Arabs who took due note of proceedings. On the night of 4 March, the three men swam the river and reported to the Turks what was taking place in Kut. Immediately the Turkish picquets were strengthened and the possibility of a surprise crossing, which was never high, was even further reduced.

On 5 March, the sappers made an attempt to float a large mine downriver to blow up one of Khalil's bridges. It seemed like a good idea at the time but after its departure from Wool Press Village it bobbed downriver until it hit a sandbank, exploded and spread several tons of sand over the surrounding district. E.W.C. Sandes was more specific and commented that it created a crater in the bank of the Shatt-al-Hai.

CVFT did nothing for his reputation that same day when he sent, by wireless, his despatches from Ctesiphon to General Lake. He named those he thought should be decorated for their service, not least Colonel Climo, and then commented, ill advisedly, that his division had:

> Suffered professionally in comparison with our comrades in the European theatres of war who, in many instances, are being promoted over our heads simply because the despatches of their operations were promptly published and promptly rewarded. I knew in my own case that several major generals junior to me in the Army had been promoted to lieutenant general over my head although these officers had not had an independent command nor such responsibilities as I had.

Sadly, and although he wrapped it all up in expressions of concern for his subordinates, the sub-text was unmistakably 'what about me? What about a decoration and what about promotion?' Townshend, despite his lifetime in the Army, did not seem to grasp the simple facts that rank is designed to be commensurate with responsibility and that promotion is dependent upon 'merit tempered by seniority'. Lake would have been disappointed in his one-time protégé.

Aylmer had intended to make another attempt to relieve Kut on 4 March but was delayed by the weather which did not moderate until 8 March, much to the disapproval of Townshend who observed that the delay gave the Turks time to continue with trench construction to close the gap between the Dejailah redoubt and the Hai River. Notwithstanding that, Townshend commented to both Lake and Aylmer that the Turkish position was undermanned and that only 8,000 men were holding a line 13 miles long. He remarked that his friend should 'easily break through'. He made Aylmer's task sound like a piece of cake – which it was not.

In Kut the garrison prepared to break out to support the turning attack that was to sweep through the desert after a night march to attack the far right of the Turkish position, some 14 miles from the river. The strongest swimmers had been briefed as the first to cross in mahailas and on rafts.[28] Getting across the river would be just the beginning. Scaling the steep, slippery and muddy banks on the far side and digging in under Turkish fire would be a major task on its own. Any subsequent advance to assist Aylmer would be entirely dependent upon the success of the bridgehead. Townshend was absolutely not going to commit himself until, in effect, Aylmer had carried the day.

To the south, and after a very long march, Kemball was in position at dawn only a mile from the thinly manned Turkish redoubt. Unfortunately his gunners were not in position and his orders were to attack only after a concentration had been laid on the Turkish lines. He challenged the order but was told to wait. The wait was fatal and as the sun rose in the sky the Turks could see their adversaries – waiting.

The extra time gifted to the Turks by the bad weather had been put to good use. When Aylmer finally mounted his outflanking attack on the redoubt, 'it failed utterly',[29] with the loss of 3,476 casualties to add to the 7,000 incurred in the earlier assaults that had all been prematurely launched at Townshend's urging.

The Turks suffered heavy losses but they did not concede the ground. They were fortunate that, with ample bridging equipment in place, they were able to move reinforcements across the river from the left bank and it was these that won the day. Aylmer was repulsed and the writing was on the wall. Generals who lose battles are invariably replaced and brave Aylmer was to be no exception.

Aylmer sent a message to Kut to say that he would have to retire from his advanced 'position on the right bank unless the Turks withdraw, which does not seem probable. We shall be unable to maintain ourselves in present position owing to a lack of water.'

This 'lack of water' was a direct consequence of the flanking movement that had taken the Tigris Corps so far from the river. In the meantime, on 10 March 1916, Townshend issued another of his communiqués, or as the soldiers called them, 'c'municks'. The document was printed and circulated to every locality. It said:

As on a former occasion, I take the troops of all ranks into my confidence again.

We have now stood a three months' siege in a manner which has called upon you the praise of our beloved King and our fellow-countrymen in England, Scotland, Ireland and India, and all this after your brilliant battles of Kut-el-Amara and Ctesiphon and your retirement to Kut, all of which feats of arms are now famous.

Since December 5, 1915, you have spent three months of cruel uncertainty, and to all men and all people uncertainty is intolerable.

As I say, on the top of all this comes the second failure to relieve us. And I ask you also to give a little sympathy to me who have commanded you in these battles referred to, and who, having come to you as a stranger, now love my command with a depth of feeling I have never known in my life before.

When I mention myself I would also mention the names of the generals under me, whose names are distinguished in the army as leaders of men.

I am speaking to you as I did before, straight from the heart, and, as I say, I ask your sympathy for my feelings, having promised you relief on certain dates on the promise of those ordered to relieve us. Not their fault, no doubt. Do not think that I blame them; they are giving their lives freely, and deserve our gratitude and admiration.

But I want you to help me again, as before. I have asked General Aylmer for the next attempt to bring such numbers as will break down all resistance and leave no doubt as to the issue.

In order, then, to hold out, I am killing a large number of horses so as to reduce the quantity of grain eaten every day, and I have had to reduce your ration. It is necessary to do this in order to keep our flag flying.

I am determined to hold out, and I know you are with me heart and soul.

'Our Charlie' was very ill-advised to write in such terms and tone. Even taking into consideration the stress that he was under, pleading for the sympathy of his soldiers was demeaning and it had quite the opposite effect to that he had hoped for. Mr R. Hague recalled hearing a gunner sergeant mutter, 'Well if General Mellis had said that I'd have dropped dead from the shock.' Events moved swiftly and Fenton Aylmer was duly sacked. A most gallant officer's career came to an abrupt and sad end. He wrote to Townshend on 12 March, as follows:

My Dear Townshend,
    The War Office says that my conduct of operations has been unfortunate, and have ordered my suspension. I need not tell you how deeply I grieve that I have not been able to relieve you; but have every confidence that my successor will be able to do so very soon. I have had a harder task than most people realise. It all looks very easy when you sit in an armchair at the WO! The business a few days ago very

nearly came off. I cannot tell you how much I admire the splendid way in which you are defending Kut. I heartily pray that you will gain your reward in speedy relief. Give my best wishes to Delamain, Mellis, and Hamilton. Goodbye and God bless you all and may you be more fortunate than myself.

Yours ever,

E.G. Aylmer

Aylmer's conduct in defeat and professional disgrace was exemplary. He did not complain and, like the good soldier he was, he 'turned to his right, saluted and marched off parade'. Later he was called to give evidence to the Mesopotamia Commission and only then did he say that he had fought his last action against his better judgment, but that he was acting under the orders of his superiors. He went on to say that he had proposed another plan that had not been accepted.

Townshend sent Aylmer a message of sympathy, noting: 'I knew his heart must be broken.' He may not have thought it through but with the loss of Aylmer, the only candidate to replace him was the Chief-of-Staff of the Tigris Corps, one Major General George Gorringe. The inevitable appointment of Gorringe as the Corps Commander and his promotion, albeit temporary, to lieutenant general was not well received by Townshend. John Boggis recalled that Charles Townshend expostulated to one of his staff officers, 'But, he's *junior* to me, its all wrong!' Later that day, and having had time to dwell on what he saw as a personal affront, the GOC 6th Division burst into tears and wept on the shoulder of another of his officers. It was not a pretty sight and, taken in combination with his recent communiqué, Townshend was starting to erode the respect of those around him.

Khalil wrote to Townshend just after this most recent reverse as follows:

Your Excellency,

The English forces which came to relieve you were compelled to retreat after giving battle at Felahiyeh and suffering 7000 casualties. After this retreat, General Aylmer, who was a month and a half making his preparations, yesterday, when he thought he was strong enough, resumed the offensive, as you saw. But he was again compelled to retreat with 4000 casualties, and I am left with adequate forces.

For your part, you have heroically fulfilled your military duty. From henceforth, there is no likelihood that you will be relieved. According to your deserters, I believe that you are without food and that diseases are prevalent among your troops. You are free to continue your resistance at Kut, or to surrender to my forces, which are growing larger and larger.

Receive, General, the assurances of our highest consideration Khalil

Khalil knew that the end was now in sight. He had seen off Aylmer and had no fears of what Gorringe might do. Townshend's food stocks were running low and as the Kuttites had little hope of salvation, he could afford to be courteous – his invitation to surrender was well judged. He expected the offer to be rejected and it was, however, the courteous tone of the letter and the phrase 'assurances of our highest consideration' sparked in Townshend the pious hope that, if he could negotiate a surrender, the possibility was that he and his men would be allowed to march to freedom through the Turkish lines, albeit without their weapons.

The snow on the mountains of the Caucasus was melting fast and the Tigris started to rise. All the participants knew that once the river burst its banks the manoeuvring of both armies would be drastically curtailed. The flood was inevitable and it would be much more damaging to the British.

The Kuttites were hungry, they were lousy, their clothes were in tatters and their boots in sore need of repair or replacement. Only their weapons were clean. The distribution of horse and mule meat was carefully watched and the Wool Press garrison, in particular, felt ill-used because they did not get a fair share. The unexpected issue of 90 lb of offal – liver and hearts, delivered across the river by the *Sumana* was greeted with disproportionate joy by the recipients. Wool Press was defended by about half of the brigade commanded by Hamilton; it was accessible by boat and *Sumana* made the trip daily, but General Hamilton only visited his men once in the four months of the siege – his men were unimpressed. The flies flourished, multiplied and bit.

The slaughter of horses and mules was raised to twenty-five a day and the officers all hoped fervently that their charger would be spared. When a favourite beast was killed even hardened soldiers wept.

The one hundredth day of the siege was marked on 13 March and there was speculation that the unenviable record of Ladysmith, which held out for one hundred and twenty days, might yet be eclipsed. The general attitude was, 'not another three more weeks of this, surely not?' Officers who knew Gorringe had little faith in his ability; he was a general out of time. He was devoid of any tactical skill who would have been better suited to warfare against the ill-armed, dissident tribesmen on the fringes of the

Empire some forty years before. Brigadier General Fraser, commenting on his commander's talents after the abortive attack at Sannaiyat on 5 April 1916, said, 'His cursed optimism, contempt for the Turks, contempt for the principles of war and for the lessons of *this* war, have again landed us in failure and run up a butcher's bill. This is culpable homicide.'

The river broke its banks and trenches, on both sides, were flooded and abandoned. The right bank, up which any assault by Gorringe was expected, was more severely flooded than the left. The tactical options were drastically reduced. The weather was now hotter, more humid and the flies seemed to have multiplied. Fleas and lice were now additional irritants. The security of rations became an issue when the ration store was surrounded by thousands of starving men.

Boggis sought some horse liver from the butcher for Townshend's supper, but the butcher demurred.

'It's full of ammonia mate,' he said.

'It'll be a bit different for Charlie,' replied Boggis stoutly

The liver was duly cooked, smelt awful and offered to the GOC.

'Sorry, Boggis,' said Townshend, his nose wrinkling, 'I'm afraid I just can't.'

'I'm sorry, Sir – thought it might make a change.'[30]

On 31 March, Gorringe wired Townshend, saying:

> Preparations for your relief are well forward and you may be assured that I shall not be a day later than is absolutely necessary. According to Baghdad records . . . the last flood was the maximum we are likely to have; another of possibly equal height may be expected 10th to 15th of next month. The floods threaten and are causing much trouble . . . to the Turks . . . their food supplies very short and casualties considerable.[31]

The *Sumana,* which was so important to the defenders as a link between Wool Press Village and the town, was damaged by Turkish gunfire and put out of action. It is surprising that she had until then come through the sieges unscathed, but her repair was a priority. A mail drop was expected and when the small aeroplane appeared overhead morale rose in anticipation of letters from home. The mail was duly dropped – into the middle of the wide, muddy wastes of the Tigris.[32] Townshend was painfully aware of what a blow this had been and belatedly authorized the sending of three hundred telegrams – but by officers only. A few days later, one of the signalmen sent a personal message to his family, which was intercepted by a Royal Navy ship at sea. The warship signalled Kut. The soldier concerned was promptly court-martialled and sentenced to imprisonment, to be served when the siege was lifted. These two incidents are so unbalanced and unfair that they will appall the modern reader but in 1916, soldiers did not ask and did not expect the same treatment as their officers. This was probably as well.

The siege wore on, signals were exchanged, intentions were mis-interpreted, the flies swarmed, the river rose again, the corpses started to float in the flood water, the stench was stomach turning, the money ran out and the Arabs would no longer accept paper money. Townshend asked for gold. Gorringe said that he would attack on 5 April.

The attack that morning got off to an encouraging start. The 13th Division made a frontal attack after a preliminary barrage and raced to the first line of Turkish trenches – they were vacant apart from derisive messages scrawled on the revetments. The attack continued and took the second line without resistance. The 13th Division was buoyed with optimism. Evidently, the Turks had heard of their reputation and fled. The third line was carried as were the fourth and fifth. The supposition was that Khalil had withdrawn and the relief of Kut was a walkover. But the atmosphere changed when the 13th Division, advancing even further over open desert, was engaged by well-sited machine guns and a formidable Turkish defensive line. The British went to ground and scraped shelters in the sand. It was only night-fall that gave respite from the lash of the machine guns but not from the myriad of biting insects. The night gave cover to the British but it provided similar cover to the Turks and they melted away to their next prepared line.

At dawn, on 6 April, Gorringe's troops took possession of the Turkish position at Felahiyeh. What had seemed initially to be 'a piece of cake' eventually cost 1,868 casualties.[33] The guns that were firing only a few miles away could be heard in Kut but the message they gave was not clear and Townshend sent urgent messages asking for situation reports. They told him that the attack had faltered and the advance had been halted.

Hunger was now acute and the Sikh soldiers started to eat the grass wher-ever it could poke a spindly head above the sand; this was unpalatable but it staved off beriberi in the short term. Paying the troops was a problem because the locals would not accept paper money.

CVFT again asked for gold to be air-dropped.

The stench from putrefied Turkish corpses permeated the front-line trenches.

For the men fighting their way to Kut, life was also miserable. The heat was crushing, flood water now affected every movement and the ever-present, unremitting flies were in the soldiers' eyes, up his nose and in his ears. To open his lips to breathe was to invite several battalions of flies to enter for a tour of his tonsils. Eating anything that could be found was shared with the flies and was unrelieved misery. In addition there were mosquitoes and sand flies that bit – often.

'Our Charlie' issued another communiqué to his troops which was more of the same with the exception that he urged his Indian troops to eat the horse meat authorized by their creed but, as yet, not taken up by the soldiers. The communiqué was long on rhetoric but short on anything else. The immediate effect, however, was that 5,135 Indians started to eat horse meat. Townshend's generals were irritated because they had told him weeks before that, if ordered, the Indians would eat horse meat.

These communiqués were a two-edged sword and there is no doubt that CVFT not only shared his thoughts with his soldiers in them, but also with the Turks, who got a copy, if not hot, then certainly lukewarm off the press. He inadvertently and unnecessarily gave away low-level intelligence in the process. Townshend wired Lake on 7 April and said that he and six or seven hundred of his fittest men could run the gauntlet downriver in *Sumana*. He would leave the remainder to surrender. He went on to suggest that perhaps Gorringe might like to open negotiations with Khalil for an exchange – say Kut in exchange for Townshend and his garrison? He said that now the floods had engulfed the Turkish trenches a breakout was impossible. The flooded trenches were an impassable barrier to exhausted troops.

An analysis of Townshend's motives after 7 February when he first asked Nixon to recommend his promotion is instructive. A pattern emerges that shows that 'Our Charlie' would be only too prepared to abandon his command and his men if it would secure his personal release and possibly his promotion. On 5 March, he raised the promotion issue again and now on 9 April he had suggested that he should escape. He had suggested negotiations be opened with Khalil three times, had himself written two ingratiating letters to the enemy commander and, of course, had proscribed attempts to blow the enemy commander to kingdom come.

Hardinge handed over as Viceroy of India to Lord Chelmsford on 10 April 1916; he had failed miserably and would not be missed. General Lake made a belated decision to resupply Kut from the air, Gorringe opted to commit his 3rd Division on 12 April and back in India it had been discovered that port arrangements in Bombay were every bit as shambolic as those in Basra.

It was thought to be a viable option to run a stripped-down but armoured

*Julna*r upriver, loaded with several tons of food. Admiral Wemyss advised against such a project as foolhardy.[34] Lake took note,[35] but he did not abandon the idea and revived it when it became clear that resupply by air could not cope with the tonnage required. Then, to ease the food problem, Lake suggested that CVFT expel all of the civilian occupants of Kut. This might have been an option three months earlier when it was proscribed, but now Khalil saw every mouth in Kut as being on his side and made it clear that anyone now attempting to leave Kut would be shot. Townshend rejected the idea as being politically catastrophic. The *Julnar* option, he said, was also unlikely to succeed given the fusillade it would face every inch of its journey.

On the night of 11/12 April it rained heavily. Under cover of darkness dozens of Arabs, living in Kut, attempted to float downriver on inflated goat skins,[36] only to be greeted by the Turks when they made landfall – and shot.

The weather caused Gorringe to delay his initiative until 15 April and then that most unimaginative of generals threw his soldiers of the 3rd Division once more into the mincing machine, starting with a night march to contact. 'March' is not the word as the men waded through knee-high water, were illuminated by lightning, eventually made contact, and fell in the mud and shallow water. If they fell into deeper water they drowned – in a desert. The 3rd Division carried some Turkish trenches. The position at Beir Aissa, when taken, contained 2,300 enemy dead, but the counter-attack regained much of the ground taken at great cost. Gorringe was not deterred and continued to hurl his men at the bulwark of Turkish defences; the execution was awful.

In order to hamper Gorringe, the Turks breached the banks of the Tigris to expand the flooded area, which posed even greater problems for a general who was already out of his depth. Air supply had some modest success and 3,500 lb of food was dropped on Kut, but that was 1,650 lb short of what was needed for a single day. The airmen who sought to sustain Kut were gallant but unskilled and risked their lives daily only to drop their burden, from 5,000 ft or more, in the river or into Turkish lines. The defenders were highly frustrated as they watched precious packages fall out of reach.

The end was very close and the last throw of the dice was to be *Julnar*'s. Volunteers were called for and under the command of Lieutenant Brook–Firman RN she was to make the 12-mile dash upriver to bring food to Kut. The exercise was far from a secret – that being the case, the little ship and her crew had no chance of success and not much chance of survival

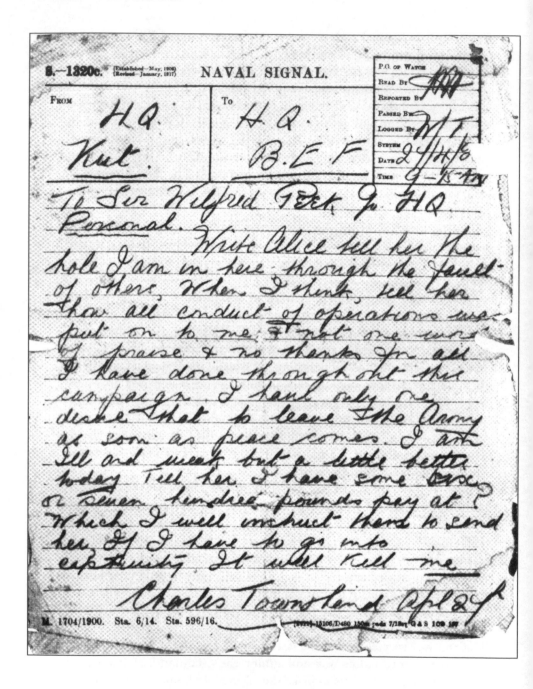

Fig 13. Townshend's last message.

either. Lieutenant Commander (N) Cowley RNVR and Engineer Lieutenant Reid RNVR were the other two officers when *Julnar* made her passage on the night of 24/25 April 1916. She was detected early in her voyage and drew heavy fire almost from the start. At Magasis she fouled a heavy chain that had been stretched across the river to foil just such a foray and was brought to a halt. Brook-Firman died on his bridge, along with many of his crew. Cowley and Reid were among those captured; the former was murdered in captivity probably because he had been a sufficiently long-term resident in Mesopotamia that he was regarded by the Turks as a Turkish national and thus a 'traitor'. Brook-Firman and Cowley were awarded posthumous VCs.

Twenty men were dying each day of starvation and CVFT had no choice but submit. Lake wired him to say he should now negotiate with Khalil saying that 'with your prestige you are likely to get the best terms'. The reality was that now everyone, and not least General Lake, wanted to distance themselves from the national disgrace that was about to happen. Townshend replied, saying that he would only meet Khalil if *ordered* (author's italics).

At 0330hrs on 26 April, Lake issued the 'order' and at 0900 that day Townshend sent a letter to the Turks requesting a ten-day armistice. Khalil told Townshend to sail upriver in *Sumana* to meet him. His first attempt to comply failed when Turkish gunners fired on *Sumana*. When that was resolved 'Our Charlie' sailed next morning.

After 147 days of flies and death in a multiplicity of forms, the siege of Kut was over.

The statistics make unhappy reading for any but a Turk. The advance of the 6th Division to Ctesiphon and its subsequent withdrawal to Kut had cost 7,000 casualties; whilst besieged the Division had lost a further 1,608 killed and 1,836 wounded; forty-eight were 'missing'. Between December 1915 and April 1916 the relieving forces under Aylmer and Gorringe suffered 23,000 casualties. The total casualties were therefore over 30,000, and now 13,000 men were prisoners of war, having achieved absolutely nothing, in either strategic or tactical terms.

Townshend dashed off a final personal signal on 27 April and that is reproduced on Page 266. It exudes self-pity and the final telling remark is: 'I have to go into captivity. It will kill me.' This is a fair indication of his attitude as he went into the surrender negotiations. Certainly, there was no talk of 'fighting to the last round.'

He issued his final communiqué on 28 April and once again drew attention to himself in seeking sympathy from his soldiers. He said:

These considerations alone, namely, that I can help my comrades of all ranks to the end, have decided me to overcome my bodily illness and the anguish of mind which I am suffering now, and I have interviewed the Turkish General-in-Chief yesterday, who is full of admiration at 'an heroic defence of five months', as he puts it.

Negotiations are still in progress, but I hope to be able to announce your departure for India, on parole not to serve against the Turks, since the Turkish Commander says he thinks it will be allowed, and has wired to Constantinople to ask for this, and that the *Julnar*, which is lying with food for us at Magasis now, may be permitted to come to us.

Whatever has happened, my comrades, you can only be proud of yourselves. We have done our duty to King and Empire; the whole world knows that we have done our duty. I ask you to stand by me with your steady and splendid discipline, shown throughout, in the next few days for the expedition of all service I demand of you.

The communiqué was very misleading and to suggest to his 13,000 men that they might expect to be repatriated was unnecessary and cruel. It achieved nothing. The surrender arrangements were conducted with a degree of civility. It was agreed that 1,100 sick and wounded were to be exchanged for the same number of Turkish POWs; the British soldiers to be exchanged were selected by Turkish doctors.

In Basra a diligent staff officer, even at this late stage, sent a signal asking for 'the number of files killed in April in Japanese fly-traps'. The starving recipient in Kut was so outraged that he scrawled 'Balls' across the message pad and sent it back to the signallers for transmission. The reply was immediate and it read: 'For files read flies.' The starving one replied: 'For balls read cock.'[37] Equipment was systematically destroyed. Weapons and particularly the guns were made inoperable. Anything that could be burnt was sent up in flames. Townshend retired to his headquarters and did not make a final round of his men as he focused on more pressing issues.

A Colonel Nizám Bey was the officer who accepted the surrender of the officers and each in turn was expected to formally give up his sword. Some did but others broke their swords and threw the pieces into the river. For Townshend, a special ceremony was staged. Khalil came to Kut himself for the event. When Charles Townshend handed over his sword Khalil, with abundant courtesy, handed it back. That was the moment when Townshend asked if Spot could be sent, with the dog belonging to General Mellis, down to Basra. Khalil agreed and Spot lived to fight another day – he was lucky not to have been eaten. Kut was abandoned to the indigenous Arabs; the weapon pits decayed and collapsed. The dead were sometimes found, the Turks exacted retribution and only the flies – millions of them – flourished. For the prisoners of war the final horror of this campaign was about to start. Captivity would be the least of their problems.

Notes

1. Mr W.J. Sherlock. Quoted by Braddon.
2. Mr E.J. Mant. Quoted by Braddon.
3. CVFT.
4. CVFT, *My campaign in Mesopotamia.*
5. Mr J. Wadham. Quoted by Braddon.
6. CVFT.
7. CVFT.
8. Ibid.
9. CVFT's italics.
10. The Mesopotamia Commission, 1917.
11. A.J. Barker.
12. Mr H.S. Soden. Quoted by Braddon.
13. Colonel G.R. Rae, personal papers.
14. *Official History of the World War I*, vol. II.
15. Mr J. Boggis. Quoted by Braddon.
16. Mr W.J. Sherlock.
17. Mr G.H Cheeseman. Quoted by Braddon.
18. The siege of Plevna took place during the Russo-Turkish war of 1877–1878. The Turks held the city and by so doing held up the Russian advance into Bulgaria. The Turks decided to break out and they crossed the River Vit and attacked the Russians but the foray was fruitless, it led to high casualties and was the prelude to the fall of the city. Osman Pasha, the Turkish commander, was treated with great honour by his captors but most of his soldiers were massacred. It is highly unlikely that any of CVFT's soldiers had ever heard of Plevna and, if they had, they would think it a poor model for their future.
19. Sherson.
20. Mr E.J. Mant. Quoted by Braddon.
21. Sir John Mellor.
22. This was a long cord with a weight on one end and loops on the other. It was used to 'pull through' the barrel of a rifle with a piece of flannelette secured in the loops in order to clean it.
23. Captain G.H.G. Burroughs.

24. Braddon.
25. Mr H.S. Soden.
26. Mr G. Roff.
27. Mr J. Sherlock, Mr A. Vanstone and Mr G.H. Allen in conversation with Braddon.
28. Mr G. Sporle.
29. Sherson.
30. J. Boggis quoted by Braddon.
31. *Official History of World War 1*. vol. II.
32. Cpl Candy (diary).
33. *Official History of World War 1*, vol. II.
34. Rosslyn Erskine Wemyss, 1st Baron Wester Wemyss GCB CMG MVO (1864–1933).
35. Mr W.S. Finch.
36. A.J. Barker.
37. Sir Joseph Napier (diary), recorded by Braddon.

Chapter 15
April 1916–October 1918
Prisoner of War

On 4 May 1916, in a sombre House of Lords, Lord Charles Beresford, an old chum of Townshend's, prompted a statement from Lord Kitchener, who said among other things:

> General Townshend and his troops in their honourable captivity will have the satisfaction of knowing that in the opinion of their comrades, which I think I may say that this House and the country fully share, they did all that was humanly possible to resist to the last. And their surrender reflects no discredit on themselves or on the records of the British and Indian Armies.

He went on to comment on the excellence of the defensive arrangements and attributed the surrender to a combination of inclement weather, starvation and ill-health. Gorringe and Lake also picked up plaudits along the way, but for Aylmer there was nothing. The tones of Kitchener's remarks were just right for the situation and he expressed the only sort of sentiment that the public would want to hear at the time. The British had been defeated in the Dardanelles in January and now, only four months later, after a further heavy defeat at Kut, the public needed a hero. At least for the time being, Charles Townshend was just that.

Kitchener had always been an active supporter of Townshend and the latter later acknowledged that the FM had been, in large part, responsible for his successive promotions from Lieutenant Colonel to Major General. However, later events were to throw doubt on this relationship.

Back in Mesopotamia the hero of the hour was placed aboard a launch with Captain Morland, his ADC, a senior staff officer, Lieutenant Colonel Parr, an Indian servant, a Portuguese cook and two soldier orderlies, one of whom was LCpl John Boggis. Meanwhile at Shamran, about eight miles from Kut, a camp had been prepared for the starving men who were concentrated there for the 1,000-mile march that awaited them and which would

271

be the death of many. They were without doctors and only a nominal one officer per regiment had been allowed to stay with them, although eventually these, too, would be extracted.

The prisoners were given a biscuit, a product so hard and unyielding that few were able to digest it until it had been soaked for hours in unfiltered water. The biscuits absorbed the water, they were duly eaten and then the consumer died. 'Frothing at the mouth, their bowels disintegrated into greenish slime, dehydrated in a few hours, they changed from lean men into leathery skeletons.'[1] It was judged to be enteritis but giving it a name did not make the dying any easier.

News of the passage of 'Our Charlie' reached the prisoners and, ignoring the whips of their guards, they thronged the river bank waiting for Charlie to appear. When the small launch steamed into sight the soldiers cheered and waved. Townshend stood at the rail, at the salute, tears streaming down his face. The launch steamed on, cheered to the echo, rounded a bend and disappeared. There was an awful moment of anti-climax on the river bank as the men fell silent. The Turkish guards were galvanized into action and, laying about them with their whips, the captives were thrashed back into order.

In 1916 and thereafter, none of his surviving soldiers ever blamed Charlie for the fate of the 6th Division. Braddon, who held Townshend in singularly low regard, was first to concede that, come what may, he had won the hearts of his men. After Braddon's book, entitled *The Siege*, was published in 1967, it brought down a storm of protest on his head from Kuttites who believed his account to be unfair to 'Our Charlie'.

Meanwhile, the launch made its stately passage to Baghdad, passing Azizieh, Lajj and Ctesiphon on the way; it was followed by other similar vessels filled with officers. Much as the officers had protested at being separated from their men, the Turks had ignored them, being quite at a loss to understand a relationship that most certainly did not exist in the Turkish Army.

After the event it was thought that, had Townshend insisted on himself and his officers remaining with their men, the effects of the horrifying death march that followed could have been greatly reduced. That is wishful thinking because Townshend would never have volunteered to put himself in such a position as he was dreading captivity in any form and, if he had to endure it, then let it be as agreeable as possible.

Walking one thousand miles was not on his agenda.

Similarly, CVFT could have pleaded on behalf of the inhabitants of Kut, who were now treated by the victors with the utmost cruelty. The Turks were determined to deter any other Arabs who might assist the British, tortured and shot 50, and hanged many more, the bodies of the unfortunate victims decorating the gibbets that were erected along the bank. It was a sign of things to come.

Townshend, on the other hand, was treated with considerable deference by his captors and was spared the company of von de Goltz who had died of typhus just a few days before. On arrival in Baghdad, Townshend and his entourage were quartered, for a week, in what had been the Italian consulate, and here he was entertained handsomely by Khalil. The Turkish general took the chance to discuss the strategy of the recent campaign with his defeated but loquacious opponent.

The dinner party was to prove to be a public relations disaster for Townshend when eventually news of it leaked out – it was seen to be in stark contrast to the privations that the men of the 6th Division were now enduring, privations that he did virtually nothing to ameliorate.

Townshend was 'invited' to move on to Constantinople and consulted with Mellis, who had now joined him. Mellis provided him with ample reason to accept the 'invitation' by telling him to 'clear out of this infernal country'.[2] This was good enough for Charlie and he embarked on the 1,255-mile journey by train, coach and lorry. On the roads he came across about forty soldiers amongst whom were survivors of the *Julnar*, whose gallant attempt to run the blockade had failed in the last days of the siege. Sub Lieutenant Reid left his erstwhile commander in no doubt as to the misery that had been imposed on him and his crew since their capture. Townshend gave Reid some money and kind words but, apart from delivering 'a severe lecture to the Turkish officer in charge of the prisoners',[3] he gave no practical help. Apparently with a clear conscience, he moved on.

Townshend's account of his journey reads like a travelogue and he recounts in his book, *My campaign in Mesopotamia*, details of a succession of interesting sights, comfortable beds with clean sheets and agreeable meals with fawning Turks. There is an unconscious irony in this account, which is so much at odds with the lifestyle of his soldiers and now his officers.

Mellis was made of stern stuff, having recovered from a bout of ill-health, and followed up behind his struggling men. Mellis was not only physically courageous but was morally courageous too. He was not a young man and was not in sound health, but he took on the responsibility for Townshend's men. He was outraged by the neglect of the marchers and distressed at the pitiful sights that he saw on the trail – young men, just skin and bone, crawling on all fours, others huddled in death. Mellis, known to the Turks as His Excellency, Mellis Pasha, was a ferocious advocate for the Kuttites.

At every stop on the interminable desert road he would assail the local commander, demanding food and shelter. Mellis was small in stature but a giant of a man in every other way. Sadly, there was much he could do nothing about.

> At Mosul they were packed into cells crawling with lice and devoid of latrine buckets. A sixteen-year old bugler refused to give himself to a Turk who wanted him and was bastinadoed for his non-compliance. The water point was just below a hospital cesspit and, as they tried to fill their water bottles, they had to avoid the turds that swam on the surface.[4]

The contrast with the progression of Townshend is considerable. He was treated like visiting royalty. Guards of honour were drawn up for him to inspect; cordial greetings and generous hospitality were the order of the day. The Turkish War Minister, Enver Pasha, met him at Bozanti and, whilst Townshend relaxed in the Minister's private train, Enver made a remark that would haunt Townshend for the remainder of his days. He said, perhaps sarcastically, that Townshend would be 'the honoured guest of his nation'. In Townshend's defence it was at this meeting that he did raise the subject of the prisoners of war and their conditions. However, Enver was laconic and nothing was achieved. 'The honoured guest' then suggested that he should be 'exchanged' and allowed to return to England. Again Enver was not to be drawn and commented dryly that being a prisoner was part of the fortunes of war. He was of course quite correct and it ill-behoved Townshend to seek further personal preferment. In practice Enver was aware that, in Townshend, he had a hostage who might be a useful bargaining chip in the future and he had no intention of freeing him.

When Enver left the meeting accompanied by a group of German and Austrian officers, Townshend commented that 'Many of them saluted me, others snap-shotting me with Kodaks.'

Enver knew full well the condition of the British prisoners, as by now the survivors had reached Baghdad and he had inspected them. He noted the rib cages, the tattered clothes, the weeping wounds and spoke to several prisoners. To one he said, 'The Turkish Army has done what nobody has done before – captured a British division. What do you think of that?'

'May I reply man to man?' asked the Englishman.

'Of course.'

'Then if the positions had been reversed, do you really think it would have taken the British Army five months to capture a Turkish division?'

'Take him out and shoot him,' snarled Enver.

'But you gave him permission to speak as man to man,' a brave young ADC protested to the Minister.

Enver glowered, cancelled the execution and stamped off.[5]

He was directly instrumental in adding to their suffering. On his orders groups were despatched every ten days or so to make the pitiless journey across the arid plains and over the mountains beyond. It was now summer. The heat was intense and unremitting; the food was hopelessly inadequate; the flies swarmed in clouds; and the guards used long, biting whips. Little wonder then that the men died in thousands. Enver was an unadulterated swine and he sullied the name of Turkey by his callous disregard for civilized behaviour.

Townshend did not know the detail of all of this pain. It was out of his sight, beyond his jurisdiction and he could not halt it. He focused on his own situation, and in Constantinople it was flattering to have a Turkish naval officer called Tewkik Bey allocated to him as an additional ADC. The arrangements in the Turkish capital bordered on farce. He was greeted as if he was an ally who had won a great victory, a sumptuous reception was held and he was then driven in an open landau through cheering crowds. It must have been very agreeable to a man with an ego like Townshend's, but in due course this extraordinary relationship that Townshend was building with the Turkish establishment would cause him to reap a bitter harvest.

It was a bizarre situation that von de Goltz, whom Townshend had spared from artillery fire, but who nevertheless had devoted his energies to defeating Townshend, and who had promised to deliver Townshend in person to Constantinople, travelled on the same train. Townshend went first class; von de Goltz was in a coffin in the guard's van!

The British party was lunched in the, now inevitable, grand manner and taken by launch to the island of Halki on the Sea of Marmara, where a large house had been requisitioned for his use. Halki was a very fashionable resort; it attracted the wealthy and influential from Constantinople society and was a convenient place to lodge a mistress. If this was imprisonment, then it was not all bad. Townshend was waited on hand, foot and finger. He wanted for nothing and was free to walk about the island at will. He swam every day and pronounced the exercise 'delicious'. The house was a handsome building, well appointed and life was very pleasant. Letters from his wife kept him up to date with events in England and he started to negotiate to get Mrs Townshend out to join him. The Turkish Government had no objection and actually raised the matter with the British Government, suggesting that the Townshends could live in the British Embassy at Pera. Whilst Charles was negotiating for his release, or at least the presence of his wife with him in Constantinople, Alice Townshend was working hard at the other end. The issue was raised to the level of the Prime Minister and on 1 August 1916. Mr Asquith wrote to Alice flatly rejecting the proposition. He did not say so but it was considered inappropriate to turn an embassy, albeit one currently abandoned, into a place of internment.

As 1916 wore on and the weather turned cold, Townshend was moved to Prinkipo, a larger island that enjoyed a more sheltered aspect. The house was the summer residence of the British Consul and 'it looked like a country vicarage with a charming garden.'[6] Just after the move he was distressed to read in a London paper that the Marchioness of Townshend, despite eleven years of childless marriage, had been delivered of a son. This boy would be the 7th Marquess and Charles Townshend would not now have the title that he had aspired to all his adult life. He was never going to be Lord Townshend, nor was he going to be a lieutenant general. Life, he thought, was a bitch; he despaired and shared his despair with his entourage.

On 16 October 1916 his despair was not much reduced when he received notification that he had been appointed a Knighthood as a Companion of the Order of the Bath (KCB). With marked lack of grace, 'not before time', he grunted at Boggis: 'I don't suppose anyone will grudge me my KCB, after thirty-five years' service in nine campaigns and nine times mentioned in despatches. It has not been awarded *too* soon.'[7]

The new Lady Townshend was her ever-supportive self, keeping up a stream of correspondence filled with the news and gossip from London. She visited wounded soldiers in hospital and on one occasion referred to a young man, late of the 6th Division, who had lost both eyes and both arms in France. When she identified herself the young and hopelessly crippled soldier said, 'General Townshend, what a fine man and nobody need say anything about him for we all know what he is.' She went on to warn her husband to be discrete in his correspondence, saying in her letter: 'Beware of your enemies at home. The slightest word or jest may be distorted by them. Your powerful friends (and you have many) are taking the greatest care of you . . . I tremble to think that, in your captivity, you might harm yourself when you have done so brilliantly on active service.'

Townshend had not given up hope of being paroled and asked the Spanish Ambassador to obtain Enver Pasha's permission to leave Turkey so he could live in Spain with his wife and daughter. Nothing came of this initiative and in the short term his courting of Turkish officials availed him little except splendid lunches. This fraternization had the effect of distorting the setting of Townshend's moral compass. He started to identify with and have sympathy for the Turks, notwithstanding their treatment of his soldiers. Until the end of his life Townshend was wholeheartedly committed to the Turkish cause and this affection for an adversary that had abused so many British soldiers was difficult for many to understand. Townshend was a shrewd man and perhaps he was looking to the longer term and the end of the war when he might yet carve out a role for himself. An amateur psychologist might wonder if he was an early example of the 'Stockholm Syndrome'.[8]

Major General Sir Charles Mellis VC was working desperately to alleviate the suffering of his men, most of whom were now employed as forced labour, either in mines or in the construction of a railway. They continued to die of malnutrition and most of the other malignant diseases common to that part of the world. Mellis wrote furious letters to Enver Pasha demanding that he do something, anything, to help, but Enver blandly denied that the prisoners were subject to any ill-treatment.

Braddon asserts and quotes A.J. Barker as follows: 'Townshend was concerned only with his own release from captivity, so much so that *he wrote to Mellis trying to exonerate Enver Pasha from any responsibility for the fate of those who had marched from Shamran, and saying everything that could be done for his troops was already being done* (author's italics).' This is an allegation for which this writer can find no supporting evidence and certainly not in A.J. Barker's biography of Townshend. Consequently, the authenticity of Braddon's account of the siege and aftermath is weakened.

The prisoners' lot was aided by the practical compassion of the American Ambassador, Mr Morgenthau, and his successor in their role as representatives of the Protecting Power. When the USA entered the war, the Dutch Ambassador assumed this responsibility. They each in turn heard what Mellis had to say and did what they could to help.

Tewkik Bey, the Turkish ADC, who had become an important player in the Prinkipo scene, was summarily sacked for passing fraudulent receipts for pay drawn on behalf of Townshend and Morland. He was replaced by Hussein Bey, a rather less compliant individual. The question of money was a matter that Townshend regularly brought up with the authorities in London, complaining of the difficulty he experienced keeping up an establishment filled with servants. He did not get much in the way of sympathy and failed to read between the lines – not for the first time

He was a prisoner of war but did not expect to be in the least inconvenienced by such a trifle. Perhaps the frequent dinners and luncheons with local notables, the free access to the beach, the adjacent hills and the leisured, very comfortable lifestyle all served to erode his grip on reality. Despite all of this, Charles Townshend was restless: he was missing out on all the great activity on the Western Front; he was frustrated and sometimes this frustration boiled over. In one incident he thought, mistakenly, that a local Greek youth had laughed at him. He sent Boggis to bring the young man to him whereupon he struck him with a whip he had collected from the house.

There were any number of abortive schemes to escape and although some were tentatively rehearsed they all came to nothing. On 24 February 1917, Kut was retaken by General Maude and Townshend noted sourly, but no less accurately, that Maude's 100,000 men in seven divisions, were 'a considerable difference in size from the force I was given to take Baghdad with.'⁹ Maude went on to take Baghdad on 11 March, about eleven months after Townshend had capitulated at Kut.

The writing was already on the wall for the Ottoman Empire and when the USA entered the war on 6 April 1917, the Turks, with whom Townshend was now on the easiest social terms, recognized that there could only be one outcome.

On 5 August 1917, the Mesopotamia Commission published its findings. The Commission was damning in its conclusions. Townshend was exonerated from any blame because his failings were as nothing compared to the failure of others. This was a comfort for Townshend who remained on very friendly terms with Enver Pasha and they met quite frequently. During one of these meetings Enver assured Townshend that if he had had his way, Townshend would have been released in May 1916, but he added darkly that 'the Germans would not agree.'¹⁰

The Commission was harsh in its judgment of the Government of India, and particularly upon Duff and the Viceroy, Lord Hardinge. Both were found to have showed '*Little desire to help and some desire actually to obstruct the energetic prosecution of the war* [author's italics]. '¹¹Also named as being inadequate, incompetent or uninformed were General Sir Edmund Barrow, the Military Secretary to the Viceroy, and Surgeon-General Sir William Babtie VC CB CMG. This latter individual, although personally brave, had moved effortlessly up through the medical ranks until he was appointed Deputy Director-General Medical Services in Mesopotamia. He was the senior doctor and the medical arrangements called his competence into question – not for the first time, as he had already failed in the Dardanelles. General Nixon, the Commander-in-Chief of the Mesopotamian

Expeditionary Force, was also held to be largely responsible for the failed campaign. Nixon withdrew into well-deserved obscurity. However, Duff was unable to live with the shame and committed suicide on 20 January 1918.

Hardinge pre-empted the Commission report and defended himself in the House of Lords on 3 July 1917. In weasel words he went through the ritual of expressing concern for the wounded. But, in a nutshell, he said it was not really his fault. It is a travesty that Hardinge suffered no punishment for his crass incompetence as, because he was the ultimate Indian authority, the responsibility for all of the ills of IEF 'D' was, undeniably, his.

Hardinge went on to greater things and in 1920, apparently without a stain on his character, he was appointed Ambassador to France, a post he held for two years. He died in 1944 fully laden with all the honours his country could reasonably have given him. His post-nominal letters were KG GCB GCMG GCVO ISO PC. Never was wanton incompetence so richly rewarded.

On 9 July 1917, Mr. Joynson-Hicks asked the Prime Minister in the House of Commons what decorations or awards had been given to individuals named in the Commission's report. Bonor Law replied that Duff had been appointed GCSI on 1 Jan 1916 and Barrow similarly in February 1916. Hardinge had also been decorated but in his case it was no less than the Garter (KG). Incredibly, Babtie was made KCMG in May 1916. The public anger that the Commission's report generated was the spur for Rudyard Kipling to write his poem *Mesopotamia*, which is to be found at Appendix A to this book.

Months in captivity were stretching into years and, in early 1918, the war was still raging by the time Townshend and his entourage entered their third year as prisoners. General Mellis was in very poor health and the India Office tried to have him exchanged, but failed. At about the same time the War Office was explaining patiently to Townshend that he could not expect parole or exchange unless the same was extended to all of the other officers in captivity.

The Germans had launched their massive final assault in France. British losses were huge and in the mayhem of the spring of 1918, the reputations of Townshend's peer group, fighting in Flanders, were won and lost. The battle in France was in the balance, but the British naval blockade of Germany was strictly enforced and it was to prove to be crucial; it was also winning the battle against the U-boats. The oil now safely secured by British bayonets in and around Basra was the strategic material that made all this naval ascendancy possible. The moribund German High Seas Fleet, meanwhile, was in a state of mutiny.

In September 1918, Marshal Foch's offensive devastated the Germans, who lost 150,000 prisoners, Berlin was in the grip of anarchy and two Bavarian divisions had mutinied. It became abundantly clear that the collapse of Germany was imminent and, with it, all the aspirations of her allies, not least those of Turkey. Townshend saw an opportunity and, determined to exploit it; he seized the moment and advised the Turkish Government that he was prepared to interface with the British Government as an intermediary when peace talks were opened, 'I flattered myself that they would have confidence in my ability to conduct such a mission,' he noted, adding, 'and would have equal confidence in the genuineness of my endeavour to obtain honourable terms for their country.'

His Turkish ADC left Prinkipo on 17 October 1918 bearing Townshend's offer in a letter addressed to Field Marshal Izzet Pasha. Townshend laid down a number of tough conditions. Entirely off his own bat he insisted that the Turks throw open the Dardanelles and the Bosporus; and that Mesopotamia, Syria, and the Caucasus, whilst still acknowledging the Sultan as their ruler, would become autonomous states. He required that all prisoners of war held by the Turks be released. He then moved into difficult country because he offered to arrange for the Allies to evacuate Mesopotamia and Syria. Turkish territory in Europe would remain under Turkish control and Britain would provide funds to prop up the, now bankrupt, state of Turkey.

Izzet knew a good deal when he saw one and needed little persuading to take Townshend on. Izzet released Townshend from captivity with a warm handshake and the General's status changed immediately from POW to diplomat. Townshend had, of course, taken upon himself responsibility and authority that vastly exceeded his station. He had no doubt that, in sporting terms, he had 'just played a blinder' but, elsewhere not everyone was so convinced.

On 18 October 1918 he set out on his mission accompanied by Captain Morland, Hussein Bey and his domestic servants. The governor of Smyrna provided a yacht and they sailed, through very hazardous minefields, to the British-held port of Mitylene. On arrival in Mitylene on 20 October, they made early contact with a motorboat commanded by a British naval officer. Townshend said exultantly, and who would blame him, 'Once more I am under the British flag.'

He was free, and from his viewpoint he had the world at his feet. He determined that he was now going to play a part on the world stage – or so he thought. To this end he sent copies of his proposed peace terms to the Foreign Office where no doubt they were received with bemusement. CIGS sent a signal telling Townshend to stay where he was until he received further orders.

A week passed and Charles Townshend was made most welcome by Admiral the Hon. Sir Arthur Calthorpe, C-in-C Mediterranean. However, when the Turkish delegates arrived on 26 October and were taken aboard HMS *Agamemnon* to begin discussions, Townshend was not invited to the table. Townshend noted: 'I remained with the fleet whilst the business proceeded, in order to help if matters came to a deadlock.'[12] In fact, had he known it, this was a sign of things to come.

Whilst these diplomatic gyrations were conducted, British prisoners were being freed. However, of the 2,592 British soldiers of the 6th Division, 755 would not be going home, nor would 3,063 of the 10,486 sepoys and camp followers. Their bones are still in Mesopotamia.

Notes
1. Braddon.
2. Barker.
3. CVFT.
4. Braddon.
5. Captain H.S.D. MacNeal, as quoted by Braddon.
6. Sherson.
7. Sherson's italics.
8. 'Stockholm syndrome' is not a medical term, but it is a phenomenon in which captives begin to identify with their captors. At first this seems to be a defensive response generated by a fear of violence. Insignificant acts of kindness by the captor are magnified out of proportion in the captive's mind, not least because in a hostage situation the captive will have lost his sense of perspective. It is an extreme case but, possibly, apposite, in the case of Townshend, that rescue attempts are seen as a threat, since it is likely that the captive would be injured during such attempts.
9. CVFT.
10. CVFT.
11. The Mesopotamia Commission report, p. 123.
12. CVFT, *My campaign in Mesopotamia.*

Chapter 16

1918–1924

Soldier to Civilian

Charles Townshend did not rush to get back to Great Britain. He stopped off in Rome and Paris where an overjoyed Alice was waiting for him. Townshend received from his friends and then from the French Government the sort of welcome that by now had become *de rigeur* for the 'Lion of Kut'. Clemenceau, whom he had known for years and who was the French Premier, made a particular effort to orchestrate the celebrations, even though he was very busy with the battles still raging in Flanders as the German Army faced inevitable defeat. Clemenceau saw fit to share with Townshend a German telegram asking for safe passage for a delegation through French lines to discuss an armistice.

Whilst in Paris Townshend was asked to give an interview to a correspondent of *The Times*. Never one to miss an opportunity for a little gentle self-advertisement, Charles Townshend readily agreed. In the interview, and among other minor indiscretions, he mentioned that he had been 'treated as an honoured guest by the Turks'. It was a mistake and it brought immediate retribution.

Townshend's arrival in England was noticeable in its frigidity. This was because his interview had attracted very high-price attention in the War Office and the file shows a series of minutes passing between the Director of Military Intelligence (DMI), the Adjutant General (AG) and the Military Secretary (MS). Their disapproval can be discerned between the lines of the tautly handwritten loose minutes. It is little wonder that he was not welcomed by any official and was accorded no public recognition. Instead Townshend was the recipient of an ice-cold letter from the War Office which enquired in the most formal terms why he had felt empowered to give a press interview at which he had released military information. His attention was drawn to King's Regulations on the subject and he was required to give answers 'in writing'.

It was from 14 Hill Street, Berkeley Square that Townshend replied to the War Office, in green ink and at great length, giving his explanation. He

282

made a telling point by quoting the Secretary of State for War who had recently announced that 'no officer or man had been prevented from speaking out as to his treatment as a prisoner of war.' This he believed justified his interview; the fact that the statement of the Secretary of State was untrue and that he had misled the House is beside the point. Then, in typical Townshend style, he went on to say:

> I would ask leave to point out that I have always done my duty to my country and to the satisfaction of my superior officers in many campaigns now – besides the last campaign in Mesopotamia – and I feel it very greatly to receive such a communication as this one before me from the Army Council, more especially in view of the trials I have undergone at having become a prisoner-of-war from no fault of mine, and from seeing all my juniors go over my head, thus ruining my career in the Army.

Foolishly, instead of obeying the military principle of 'maintaining the aim' which, in this case, was defending his *Times* interview, Charles moved off into a gripe about his career and the injustice of it all. It was an argument that cut no ice and it had the opposite effect to that he desired.

As this narrative has illustrated, time and again Townshend had done more than enough during his thirty-seven years service to alienate people and, along the way, had contrived to add to the list Field Marshal Sir Douglas Haig and Field Marshal Sir 'Wully' Robertson. He had never served under either man and so their disapproval was earned second-hand, but was, nevertheless, professionally lethal. Failing to find favour with just one field marshal would normally be terminal for a military career. However, to be disparaged by two is disfavour of gargantuan and probably unique proportions. Incidentally, Haig and Townshend had been close contemporaries, in 1914, when both were major generals.

There were other, less exalted but no less dangerous, opponents and there existed a loose and uncoordinated anti-Townshend faction at the top of the Army. Townshend's career was as dead as the dodo but as yet he did not know that and, had he had sight of Haig's diary, he would have been mortified. In it, Douglas Haig recorded a discussion he had with King George V when the Monarch visited him at Montreuil on 22 November 1918. Haig wrote:

> The King said to me that he had told the PM to offer me a peerage. I replied that I had been offered a Viscountcy, but had requested leave

to decline accepting the reward until adequate grants for our 'disabled' had been voted. I wished to remain with my Armies. HM then went on to tell me how General Townshend of Kut fame should have remained to share the fate of his fellow prisoners instead of taking his liberty in order to help the Turks get a satisfactory peace. Townshend, he thought, 'was an advertising sort of fellow'. I agreed, and a semi-lunatic as well.

By late November 1918, the returning POWs were telling the world about the privations they had suffered at Turkish hands and among the informed members of the public a ground swell of anti-Turk resentment quickly built up.

Townshend went to the theatre, as was his wont, and, when his presence was noted, the audience, which was perhaps less well informed, greeted him with a standing ovation. He had to leave at the end of the performance by a side door as it was feared that he would be mobbed. This convinced Charles that there still remained a lot to play for; he expected to be appointed to a senior command in the near future but decided that he would help the process along by some of his trademark lobbying.

He wrote to Curzon, now the Foreign Secretary, asking him to take up cudgels on his behalf and to help him gain recognition for his services in Mesopotamia. He conceded in this letter to Curzon that 'there is actually a hostile feeling in some influential quarters against me.'[1] Curzon invited Townshend to come and see him and at that meeting Curzon said, 'the government knows well the good work you have done for the Empire.'[2] He also allegedly added that 'some members of the Government had suggested that [he] should be promoted to lieutenant general but Lord Kitchener had said that promotion should be deferred until afterwards.'[3]

On 7 January 1919, the War office replied to Townshend's latest request for employment with a hammer blow. The Military Secretary said that there was no employment available for which he could be selected and furthermore he would be placed on half pay from two days hence.

It did not end there.

Yet another letter followed straight on the heels of the first. This second missive from the War Office said that Townshend's 'qualifications for promotion to lieutenant general had been fully considered and although the good services he had rendered had been fully appreciated his request for promotion could not be approved'.[4]

These two letters would have utterly crushed anyone else. The scale of the rejection was huge, but it merely bounced off Charles Townshend. He returned to the fray seeking to identify the reasons that were inhibiting his march ever onwards and upwards. He dug deep into his past and came up with a likely incident that might have had a bearing. He wrote to the War Office in these terms:

> I have been privately informed that a letter which I wrote to an Austrian friend of mine (who was Military Attaché in Paris when I was British Military Attaché in 1905) on learning of the assassination of the Austrian Archduke and Archduchess, written before war was even contemplated with Germany and Austria, came into the hand of the War Office, and is in existence there. I personally will not believe that such a private letter, which I had every right to write, could be used, privately against me. It was a private letter written to a friend, in which I remember I expressed horror and detestation of the assassination, and which was written by me with no knowledge whatever that war would break out between my country and his. Moreover, if it was considered wrong of me to write this letter why have I never been reprimanded or my reasons asked for in writing it, and why was I selected to command a force on the Tigris, and left in ignorance of having committed a fault, if such ever can be called a fault?

It is a poorly drafted letter and would not impress any reader in 1919, and probably even fewer ninety or so years later. The letter rambled on and culminated in Charles Townshend asking for an interview with the Secretary of State for War.[5]

That the letter to the Austrian had been written is not in dispute and Sherson draws attention to the indiscrete remarks it contained. Townshend had criticised 'bad government', and specifically Lloyd George. He said that he 'wished he could transfer to the Austrian service so as to get to the front where he might be less unjustly treated.' This was no more than a social nicety and a superficial aspiration. It was a routine Townshend gripe and, as it was contained in a private letter, none of it is matter of the least consequence.

It was a private letter, written to a foreign national, at a foreign address and if it was later to be found in the public domain it begs the question, how did this come about? This curious little vignette in the life and times of C.V.F. Townshend does however still have some elements worth considering. It appears that Mr H.A. Gwynne,[6] the Editor of the *Morning Post*, informed Townshend, probably in early 1915, that he had dined with a

Colonel Fitzgerald, the Military Secretary to Field Marshal Lord Kitchener, told Gwynne that, in late 1914, Lord Kitchener had come into the possession of a letter written by Townshend in which he had offered his services to Austria. Gwynne immediately protested to Fitzgerald that he knew Townshend well and that the General was a completely committed patriot. Gwynne moved onto the offensive and asked Fitzgerald if he had actually *seen* the offending letter (author's italics). The Colonel said that, although he had not had sight of the letter, he 'knew it was alright'.[7] Very significantly, he added that Gwynne was free to repeat the story if he so chose.

That is not the end of the story because Gwynne added that, about nine months later, whilst Townshend was enjoying unparalleled success during his advance up the Tigris to Ctesiphon, he, Gwynne, was lunching at the Ritz Hotel in London with Mrs. Alice Townshend, an old friend of long acquaintance. An enjoyable lunch having been completed, Alice Townshend left. On her departure, a member of the Army Council, by definition one of the most senior members of the Army hierarchy, and who had been at a nearby table, approached Gwynne. The officer got straight to the point and said to Gwynne, 'Well, you were lunching in dangerous company.' Gwynne demurred, remarking that Alice and her husband were his friends. At this the officer, having first enjoined secrecy, repeated substantially the same story as that of Colonel Fitzgerald.

Mr Gwynne was a seasoned journalist, the Editor of a prominent newspaper, and his well-known position was that he owed secrecy to no one. One wonders why, on two separate occasions, well-connected individuals should spread inaccurate information wholly to the discredit of C.V.F. Townshend and to someone well placed to disseminate the story? The letter had indeed been intercepted, as later events would confirm, and someone wanted to publicize the contents down unofficial channels. That prompts the next question: why?

If Charles Townshend was judged to have made a serious error, then the disciplinary machinery of the Army was sufficiently sophisticated to deal with him. He could or should have been charged with a specific offence and brought to trial by court martial, and if found guilty he would have been awarded an appropriate punishment. He could have been summarily removed from command of the 6th Division. Alternatively, the Army Council could have called for his resignation and at the very least, the absolute minimum, he should have been asked to explain himself. No official action was taken and it can safely be presumed that that was because there was, in actuality, no case to answer.

Lord Kitchener was all-powerful whereas in contrast, Townshend was a very long way down the military food chain. He was of no consequence on the national stage and Kitchener, who had been one of Townshend's most effective patrons over many years, had merely to express his displeasure to ruin 'Our Charlie'. It beggars belief that Kitchener would be party to the sordid skullduggery described above, yet would have still given the generous tribute to Townshend in the House of Lords on the fall of Kut.

All of the players in this drama are long dead and although speculation is generally inconclusive there is a small matter, perhaps worth reflecting upon, when considering the motivation of Fitzgerald. Townshend was, without the least shadow of a doubt, a very active heterosexual and as such, probably held homosexuals in ill-concealed contempt. However, there are profound doubts, on the heterosexual score, about Kitchener and his relationship with Fitzgerald.

Oswald Fitzgerald was the Field Marshal's 'constant and inseparable companion,' having been appointed his aide-de-camp as a captain. The great man gathered around him a cadre of eager, young and unmarried officers, who became known as 'Kitchener's band of boys'.[8] That, in itself, is not damning but, 'when the great Field Marshal stayed in aristocratic houses, the well-informed young would ask servants to sleep across their bedroom threshold to impede his entrance. His compulsive objective was sodomy, regardless of gender.'[9]

Fitzgerald rose to the rank of colonel alongside his master until they met a common death on their voyage to Russia.[10] Could it be that Townshend, in one of his waspish asides or intemperate letters, had commented on Kitchener and his predilections in the usual, disapproving, homophobic manner of the day? Was such an observation repeated to Kitchener or Fitzgerald? Who knows where the unnamed member of the Army Council fits in all this? The people spreading this story obviously despised Townshend; they were not alone in this.

On 21 March 1919, Townshend had his day in court with his erstwhile subordinate officer, W.S. Churchill. The years had transformed their relationship and Churchill was no longer the subaltern asking the advice of a distinguished colonel. He was now near the head of government, world famous, a power in the land and operating on a vastly different plane to his visitor.

Townshend unburdened himself to Churchill, probably in great detail and with sparse dignity. He was pleading for his future. It came as a shock to him to be told that the famous 'letter' had not been seen by 'The Selection Board for regulation and promotions'. And so his supposition was incorrect. The death of Kitchener, in June 1916 whilst Townshend was a prisoner, had terminated any interest in the matter. Nevertheless, Churchill did confirm the existence of the letter and said that only he and his predecessor, Lord Milner, had seen it. Churchill allegedly told Townshend that 'although the letter was indiscreet there was nothing in it in any way to prevent his promotion and he, Churchill, would have been happy to support such a promotion if the Board had not been unanimous in not selecting him.'[11]

Churchill had enquired as to why Townshend had not been selected and was told that neither Lieutenant General Sir John Nixon nor Lieutenant General Sir Percy Lake had recommended his promotion. That was devastating news for Charles. He had carried out Nixon's asinine strategy loyally and efficiently, and he had served Lake with great diligence, but both of these generals had made a professional evaluation of Townshend and he had been found wanting. Little wonder that he was on half pay with his career at an end. At the end of the interview Townsend asked if he was to consider his career ruined. This was an absurd question considering the circumstances and the revelation he had just heard. Churchill, however, responded by saying, 'Why ruined? I am looking for a command for you now.'[12]

It is appropriate to examine Townshend's claim that the system had done him down. An officer in the Armed Forces has to meet the following criteria if he is to be promoted: he has to be physically fit, professionally qualified, of appropriate seniority, *recommended by his superiors without equivocation, and he has to be available for employment in the higher rank* (author's italics). It had now emerged that Townshend failed to make the grade on two counts. Firslty, he was not recommended by two former reporting officers – one non-recommendation would have been enough to stop him in his tracks. Secondly, he was locked away in Kut and unavailable to serve elsewhere in the higher rank. On that basis he had absolutely no cause for complaint and his constant whingeing that he was the victim of an injustice was not only counter-productive but it demeaned him.

It is useful to fit Charles Townshend into his niche in the structure of the Army and to demonstrate the degree of his influence on national issues. In 1914, the British Army had 247,432 regular soldiers and just under 500,000 reserves of all sorts. In addition the Indian Army was 174,725 strong. The British and Indian Armies combined had the following senior officers:

Field Marshals – 11 (+ 3 Royal)
Generals – 18 (+3 Royal)
Lieutenant Generals – 28
Major Generals – 114

The total number of active major generals and above, including medical officers, was 165. [The above total 171]

It is of only academic interest because seniority is not, in itself, the criteria for promotion. Nevertheless, Townshend was 66th on the major generals' list and was thus, in 1914, the 117th most senior officer in the Army – for what that was worth. He was senior to many officers older than he.

In late 1918 the strength of the Army had risen to 3,563,466 and the senior officer situation was as follows;

Field Marshals – 8 (+1 Royal)
Generals – 31 (+ 1 Royal)
Lieutenant Generals – 46
Major Generals – 255 (includes 13 x medical)

Townshend was now the 24th senior major general and 101st in seniority in the Army. However, of the forty-six lieutenant generals, forty-four of them had been junior to him as a major general, as had three of the generals. The total of active general officers including medical officers was 338. In effect, despite vast changes in the officer structure consequent on a world war, Townshend had not progressed.

Townshend's ire at being overtaken is a natural human response to a disappointing and irritating situation. However, it was a combination of circumstances and, specifically, his failure to win a recommendation from either Nixon or Lake that ditched his career.

It is interesting to note that in 1918, when Charles Townshend was fifty-seven, the five army commanders (generals) were aged between fifty-three and sixty-one. The sixteen lieutenant generals, commanding corps, were between forty-eight and sixty. Their average age was only fifty-four. Twelve of these officers started the war as brigadiers and one had been a lieutenant colonel (Butler); they all, of course, went past Townshend. In the ranks of the major generals, the accelerated promotion of younger men was most marked. Most of them were in their forties and Jackson was only thirty-nine, an eye-watering eighteen years younger than Chitrál Charlie. There was only one other major general who did not win substantive promotion during the First World War besides Townshend – and that was the charmless Gorringe.

Townshend could take some comfort that he survived the war because four lieutenant generals, twelve major generals and eighty-one brigadiers were killed. Townshend was one of the 146 who were captured or wounded.[13]

That all serves to put Townshend's position into an Army perspective and in 1918 opinions of him varied. His returning soldiers adored him, his officers less so and his generals not at all. Rumours abounded that a deputation led by the redoubtable Mellis had approached the War Office and suggested that Townshend's behaviour be investigated.[14] If indeed such a delegation ever existed nothing, ever became of it. The press had been generally supportive and in March 1919, *The Sunday Times* commented that: 'three months have elapsed since Chitrál Charlie returned to England but he has had no official recognition and he is still unemployed.' The newspaper went on to observe that 'Townshend's recommendations for honours and promotions for those under his command has been ignored and that his own promotion has been stopped while at least half a dozen major generals have been promoted over his head.'

In fact, it was very many more than 'half a dozen major generals' who had been promoted over CVFT's head. No less than forty-seven officers had passed him by and that, of course, was a source of major irritation and frustration for him.

The General was not entirely spurned and was in demand as a speaker, when his ebullient personality and sense of humour served his audiences well. He spoke at the dinner of the Society of St George in May 1919, and followed Lord Birkenhead, then Lord Chancellor. Birkenhead, in introducing Charles, spoke of him in the most generous of terms, his words being greeted with a tremendous ovation. Birkenhead said, after the dinner, that he had tried to redress the balance in Townshend's favour as he had received scant justice. In practice it had no effect.

Townshend continued to pursue the War Office, writing on 19 May to ask for his case to be reconsidered. The reply was peremptory in the extreme and said: 'The former decision conveyed to you on 12 February must stand.'[15]

But Townshend would not let go and wrote again at length, listing his grievances and saying: 'Herewith I resign my commission.' This was a mistake and a Lieutenant Colonel P.W. Chetwode, writing with his tongue firmly in his cheek and on behalf of the Military Secretary, asked if he really meant to *resign*, in which case he would forfeit his rank and pension, or did he mean to *retire* in the normal way with retired pay (author's italics)? If it was the latter and more sensible course then he would have to wait until he was sixty. He was already on half pay and so, in effect, the War Office had him under command for another year – a year in which he would remain subject to The Army Act and the military discipline that the Act enshrined.

In July 1919, there was unrest in Poland and Townshend reacted to a rumour, anticipated that there might be opportunities there and, despite his status, wrote straight to Churchill asking for employment. But he had over-played his hand by now and Churchill had had enough. On 7 July, WSC instructed the Military Secretary to tell Townshend: 'We know nothing of 500 British officers being sent to Poland; that Poland as far as we are aware is under the charge of the French. And so it is presumably to Marshal Foch that he should apply.' The sting was to be in the tail for Churchill's memo continued: 'No objection would be raised to his entering the Polish service provided he was first of all placed on the retired list.'

Townshend decided that he had a story to tell and turned his hand to writing his book, which was to be entitled *My campaign in Mesopotamia*. In it he set out to refute the rumours that he now knew surrounded his name and probably because of these very rumours he had no difficulty in finding a publisher. With time on his hands he addressed his authorship with his usual brand of diligence. The book gets off to an unfortunate and rather patronizing start in which Chitrál Charlie advises his reader that they will be 'unable to judge military operations unless they have a sound knowledge of the six great Fundamental Principles of War as established by Napoleon.' He then spends twenty pages explaining these principles. The explanation does not add to the 'readability' of the tome, and thereafter the book is painstakingly detailed. Just as Robertson had shaded his account of the siege of Chitrál, so now did Townshend shade his account of the events of 1915–1918. However, Townshend was sufficiently self-assured that he did not edit out any content that would give ammunition to his detractors, which was a mistake. Sadly, his vanity and insensitivity are displayed throughout the book. By August 1919, the book was in draft form – a good friend should have read it and advised him of its deficiencies.

A further seven months elapsed before, on 23 October 1919, three and a half years after the surrender of Kut, the *London Gazette* published honours and awards in connection with the defence of the town. It was noted with incredulity by the general public that Townshend's name was not included. The Establishment's rejection of the GOC 6th Division was now complete and very public. Realistically what could Townshend have hoped for? Promotion to GCB or perhaps a knighthood in another order of chivalry? Whatever his aspirations were the Establishment judged him and gave him nothing.

Townshend picked up the atmosphere that surrounded him and in a speech given at Norwich, it was too late when he averred, 'I knew nothing of the horrors that happened to my men during the march, but I was able to shorten their captivity by helping to bring about peace with Turkey.'

His critics said that if he did not know about the conditions to which the garrison of Kut was committed, then it was his bounden duty to find out. Certainly Townshend cannot escape censure on this score since he actually met the survivors of the ill-fated *Julnar* trudging into captivity during his own more comfortable journey. But even if he is to be excused on account of ignorance of the barbarous treatment his men were undergoing in the early stages of their captivity, it is difficult to understand his continued obsession for the Turks after the war.

Frank Scudamore, a war correspondent who had met Townshend many years before in 1884 in the Sudan, went to see him for the material for an article which was duly produced after a lengthy, rather pathetic interview. The piece appeared on 24 January 1920 in *Thomson's Weekly News* under the headline 'Townshend, Hero of Kut, hits out at his traducers.' The reporter recorded Townshend's words verbatim and for those making a judgment on Townshend, many years later, his own words sum him up. They are damning and in modern parlance he comes across as a 'whinger'.

The greater part of Scudamore's article is reproduced below but its length necessitates its editing. The flavour of the piece is retained but the reader has to imagine the tone of Townshend's voice as he enumerates his qualities and the perfidy of those who do not recognize them. He embraces the role of victim and wallows in it. All in all, as a summation of his last years of his uniformed service, it is a very sad but revealing document:

> To you [Scudamore] . . . a comrade in arms in many campaigns, it is natural that I should be able to expose a little of the feelings that almost overpower me and that I have been obliged to keep subdued during many years. I cannot speak freely[16] but I will be glad to talk to you upon the subject of the stories that have been circulated and broadcast about me, especially in regard to the rumour subtly circulated as to my connection, when a prisoner in Constantinople, with the appalling sufferings undergone by the officers and men under my command. Moreover, I can hint to you things I may not say openly as to the treat-

ment meted out to me ever since my return from captivity – a captivity during which, having no powers beyond those of any other prisoner of war, I had been successful in obtaining the assistance of the American and the Dutch Governments,[17] whose magnificent and untiring labours had been successful in sending to our prisoners . . . comforts.

After referring to his role in the negotiations, 'which took Turkey out of the firing line,' and quoting M. Clemenceau's greeting, 'By your endeavours, Townshend, you have saved the world many thousands of lives and many millions of money', the General added, 'No such comment has been made by any person in authority in this country.' Proudly, Townshend went on to describe his triumphant reception at Constantinople. 'I can but feel that I was better treated by our enemies than I have been since my return by my friends at home.' The article then covered at length the trial and misery of his captivity, but there was no reference to his unavailing initiatives to live on parole in Spain or of his attempts to share his incarceration with Lady Townshend. The issue of his apparent abandonment of his men after the surrender was raised again and the General commented as follows:

During all this time I was absolutely barred from any sort of communication with the forces that had been under my command. I never knew anything as to the stories of their appalling hardship and suffering, until in late 1917, I heard by means of a private letter from Lord Curzon, which reached me by a roundabout means, of what had happened to my men during their march into captivity.

Immediately upon the receipt of that letter I insisted upon an interview with Enver Pasha, to whom I made strong and indignant representations, pointing out that he had broken the word given to me by Khalil Pasha and himself. [He responded by saying] . . . it had been impossible to treat my men better than had been done . . . That so far as supplies were concerned the Turkish Armies were themselves in a condition of starvation, and his own men were literally dying in thousands of typhus, brought about by starvation. This was . . . the truth for, daily, [Turkish] soldiers in rags and in the last stages of emaciation used to beg for bread at my door. Do not let it be thought that, because I could get to know nothing of the conditions of captivity of my men, I did not endeavour to do as much as I could to relieve the sufferings which I knew they must inevitably be enduring.

These allegations by inference that suggest that I was indifferent to the fate of my men while I was living as a technical prisoner in comfort and maybe luxury in Constantinople, have cut me perhaps more bitterly than any other aspects of what at this moment I will merely call the indifference which I have encountered since my return to this country. Nothing, of course, has been said to my face.

My enemies are too shrewd for that, but you can imagine my indignation when I find – as I am beginning to do – vague and cryptic stories put about to this effect, not openly, but with the customary courage of the anonymous critic, whispered by certain of my special enemies to their lady friends at the Ritz in obscure corners.

He expanded on the plots against him and complained that if he had been faced with a direct accusation he could have refuted it, but he had no means of rebutting malicious rumours. He compared himself to Dreyfus, the French officer famously maligned.[18] This was not, by any stretch of the imagination, remotely comparable to Townshend's circumstances. Nevertheless, he continued:

Take even this censure by implication as to my residence while a prisoner on Prinkipo Island. There is a hinted suggestion that I was living in luxury during those two years. I can assure you that the contrary was very much the case. Everything that could be obtained in Constantinople and this was but the barest necessities of life had to be paid for at a fabulous price with which your wartime ration prices cannot be compared. I, of course, had to maintain the establishment that included my jailer, officers, and numerous orderlies.

The General then went into considerable detail about the economics of captivity and said that he was constantly short of money, and that a parsimonious government did precious little to help. Having got the cash issue off his chest he returned to his role as the victim of a powerful group of unnamed enemies. He said that his poor relationship with one of his adversaries dated back ten years:

I cannot go into that matter with any definiteness at present, but there had been several causes – causes, it may be said, that are so completely technical from the point of view of military procedure and War Office practice that, even if explained, the public could not readily understand – which had made me a marked man – and not marked for promotion either – in a certain powerful coterie.

So far back as 1910 I fell foul, through a perhaps unfortunate frank-
ness, with an extremely prominent personage in the High Command
whose hobby of predilection was the Territorial scheme. I received a
letter which asked me to call upon him, and on arrival was requested
to state my views on its proposed formation. I said, 'If I am to reply I
must be permitted to give bluntly my considered opinion, which is
that the reform you have in consideration appears to inevitably involve
the most complete economic waste of man-power that could be
conceived.' I gave my reasons, and one of them I instanced was the
fatal result in France in 1870 that was brought about chiefly by her
adoption of a territorial system on similar lines.

My interlocutor looked at me surprised, and obviously chagrined.
'I may tell you, Townshend,' he said, 'that the extraordinary view you
have just put forward is diametrically opposed to that of fourteen
officers senior in rank to yourself, whose opinions I have solicited in
this matter.'

'Well, sir,' was my reply, 'I have nothing to do with the opinions of
other men. You asked me for mine, and I have given it you.'

I should not perhaps go so far as to suggest that this episode had any
definite effect in causing to be placed on the records the sort of black
mark that has for a long time figured against my name It was, however,
one link in a long chain of circumstances that did not make for my
greater popularity in certain high quarters.

There has been in the course of my later career a variety of such
instances – occasions when, my views having been sought by my
superiors in certain definite circumstances, the considered opinion at
which I arrived after long years devoted assiduously to the closest
study of the art of war, have so utterly conflicted with those adopted
by my questioners as to put me very much at loggerheads with them.

I am a long-time student and close friend of Marshal Foch, who is
acknowledged to be the greatest living authority – possibly the greatest
authority of all time – upon the art and science of war.

In 1911 it was my privilege to make a study with Marshal Foch of
those parts of Belgium and Northern France against which, in his
considered estimation, the chief attack of the enemy must assuredly
be made in the war with Germany which he then considered to be
inevitable. The Marshal was good enough to ask me to read the frontier map for him and give my views of likely happenings, and he
congratulated me upon the fact that they coincided in the minutest
particulars with the conclusions at which he himself had arrived.

There was at least the likelihood that this would be the case, seeing that I had spent years in studying under his guidance, but I have always considered his appreciation to be the greatest compliment that has ever been paid to me. Of course, the war has shown that in every instance Foch's predictions have proved to be correct.

The study of the science and art of war has, to be sure, always been admitted by great men at the War Office as essential to a military training, but I should not like to assert that it has made for the popularity in certain circles of its practitioners. In my own case certainly I have found it definitely detrimental to my advancement. For instance, for years I had devoted all the time I could spare from my immediate military duties – and I was in continuous active employment abroad – to the study of the French frontier provinces with a view to the coming war with Germany. Moreover I was constantly in close touch with prominent officers of the French Army and with members of the Government and of the Chamber in France. I have always maintained a home in Paris, though my use of it from time to time suffered intermission, as, for instance, when I have been on service in India or elsewhere. I am very familiar with the French language, which I speak practically as I do English. Now, these are all reasons why, in my opinion, I had a right to expect that on the outbreak of war I should at once be given an opportunity to apply where it was urgently needed the knowledge to whose acquirement I had devoted long years of study – and study on the spot. I expected a command in France, and I may tell you that my friends in the French High Command had formed the same expectation, and had cherished the hope of finding me beside them, where they felt that my knowledge of the language and of the terrain must give a high value to my services.

What happened?

I was sent, as you know, to Mesopotamia,[19] and in conditions as regards the numbers, armament, and equipment of my forces such as to render inevitable the result that ensued. Well, let that pass. What happened at Kut is history, and I am not suggesting that there has ever been any attempt made in any quarter to disparage my conduct of the operations on the Tigris. Kut had to fall for reasons into which I need not enter. They are so well known. But the holding of Kut played an enormous part in the conquest of Palestine. For the victories that crowned Lord Allenby's endeavours in that country fitting praise and honour have been accorded to that successful commander, as was in every way right and just. No man can appreciate more highly than I do the value of the triumphs he achieved. But what has been my case? Why, the deadly silence that has covered me as with a pall ever since I landed in this country.

Compare the difference in the reception that was given to me in Paris when I passed through the city on my return from Turkey with the absolute lack of the greeting that I had every right to expect at the hands of my superiors when and after I reached this country.

In Paris I was received by M. Clemenceau, who congratulated me, with a warmth that sent a glow through my heart, both on my defence of Kut and on those efforts to which I have already referred, which brought about the peace with Turkey that was really the main factor which led to the German demand for an armistice. Marshal Foch hastened to me to express his generous appreciation of my work. There was surely no vanity, no overweening conceit, or undue show of confidence in the hope that I cherished, as I crossed the Channel, that in my own land some similar evidence of my country's appreciation would be vouchsafed me.

I need not say more, for you know what happened here and how bitter has been my deception throughout the year that has passed. My best friends, it is true, are now no more, but I had thought I possessed others. Mr Churchill I have always believed to be well affected towards me. That is a modest estimate of what I have hoped was the extent of his regard. Some months ago Mr Churchill gave me definitely to understand that he had in prospect for me a position which I could accept with satisfaction as perhaps commensurate with my rank and past services. But, the months have elapsed, and I have heard no more from the Secretary for War, and must therefore draw from his silence the conclusion, not that he has forgotten, but that under influences which I will not discuss he has evidently been induced to change his mind.[20]

I have waited for months, hoping against hope for just the appreciation which I feel to be my due, but after closely analysing the signs and portents that surround me I am inevitably forced to the conclusion that for reasons quite alien to my service the road is definitely blocked.

I will not go so far as to definitely assert that the cabal against me is one of absolute ill-will, but I cannot but feel that there are those within the inner circle who have built up against me a wall of prejudice which no effort of mine can break down. Throughout the whole of my life as a soldier the best interests of the Army have been my constant pursuit, and it is with a grief and a pain that I am powerless to express that I am forced to the conviction that the path of possible future service as an officer of His Majesty's Forces is definitely denied to me.

The men who knew and appreciated the work I strove to do are now no more. There were three of them who always gave me their cordial support and their thanks – Lord Kitchener, Sir Redvers Buller and Lord Wolseley. Alas! they are all gone, and I have now no powerful friends. Were those three great men still living I should not be in the position in which I find myself today.

Just a few days after the publication of this illuminating and undignified interview, which in its unedited form is even more toenail-curlingly awful, in February 1920, Charles Townshend's version of events in Mesopotamia was in the bookshops. The book attracted encouraging sales but no offer of employment and no reaction from the War Office which, it must be presumed, had sanctioned the writing of it.

On 5 August 1920, Charles wrote yet again directly to Churchill. He suggested that if WSC read his book it might assist in the solution of several international problems, and it offered political advice – this to a master of that craft. The letter is a repetition of so many others that its contents are not included here.

Townshend was not sixty until February 1921 when he would be placed firmly on the retired list. However, events overtook him when the Member of Parliament for The Wrekin died suddenly. Although he had never contemplated a political career, Townshend was flattered to be approached by Mr Horatio Bottomley[21] and asked to accept a nomination to stand in the by-election. Bottomley had made a reputation as 'the soldier's friend' and carried weight with the Conservative Party organization in The Wrekin. There was no difficulty in getting Charles adopted as the candidate. Indeed, Bottomley no doubt saw him as a useful acolyte.

Townshend stood for election in November 1920 and his retirement was accelerated by three months to allow him to stand. Sherson is silent on the administrative details but the probability is that the War Office was now only too happy to be rid of CVFT.

He cantered home in the election, took his seat in the House and made his maiden speech in December 1920 in a debate on Mesopotamia. The speech was heard with the customary courtesy and the Prime Minister, Lloyd George (who Townshend had vilified in the famous letter of 1914) rose to reply. Lloyd George said, in his lilting Welsh accent, that he had:

Great sympathy with what was said by my honourable and gallant friend below the gangway, whom we welcome to the House and who rendered such a very conspicuous service at a critical moment with very inadequate resources. The defence he put up against over-whelming forces is one of the glories of the Army of which he is a member.

One might have expected that a man like Townshend, who was only too happy to share his view on anything and everything, and who loved to be the centre of attention, would have basked in the spotlight that the House could provide. In fact he spoke very rarely and then only on military topics. Charles Townshend found himself in the company of men and women who were worldly, his intellectual equal or better and, for the most part, not particularly impressed by 'nine mentions'. He was ill at ease and opted to seek some form of appointment with diplomatic overtones. He felt that he still had significant influence in Turkish affairs and that, if sent to Turkey as an envoy, he could play a part to the benefit of both countries.

The Foreign Office could not have agreed less, did not want an amateur interfering in its affairs and what was more it said so in robust terms. Townshend was never one to take 'no' for an answer and decided to go to Turkey as a private individual. He made repeated applications for a visa, all of which were rejected, albeit courteously. Townshend took the matter up with any senior member of the Government who would listen – most would not. Austin Chamberlain, the Lord Privy Seal, eventually wrote to him and told him: 'A journey to Turkey at the present time by one who was known to be keen to negotiate with Turkey on behalf of the British government would be the reverse of opportune as it could not fail to be misunderstood by both our allies and by Turkey.'

The Government's position was difficult enough and the British position was by no means either firm or clear. Curzon wanted to expel Turkey from Europe – and at the same time remove the Turks from control of Constantinople and the Dardanelles, but allow them to remain an entity. Lloyd George's view ran counter to that and he thought that Turkey was no more than available space on the map to be parcelled up among other Powers as compensation for its misdeeds. The views of the Allies had also to be factored into the political equation. Agreements entered into during the war further complicated the issue; Lloyd George was much influenced by an offer made to Greece in 1915 – 'large concessions on the coast of Asia Minor'. He felt that the British Government could not renege on this offer.

Curzon had once been an active supporter of Townshend since they had first met in 1893 in Gupis. Now Curzon found himself the recipient of the political outpourings of a man who simply would not accept that his views and his services were not required in a world that had moved on. Curzon did not agree with his Prime Minister, however, both men were united in their determination to keep Townshend's fingers out of the Turkish pie. Accordingly, CVFT found it impossible to obtain a visa to visit Turkey. His every application was rejected. He did not accept that, as an MP, he had a duty to the House and to the nation, and when it suited him, he opted to conduct his affairs as a private citizen.

Austin Chamberlain was the recipient of a letter from Townshend that explained that his Turkish friends, including Izzet Pasha and Yusuf Kemal, wanted him to be Ambassador to Turkey, or failing that the Governor of Smyrna. He explained that the Turks trusted him but had little respect or confidence in other Englishmen. He closed by saying: 'I have made up my mind to go to Turkey directly the peace is signed. Kemal has invited me to Angora and says they will give me a reception never equalled to any Englishman before. I am crossing to Paris tomorrow.'

The letter was ignored by Chamberlain but Curzon, who must have been close to the end of his tether, eventually wrote again and this time said:

> I seem quite unable to convince you that, while not in the least questioning your sincere and patriotic intentions, we do not wish to send anyone to Angora at the present stage at all – in fact it would be directly contrary to my pledges both to the French and the Italians. I may further add that the opinions you express on certain aspects of the proposed settlement are so sharply in contrast with the views entertained by His Majesty's Government and by the allies, now acting, I am happy to say in complete unison, that the last thing we desire is to authorise the despatch of a delegate unofficial or otherwise who does not agree with us.

The message was loud and very clear but Townshend did not get it. He decided that, notwithstanding the delicate negotiations in the hands of experts that were underway and which were designed to create a lasting peace, he could make a useful and unique contribution. He applied for a passport for a visit to France and 'other countries'. The presumption is that his passport had expired whilst he was a POW.

The reply was to the effect that he would only be given a passport if he furnished a signed undertaking that he would in no circumstances attempt to enter Turkey. Townshend was outraged at what he considered an insult, but others might think the action of a prudent government. The following gentlemanly exchanges were recorded in *Hansard* on 3 May 1922:

Sir CHARLES TOWNSHEND asked the Lord Privy Seal, with regard to the refusal of the Secretary of State for Foreign Affairs to grant a passport to the Hon. Member for The Wrekin to visit Turkey, why the Hon. Member, who would proceed there in a private capacity, may not have the same privileges as are extended to other Members of this House and to other subjects of His Majesty generally.

Mr. CHAMBERLAIN My Hon. and gallant Friend has repeatedly proffered his assistance to the Foreign Office during the last three years to conduct negotiations, either in a private capacity or on behalf of His Majesty's Government, both at Angora and at Constantinople. While convinced of the entirely patriotic spirit in which these offers have been made, the Secretary of State for Foreign Affairs has been unable to take advantage of them, because he did not feel that the presence of my hon. and gallant Friend would not conduce to the ends which, His Majesty's Government have in view. Nevertheless, my hon. and gallant Friend has continued to press for passport facilities for Turkey, though he knew well that his intervention was not desired. In these circumstances, the Secretary of State had no alternative but to inform him, as he did on the 27th March last, that such a journey undertaken by my hon. and gallant Friend at the present time would be the reverse of opportune, since it could not fail to be misconstrued, both by our Allies and by Turkey, as an official mission, and, consequently, to prejudice the present negotiations and to delay still further the re-establishment of peace with Turkey; and that in these circumstances he regretted that he must postpone the grant of a passport to those places until a more suitable moment.

Lieut.-Commander KENWORTHY Do not His Majesty's Government sometimes regret that they have not taken the advice both of myself and the hon. Member for The Wrekin with regard to Turkey?

Mr. CHAMBERLAIN I have never had occasion to regret not following the advice of the hon. and gallant Gentleman . . . My hon. Friend occupies such a position in those countries that his visit would necessarily attract great attention, and after the proposals which he has made the presence there of a man of such distinction as he could not but embarrass the negotiations and the prospects of peace. It was on these grounds that the Government felt bound to refuse the passport.

Captain <u>GEE</u> Are passports refused to Members of this House who are not in agreement with the policy of the Government?

<u>Mr. CHAMBERLAIN</u> Passports have been issued to Members of this House who are very far from being in agreement with His Majesty's Government. The granting of passports is regulated, not by the feelings of His Majesty's Government, but by the interests of the public service.

Townshend's position was becoming more extreme and his unqualified support for the Turks was countered by his violent hostility to the Greeks. On 15 June 1922, he spoke vigourously in the House in a sustained attack on the Government's Eastern policy. This speech drove him further into the political and to some extent social wilderness.

This biographer is loath to burden the reader with the details of Charles Townshend's machinations over the next few months; suffice it to say that he conducted his affairs entirely to his own satisfaction and, by devious means, inserted himself onto the outer fringes of the diplomatic scene in Europe. He made it his business to meet anyone who might share his Turkophile views and quite expressly avoided being exposed to anyone likely to defend the Greek position.

He socialized with the great and the good in Paris, Marseilles, Alexandria, Haifa, Beirut and Aleppo. In Beirut, on 17 July 1922 (CVFT's passport having been issued), the British Consul-General, who had been alerted by the Foreign Office, called on him and reminded him of his national responsibilities and his earlier agreement (March 1922) not to enter Turkish territory. Townshend justified his non-compliance by arguing that events had overtaken him and that his earlier agreement had only been 'provisional'. Not for the first time Townshend proved himself to be a semanticist.

Townshend went to Turkey and was greeted in great style, although not sufficiently so to inhibit him asking for a private train for the last leg of his journey. This was immediately provided and, at journey's end, Chitrál Charlie had his meeting with Kemal Pasha at Angora. A French naval officer acted as interpreter whilst Townshend elaborated on his ideas of an equable peace that had not one whit of government backing. He had previously offered Kemal his 'services and his sword' but he was told that it was now Turkish policy not to give command to foreign officers. This was a policy obviously agreed upon after the disagreeable association the Turks had with German officers commanding their troops. The Turks reiterated that they would welcome Townshend as HM's Ambassador, or failing that as Governor of Smyrna – this was heady wine. The next day he cabled

Captain Gee VC MP in which he said that immediate peace with Turkey was possible on the evacuation by the Greeks of Smyrna and Turkish territory in Asia Minor. He asked Gee to publicize his views to the Cabinet and the press.

The meeting was followed by much wining and dining and Townshend's diary is filled with pages and pages of tedious detail of where he went and who he met, especially attractive women who unfailingly attracted his attention and admiration. Sherson, who had ploughed through all of the diaries, commented:

> His old habit of jotting down every little detail clung to him still. He writes page upon page daily, and again one wonders how he could possibly find time to put it all down. It can only be supposed that his temperament was such that he could not be idle for a single moment, not even in the hottest and most trying weather, and under trying circumstances must out with his pen and jot down everything!

The visit to Turkey confirmed for Townshend his estimation of that nation. He was impressed with the state of the Army and the excellence of public facilities. His unquestioning enthusiasm for all things Turkish remained with him for the rest of his life and it tilted his approach to public life out of balance. The Turks for their part were only too happy to have an unpaid advocate in the House of Commons and made it clear that he would be welcomed if appointed HM's Ambassador. He spent time in France and there he was made more welcome in official circles than he ever was at home in Britain. His views were treated with respect and he was accorded considerable deference – much to his liking.

In August Lloyd George made a pro-Greek speech in the House and this encouraged the Greeks to such an extent that copies of that speech were distributed to the Greek Army as a Special Order of the Day. The events that followed were tragic, the Turks attacked and took Smyrna, and in Greece revolution broke out and the King abdicated.

Charles Townshend devilled on through the summer of 1922 and on 31 August was in correspondence with the Prime Minister who said that he would consider Townshend's report on his trip to Angora and discuss it with the Foreign Secretary, but nothing came of it. However, on 20 September, the newly appointed Mr Worthington-Evans, the Secretary of State for War,[22] asked Townshend to come to see him to discuss the 'Chanak Situation'[23] and in the course of the conversation Townshend refuted the suggestion that the French were 'running away'; he said shrewdly that they were not going to risk the loss of the Colonial Empire in a holy war with Islam even if we, the British, were foolish enough to do so. Some of Townshend's pragmatic political thinking would have served his nation well some eighty years later.

Later in the year Townshend was giving direct advice to the Turkish Government that ran counter to the British opposition to the fortification of Constantinople. Ismet Pasha asked Townshend what he should do in the face of this opposition and Charles Townshend MP told him to ask for British and French guarantees for the security of the city. Townshend was now treading a dangerous path.

Sherson, searching for the positive, asserted: 'it could be justly claimed that Townshend did much toward settling the terms of the Treaty of Lausanne.[24] His opinion was highly valued and not least by Ismet Pasha, who represented them at Lausanne. He listened to his advice – and what is more he took it.'

On 19 October 1922, the Government resolved to call a General Election and to go to the country as a Conservative Party with Conservative policies. Townshend, although the sitting MP for The Wrekin, had aspirations to represent a Norfolk constituency in the new Parliament. He made a start in finding a seat but it was an uphill task and then as now the local party organizations held the whip hand in the candidate selection process.

He was distracted from matters political when his daughter Audrey was married on 22 November to Comte Baudoin de Borchgrave D'Altena. The event took place in Paris at the residence of Count Cahen D'Anvers and it was obviously one of the society weddings of the year. Townshend could now hope for a grandson.

On 6 December 1922, the General Election took place but Townshend was not a player as he had been unsuccessful in finding a seat. Richmond, Surrey, would have been happy to take him but it was too far from Norfolk. He retired to Vere Lodge contenting himself by taking up his prolific letter-writing.

In Athens the late Prime Minister Gounaris and his colleagues were executed to international disapproval. Townshend found that he missed the opportunities that Westminster gave him to be well briefed and travelled frequently between Norfolk, London and Paris. He and Lady Townshend finally decided to buy Vere Lodge which hitherto they had had on a lease. Once the business was concluded they started to invest time and money in adapting it to their long-term needs. The house had been built by Lord Charles Townshend, the heir presumptive to the 3rd Marquess. Family portraits that had been purchased by Count Cahen D'Anvers in the great sale of 1904 were returned to Norfolk and Townshend had the pleasure of hanging them once more in family property.

Sherson incorrectly attributes the publication of CVFT's book, *My campaign in Mesopotamia*, to this period in early 1923. In fact the book had been published, long before, in February 1920. Charles Townshend had always had a bee in his bonnet about Canada; it was a subject that he studied at some length at the beginning of the century – now he decided to write a book to be entitled *The Gateway to Canada*, dealing with the seizure of Canada from the French, in part due to the efforts of the 1st Marquess Townshend. It has never been published.

On 8 July 1923, a black day for Townshend, his little dog Spot, who had been by his side during his time in Mesopotamia, had to be put down. Spot had been evacuated from Kut with the dog of General Mellis, both having been present at three major battles. The General was misled by his family who told him that Spot had been found dead in the garden; in fact he was discreetly put to sleep. Charles Townshend was predictably very distressed at the loss of his beloved dog.

The peace treaty was signed in Lausanne and once more Townshend asked the Prime Minister to send him out to Kemal to 'square things'.[25] When there was no response from Downing Street he decided to go anyway. The evidence suggests that he went at the behest of a financial consortium, which saw rich pickings in post-war and stable Turkey. He went to Constantinople where he met up with old friends and offered advice as to how best the new Turkish Government could fund its activities. He was given the chance to walk down memory lane and in the process visited places that he knew well, not least the house of Enver Pasha (now dead) and Izzet Pasha's villa where he and Captain Moreland sometimes went for lunch. He went back to Prinkipo and wandered round what had been his 'prison'. Khalil Pasha, who had defeated him at Kut, sent him a warm cable of friendship and in between times Townshend found time to record in his diary meeting 'young and beautiful' ladies.[26] He met Ismet Pasha, now a member of the Turkish Cabinet, who left a cabinet meeting in order to see him. The matter of his Ambassadorship was raised yet again and the reasons why it would be mutually beneficial to both countries were rehearsed.

The journey home was uncomfortable – no private train this time but a crowded, dirty carriage in which he gave up his seat, noting that the compartment housed some Turkish ladies 'three of them very pretty'.

On his return from Turkey, tired by the travelling, Lady Townshend realized that Charles was below par. He was just a few weeks short of his sixty-third birthday and it soon became apparent that he was a sick man. He was diagnosed with a 'serious spinal disease brought on by war strain and doubtless mental strain', according to Sherson, but, with hindsight, he had almost certainly contracted cancer. He was well enough to welcome his first grandchild on 24 January 1924.

In early May 1924, the Townshends were in Paris, but Charles's voluminous diary now received scant attention and sparse notes. Sherson draws attention to the entry for 6 May: 'Present for Rutter for having tended my kit since Raven left on 26 March.' Sherson adds: 'but he never lost heart and as usual was always thinking of other people.'

Charles Townshend arranged to have lunch at the Ritz and his friends advised him not to take any risks. He returned from lunch and made a final entry in his diary which read: '*Je serai*. I'm alright.' He never took up his pen again and the following day he was taken with a paralysis of the throat.

His condition worsened rapidly.

Just before midnight, on 17 May 1924, Chitrál Charlie died.

Notes

1. A.J. Barker.
2. Sherson.
3. Sherson's book carries this assertion but not as reported speech. The text can only have come from CVFT's diary.
4. Sherson.
5. W.S. Churchill.
6. A man well acquainted with Charles Townshend with whom he had worked alongside during the campaigns in Egypt. He was drowned with Kitchener when HMS *Hampshire* struck a mine off the Orkneys.
7. Sherson.
8. Ronald Hyam, *Empire and sexuality: The British experience.*
9. A.N. Wilson, *The Victorians*, 2002.
10. H. Montgomery-Hyde, *The love that dare not speak its name.*
11. E. Sherson.
12. E Sherson.
13. Includes some statistics taken from Corrigan, *Mud, Blood and Poppycock.*
14. A.J. Barker. He does not identify a source for this rumour.
15. A.J. Barker.
16. This was a reference to the fact that as a serving soldier, he was restricted in his dealings with the press. No doubt he had learned from the interview with *The Times*.
17. It is a matter for conjecture that CVFT had done anything at all to ease

the burden on his soldiers. This assertion that he obtained the support of two foreign governments is made here for the first time. Interestingly, Erroll Sherson makes no mention of this very significant claim in *Townshend of Kut*.

18. Captain Alfred Dreyfus of the French Army was unjustly convicted of treason in 1894 and imprisoned. The culprit was found but a corrupt government manipulated the justice system and Dreyfus was not released and exonerated until 1906. He served throughout the First World War and ended as a Lieutenant Colonel.

19. He was of course an officer in the Indian Army and Mesopotamia, under the aegis of the Indian Army, was where it fought. CVFT had been overjoyed to be given command of 6th Division.

20. This thinly veiled, public criticism of the Secretary of State for War was, in itself, sufficient to draw more fire.

21. Horatio Bottomley (1860–1933), an entrepreneur, proprietor of *John Bull*, a discharged bankrupt and by most standards could be described as 'a wide boy'. He had great public support but subsequently, in 1922, was sent to prison for seven years for fraud.

22. Sir Worthington Laming Worthington-Evans, 1st Baronet, GBE (1868–1931), Secretary of State for War 1921–2.

23. The Chanak Affair of September 1922 was the threat by Turkey to attack the British and French troops stationed near Chanak guarding the Dardanelles neutral zone. The Turkish troops had recently defeated Greek forces and recaptured Smyrna. The inept handling of the crisis by the British Cabinet was a major contributor to the downfall of British Prime Minister David Lloyd George and it led to the General Election later the same year.

24. The Treaty of Lausanne was a peace treaty signed in Lausanne on 24 July 1923. It settled the Anatolian and East Thracian parts of the partitioning of the Ottoman Empire by annulment of the Treaty of Sèvres (1920). The Treaty also led to the international recognition of the sovereignty of the new Republic of Turkey as the successor state of the defunct Ottoman Empire.

25. E. Sherson.

26. E. Sherson.

Chapter 17

1924–2010

Epilogue

The passing of Charles Townshend at the relatively early age of sixty-three was not front-page news in the UK and only *The Daily Express* saw fit to give his death any prominence. A memorial service was quickly arranged at the British Embassy church in Paris – the Ambassador attended as did the Military Attaché, and for both it was probably a matter of duty. Charles Townshend was not buried in France; his body was enclosed in a lead enve-lope and a plain oak coffin. The coffin bore a plate inscribed 'Townshend of Kut'.

The funeral took place at East Raynham in Norfolk. There were no official representatives of HM Government or the Army present and the Marquess was noticeable by his absence. Lady Townshend and her daughter, now the Countess Baudoin de Borchgrave D'Altena, together with Lord St Levan and his wife, were the family mourners. The church was packed with old soldiers, most of whom had served with Charles in the Sudan, India or Mesopotamia. His theatrical friends came to his last show to see the final curtain come down.

The funeral was a simple affair. The coffin was shrouded in the Union flag; there were masses of flowers, some in the form of a French tricolour from Alice Townshend. The Royal Norfolk Regiment was present in strength and the bearer party was made up of much-medalled veterans, some of whom had served at Kut. The service was conducted by the Bishop of Thetford who, as custom dictates, spoke of the dead man in the most generous terms. Having said that Charles was 'absolutely devoted to duty and to the great profession to which he belonged', he concluded his address by saying, 'Townshend was the type of man who made for the real greatness of the British Empire.' There are few churlish enough not to say 'amen' to that.

It had poured with rain during the service but the weather cleared as the cortège made its way to the grave side. Brigadier-General W.G. Hamilton CB DSO carried Townshend's sword, the very weapon returned to him by Khalil in April 1916. Lieutenant Colonel C.D. Seymour bore his decorations and medals, of which there was a profusion gathered over thirty-seven years of campaigning. The non-attendees at the funeral were significant. Only Hamilton of his generals was there and only a sprinkling of his officers.

The obituaries that were published were reserved, even muted. On 19 May 1924, *The Times* commented: 'Major General Sir Charles Townshend cannot be considered a great soldier, but will always be remembered for his defence of Kut in the Great War.' Having made a somewhat negative start, the writer went on in a critical tone implying that Townshend saw the siege of Kut as 'a last torch to illumine this once resplendent region'. These were high-sounding words but they made clear that Townshend was a seeker after glory – at least in the opinion of *The Times*.

The obituary in *The Daily Telegraph* was much more generous, the author being Colonel Repington, an old friend of Townshend. He ventured to say that he was 'a very intrepid man, a good leader in the field'. However, Repington did not dodge the issue and added: 'After the surrender of Kut, General Townshend committed an error of judgment in allowing the Turks to separate his fate in captivity from that of his men.'

The contrast in style of his captivity and that of his men was obviously a major talking point after the war. Despite all the gossip and innuendo the charge that he had conducted himself dishonourably was never levelled at Townshend, officially or unofficially. In the modern vernacular. 'The issue was the elephant in the room.' He raised the matter himself in interviews and in his book, and made reference to it in the House, but, until accused publicly, he could not be tried and, perhaps, acquitted.

In fact he was tried by the court of public opinion, found guilty and his name is forever besmirched as a result. Any researcher looking into the life and times of Charles Townshend is unlikely to find a cogent defence of his comfortable period in captivity, and it must be concluded that he did fail his soldiers, the gravest and most unforgivable offence that an officer can commit.

He had made it clear that he dreaded being a prisoner, when he even suggested that captivity would kill him; this was an extreme position to take. However, given that attitude and faced with the option of being an 'honoured guest' rather than submitting to some, as yet unknown, alternative, his decision is at least understandable. The overwhelming consensus is that he made the wrong decision. *But having made it, he did nothing to correct it* (author's italics). Therein lies the ruin of his reputation.

The reason for his espousal of the Turkish cause is difficult to fathom. It surely must have been motivated by something deeper than a comfortable bed and 'three squares' a day. But if so – what? The Turks certainly knew their man and they played, with great skill, to Townshend's vanity. They flattered him; they treated him with deference and consideration, appointed a Turkish ADC and then, like a hungry trout, Townshend rose to the bait. In an unsophisticated but effective way the Turks successfuly enlisted him as willing agent and, for the rest of his life, he was their man.

In 1975 Dr Norman Dixon wrote a stimulating book entitled, *On the Psychology of Military Incompetence*. Two of his many case studies are from the same family, albeit related only by marriage – they are Buller and Townshend. Dixon writes persuasively about Townshend and damns him as an incompetent. His judgment, although interesting, has to be taken with a pinch of salt as he acknowledges that his prime source is Russell Braddon's *The Siege*. Braddon's book is immensely readable, well researched and entertaining – it is also biased against Townshend, no doubt, at least in Braddon's view, for perfectly valid reasons. John Laffin, in his book,[1] also made up his mind from the same source and observed: 'Townshend's troops in Mesopotamia gave him their loyalty, their strength and finally their liberty and their lives. He betrayed them.' Laffin did not pull his punches and added: 'Townshend was vain, egocentric and suffused with an almost Gallic desire for *la gloire*.'

Laffin judged that Townshend 'had plenty of time to retreat to the safety of Amara and his men were fit enough. But he was more interested in his grand ambition than in the welfare of his men.' That is a simplistic judg-ment and not entirely fair. The reality was that Townshend's troops were exhausted and his decision to stop in Kut could easily be justified on mili-tary grounds.

Braddon provided both Laffin and Dixon with any amount of irrefutable factual and anecdotal evidence for them to evaluate. Among Dixon's comments on Townshend are the following:

> As the person most responsible for the disaster at Kut and the misery inflicted on his troops, Townshend might well have experienced and tried to expiate some modicum of guilt. That he did not raises several interesting issues, not least of which being the suggestion that member-ship of a hierarchical authoritarian organisation in some way absolves the individual from being hampered in his actions by this tiresome emotion. Townshend was by no means unique in apparently being devoid of a sentiment most people experience. Nixon too seemed unmoved at what his bid for glory had cost the soldiers under him.

Further relevant extracts are to be found below:

A second group whose besetting sin was overweening ambition coupled with a terrifying insensitivity to others. These, men like Haig, Townshend, Walpole, Nixon and Joffre, seemed dedicated to one goal – self-advancement. Vain, devious, scheming and dishonest, they were certainly not inactive in the courses they pursued nor, of course, were they necessarily without military talents.

It is hardly surprising that even the most incompetent generals were often effective social leaders. No one took greater risks than Townshend, no one was more concerned to indulge his troops than Buller . . . it may seem scarcely credible that the riskiness of Townshend and the indulgence of Buller could have compensated for their other characteristics.

Dixon compares Townshend with Montgomery, another egoist of the first order, but he concludes that when speaking of Montgomery, who had had a joust with authority: 'There can be no doubt that to Montgomery's act of intelligent effrontery a good many men owe, if not their lives then at least salvation from five years in a German prison camp.' This sort of personal risk-taking for the sake of larger issues was not a feature of Townshend's make up. For him it was self first, Army second.

Dixon goes on to say:

Even men like Elphinstone [the instigator of the retreat from Kabul in 1842], Townshend and Buller, about whose flagrant incompetence in the role of decision maker there can be no possible doubt, earned a loyalty and affection, albeit far beyond their deserts, which maintained the morale and fighting spirit of their men almost to the end . . . While a man like Townshend would not be likely to survive for very long in a modern civilian firm, his autocratic mien was lovingly accepted by men whose lives were hanging by a thread.

For all of Dr Dixon's scholarship and his bleak view of Townshend, it is strongly suggested that in one respect his judgment is flawed. It is true that Charles Townshend was fallible – perhaps particularly so, but for all that, he was a thoroughly competent general.

Chitrál Charlie knew his business and he was an expert practitioner. His progression until December 1915 had been one of unalloyed success and as a result he was fêted and his successes were trumpeted abroad. He spent the lives of his men with care and he was acknowledged, even by the Turks, to have been the victor at Ctesiphon. Had he fallen to a Turkish sniper at Ctesiphon he would have died a hero and this book would have a different tenor – and it would have been a deal shorter too!

CVFT survived to make the momentous decision to stand at Kut with his depleted division, a decision that the pundits now rule was an error. Dixon adds academic weight to Braddon's view by saying of the selection of Kut:

> Townshend's new-found delusion regarding the virtues of Kut may well have its origins in a much earlier event, the siege of Chitrál. This is a highly plausible hypothesis. When intractable desires are thwarted by reality there is a tendency to hark back to the memory of earlier gratification and Chitrál epitomised for Townshend such gratification.

However, there is ample evidence that his men were exhausted and no matter how desirable it might have been to march on to Amara, there was the possibility that the column would be overtaken and brought to battle on ground not of Townshend's choosing. On that basis, his decision was not entirely unreasonable.

Townshend's additional reasons for standing at Kut – where by so doing he would command the confluence of the Tigris and the Hai, and stem any southward advance by Khalil around Kut – are less convincing; the reality is that the Hai was of no strategic importance and the Turks outflanked Kut easily, without being opposed.

Townshend was fortunate to be given an independent command on ground that gave him room to manoeuvre. He demonstrated that he was a skilled tactician and as the opening of this book remarks that a general's reputation is influenced by the skill and tenacity of his opponents. Townshend out-thought his enemy but his failure was not to have the moral strength to challenge Nixon and be prepared to resign his command if necessary. To do that would have been an end to his career. It was not a gamble he was prepared to take because he would not have become a field marshal in those circumstances – or even a lieutenant general.

There is speculation that had Townshend commanded a division on the Western Front he would have been more successful. This is highly unlikely. There was literally 'no room to manoeuvre 'in the static trench warfare that developed in Flanders, and Townshend would have been frustrated not to be able to put into use the tactics upon which he and Napoleon were agreed. He would have been appalled by the unsophisticated frontal attacks that he would have been compelled to mount. However, the chances are that he would certainly have risen one level and possibly two. His near-contemporary Haig went up three.

It has to be conceded that, whilst in Kut, Townshend deliberately lied about his food stocks in order to hasten both Aylmer and Gorringe in their plans for his relief. It is axiomatic that two generals with a common aim and who share intelligence will be ruthlessly honest with each other. To be otherwise is to put their mutually supporting operations in jeopardy. In this case Aylmer committed his troops prematurely and many brave and unquestioning men died as a result. Townshend has a lot to answer for in this regard.

Erroll Sherson, his first biographer, comments on his cousin in the following way:

> He was a broken old man. Old really before his years actually entitled him so to be called. His mercurial temperament and the incessant worry of struggling against all of those whom he firmly believed to be responsible for the termination of his military career, combined to give the finishing touches to the break up of a constitution naturally strong, but much weakened by the terrible strains and privations he had undergone in Mesopotamia . . . who shall say that he did not die of a broken heart?

In reflective mood, Braddon, in an unusually compassionate tone, has this to say:

> Poor Townshend. His wife and daughter loved him. His friends loved him. His dog 'Spot' – repatriated, as promised by Khalil – loved him. Society accepted him and knew him simply as 'Kut'. A fashionable artist painted his portrait, and actors and actresses still enjoyed his company. But denied his family title and denied his field marshal's baton he had to have something else. Like the adulation of the Turks as he decided their fate on behalf of the British Government . . . [He] was denied [this].

A.J. Barker, himself a soldier, made this assessment when he completed the second biography of Charles Townshend:

Because the Mesopotamian Campaign was 'Nobody's Child' and a near Crimean disgrace, Townshend became the scapegoat and suffered for a series of mistakes which were not . . . his own fault. He was a courageous soldier and a good general; a mediocre Member of Parliament, but a real-life character. In another era he would have been treated more generously – kicked upstairs with promotion and a title . . . he could have made a first-class governor of one of Britain's colonial possessions.

Field Marshal Lord Harding, whilst not commenting on Townshend specifically, made some pertinent remarks when he was speaking about 'Leadership' to the cadets at the RMA Sandhurst in 1953. He said, 'You have to have *complete integrity* (Harding's italics). You have got to be honest, not only with yourselves but with the men you lead . . . honesty and integrity are things you cannot compromise with – you cannot alter; if you do . . . you will not be able to lead.'

The fact is that Charles Townshend did not have that 'complete integrity' and, given that fundamental deficiency, his eventual failure and fall from grace were inevitable.

This, his third, biographer concludes that Charles Townshend was a psychologist's dream. That he was egocentric there can be no doubt and as a result his conceit, selfishness and overweening ambition scarred his life. His insensitive, single-minded pursuit of power and, if possible, glory failed to win him many friends among his peers, and eventually his superiors called a halt to his further advancement. He was however a skillful general, an innovative leader and an engaging man. His extrovert personality was a useful tool and he employed it to very good effect, especially in his superficial relationship with his soldiers. It is little wonder that he fitted easily into the London theatrical scene. He was a man with ample talent and, had he conducted himself in a less aggressive and more honourable manner, the chances are that he would have reached the rank of at least major general anyway. He was never the high-flyer he thought he ought to be and, perhaps, he paid the price for parading his military education to those of his seniors who lacked the same. Comparing himself with Napoleon is a grotesque manifestation of his mis-appreciation of his own worth.

It would be a mistake to be duped by the bogus claim that Townshend was a hero. He was not. At Chitrál he performed efficiently in a situation not of his choosing. His withdrawal to the fort under fire on the night of

3 March 1895 was well done, but that then was his business for which he had been trained. He did nothing that could be described as heroic (Harley did) and his being recognized as a 'hero' had more to do with the political situation in India as it was viewed around the world, and precious little to do with personal gallantry.

Similarly, his withdrawal from Ctesiphon to Kut was conducted in the most exemplary way and he is correctly recognized for that. Once incarcerated in Kut he replayed his performance at Chitrál. He was competent and efficient – no more. He did not expose himself in the front-line trenches and never visited Wool Press Village. He may be described as 'the Hero of Kut, but that is a misnomer – the heroes of Kut were the starving British and Indian soldiers who manned wet, fly-blown trenches and who gave their lives in a hopeless cause.

Although not a 'hero', Charles Townshend did not lack physical courage, and particularly as a young officer he was anxious to be in the middle of the action, as this narrative has demonstrated. Sadly, all the physical courage in the world is no substitute for moral courage and this was a quality that Townshend lacked. He failed to face up to Robertson at Chitrál and, fatally, he failed to confront Nixon after he had taken Kut. Had he told Nixon that he would go no further unless he was reinforced, he might have been sacked, but then Nixon too would have been exposed. Whatever the result, had Townsend taken that position he could rightfully be termed 'the Hero of Kut'. Alternatively, if Townshend had been killed at Ctesiphon, the probability is that he would now be remembered with respect and admiration. However, his conduct from November 1916, until his repatriation in 1918, and his subsequent espousal of the Turkish cause, undid all the good that went before.

Townshend has been resting in his grave for eighty-six years and, over time, the stone above the grave has been broken. Lichen has invaded the surface but close examination shows that the inscription reads: 'Townshend of Kut' – an epitaph that is the least that this sad, tormented man deserves.

Note
1. *British Butchers & Bunglers of World War1.*

Appendix I
'Mesopotamia'

by
Rudyard Kipling

They shall not return to us, the resolute, the young,
The eager and whole-hearted whom we gave:
But the men who left them thriftily to die in their own dung,
Shall they come with years and honour to the grave?

They shall not return to us; the strong men coldly slain
In sight of help denied from day to day:
But the men who edged their agonies and chid them in their pain,
Are they too strong and wise to put away?

Our dead shall not return to us while Day and Night divide –
Never while the bars of sunset hold.
But the idle-minded overlings who quibbled while they died,
Shall they thrust for high employments as of old?

but

Shall we only threaten and be angry for an hour:
When the storm is ended shall we find how softly
how swiftly they have sidled back to power
By the favour and contrivance of their kind?

Even while they soothe us, while they promise large amends,
Even while they make a show of fear,
Do they call upon their debtors, and take counsel with their friends,
To conform and re-establish each career?

Their lives cannot repay us – their death could not undo –
The shame that they have laid upon our race.
But the slothfulness that wasted and the arrogance that slew,
Shall we leave it unabated in its place

Bibliography

Braddon, R., *The Siege*, Jonathan Cape, 1969.

Candler, E., *The long road to Baghdad*, Cassell, 1920.

Corrigan, G., *Mud Blood and Poppycock*, Cassell, 2003.

Dixon, N., *'On the Psychology of Military Incompetence'*, Jonathon Cape, 1976.

Durand, Col A.G., CB CIE, *The making of a frontier*, 1900.

Hansard, Various entries, such as Mr Hicks, J./Mr Law, B., 9 July 1917.

Harris, J. *Much Sounding of Bugles*, Hutchinson & Co., 1975.

Hastings, M., *Warriors*, HarperCollins, 2005.

Henty, G.A., *Through three campaigns – The story of Chitrál, Tirah and Ashanti*, n.d.

Hunter, Maj C., RLC, *Eight Lives Down*, Transworld Publishers, 2007.

Jones, E.E., *Memoirs and Diaries*, John Lane, 1920.

John Keay, J., *Exploration of the western Himalayas*,, 1895.

Kingsmill, A.G., *The Silver Badge*, Stockwell, 1966.

Kipling, R., *Mesopotamia*,, 1917.

Knight, E.F., *Where three empires meet*, Sang-e-Meel, 1892.

Laffin, J., *British Butchers & Bunglers of World War 1*, Sutton Publishing Ltd, 1988.

London Gazette, various entries.

Moore, J., *Mesopotamia*,, 2006.

Mousley, Capt E.O., RFA, *The secrets of a Kutite*, John Lane, *1920*.

O'Connor, Maj J.O., USAF, *WW1. British Mesopotamia Campaign*, USAF Staff college, 2006.

Robertson, Sir George, *Chitrál. The story of a minor siege*, Charles Scribner's Sons, 1899.

Sandes, E.W.C., *In Kut and Captivity*, Murray, 1919.

Saunders, J., *The Psychology of Military Incompetence*, 1988.

Scudamore, F., *Thompson's Weekly News*, 1920.

Sherson, E., *Townshend of Chitrál and Kut. A biography*, William Heinemann Ltd, 1928.

Steevens, G.W., *With Kitchener to Khartoum*.

Sykes, Sir Mark, MP,, *Daily Telegraph*, 22 November 1915.

Thomson, H.C., *The Chitrál Campaign*, 1895.

Townshend, C.V.F.T., *My campaign in Mesopotamia*, Thornton Butterworth, 1920.

Index

AAG 121, 124, 127, 132, 139, 143, 144, 148

Abadan Island 160, 161, 165, 166, 179

Abattis 42

Abdul Majid Khan 62, 73, 76, 80, 81, 84

Abu Klea 15, 16, 18, 21, 22, 23, 24, 25, 68, 72

Abu Klea, steamship 102

Abu Kru, battle of 23, 24

Aeroplane 174, 181, 186, 189, 204, 209, 232, 251, 255, 262

Agent, political 32, 33, 37, 56, 63, 69, 86, 91, 136, 233

Ahwaz 179, 184, 185, 198

Alexandra, HMS 20

Ali-al-Gharbi 189, 239

Amara, Amarah 177, 178, 179, 181, 185, 186, 187, 207, 215, 217, 220, 221, 223, 246, 247, 312.

Amán–ul-Mulk 56, 57, 58

Ambassadors (various) 276, 277, 279, 300, 302, 303, 305, 308.

Amir-ul-Mulk 59 61, 62

Annesley, Lieutenant Col. AC. RF 132, 133, 134, 135, 136, 141

Armenian, troopship 124, 125

Artillery, The Royal, French and Turkish 9, 17, 20, 98, 113, 146, 167, 172, 173, 178, 180, 186, 190, 192, 204, 207, 208, 211, 214, 226, 227, 229, 232, 235, 238, 253, 275.

Army Act, the 133, 162, 163, 291

Atbara, the town, the battle of 102, 106, 107, 108, 109, 114, 115, 120, 124

Aubyn, J 1st Baron St Levan 93, 94, 119, 121, 123, 129, 131, 148, 308

Aylmer, Lieutenant Gen. Sir Fenton

VC KCB 41–43, 47, 52, 96, 191, 235, 236, 239- 248, 250 –261, 267, 271, 313

Azizieh 199–202, 204, 205, 220–223, 272

Baker, Colonel Valentine 9

Baden-Powell, Lord Robert 3

Bahran 169, 174

Baird, Captain J, 24th Bengal Infantry 45, 46, 63–68, 79, 82, 89

Badri Nar Singh 65, 79

Baghdad 169, 179, 181, 185, 187, 189, 194, 196 –202, 204, 209, 210, 217, 218, 220–223, 230 234, 236, 237, 246, 262, 272–274, 278, 317

Balls Park 94, 119, 134, 147

Basra 161, 166, 168–170, 174, 179–182, 185–188, 198, 200, 201, 204, 209, 215–218, 220, 223, 230, 233, 245, 246, 248, 250, 253, 264, 268, 279

Baring, Evelyn. 1st Earl Cromer 96

Bayonet 16, 17, 19–21, 23, 33, 42, 47, 56, 66, 79, 88, 98, 102, 105, 170, 173, 175, 192, 199, 200, 210, 211, 214, 279

Bayuda desert 16, 26

Beech, Mr 40, 41

Bellums 166, 170, 172–174

Berber 101, 102, 109, 117

Beresford, Lord Charles 20, 23–25, 271

Bhistis 238, 249

Bloemfontein 126–128, 150–152

Boisragon, Brigadier. GH. VC 42, 43, 47, 52

Bonaparte, Napoleon 2, 48, 55, 69, 70, 199, 209, 218, 236, 291, 313, 314.

Banjo Playing of 7, 8, 15, 30, 55, 142

Blosse Lynch, HM Steamer 170, 204

Braddon, Russell 31, 52, 168, 179, 182, 184, 194, 200, 218–222, 228, 235, 238, 243, 270, 272, 277, 281, 310, 312, 313, 317

Brevet rank 91, 92, 100, 124, 132, 139, 143, 147

Britannia RNC 6, 127

Buller, General Sir Redvers VC GCB GCMG 3, 26, 29, 31, 51, 55, 93, 94, 96, 120–123, 129, 136, 147, 148, 298, 310, 311

Burnaby, Colonel F RHG 15, 19, 23

Boats, Gun. 24, 97, 106, 108–111, 211, 213

Boggis, LCpl. R Norfolk 163, 168, 194, 209, 210, 212, 218, 221, 225, 228, 243, 260, 262, 269, 270, 271, 276, 278

Bombay (now Mumbai) 7, 141, 181, 223, 264

Cahen D'Anvers, Count, Comtesse. 100, 116, 138, 144, 304

Cahen D'Anvers, Alice. (Later Lady Townshend) 109, 116

Cambridge, Prince George, Duke of 55, 93, 116

Camel(s) 13–20, 22–24, 29, 94, 98, 105, 114–116,

Campbell, Captain CP CIH 56, 60–66, 68, 72, 73, 77, 89, 91, 94

Canada 136, 137, 153, 164, 305

Carts, unsprung 186, 190, 193, 215, 229

Casualties 20, 23, 40, 41, 43, 65–67, 71, 75, 78, 87, 104, 167, 184, 213, 214, 217, 221, 222, 228, 236, 237, 239, 244, 248, 252, 258, 260, 262, 263, 267, 269

Cape Town 124, 125, 152

Civilian, Civilians 27, 40, 69, 159, 162, 233, 235, 256, 265, 282, 311

Central Indian Horse (CIH) 28, 31, 32, 51, 129, 131

Chain of Command, the 11, 14, 50, 126, 134, 149, 200, 235

Chalt 35–37, 44

Chamberlain, Colonel N. 126, 127, 131

Chamberlain, Sir Joseph 164, 180, 185, 202, 235, 299

Chitrál 35, 54, 56–73, 75–87, 89–95, 103, 117, 149, 180, 187, 229, 230, 232, 235, 238, 247, 291, 312, 314, 315

'Chitrál Charlie' 5, 190, 195, 199, 200, 209, 210, 212, 1213, 220, 223, 227, 241, 254, 289, 290, 291, 302, 306, 311

Cholera 35, 77

Churchill, Sir WS. 57, 112, 120–122, 287, 288, 291, 297, 298, 306

Clemenceau, CB. 282, 293, 297

Climo, Colonel SH CB. DSO 172, 189, 210, 211, 214, 257

Clio, HM Steamer 170, 174, 175

Ctesiphon 87, 195–199, 202–206, 209, 210. 215, 216, 218, 220–222, 229, 236, 242, 246, 247, 250, 257, 258, 267, 272, 286, 312, 315

Column 15, 16, 22, 46, 61, 85, 110, 112, 135, 204, 205, 207, 208, 210, 211, 213, 220–222, 224, 227–230, 233, 312

Communiqués 190, 220, 232, 258, 264

Comet 170, 176–178, 181, 186, 189, 202, 227

Commander-in-Chief 14, 16, 92, 104, 116, 121–123, 135, 138, 156, 157, 164, 183, 185, 194, 217, 245, 278

Constantinople 187, 293, 301, 304

Cooper, Lieutenant Col. RF 141

Coolies 34, 50, 51, 186

Court Martial 87, 99, 202, 239, 254, 263, 286

Crewe, Lord 151, 167, 178, 179

Curzon, GT. 1st Marquess Curzon of Keddlestone 55, 69, 93, 96, 122, 284, 293, 299, 300

Demolition 42, 236
Debbeh 15, 100
Defecation 77, 251
Delamain. Major Gen. Sir Walter.
    KCB KCMG DSO 165, 166, 176,
    183, 188, 192, 200, 208, 210–214,
    226–228, 234, 239, 260
Delhi 83, 95, 166
Dervish 16, 17, 19–23, 98, 102–104,
    106, 107, 109–115
Diary, CVFT 8, 11, 12, 22, 30, 31, 33,
    37, 43, 46, 49–51, 54, 56, 59, 66,
    72, 83, 86, 93, 97–101, 109,
    115–119, 121, 122, 125–128, 138,
    144, 158, 175, 181, 182, 189, 209,
    230, 233, 254, 303, 305, 306
Distinguished Service Order (DSO) 1,
    52, 91, 116, 117, 134, 147, 158,
    188, 219, 225, 237, 308
Diplomat/Diplomatic 32, 36, 49, 69,
    149, 194, 280, 281, 299, 302
Disease 33, 76, 260, 277, 306
3rd Division 264, 265
6th Poona Division 161, 165, 168, 169,
    174, 180, 182—184, 186, 189,
    190, 194–197, 200–202, 207, 213,
    214, 217, 218, 221, 222, 225–230,
    237, 246, 247, 252–254, 260, 267,
    272, 273, 276, 281, 286, 291, 307
12th Division 167, 169, 179, 184, 197,
    241
13th Division 251, 253, 263
Dobbie, Brigadier Gen. WH CB 166,
    172
Dogras 76, 251
Dongola 15, 97, 99, 106
Dorsets, (Dorsetshire Regiment, The)
    166, 168, 177, 199, 211, 213,
    227–229, 249
Dover 132, 133
Duff, General Sir Beauchamp, GCB
    GCSI KCVO KstJ. 164, 166, 180,
    183, 185, 187, 194, 196, 197, 201,
    245, 251, 278, 279
Durand, Colonel A G. 32–34, 36, 37,
    38, 40, 41, 44, 45, 47, 49, 51, 52,
    56, 57, 69, 96

Education 100, 162, 199, 314
Egypt / Egyptian Army / Egyptian
    Police 5, 7–11, 14, 27, 29, 31, 48,
    95– 98, 104, 109, 110, 112, 115,
    116, 133, 306
Egypt P&O Ship 122
El Teb 9
Enver Pasha 274, 276–278, 293, 305
Escape (various) 9, 12, 15, 43, 46, 47,
    60, 80, 101, 106, 146, 228, 252,
    264, 278, 292
Essinn 186, 189, 242, 246, 354
Espiègle HMS 160 166, 170, 172–176
Euphrates River 161, 166, 179
Examinations, promotion 51, 144
Ezra's tomb 175, 176

Felahiyeh 260, 263
Ferkeh, battle of 97, 98, 117
Fireball 45, 78
Fitzgerald, Colonel O 286, 287
Flies 12, 13, 164, 168, 169, 175, 180,
    188, 193, 201, 211, 217, 234, 252,
    261–264, 267–269. 275
Flood, River Tigris 109, 172, 173, 238,
    250, 252, 261–265
Frazer's Post 202
French, Field Marshal JDP, 1st Earl of
    Ypres KG GCB CMG CVO KCMG
    PC 2, 125, 158, 159
French Army 137, 146, 296, 307
French, language, people, customs, 2,
    11, 29, 100, 142, 149, 152, 155,
    178, 184, 207, 236 282, 291, 294,
    296, 300, 302, 304, 305, 307, 308
Firefly, HM Gunboat 202, 227, 240
Fry, Brigadier CB 166, 188, 190–193
Foch, F. Marshal of France 2, 152,
    155, 157, 280, 291, 295–297
Food, availability, variety, supply,
    scarcity of 29, 33, 75, 82, 87, 89,
    170, 177, 181, 182, 188, 215, 220,
    223, 228, 229, 232, 240, 243–249,
    256, 260–262, 265, 268, 274, 275,
    313
Fortification 24, 72, 77, 78, 222, 304

Gakdul 16 25, 26

Gardner machine gun 15, 17, 18, 20, 23–25

Gilgit 32, 34, 34–37, 45, 48, 51, 52, 54, 58, 60, 62, 69, 79, 80, 83, 89–91

Goltz, Field Marshal M Von de 210, 230, 232–235, 237, 242, 243, 246, 273, 275

Golf 40, 41, 108

Gordon, Major Gen. CGG CB 3, 12, 14–16, 22, 24–26, 115

Gorringe, Lieutenant Gen. Sir George KCB KCMG DSO 240, 241, 265

Grain 43, 77, 244, 249, 259

Greatcoats 72

Great Game, the 34, 44

Gupis 72, 54–56, 59, 72, 78, 118. 127, 300

Gubat 24, 25, 68

Guns, (including mountain, field, Turkish) 17, 23, 35, 38, 41, 44, 52, 90, 97, 105, 107, 110, 111, 166, 168, 169, 170, 173–175, 178, 181, 183, 187, 189, 191, 193, 199, 205, 208, 211, 220 232, 241, 243, 247, 253, 255, 263, 268

Gunboats 24, 99, 108–111, 211, 213

Guns, 4.7" 172, 176, 204, 227, 240

Gurdon, Lieutenant 59, 61, 63, 64, 65, 68, 73, 82, 89, 91

Gurkha (s) 32, 37, 41–43, 65, 67, 75, 76, 212, 213, 236

Gwynne, HA 128, 285, 286

Hai River/ Shatt al Hai 179 180 241 254, 257

Haig, the Rt. Hon. the Earl KT GCB OM GCVO KCIE 2, 163, 283, 311, 313

Harley, Lieutenant DSO 60, 73, 76, 77, 80, 88, 89, 91, 102–104, 106, 117

Hamilton, Brigadier. WH CB DSO 205, 208, 210, 211, 214, 226, 234, 260, 261, 308, 309

Hardinge, Lord, of Penshurst 164, 166, 185, 194, 196, 197, 200, 201, 202, 242, 264, 278, 279

Hero 2, 3, 26, 48, 68, 89, 91, 94, 131, 209, 218, 238, 271, 292, 312, 314

Hindu Kush 32–34, 36, 40, 54, 73

HM Government 35, 235, 308

Hoghton, Brigadier FA 188, 192, 195, 207, 210, 211, 213, 214, 229, 234

Horsemeat 251

Hospital, (includes field, civilian, ship) 25, 50, 55, 61, 87, 164, 168, 181, 182, 186, 196, 204, 216, 240–242, 245, 248, 249, 252–256, 274, 276

Hounslow 135–137, 139, 141, 145, 146

Hunter, General Sir Archibald GCB GCVO DSO 102–104, 120, 144, 145, 149

House of Commons 279, 303

House of Lords 271, 279, 287

Hunza 28, 34–37, 47–49, 55, 68, 72, 73, 78, 89, 100, 180

IEF 'D' 179, 279

Indian Army 7, 29, 31, 48, 50, 58, 70, 94, 115, 124, 129, 156, 158, 164, 179, 184, 189, 197, 288, 307

Indian Empire 35, 56, 164

Indian Staff Corps 7, 11, 14, 28, 132

India Office 30, 94, 95, 124, 279

Isle of Wight 145, 147

Julnar HM steamer 204, 265, 267, 268, 273, 292

Kabul 3, 57, 83, 311

Kanjut River 35, 36, 38, 54

Kashmir, Kashmiris 32, 34, 35, 40, 46, 48, 52, 58, 60–62, 66, 67, 71, 76, 79, 86–88

Kelly Lieutenant Col. JG 83, 85, 89–91

Kemball, Major Gen GV 217, 240, 258

Kila Drosh 60, 61

King George V 196, 283

King's Shropshire Light Infantry 147

Kitson, Major Gen. Sir George 158

Kitchener, Field Marshal Lord
    94–102, 108, 109, 112, 115, 117,
    120, 123, 126, 133, 138, 139,
    141–143, 145, 147, 148, 158, 159,
    271, 284, 286, 287, 288, 298, 306
Khalil, General 210, 213, 242, 243,
    256, 260, 261, 263–265, 267, 268,
    273, 293, 305, 308, 312, 313
Khartoum 3, 12, 14, 15, 16, 18, 24–26,
    91, 101, 108, 109, 117, 138, 230
Khedive 29, 96
Kipling, Rudyard 21, 279, 316
Knight, EF 36, 39–41, 43, 46, 52, 100,
    153
Kunar River 54, 64, 72, 78, 90
Kurna 166, 167, 171–174, 177–182,
    186, 187, 197, 220
Kut el Amara 2, 179, 183, 185, 186,
    191, 195–198, 201, 202, 205, 2–7,
    209, 217, 220, 222, 223, 229–253,
255–258, 160, 261, 263–265, 267–269,
    271–273, 282, 284, 287–292, 296,
    297, 305, 308–310, 312, 313, 315
Kuttite 248–253, 255, 261, 272, 273

Labouchère, H, Du Prè, MP 49
Ladies 11, 31, 100, 142, 184, 240, 305
Mrs, (Lady) Townshend 275, 276,
    293, 304, 305, 308,
Lajj, Llaj 209, 210, 215, 220–222, 272
Lake, Lieutenant Gen. Sir Percy KCB
    KCMG 156, 157, 245, 246,
    250–253, 257, 264–267, 271, 288,
    289
Latrines 76, 77, 89
Lansdowne, Lord, KG GCSI GCMG
    GCIE PC 93, 129, 130, 135, 137,
    152
Lawrence, HM Minesweeper 170
Leadership 33, 88, 99, 212, 314
Lee-Metford rifle 105, 110
Lewis Pelly, HM Armed tug 170, 174,
    176
Lies, Lied 2, 196, 313
Loophole 41–43, 73, 238
Low, Major Gen. Sir Robert GCB 90

Mackenzie, Captain C, Seaforth
    Highlanders 45, 46
Macdonald, Major Gen, Sir Hector
    KCB DSO 95, 98, 99, 107, 109,
    110, 112- 114, 117, 120–122
Magasis 267, 268
Mahailas 176, 189, 202, 245, 253, 257
Mahdi, Mahdists 9–11, 16, 20, 21, 23,
    24, 26, 96–98, 115
Maiun 36, 38, 39, 43, 45, 47
Manners-Smith, Lieutenant Col. J VC
    CIE CVO 44, 46, 47, 51
Marble rock 72, 80
Mardacq, Commandant 152, 155
Marksmen 46, 66
Marmarice, Turkish gunboat 169, 175
Martini-Henry rifles 75, 78, 87, 111
Maxim gun 97, 105, 110
Mention in despatches 26, 47, 49, 91,
    96, 98, 104, 234, 276, 299
Marine (s), Royal Light Infantry 6, 7,
    11, 12, 14, 17, 21, 23, 27, 28, 29,
    94, 132, 200
Medal (s), 11, 27, 52, 79, 126, 127,
    152, 234, 308, 309
Mejidieh, HM Steamer 170, 189, 204,
    209, 212, 216, 228
Mellis, Major Gen. Sir Charles VC
    KCB KCMG 167, 168, 208, 210,
    213, 223–225, 227234, 239, 253,
    254, 259, 260, 268, 273, 274, 277
    279, 290, 305
Mesopotamia Commission, the 194,
    209, 214, 216, 218, 260, 269, 278,
    281
Metemneh 15, 27, 28, 34, 36
Methuen, Field Marshal, Lord GCB
    GCMG GCVO 126, 138, 152
Military Secretary, the, 122–124, 130,
    133–135, 158, 278, 282, 284, 286,
    290, 291
Military attaché 128, 146, 159, 258,
    308
Mine, mining, miners, minefield 88,
    103, 172, 173, 175, 236, 256, 277,
    280, 306,
Miner, HM Minesweeper 170

MP, 49, 204, 300, 303, 304
Montgomery, Field Marshal,
    Viscount, KG GCB DSO PC 2, 184,
    311
Morale 78, 79, 89, 136, 144, 200, 220,
    223, 234, 237, 239, 241, 254, 262,
    311
Mosul, Turkish gunboat 175, 176, 204
Muslim 21, 58, 199, 210
Mutiny 83, 143, 144, 159, 195, 280

Nagar 28, 34, 35–38, 43, 44, 47, 49, 52,
    55, 68, 72, 73, 78, 89, 100
Nagdu, Sepoy 45, 46
Nasariyeh 179–186, 198, 201
Negotiations 50, 80, 81, 84, 138, 249,
    264, 267, 268, 293, 300, 301
Nicholson, Lieutenant Gen. Sir
    William GCB 137, 138, 150, 151,
    153, 163
Nile, river 14–16, 21, 22, 24, 27, 38,
    54, 68, 97–99, 106, 109, 110, 115
Nilt 135, 38–41, 43–45, 47, 52
Nixon Lieutenant Gen. Sir John
    GCMG 2, 157, 158, 167–170, 172,
    174, 178–188, 190–193, 196, 197,
    199–202, 204, 205, 209, 210, 213,
    217, 218, 22–223, 229, 230,
    233–236, 240, 241, 244, 245, 264,
    278, 279, 288, 289, 310, 311, 312,
    315
Nizám-ul-Mulk 58
Royal Norfolk Regiment, Norfolks,
    163, 168, 182, 199, 213, 226, 301
Norfolk 6, 94, 304, 305, 308
North West Frontier 28, 32, 34, 37, 58,
    60, 61, 116, 127, 148, 159
Nunn, Capt. Wilfred RN 172, 175,
    176, 178, 224, 225
Nur-ur-Din, General 186, 189–191,
    193–196

Odin, HMS 160, 166, 170, 174–176
Oil, Oilfields 160, 165, 167, 179, 185,
    196, 230, 249, 279
Omdurman, Battle of 103, 106, 110,
    112–115, 120

Orange River Colony 149–152
Order of Merit 79, 236
Osman Digna 9, 14, 105, 114
Oxfordshire and Buckinghamshire
    Light Infantry (Ox and Bucks)
    173, 199

Pakistan 54, 70
Paris 55, 101, 109, 132, 142, 145–147,
    159, 245, 282, 285, 296, 297, 300,
    302, 304, 306, 308
Parole 268, 276, 279, 293
Peshawar 28, 32, 58, 83, 85, 90
Political officer 47, 51, 54, 58, 63, 187,
    204
Pontoons 204, 205, 228, 236
Poonah, P& O troopship 8, 9
POW 228, 268, 280, 284, 300
Pretyman, Major Gen. GT CB 127,
    128, 130, 132, 136. 138, 148, 150
Prime Minister 131, 276, 279, 298,
    300, 303–305
Principal mass 189, 194, 207, 208, 210,
    211
Prinkipo 276, 277, 28, 294, 305
Promotion 3, 8, 27, 51, 79, 91, 100,
    148, 150, 153, 234, 240, 251, 257,
    260, 264, 271, 184, 288–290, 292,
    294, 314
Psc 55, 118

Quebec 5, 94, 130, 136–138
Queen, the 6, 34, 49, 91, 94, 104, 116,
    122, 135

Railway 9, 34, 97, 101, 102, 108, 160,
    166, 180, 189, 204, 277
Ragu Pertab Regiment 43
Rakaposhi, Mount 38, 52
Rations 26, 50, 75, 76, 78, 230, 234,
    236, 243, 244, 246, 248, 262
Rawal Pindi 34, 158, 159, 161
Redoubt 44, 46, 115, 169, 173, 184,
    209, 213, 244, 254, 255, 257, 258
Resident, the 60, 61, 67, 73, 75, 76
Reconnaissance 45, 63, 168, 176, 181,
    189, 196, 217

Robertson, Sir George, KCSI 32, 47, 56, 58, 60–82, 84, 86, 91, 96, 187, 229, 283, 291

Roberts Arthur 94, 118, 123

Royal Navy 6, 7, 20, 149, 160, 165, 170, 185. 263

Raynnam Hali, Norfolk 6, 94, 119, 134, 136, 138, 155

Royal Fusiliers 130, 132–134, 139

Russia, Russian(s) 34, 35, 44, 47, 83, 160, 234, 246, 253, 269, 287

Sandhurst, RMC 6, 27, 162, 314

Sannaiyat 242, 262

Sally 26, 86, 88, 89, 178

Samana, HM Armed Tug 174, 176, 202

Sangar (s) 38, 42–47, 78, 80, 82, 84, 88, 89, 173

Sappers, sapping, sap 23, 38, 41, 42, 73, 84, 204, 205, 229

Scott, Sir Percy 187, 204, 233

Secretary of State for War 130 133, 154. ʼʼʼ. 303, 307

Sewage 77, 84

Sirdar, the 95, 98, 100, 102–104, 106, 108, 113, 114, 116, 120

Shaitan, HM launch 170, 173, 174, 176, 177, 204

Sherson, Erroll 30, 48, 118, 128, 131, 136, 138, 140, 144, 145, 147, 148, 157, 159, 161, 162, 182, 235, 248, 269, 270, 281, 285, 298, 303–307, 313

Sher Afzul 57, 58, 60, 62, 63, 65, 66, 79–84, 89, 90, 232

Shuja-ul-Mulk 61, 62, 69

Sentry 48, 87, 239, 240

Shaiba, Battle of 167, 168, 247

Shabluka gorge 108, 109

Shatt-al-Hai 179, 180, 241, 257

Sheikh Saad 189, 241, 242

Siege (s) besieged, besiegers 3, 14, 24, 26, 27, 52, 57, 69, 71, 72, 73, 75–84, 86–91, 125, 130, 138, 220, 230, 232, 233, 237, 241, 243, 249, 251–253, 255, 256, 258, 261- 263,

267, 269, 272, 273, 277, 291, 309, 310, 312

Sikh (s) 58–61, 76, 77, 80, 86, 88, 159, 160, 251, 263

Simla 30, 51, 119, 123, 181–183, 185, 201, 251

Sinkat garrison 9

Sifat Badádur 75

Skardu 48–50

Smith-Dorrien, Major Gen. Sir Horace GCB GCMG DSO 139–142

Smith, Brigadier GB 189, 234

Snider rifles 33, 68, 75, 78

Snipe, sniper 87, 238. 239, 249, 251–253, 312

South Africa 3, 52, 66, 118, 121, 122, 124, 126, 128–130, 133, 138, 142, 149–153

Square, British infantry 14, 17–24, 3

Starve, starvation 27, 80, 111, 161, 232, 240, 243, 251, 267, 271, 293,

Steamers, river, paddle 22–24, 175, 186, 204, 215

Stewart, Brigadier, Sir Herbert KCB 15–18, 21–24, 26

Stewart, Captain, 'Curly' 32, 35, 38, 51, 54, 95

Stiffkey Hall 134, 147

Sophia, steamer

Splints 193, 216

Spot (dog) 209, 210, 245, 268, 303, 313

Srinagar 34, 48, 50

Steevens, GW 104, 117

Suakin 9, 12–15, 109, 180

Sudan, Sudanese 5, 9, 10–12, 16, 21, 27, 28, 93, 95–98, 101–104, 109–113, 115 116, 120, 292, 308

Suwada marsh 189–191

Sword 2, 17, 19, –21, 25, 114, 181, 236, 264, 268, 302, 308

Sykes, Sir Mark MP 204

Tamai, battle of 9

Thayetmyo 142, 143

Theatre, operations of 2, 18, 26, 29, 62, 126, 132, 142, 166, 167, 174, 185, 220, 240, 252, 257

Theatre, entertainment 30, 94, 145–147, 156, 161, 184, 212, 284

Territorial Army, TA 154, 156

Thornton Butterworth Ltd 1, 317

Thol 39, 41, 43–45, 47

Thum 36

Tigris river 54, 161, 165, 166, 168, 169, 174, 179–180, 185–187, 190, 194, 197–199, 202, 204, 217, 218, 223, 230, 235, 244, 249, 250, 252, 254, 258, 260–262, 285, 286, 296, 312

Tirich Mir 73

Truce 82–84, 237

Torres Vedras, Lines of 26, 243

Tower 40, 41, 72, 73, 77, 80, 82, 84, 86, 87, 89, 169, 190, 191

Townshend, Audrey 26, 124, 139, 145, 151, 304

Townshend, Major Gen. Sir Charles
KCB DSO

  Ambition; social, military, strategic 2, 5, 13, 48, 96, 103, 129, 130, 139, 143, 155, 187, 241, 310, 311, 314

  Appeals, appealing 14, 121, 134, 148, 150, 156

  Aspiration to be Lord Townshend , 7th Marquess, 6, 47, 94, 119, 123, 134, 144, 146, 147, 276

  Banjo, entertaining on 7, 8, 30, 55, 142

  Birth, parenthood, family background 5, 6

  Bonaparte, Napoleon, admiration for 48, 55, 170, 199, 209, 218, 236. 291, 313, 314

  Canada, visit to, writing about 136, 137, 153, 305

  Command, the exercise of, lobby for, performance in 13, 18, 24, 29, 31–34, 37, 41, 43, 47–51, 54, 55, 66, 68, 72, 75, 77, 95, 108, 116, 124, 125, 128, 129, 132–137, 139, 141–151, 154, 156, 157, 159, 161, 168, 175, 183, 187, 188, 196, 198–200, 204, 284, 285

  Despatches, mentioned in 26, 49, 100

  Diary, multiple entries See 30, 37, 49, 50, 56, 93, 98, 99, 119, 128, 181, 209, 230, 280, 305, 306

  Enlistment, training RMLI 6

  Gallantry, personal courage, bravery 2, 26, 33, 96, 150, 160, 179, 187, 213, 314, 315

  Insensitivity, arrogance 48, 142, 291, 311

  Integrity 314

  'Ladies man' 11, 30, 141, 142, 184, 240

  Morale courage 179, 187, 315

  My *campaign in Mesopotamia* 1, 166, 208, 269, 273, 281, 305

  Personal file 27, 29, 130, 134, 136, 148

  Personality 2, 6, 7, 48, 96, 137, 142, 152, 163, 210, 234, 290, 314

  Relationship with:

    Annesley 132–135

    Buller 26, 29, 31, 51, 55, 93–96, 120–123, 129, 136, 147, 148, 298

    Churchill 121, 287

    Curzon 55, 93, 122, 123, 284, 293, 299, 300

    Haig 283

    Kitchener 19–96, 100, 120, 123, 126, 138, 141–143, 145, 147, 148, 158, 159, 271, 284, 286–288, 298

    Lake 156, 157, 246, 251, 253, 257, 267, 288

    Macdonald 98, 99, 120–122

    Nixon 157, 158, 168, 170, 178, 179, 181, 186–188, 197, 19201, 213, 221, 222, 233–235, 244•

    Pretyman 128, 130, 138

    Robertson 63, 69, 71, 72, 75, 86, 96, 315

  Service in RMLI 6, 7, 11, 12, 14, 27, 28,

  Service in ISC/ CIH 7, 8, 11, 14, 28, 32, 51, 60, 129

  Service in RF 130, 132–134, 139, 143

  Service in KSLI 147

Transfer of arm, service or theatre 7, 8, 11, 14, 48, 94, 118, 121, 124, 129, 130, 135, 285
Townshend Charles Thornton (1840–1889) 5, 6, 30
Townshend. Field Marshal, George, 1st Marquess 3, 6, 94, 119, 130, 134, 136–138, 144
Townshend, John Villiers Stuart, 5th Marquess 5, 119, 122, 123
Townshend, John James Dudley, 6th Marquess 6, 123, 134, 144, 146, 147
Townshend, Rev Lord George 6
Townshend's regatta 173
Transfers, regimental 7, 8, 11, 14, 48, 94, 118, 121, 124, 129, 130, 135, 285
Turkey 160, 161, 275, 280, 292, 293, 297, 299–303, 305, 307

Umra Khan 58–62, 69, 79–82, 90

Vere Lodge 155, 304
Viceroy of India 32, 69, 122, 123, 132, 164, 167, 180, 182, 183, 185, 196, 197, 200, 242, 264, 278
Volley, volleys 18, 23, 24, 64, 65, 102, 105

Wadi Halfa 27, 97, 99, 114
War Office, The 29, 91, 124, 130, 132–134, 137, 146, 150, 152, 153, 155, 156, 159, 166, 252, 259, 279, 282, 284, 285, 290, 291, 294, 296, 298
Whitehall 29, 161, 164, 180, 185, 242
Whitmore, Private, R Norfolk 153, 156, 170, 182
Wilson, Colonel, Sir Charles 23–26
Whitchurch, Surgeon Captain HF IMS VC 60, 61, 63, 65, 67, 68, 70, 73, 75, 79, 87, 91
Wolseley, Field Marshal Sir Garnet KP GCB, OM, GCMG, VD, PC 14, 15, 28, 118, 188, 298
Wolfe Murray, Lieutenant Gen. Sir James KCB 148
Women 11, 12, 27, 48, 50, 58, 96, 98, 101, 105, 106, 115, 116, 120, 141, 187, 233, 256, 299, 303
Wool Press Village 231, 248, 249, 253, 256, 262, 315

Younghusband, FC 94, 95, 100

Zariba 16, 17, 22, 23, 25, 102–106, 110